CAMBRIDGE IBERIAN AND LATIN AMERICAN STUDIES

GENERAL EDITOR

P.E. RUSSELL F.B.A.

Emeritus Professor of Spanish Studies
University of Oxford

ASSOCIATE EDITORS

E. PUPO-WALKER

Director, Center for Latin American and Iberian Studies
Vanderbilt University

A.R.D. PAGDEN

Lecturer in History, University of Cambridge

The Strife of Tongues

This is the first full-length study of Fray Luis de León (1527–91) to appear in English for over sixty years. Today, Fray Luis is known chiefly as the author of some of the finest poetry of the Spanish Golden Age, but he also wrote important prose works in both Latin and Spanish, and produced eloquent translations into Spanish of Biblical and classical texts. He spent five years imprisoned in solitary confinement by the Spanish Inquisition, fighting to clear himself of a series of accusations against his views on the Bible. Acquitted on all counts, he returned to teach at the University of Salamanca.

This book examines the controversies in which Fray Luis was caught up, and investigates the complex influences upon his writings of his prison experiences, his indebtedness to Judaism, his interests as a linguist, and his work as a Biblical scholar and theologian. Colin Thompson looks afresh at Fray Luis's most famous poems and prose works, and explores his understanding of language as a means of enabling God to speak to humanity and humanity to rise to God.

CAMBRIDGE IBERIAN AND LATIN AMERICAN STUDIES

HISTORY AND SOCIAL THEORY

ROBERT I. BURNS: *Muslims, Christians, and Jews in the Crusader Kingdom of Valencia: Societies in symbiosis*

MICHAEL P. COSTELOE: *Response to Revolution: Imperial Spain and the Spanish American revolutions, 1810–1840*

HEATH DILLARD: *Daughters of the Reconquest: Women in Castilian town society, 1100–1300*

JOHN EDWARDS: *Christian Córdoba: The city and its region in the late Middle Ages*

LEONARD FOLGARAIT: *So Far from Heaven: David Alfaro Siqueiros' 'The March of Humanity' and Mexican revolutionary politics*

DAVID THATCHER GIES: *Theatre and Politics in Nineteenth-Century Spain: Juan de Grimaldi as impresario and government agent*

JUAN LÓPEZ-MORILLAS: *The Krausist Movement and Ideological Change in Spain, 1854–1874*

MARVIN LUNENFELD: *Keepers of the City: The corregidores of Isabella I of Castile (1474–1504)*

LINDA MARTZ: *Poverty and Welfare in Habsburg Spain: The example of Toledo*

ANTHONY PAGDEN: *The Fall of Natural Man: the American Indian and the origins of comparative ethnology*

EVELYN S. PROCTER: *Curia and Cortes in León and Castile, 1072–1295*

A.C. DE C.M. SAUNDERS: *A Social History of Black Slaves and Freedmen in Portugal, 1441–1555*

DAVID E. VASSBERG: *Land and Society in Golden Age Castile*

KENNETH B. WOLF: *Christian Martyrs in Muslim Spain*

LITERATURE AND LITERARY THEORY

STEVEN BOLDY: *The Novels of Julio Cortázar*

ANTHONY J. CASCARDI: *The Limits of Illusion: A critical study of Calderón*

LOUISE FOTHERGILL-PAYNE: *Seneca and Celestina*

MAURICE HEMINGWAY: *Emilia Pardo Bazán: The making of a novelist*

B.W. IFE: *Reading and Fiction in Golden Age Spain: A Platonist critique and some picaresque replies*

JOHN KING: *Sur: A study of the Argentine literary journal and its role in the development of a culture, 1931–1970*

JOHN LYON: *The Theatre of Valle-Inclán*

BERNARD MCGUIRK & RICHARD CARDWELL (eds.): *Gabriel García Márquez: New readings*

JULIÁN OLIVARES: *The Love Poetry of Francisco de Quevedo: An aesthetic and existential study*

FRANCISCO RICO: *The Spanish Picaresque Novel and the Point of View*

HENRY W. SULLIVAN: *Calderón in the German Lands and the Low Countries: His reception and influence, 1654–1980*

COLIN P. THOMPSON: *The Strife of Tongues: Fray Luis de León and the Golden Age of Spain*

DIANE F. UREY: *Galdós and the Irony of Language*

MARGARITA ZAMORA: *Language, Authority, and Indigenous History in the Comentarios reales de los incas*

The Strife of Tongues

Fray Luis de León and the Golden Age of Spain

COLIN P. THOMPSON

University Chaplain and Lecturer in European Studies
University of Sussex

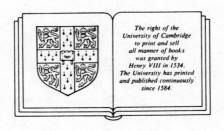

*The right of the
University of Cambridge
to print and sell
all manner of books
was granted by
Henry VIII in 1534.
The University has printed
and published continuously
since 1584.*

CAMBRIDGE UNIVERSITY PRESS

CAMBRIDGE

NEW YORK   NEW ROCHELLE   MELBOURNE   SYDNEY

Published by the Press Syndicate of the University of Cambridge
The Pitt Building, Trumpington Street, Cambridge CB2 1RP
32 East 57th Street, New York, NY 10022, USA
10 Stamford Road, Oakleigh, Melbourne 3166, Australia

First published 1988

Printed in Great Britain at the University Press, Cambridge

British Library cataloguing in publication data
Thompson, Colin P.
The strife of tongues: Fray Luis de Léon
and the golden age of Spain – (Cambridge
Iberian and Latin American Studies).
1. Spanish literature. León, Luis. Critical studies
1. Title
868'.309

Library of Congress cataloguing in publication data
Thompson, Colin P.
The strife of tongues: Fray Luis de Léon and the Golden Age of
Spain/Colin P. Thompson.
p. cm. – (Cambridge Iberian and Latin American studies.
Literature and literary theory)
Bibliography.
Includes index.
ISBN 0 521 35388 2
1. León, Luis de. 1528?–1591 – Criticism and interpretation.
1. Title. 11. Series.
PQ6410.L3T46 1988
862'.3 – dc 19 88–4104 CIP

ISBN 0 521 35388 2

SE

This book is dedicated to all those who work to heal the wounds of the sixteenth century in the Christian Church of the twentieth.

Protege eos . . . a contradictione linguarum.   Psalm xxx. 20 (Vulgate)

Thou shalt keep them . . . from the strife of tongues.   Psalm xxxi. 20

Contents

Preface   *page* viii

List of abbreviations   x

A note on translations   xii

Introduction   1

1   Seeing through words   4

2   The strife of tongues   36

3   The language of revelation   86

4   The language of mystery   140

5   The names of the Word   171

6   The language of heaven   232

Notes   263

Bibliography   277

Index of Biblical references   292

General index   296

Preface

This book has been some years in the making and would never have been completed without the generous support of institutions and individuals. The Research Lectureship I held at Christ Church, Oxford from 1974–8 enabled me to lay a solid foundation for it in the most congenial and stimulating of environments. Research in Spain and Portugal was made possible by the award of a Denyer and Johnson Travelling Fellowship by the Faculty of Theology in Oxford in 1977, and by a subsequent grant from the British Academy.

I shall not forget the friendship and hospitality of the Augustinian communities which received me in Madrid, Salamanca and El Escorial, and I am deeply grateful to the Provincial, Father Vicente Gómez Mier, OSA, for inviting a Reformed minister to live and work in the Escorial, the heart of Counter-Reformation Spain. Nor shall I forget the courtesy of Father José Goñi Gaztambide of Pamplona Cathedral and of others like him, who allowed me to consult precious manuscripts and to work on undisturbed.

I should especially like to express my gratitude to Dr R.W. Truman of Christ Church and to Professor Peter Russell for their unfailing encouragement and many valuable suggestions, and to Eric Southworth of St Peter's College, Oxford for the help he has given me in revising and improving my drafts. I am also very grateful to Fr Bruce Harbert, Roman Catholic Chaplain at the University of Sussex, for his help with the translation of the Latin quotations. The world of Hispanic studies is not represented at the University of Sussex, which is especially sad as Spain and Portugal resume their historic role as part of the Western European community. But Sussex has always supported my unusual academic interests, which must compete with

the more pressing demands of the University Chaplaincy. Its commitment to the inter-disciplinary study of the arts has helped me to set my
own interests in a wider context, and I therefore pay tribute to the
vision of its founders, which has stood the test of time.

University of Sussex   Colin Thompson

Abbreviations

Periodicals

AA	*Archivo Agustiniano*
AHHA	*Archivo Histórico Hispano-Agustiniano*
AnalAug	*Analecta Augustiniana*
BBMP	*Boletín de la Biblioteca de Menéndez Pelayo*
BHR	*Bibliothèque d'Humanisme et Renaissance*
BHS	*Bulletin of Hispanic Studies*
BRAE	*Boletín de la Real Academia Española*
BSS	*Bulletin of Spanish Studies*
CD	*La Ciudad de Dios*
CT	*La Ciencia Tomista*
EHR	*English Historical Review*
HR	*Hispanic Review*
MC	*El Monte Carmelo*
MLR	*Modern Language Review*
RAE	*Revista Agustiniana de Espiritualidad*
REEB	*Revista Española de Estudios Bíblicos*
RET	*Revista Española de Teología*
RH	*Revue Hispanique*
RR	*Romanic Review*
RyC	*Religión y Cultura*

Other abbreviations

AHN	Archivo Histórico Nacional
BAC	Biblioteca de autores cristianos
BAE	*Biblioteca de autores españoles*
BM	British Museum
BNM	Biblioteca Nacional de Madrid
CC	*Clásicos castellanos*

CDIHE	*Colección de documentos inéditos para la historia de España*
CHB	*The Cambridge History of the Bible*
CSIC	Consejo Superior de Investigaciones
CUP	Cambridge University Press
FUE	Fundación Universitaria Española
OUP	Oxford University Press
PG	*Patrologia Graeca*
PL	*Patrologia Latina*
RAH	Real Academia de la Historia
SCM	Student Christian Movement
SPCK	Society for Promoting Christian Knowledge

A note on translations

All unacknowledged translations, both prose and poetry, are mine. The *Nombres* has recently appeared for the first time in a full English translation (see bibliography). Because this translation does not always accurately convey the theological precision or the rhetorical power of Fray Luis (see my review in *New Blackfriars*, 66 (1985), 201–2), I have not felt able to use it, but it provides a valuable introduction to Fray Luis for those who would like to become more familiar with his work.

The Bible presents particular difficulties. I have quoted from the Authorized Version (the King James Bible) because of its classical status in English. The numbering of the Psalms in the Vulgate and the English Bible is slightly different, and I have normally given both. Occasionally there are discrepancies of a verse or two between the AV and the Vulgate in other books, and these have been noted where any problem might arise.

Introduction

When George Borrow travelled through Spain in the 1830s, attempting with mixed fortune to distribute vernacular Bibles, he obtained an interview with the Primate of Spain, the Archbishop of Toledo. 'Does your Lordship think', Borrow asked the great man, 'that a knowledge of the Scripture would work inestimable benefit in these realms?' 'I don't know', replied the Archbishop.

Spain is not a country we associate with a culture based on a great vernacular Bible, nor is Spanish a language influenced by one. Borrow's journeyings reveal how firmly the prohibition against the Bible in Spanish had been enforced through the centuries. For many people, sixteenth-century Spain brings to mind the intolerance and fanaticism symbolized by the Inquisition, the cruelty and greed of the *conquistadores* and the imperial designs of the Armada. But it is important to remember that there was another side to the story.

It is not just that there was a flowering of all the arts which makes it so appropriate to speak of the Golden Age of Spain. Alongside the Inquisition went a vitality of religious life and controversy within Roman Catholicism and sometimes outside it which was not stifled by the threat of imposed silence or persecution, and which certainly did not lead to a dull uniformity or an unquestioning orthodoxy. Alongside conquest went exploration, and with the discovery of new lands and peoples came new ideas and challenges to received opinions. Alongside the empire-makers were to be found quiet and devoted servants of Christ's gentler rule.

In Fray Luis de León we find these other faces of the age. Though he was its victim, the Inquisition we encounter betrays a ponderous bureaucracy which moves towards his eventual release, rather than the horrors of Edgar Allan Poe's pit and pendulum. In his life and work, Fray Luis sums up many of the glories and tensions of the Golden Age of Spain. He shared fully in the theological controversies of the Europe of his time, which were by no means limited to the Protestant threat. But he refused to countenance bigotry and intolerance. He loved the Bible and, unlike Borrow's primate, was persuaded of the benefits it would bring if those who knew no Latin could read it in their own tongue. His was a minority view; he had to accept that it would continue to be prohibited in Spanish. The result of this tension was one of the glories of Golden Age Spanish prose and his greatest work of Biblical scholarship, theology, spirituality and art – the *Nombres de Cristo*. His life testifies to the courage of those prepared to fight and suffer for the truth as they see it; his work, to the creative power of controversy and of the harmonious joining of intellect with craftsmanship.

In the twentieth century, it is as a poet that he is chiefly honoured, though his own poems are few in comparison with his Biblical and classical translations, and the volume of his whole poetic output small in comparison with that of his Latin and Spanish prose works. The chief study in English remains Aubrey Bell's *Luis de León* (Oxford, 1925). Since then, a good deal of research has been done on Fray Luis, but while there have been several good studies of his life and his poetry in recent years, little attention has been given to the full measure of the man, to his work as a Biblical scholar and a theologian and to the way in which his more accessible writings are enriched by this. That is not surprising. He is a difficult man to characterize or introduce, because there are so many sides to him. Yet it is that very difficulty which inspired my attempt to provide this fuller portrait.

I have chosen to concentrate on what seems to me to be a point of union between the various Fray Luises – the scholar, the poet, the prisoner. It is his interest in language, its theory and its practice. I begin by establishing his fundamentally theological approach to language and his Biblical hermeneutic, before passing to his work as a Biblical expositor within a rich tradition which has all but vanished. That is the ground bass. But it has two principal counterpoints. His life, and especially his long imprisonment and his Jewish ancestry, cannot be separated from his writing, though the relationship between them is less simple than is sometimes supposed. Above all – for this is the reason why he may still be read with such delight – his professional skills as a linguist and a theologian were never ends in themselves. He wrote to share with those who could never aspire to such learning the essential truths he believed he had uncovered. His artistic vision purified and polished the raw materials his mind had mastered and turned them into classics of Golden Age literature. Rarely are the scholar and the artist so much at home together as they were and are in Luis de León.

I

Seeing through words

Fray Luis de León

Visitors to the old university city of Salamanca in the west of Spain often come across Fray Luis de León unexpectedly. A nineteenth-century statue of him gazes across a small courtyard towards the splendid plateresque gateway of the university. If they pass through this, they may be shown the hall where he used to lecture, complete with some of its original furnishings. At sunset, when the crowds have departed and the light deepens on the honey-coloured stones, it is easy to sit quietly and imagine that Fray Luis may come scurrying through the gate on his way back to supper.

His statue does not stand there simply because he taught at Salamanca for thirty years. Fray Luis was one of the foremost poets and prose stylists of the Golden Age of Spanish literature. He was destined to spend almost five years in his prime of life in the cells of the Spanish Inquisition, fighting to clear his name of a long series of accusations brought against him by some of his colleagues. After his release, he returned to Salamanca and became one of its most distinguished professors and famous sons. Though he is little known in the rest of Europe, his fame has remained undiminished in Spain into our own time.

Luis de León was born into a prosperous, professional family at Belmonte, a small town in the province of Cuenca and a local centre of devotion to Mary, probably in 1527.[1] His father, Lope de León, became a judge (*oidor*) in the Royal Chancellory of Granada and his uncles were courtiers, lawyers and churchmen. One of them, Francisco, held the Prime Chair in Law at Salamanca during the 1550s. Lope had married Inés de Valera, the daughter of Juan Valera, a local landowner, and they had two daughters and four sons. Jewish blood flowed in the veins of the young Luis through one of his great-

4

grandmothers, Leonor de Villanueva, who with her sister had been in trouble with the Inquisition in 1512 for reverting to their ancestral faith.

Luis de León himself tells us that when he was five or six the family moved to Madrid, then Valladolid.[2] At the age of fourteen he was sent to study canon law at Salamanca, where he was probably looked after by his uncle, his father having left for Granada in 1541. Four or five months later he abandoned his studies and instead entered the Order of the Hermits of St Augustine. After a novitiate of uncertain duration he made his solemn profession on 29 January 1544. Apart from six months of teaching at the Augustinian house in Soria, followed by a year and a half of further study at Alcalá, Salamanca was to remain his home.

The Augustinians, or Austin Friars, had been established in Salamanca since 1377, though they had never played as significant a part in the life of the university as the Dominicans and Franciscans. Their eclectic theological tradition looked back to Giles of Rome (Aegidius Romanus, c. 1247–1316), a pupil of St Thomas Aquinas (c. 1225–74), and to Gregory of Rimini (d. 1358), who had developed the nominalist philosophical teaching of William of Occam (c. 1285–1347). The Spanish Augustinians were divided into four provinces (Castile, Toledo, Aragón and Andalusia), each with its own Chapter and with little central authority except that of the General, who was invariably an Italian. During the fifteenth century, though observant movements began to foster spiritual renewal among them as in other Orders by a return to the rigours of the primitive Rule, intellectual life among the Spanish Augustinians was at a low ebb. Egidio de Viterbo (1465–1532; General 1506–15) was so concerned at the lack of educated friars that he gave many Spanish students in the Order permission to study at Alcalá and Paris, and the 1511 Chapter of the newly-united Province of Castile and Toledo legislated for a more adequate intellectual formation of its members. This commitment to scholarship was renewed under the energetic leadership of Girolamo Seripando (1492–1563; General 1539–51), during whose generalship the young Luis de León entered the Order. He was to be one of the first to benefit from and to show the desired fruits of Seripando's reforms, and Augustinian records were already singling him out as a young friar of great promise some years before his trial.[3]

Salamanca, one of the leading universities of Europe, was enjoying its own golden age of theological study under such scholars as Francisco de Vitoria (*c.* 1485–1546), often regarded as the father of international law, Melchor Cano (1509–60) and Domingo Soto (1494–1560), who from 1526 to 1560 successively occupied the Prime Chair in Theology. A reinvigorated scholasticism dominated the discipline, especially after the Council of Trent, which had enhanced the authority of Aquinas in the Church.[4] At Alcalá, the university founded early in the sixteenth century by Cardinal Cisneros de Ximénez (1436–1517), who had overseen there the printing of the great Complutensian Polyglot Bible, Fray Luis learnt Hebrew from a young Cistercian scholar, Cipriano de la Huerga (1527–60), and this was to prove decisive for the future course of his work.[5]

In 1560 Fray Luis took his licentiate (7 May) and then his master's degree in theology (30 June), in a ceremony vividly evoked by Bell.[6] The following month Gaspar de Grajal, who was to become one of his closest friends and a fellow-victim of the Inquisition, beat him by 536 votes to 332 in the public examination (*oposiciones*) for the Prime Chair of Bible. It is hardly surprising that the most recent of the Salamanca masters of theology should have failed to win one of the most senior chairs, and in any case consolation was soon on its way. Late in 1561 he won the Chair of St Thomas, one of the *cátedras menores* (minor Chairs, with a limited four-year tenure), beating his Dominican rival Rodríguez by 108 votes to 55. He rubbed salt in wounded Dominican pride by referring in a speech to the heresies recently discovered in that Order – an allusion to the case of Domingo de Rojas, of the Dominican Colegio de San Esteban, who had been burned at Valladolid in 1559. In 1565 he won the Chair of Durandus, named after the scholastic philosopher Durandus of Saint Pourçain (*c.* 1275–1334), to which he was re-elected four years later. He was still holding it when he was arrested (27 March 1572), but while he was in prison and unable to contest it a third time, he lost it, despite his pleas. Shortly after his acquittal, at the end of 1576, he was awarded a special chair, and finally, in December 1579, he won the tenured Bible Chair, which he was to hold till his death in 1591. In the speech he was required to make before the electors, he said of the Bible: 'Los que me conoscen . . . saben que ha sido aqueste mi principal estudio desde mi primera niñez' ('Those who know me . . . know that this has been my principal study from my earliest age').[7] Since 1561 he had lectured mostly on scholastic theological texts. He was now free to devote all his energies to his greatest love, the Bible.

The trial and imprisonment which threatened to cut short his promising university career in fact became the prelude to a period of great creativity and increasing renown. Most of his Spanish and Latin works were published during the 1580s, some having been begun in prison. In the middle of that decade the great Cervantes, in Book VI of his *Galatea*, could write of Fray Luis as one 'a quien yo reverencio, adoro y sigo' ('whom I revere, worship and follow'). Cervantes was thinking primarily of Fray Luis as a prose writer: his reputation as one of Spain's finest lyrical poets developed only after 1631, when another poet, Francisco de Quevedo (1580–1645), edited and published the first edition of the original poems and translations of Fray Luis, in an attempt to show how poetry ought to be written in an age much given, as Quevedo believed, to excesses of various kinds.

The fullest description of Fray Luis the man that we have likewise dates from some years after his death. Francisco Pacheco (1564–1644), the artist and art theorist, in his collection of literary portraits of the great men of the realm, writes of Fray Luis as a quiet, abstemious, trustworthy man, much given to prayer and personal austerities, and with a deep devotion to Mary; but also witty in conversation and choleric in temperament. Even allowing for the fulsomeness of his eulogy, especially in his comments about Fray Luis's skills as a mathematician, astrologer, lawyer and artist, the picture he gives of his intellectual abilities remains an impressive testimony to the regard in which he had come to be held:

Fue la mayor capacidad de ingenio que se a conocido en su tiempo para todas ciencias i artes. . . . La lengua latina, griega i hebrea, la caldea i siria supo como los maestros della; pues la nuestra, ¿con cuánta grandeza?, siendo el primero que escrivió en ella con número i elegancia. Dígalo el *Libro de los nombres de Cristo* i *Perfeta casada* . . . Al passo destas grandezas fue la invidia que le persiguió, pero descubrió altamente sus quilates, saliendo en todo superior i con el mayor triumfo i onra que en estos reinos se a visto.[8]

His was the greatest capacity of mind known in his time for all the arts and sciences. . . . The Greek, Latin, Hebrew, Chaldean and Syriac languages he knew like their masters; and as for ours, with what greatness! He was the first to write in it with measure and elegance. Let the *Book of the Names of Christ* and the *Perfect Wife* bear witness to this . . . Alongside such greatness came the envy which persecuted him, but it served to reveal to a high degree his excellent qualities, for he rose above it all with the greatest triumph and honour ever seen in these realms.

A theology of language

Through all his working life, Fray Luis was to be preoccupied with a range of problems connected with language and literature: what correspondence there might be between a word and the reality it signified; what difficulties arose in translating from a classical or Biblical language into the vernacular; what principles and techniques should be adopted to interpret the Bible, a literary text of the highest authority for the most important aspects of human life but with a multiplicity of meanings; and how he might best use his own language to enable those not educated in such matters to read with profit and pleasure the truths he had discovered and wanted to communicate. Fray Luis therefore became a thinker about the nature of language, an interpreter of literature in several languages, and an artist in his own. Some of his work proved to be controversial and both he and it were attacked.

Such theoretical statements as we have from him about these concerns are few in number and not very extensive, and generally come in introductions to his exegetical and literary works. Nevertheless, there are sufficient indications of his main ideas for us to establish accurately certain significant features about his understanding of language, even from his earliest works. It is to one of these that we now turn, to explore a subject fundamental to his own art, the nature of metaphorical language.

Among the first known works of Fray Luis are three Latin sermons which already display a considerable mastery of rhetorical devices.[9] The one which has attracted the most attention was preached at the Provincial Chapter at Dueñas in 1557.[10] In it he fiercely attacked moral laxity in the leadership of the Province and the assembled brethren, if impressed, must also have been piqued. More approachable because of its more personal and elegiac tone is the funeral oration for Domingo Soto, the preaching of which fell to Fray Luis, as the last candidate Soto had sponsored for the master's degree. But it is from the Panegyric to St Augustine, preached on his feast (28 August), probably in the late 1550s, that the first signs of the young friar's interests in the workings of language come.[11] The sermon is based on Ecclus. xxvii. 11, which includes a double simile in the Vulgate, the official Latin Bible of the Church: the wise conversation of the pious is likened to the sun, with its inward and unchanging light; the mutability of the fool to the moon, its light borrowed and inconstant. From it, Fray Luis passes on to examine the nature of metaphorical language and its theological implications. Metaphors, he argues, are possible only because in God's creation each thing is related to every other thing through a common divine origin. There is therefore a relationship between any two things in the created order which exists before they are expressed in words, and indeed makes such expression possible. Fray Luis means that metaphorical language is more than a poetic device. It is possible only because the universe was created by God, and it becomes the literary representation of the nature of that creation, in which any one thing can be described in terms of another through their shared unity of origin.

He goes on to explain that some things are better suited to the generation of metaphors than others, and that though he does not know why this is so, he does know which these things are:

Et quamvis res omnes aliae aliis sint similes, tamen nescio quo pacto fit, ut quo alia res melior praestantiorque est, & quo magis bonitate, dignitate, splendore distat à caeteris, eo illius similitudo, atque imago aliqua extet in pluribus. (p. 51)

And although all things are similar to one another, nevertheless by some means it happens that the better and more excellent a thing is, and the further it is distant from the rest in goodness, dignity and splendour, the more its likeness and image exists in many things.

His reticence is unconvincing, especially as he uses the same words ('imago', 'similitudo') as the Vulgate text of Gen. i.26 for the creation of male and female in the image and likeness of God. The reason why God is the best example of the linguistic phenomenon he cannot apparently account for is that in classical Christian teaching everything reflects his glory, and human beings supremely so. Everything tends towards God by imitating his perfection, and each is at one with the other in this process. Fray Luis says as much when he observes that all things stand, each according to its own being, in relationship to the perfect and absolute which is God. All things, therefore, have the capacity to be metaphors for some part of the divine truth. That he articulates in this sermon an understanding of the essential unity of the matter of creation should cause no surprise, for it is a linguistic version of the 'great chain of being', so familiar to sixteenth-century philosophers and theologians.

Fray Luis continues by noting how many metaphors the Bible contains for wisdom, God being the highest wisdom of man – waters, gold, precious stones, and in this text, the sun. Man is a union of three worlds of being, vegetative (as a tree, for example, which merely lives), sensitive (as a horse, which lives and feels), and intellective (man alone). The first two are blind worlds which lead him astray. They need to be governed by the third, reason, hence the importance of the

Delphic inscription, 'know thyself'. The wise man's mind makes right use of reason and can be raised to perceive the unity inherent in all the variety of creation and the first mover, God, according to whose will all things work:

Rationem dico, & intelligentiam quae aethereo, & divino genere, atque statu edita, cum se erexeri ad contemplandas sibi, similesque naturas aethereas, & immortales contemplandas, & illarum rapidissimos motus rara proportione concordes, consentientesque conspexit, atque illum mundi ornatum, & universi ordinem, seriemque innumerabilium rerum nexarum inter sese atque nodis amabilibus illigatarum animadvertit; & inde ad universi auctorem gradum faciens studioque elata ipsum omnis boni, atque pulchri fontem videndi, aciem mentis suae defixerit in Deum ipsum, probeque didicerit omnia supera, media, infima ab immoto eo cieri, & in suos quaeque fines agi, universaque regi summa aequitate summaque justitia.   (p. 56)

By reason and intelligence I mean that which, having its origin in a heavenly and divine nature and status, and having raised itself up to the contemplation of heavenly and immortal natures known and similar to itself, seeing their swiftest motions concordant and harmonious in due proportion, and observing the beauty of the world, the order of the universe and the chain of countless things connected among themselves and yoked in lovely bonds, and ascending thence to the Author of the universe, elated by the desire of seeing the source of all good and all beauty, has fixed the gaze of his mind on God himself, and will rightly have learnt that all things above, between and below are moved by unmoved Being, each guided to its proper end, and that all things are ruled by the supreme equity and justice.

Metaphor is not only traced back to a theology of creation; it here becomes a means of ascent towards God. To ponder those metaphors for divine being which creation in all its variety reveals, and especially those which carry Biblical authority, is to be lifted up to their source. Metaphorical language becomes a form of contemplation of God.

Fray Luis is not alone in this belief. The evocative thirteenth stanza of the first redaction of the *Cántico espiritual* of the great Carmelite poet and mystic St John of the Cross (1542–91) grows out of a similar response to the rich imagery of the Song of Songs:

> Mi Amado, las montañas,
> los valles solitarios, nemorosos,
> las ínsulas extrañas,
> los ríos sonorosos,
> el silbo de los aires amorosos.[12]

> My Beloved, the mountains,
> the solitary, wooded valleys,

the strange islands,
the sonorous rivers,
the whistling of the amorous breezes.

The Bride is evoking the beauty of the Bridegroom through elements from the natural creation. It is entirely appropriate for these different parts of it to be brought into a metaphorical relationship, for in God's world each thing is related to every other thing and all ultimately derive from him, depend on him and may reveal him. The equation of the Bridegroom (Christ) with mountains, woods and streams has nothing to do with pantheism, as a superficial reading might suggest, but is rather a poetic expression of the immanence of the Creator in all that he has made, a doctrine which is at least as old and as orthodox as St Augustine (*Confessions* x, 6).

It is essential to grasp the significance of Fray Luis's understanding of metaphorical language at the beginning of our study, because it will influence the way we read him. One not uncommon reaction to his poetry is that while it possesses formal precision and elegance, its themes are commonplace and it lacks the depth of personal feeling and experience, except perhaps where he reflects on his prison ordeal or laments his earthbound state when the wings of his soul long to soar aloft. On such a reading, metaphor and all figurative language has a decorative purpose and no real relationship with the content of the poetry, whatever that might be. Fray Luis then becomes a kind of precursor of the poet Luis de Góngora (1561–1627), whose extravagant and sometimes almost impenetrable style betrays, so the conventional view runs, a greater concern with the expressive potential of language than with its conceptual power. The parallel seems the stronger in view of the Latinate syntax and vocabulary both poets use (though Góngora to a much more complex degree).[13] But such a judgement must beg many questions about the relationship of form and content, and in particular about whether the use of language can be so separated from what it seeks to convey. Any intensification or disruption of its normal flow might equally well be taken to indicate conceptual difficulty, an attitude assumed by many ancient, medieval and Renaissance commentators on the Bible and by poets who deliberately cultivated an obscure style.[14]

Fray Luis's short discussion of metaphor in his sermon was not an end in itself, but rather a means of working towards its point, an exposure of the contrast between outward show and inward corruption to be found in the world at large and in the Order in particular. But it makes quite plain that for him metaphorical language carries a good deal of implicit theology which is easy for us to miss, especially where at first glance his imagery seems quite conventional. We can best demonstrate the influence of such ideas by seeing how they are present in two examples from his most widely read works – the beautiful natural location in which he sets the *Nombres de Cristo*, and the patterns of imagery which some of his original poems reveal.

The three books of the *Nombres*, his greatest masterpiece in Spanish prose, are cast in dialogue form. Three friends, Marcelo (to whom the greater part of the exposition falls), Sabino and Juliano discuss fourteen of the Scriptural names of Christ over a period of two days in a country retreat. The setting is both real and symbolic, both a background to the dialogues and an illustration of their themes. The *granja* (estate) to which the friends have retired towards the end of June is La Flecha, near Salamanca and bordered by the river Tormes, then in Augustinian hands but still existing, in private ownership, apparently much as described by Fray Luis.[15] But he is also working within a long literary tradition. The dialogue form is as old as Plato, with whose works he was familiar. St Augustine's earliest writings, his *Dialogues*, are generally regarded as idealized versions of conversations he shared, and Repges believes they are the nearest model for the *Nombres*.[16] They take place on consecutive days, the first of which is a feast; they have forewords and dedications, and they are set on an estate (Cassiacum) outside a university city (Milan), in a meadow with a tree and a brook, though bad weather occasionally interrupts the conversation. The dialogue form enjoyed a revival in the Renaissance: Bembo's *Prose* (in three books, Venice, 1525) has a structure similar to that of the *Nombres*, though its setting is Bembo's house in Venice during the winter. In Spain, the dialogues of Erasmus became popular and his followers Alfonso and Juan de Valdés both used the form for political and doctrinal purposes.[17] But merely to establish their ancestry tells us little about the artistry of the *Nombres*. The setting, like the 'paper' on which the dialogues are ostensibly based and the characters, each of whom at various times represents the voice of Fray Luis, may have had a historical genesis, but the *Nombres* is a work of art in which fact, event and invention are woven together so skilfully that we cannot tell where their boundaries lie.

The natural beauty of the location contrasts with the bustle of Salamanca as term ends:

Es la huerta grande, y estaba entonces bien poblada de árboles, aunque puestos sin orden; mas eso mismo hacía deleite en la vista . . . Pues entrados en ella, primero, y por un espacio pequeño, se anduvieron paseando y gozando del frescor; y después se sentaron juntos a la sombra de unas parras y junto a la corriente de una pequeña fuente, en ciertos asientos. Nace la fuente de la cuesta que tiene la casa a espaldas, y entraba en la huerta por aquella parte; y corriendo y estropezando, parecía reírse. Tenían también delante de los ojos y cerca de ellos una alta y hermosa alameda. Y más adelante, y no muy lejos, se veía el río Tormes, que aun en aquel tiempo, hinchiendo bien sus riberas, iba torciendo el paso por aquella vega. El día era sosegado y purísimo, y la hora muy fresca.[18]

The orchard is large and was then well planted with trees, though not in an ordered way; but this itself was a delight to the eye . . . Once they had entered it they first walked around for a short while, enjoying the coolness; then they sat down together in the shade of some vines on some seats by the jet of a small fountain. The fountain's source is on the hillside at the back of the house, and from there it entered the orchard; running and stumbling along, it seemed to be laughing. Nearby, before their eyes there was also a lofty and beautiful grove. And beyond this, though not far, the river Tormes could be seen, even at this season running high between its banks and twisting its way through that plain. The day was calm and very clear, the hour cool.

Here is the *locus amoenus*, the pleasant place of classical and Renaissance tradition, with hints of the Garden of Eden in the complete tranquillity and perfection of the scene. Here too is Castile in summer, with the sound of the water and the shade of the trees providing a refreshing coolness early in the day. But the details tell us more than that. Each thing is in its proper place and in harmonious relationship with each other and the whole. Even the trees which are naturally grouped are pleasing to the eye. Human art has intervened to co-operate with nature (the shady vines, the seats, the fountain jet) to provide a visible image of one of the central themes of the dialogues, that nature witnesses to its Creator and man can be in harmony with it and him as well as with his fellow-man when he has found his true centre and harmony in Christ, through whom all things came to be.

The second book begins after lunch and a siesta, as the heat moderates and the friends take a boat out to an island thicket in the middle of the river. There they resume their conversation:

Era el soto, aunque pequeño, espeso y muy apacible, y en aquella sazón estaba muy lleno de hoja; y entre las ramas que la tierra de suyo criaba tenía también algunos árboles puestos por industria, y dividíale como en dos partes un no pequeño arroyo que hacía el agua que por entre las piedras de la presa se hurtaba del río, y corría cuasi toda junta.   (I, 543)

Though small, the thicket was dense and very peaceful, and at that season very leafy; and among the branches which earth itself had nurtured were some other trees planted by human industry; and it was divided as into two parts by a sizeable brook formed by the water which escaped from the river between the stones of the mill-press, running as if all one.

Now there is more sign of human intervention: some of the trees have simply grown there, others have been deliberately planted; and some of the water has been put to the service of human industry. The spot is cool, and they sit beneath the shade of a tall poplar, their feet dangling in the water. They talk till night falls, for by the beginning of the name 'Príncipe de la paz' the stars are out, and in one of the most lyrical moments of the whole work Marcelo derives his understanding of Christ's peace from contemplation of the order and harmony of the night sky. Like the trees and the mill, the dialogues themselves are a human artifice, channelling into a literary form such of the energies of divine bounty and grace as may so be captured and rendered intelligible. Nature and art, the well-worn classical and Renaissance antithesis, are united to testify to the same truth, that God may be read in the book of nature but needs to be interpreted by human art to be more fully known and loved. Art, both in the setting of the dialogues and in their stylistic beauty, becomes the interpreter of nature and reveals the presence of Christ through the whole creation, as it expounds the divinely inspired language of Scripture in such a way that people may not only learn but also love the truth.

Very early the next morning, the feast of St Paul, Sabino encounters Juliano in the orchard. Juliano has been unable to sleep because of the loftiness of the previous evening's discourse and has been up and about on the hills before dawn. They return to find Marcelo still resting, so they agree to meet again in the thicket after the siesta. These touches add both realism to the setting and humanity to the characters – Marcelo is exhausted by his expository labours, Juliano too excited by them to sleep. But they also shift the focus of attention from the setting to the participants and their reactions to what they have said and heard. Sabino reports that Juliano has spent the whole siesta in the grove, walking up and down deep in thought, preparing himself to expound the next name. The third book ends, like the other two, with a psalm translation by Fray Luis, followed, as in several of the dialogues, by the words 'Y calló', 'And he fell silent'. It is the silence of adoration, beyond words yet brought about by their power:

A sacred reverence checks our songs,
And praise sits silent on our tongues.[19]

If the setting of the *Nombres* itself is caught up into the work's
theology, it is equally true that the apparently conventional imagery
of Fray Luis's poetry is much more integrated with its themes than is
often supposed. His short Ode to Felipe Ruiz on avarice (v) may serve
as a first example. In twenty-five lines of tightly constructed verse,
Fray Luis heaps up images and allusions, under the controlling
metaphor of voyages of trade, which demonstrate how material
wealth can never deliver the peace it promises:

En vano el mar fatiga
la vela portuguesa: que ni el seno
de Persia, ni la amiga
Maluca da árbol bueno,
que pueda hacer un ánimo sereno.
    No da reposo al pecho,
Felipe, ni la mina, ni la rara
esmeralda provecho;
que más tuerce la cara
cuanto posee más el alma avara.
    Al capitán romano
la vida, y no la sed, quitó el bebido
tesoro persïano;
y Tántalo, metido
en medio de las aguas, afligido
    de sed está; y más dura
la suerte es del mezquino, que sin tasa
se cansa a sí; y endura
el oro, y la mar pasa
osado, y no osa abrir la mano escasa.
    ¿Qué vale el no tocado
tesoro, si corrompe el dulce sueño;
si estrecha el ñudo dado,
si más enturbia el ceño,
y deja en la riqueza pobre al dueño?[20]

In vain the Portuguese sail
wearies the waves: for neither Persian sea
nor fair Molucca avail
to yield that precious tree
which has the power to make a soul serene.

Philip, the mine in vain,
brings forth for troubled breast a restfulness,

nor can rare emerald's gain:
the face shows more its stress
the more the greedy soul grasps to possess.

The Roman captain of old
quenched his life, but failed to quench his thirst
drinking Persian gold;
and Tantalus, accursed
amid the waters, and in thirst untold

suffers; harder still
is the miser's fate, who ceaselessly
exhausts himself, and will
shut up his gold, and dares to cross the sea,
but nothing from his mean hand dares let free.

What value treasure's heap
untouched, if it constricts the knot the more?
if it corrupts sweet sleep,
if brow be troubled sore,
and master left amid his riches poor?

Merchants may travel far, to Persia or to the Moluccas, but the valuable spices they return with cannot bring serenity to the soul. The idea is repeated with a change of images: the treasures of the mine, the precious emerald, bring only greater worry. The third verse offers two classical allusions to greed, and from waters as a highway we move to waters as refreshment: Marcus Licinius Crassus, condemned to drink molten gold, and Tantalus, condemned to everlasting thirst in the midst of water. The more the greedy soul possesses – and avarice is a spiritual sin – the more it 'tuerce la cara', 'twists the face'; even outward appearance betrays the disorder it engenders. Another consequence, miserliness, is shown in the penultimate verse. What is all this treasure for, if one is too mean to spend it? The moral is drawn together in a series of questions in the last verse: what is untouched treasure worth if it corrupts sweet sleep, tightens the knot and leaves the owner poor amid his riches? The paradox makes clear that this is not material poverty, yet the questions remain unanswered and the paradox unresolved, so that the onus is on the reader to draw the required conclusion.

Only three images of tranquillity are found in the poem, and each of these is in a negative setting: the 'serene soul' of the first verse, which no treasures of foreign trade can provide, the repose of the second, which no precious stones can bring, and the 'sweet sleep' of the last, corrupted by possessions which remain untouched. These images of repose are in each case negated by images expressing anxiety and despair, derived from the very objects sought to achieve peace. Greed, we should conclude, is sinful not so much because it is wicked as because it cannot satisfy the desires it arouses and only removes us further from their fulfilment.

An opposite process may be seen in the Ode to Salinas (III), which has music as its fundamental metaphor, and is notable for its allusions both to the Platonic theory of *anamnesis* and to Pythagorean notions of the music of the spheres. Here almost all the images are positive, representing music as a means towards contemplating divine harmony and overcoming ignorance and folly. On the one hand there is gold which 'el vulgo ciego adora', 'the blind mass adores' (idolatry), which is 'la belleza caduca, engañadora', 'decaying, deceitful beauty' in the realm of the senses, where 'todo lo demás [visible] es triste lloro',[21] 'all the rest [the visible] is sad weeping'. On the other stands the harmony of the music played by the blind musician Salinas, reawakening the soul to its noble origin and bathing it in a 'mar de dulzura', a 'sea of sweetness' which leads to ecstasy. The ecstasy may not be sustainable, but the imagery shows how the real music has the metaphorical power to overcome base desires and instincts and to open the eyes of the soul to eternal beauty. In his study of the metaphors of music, wisdom and friendship in this poem, O'Reilly shows how Fray Luis uses them as medieval spiritual writers did, as images for contemplation.[22]

Fray Luis's ode on avarice may have Horatian overtones, but it is also the voice of a Christian moralist. At the beginning of the name 'Príncipe de la paz' in the *Nombres*, Marcelo provides what is in effect a gloss on its message. He explains that peace is the fulfilment of our desires, but that if our desires are themselves misdirected our search for peace through them will inevitably be frustrated. 'Porque si navega el mercader y si corre las mares es por tener paz en su codicia que le solicita y guerrea' (I, 614), he says: 'For if the merchant sets sail and crosses the seas it is to pacify the greed which worries and besets him'. Later, as Juliano and Sabino converse about the quest for happiness, which some find and some do not, Juliano asks:

El avariento, decidme, ¿ama algo?
– Sí ama – dijo Sabino.
– ¿Qué? – dijo Juliano.

– El oro sin duda – dijo Sabino – y las riquezas.
– Y el que las gasta – añadió Juliano – en fiestas y en banquetes . . . ¿busca y
apetece algún bien?
– No hay duda de eso – dijo Sabino.
– ¿Y qué bien apetece? – preguntó Juliano.
– Apetece – respondió Sabino –, a mi parecer, su gusto propio y su contento.
– Bien decís, Sabino – dijo Juliano luego –. Mas decidme: el contento que
nace del gastar las riquezas, y esas mismas riquezas, ¿tiene una misma
manera de ser? ¿No os parece que el oro y plata es una cosa que tiene
substancia y tomo, que la veis con los ojos y la tocáis con las manos? Mas el
contento no es así, sino como un accidente que sentís en vos mismos, o que os
imagináis que sentís. Y no es cosa que o la sacáis de las minas, o que el campo o
de suyo o con vuestro labor la produce, y, producida, la cogéis de él y la
encerráis en el arca, sino cosa que resulta en vos de la posesión de alguna de las
cosas que son de tomo, que o poseéis u os imagináis poseer.   (1, 638–9)

'Tell me, does the miser love anything?'
'Of course he does', said Sabino.
'What?' said Juliano.
'Gold and riches, naturally', said Sabino.
'And', Juliano added, 'the man who spends them in feasts and banquets . . . is
he seeking and desiring some good thing?'
'That is beyond doubt', said Sabino.
'What good thing is he desiring?' said Juliano.
'He is desiring', Sabino answered, 'in my opinion, his own satisfaction and
contentment.'
'Well said, Sabino', Juliano replied. 'But tell me: are the contentment which
comes from spending riches and the riches themselves the same kind of thing?
Don't you think that gold and silver are something with substance and
weight, which you see with your eyes and touch with your hands? But
contentment is not like that, it is like something you feel in yourself or imagine
you do. It is not something you mine or something the land produces by itself
or through your labour, something which once produced you take and shut
up in the chest, but something which is the result of your possessing or
imagining you possess one of those things which has weight.'

The argument is then developed to the point where Juliano can prove
that Christ is the only source of true fulfilment. Although the *Nombres*
is not intended to be a commentary on his poetry, passages such as
these encourage us to see that Fray Luis's poetic language must be
carefully pondered in order for its meaning – in this case a moral
questioning of the whole concept of material wealth as the road to
satisfaction – to be grasped. In place of the simple prose technique of
questions, answers and exposition, the ode uses a less direct form of
communication, with allusions, patterns of images and unanswered
final questions, left for the reader to interpret and respond to.

The search for true peace was to preoccupy Fray Luis greatly, and it inspired one of his most popular poems, the ode '¡Qué descansada vida!', sometimes called 'Song of the Solitary Life' and usually printed first in editions of his poetry. Though modelled on Horace's epode 'Beatus ille', it is a very different work:

VIDA RETIRADA

¡Qué descansada vida
la del que huye el mundanal ruïdo,
y sigue la escondida
senda por donde han ido
los pocos sabios que en el mundo han sido!

    Que no le enturbia el pecho
de los soberbios grandes el estado,
ni del dorado techo
se admira, fabricado
del sabio moro, en jaspes sustentado.

    No cura si la fama
canta con voz su nombre pregonera;
ni cura si encarama
la lengua lisonjera
lo que condena la verdad sincera.

    ¿Qué presta a mi contento
si soy del vano dedo señalado?
si en busca de este viento
ando desalentado
con ansias vivas y mortal cuidado?

    ¡Oh campo, oh monte, oh rio!
¡Oh secreto seguro deleitoso!
Roto casi el navío,
a vuestro almo reposo
huyo de aqueste mar tempestuoso.

    Un no rompido sueño,
un día puro, alegre, libre quiero;
no quiero ver el ceño
vanamente severo
del que la sangre sube o el dinero.

    Despiértenme las aves
con su cantar süave no aprendido;
no los cuidados graves
de que es siempre atendido
quien al ajeno arbitrio está atenido.

    Vivir quiero conmigo,
gozar quiero del bien que debo al cielo,
a solas, sin testigo,

libre de amor, de celo,
de odio, de esperanzas, de recelo.
 Del monte en la ladera
por mi mano plantado tengo un huerto,
que con la primavera
de bella flor cubierto
ya muestra en esperanza el fruto cierto.
 Y como codiciosa
de ver y acrecentar su hermosura,
desde la cumbre airosa
una fontana pura
hasta llegar corriendo se apresura.
 Y luego, sosegada,
el paso entre los árboles torciendo,
el suelo de pasada
de verdura vistiendo,
y con diversas flores va esparciendo.
 El aire el huerto orea,
y ofrece mil olores al sentido,
los árboles menea
con un manso rüido,
que del oro y del cetro pone olvido.
 Ténganse su tesoro
los que de un flaco leño se confían:
no es mío ver el lloro
de los que desconfían
cuando el cierzo y el ábrego porfían.
 La combatida antena
cruje, y en ciega noche el claro día
se torna; al cielo suena
confusa vocería,
y la mar enriquecen a porfía.
 A mí una pobrecilla
mesa, de amable paz bien abastada,
me baste; y la vajilla
de fino oro labrada
sea de quien la mar no teme airada.
 Y mientras miserable-
mente se están los otros abrasando
en sed insacïable
del no durable mando,
tendido yo a la sombra esté cantando.
 A la sombra tendido,
de yedra y lauro eterno coronado,
puesto el atento oído
al son dulce acordado
del plectro sabiamente meneado.

QUIET LIFE

How peaceful is that life
of him who would all worldly clamour shun
and take the hidden path
whereon have walked alone
those few wise men the world has ever known!
    No troubles fill his breast
as proud and haughty men in their estate,
nor is he yet impressed
by roof of gold, its weight
on jasper borne, with Moorish craft ornate.
    He nothing cares if fame
with herald voice of his own name makes song;
no longer need he blame
the praise of flattering tongue
for what sincere truth condemns as wrong.
    What pleasure does it lend
if the vain finger indicate my worth,
if searching for such wind
I journey out of breath
beset by living woes and cares of death?
    Oh field, oh hill, oh beck!
Oh secret place of sweet tranquility!
The ship's almost a wreck;
to your dear rest I flee
from ravages of this tempestuous sea.
    I want to lay me down,
in sleep unbroken, calm, glad, free the day,
and not to see the frown,
severe yet all in vain,
of him by honour roused or love of gain.
    Let birds awaken me,
with their untutored song of gentle sound,
not grave anxiety
which ever must be found
with him who to another's will is bound.
    I want to live alone,
free to enjoy the gifts of heaven's light,
my company my own,
free of love, of spite,
of hatred and of hopes and rivals' fight.
    Upon the mountain side
I have an orchard by my own hand made
where newly each springtide
fair flowers are arrayed,
the certainty of fruit in hope displayed.

And covetous, it seems,
to see such beauty and to make it grow,
a pure and running spring
hastens there to flow
from lofty summit where the breezes blow.
  And calmly on it presses,
twists its passage in among the trees
and as it flows it dresses
the countryside in green
and scatters varied flowers on the scene.
  The breeze blows through the groves,
offering a thousand perfumes to be found;
among the trees it moves
with soft and gentle sound,
gold and sceptre lulled to sleep profound.
  Let those their treasure keep
who trust the fragile timber will reach shore;
I shall not see them weep,
those who labour sore
when north and south winds stormily make war.
  Then the stricken mast
creaks; clear day is turned into blind night;
their terror cries aghast,
piercing heaven's height,
the sea alone the richer through their plight.
  For me, a humble board
which kindly peace has furnished is enough;
let him afford the price
of finely-wrought gold cup
who does not grow afraid when seas turn rough.
  And meanwhile, as the rest
are pitifully burning all with fire
of an insatiable thirst
vain power to acquire
may I lie in the shade to hear the lyre;
  stretched out beneath the shade,
with ivy and eternal laurel crowned,
my full attention paid
to the harmonious sound
which skilled musician's art has sweetly found.

The metaphorical structure of this poem is more complex than its apparent simplicity would suggest. Its foundation is the antithesis between two ways of living, characterized as the 'escondida senda' (hidden path) of the few and the 'mundanal ruïdo' (worldly clamour) of the foolish majority, from which they flee – a theme present in the sermons and poems we have already mentioned. But if we look more closely at the images which form the framework of the poem and carry forward this metaphorical antithesis, we discover two further significant contrasts. One is between the manmade and the divinely created, metaphors in general for imprisonment and freedom; the other, more precise but pervasive, is between the manmade which is disordered because it arises out of purely sensual gratification, and the manmade which is simply and reverently ordered towards the love and worship of the Creator. It is the classical contrast between idolatry and worship of the one true God, between manmade gods and images used to awaken devotion; between the Golden Calf (Exod. xxxii) and the Brazen Serpent (Numb. xxi.6–9). From these contrasting images the poem gains its conceptual strength and originality.

Consider, for example, the concrete images which illustrate the abstract qualities of worldly clamour. In the second and third verses status and fame represent the quest for honour which obsessed so many Spaniards and which depends on flattery and hypocrisy to overcome sincere truth (a possible allusion to the 'unleavened bread of sincerity and truth' of I Cor. v.8). The wise man is unmoved when fame sings aloud his praises and the flattering tongue deceives. Fame and flattery are personified by the voice and tongue ascribed to them. The wealth and luxury which surround the powerful are symbolized more materially by the coffered ceiling of Moorish craftsmen, gilded and supported on jasper columns. But what are such things worth, asks the poet:

> ¿si en busca de este viento
> ando desalentado
> con ansias vivas y mortal cuidado?

Both the wind and the breathlessness ('viento', 'desalentado') have various levels of meaning. The wind is the air we breathe and which gives us life; but it is also the wind of fame, and those who seek this find that they are out of breath. 'Desalentado' is also a play on words, since it can mean 'dispirited', 'discouraged', 'deprived of vital energy'. Since the Hebrew *ruah*, like the Greek *pneuma*, means wind, breath and spirit, Fray Luis may again have Biblical imagery in mind, perhaps the dry bones clothed with flesh but lacking the breath of life of the vision of the valley of dry bones (Ezek. xxxvii), which depends on this multiplicity of meaning. In this breathless state, the only things which are alive are anxieties: the adjective, 'ansias *vivas*', has been chosen for full effect; anxieties which are living but which contain the power of death, '*mortal* cuidado', the adjective again deliberately weighted.

This life of worldly clamour, expressed through the ambiguous metaphor of wind, is swept up into the new but related metaphor of the tempestuous sea from which the poet flees in the fifth verse ('huyo') as the wise man flees ('huye') from clamour at the beginning. The point of connection is the wind, because it is the cause of the stormy sea. The almost broken ship is surely a life almost wrecked by the search for the wind of fame and riches, which now seeks refuge in the haven of the countryside. But the tempest metaphor reappears and is expanded towards the end of the poem (lines 61–70): those who cross the seas for gain may find that they lose it in the storm, and that only the sea is enriched by the cargo they must jettison in their plight. The metonymy of 'falso leño' (false wood) for the ship is one which Góngora was to develop, as in his attack on voyages of trade in the first of his *Soledades*:

> Piloto hoy la Codicia, no de errantes
> árboles, mas de selvas inconstantes . . .
>
> Covetousness the pilot is to-day
> Of wandering forests not of shifting trees . . .[23]

The falseness lies not only in the inability of the ship to protect its treasure but also in the misuse of the tree, part of God's creation, for greedy and idolatrous ends.

This same error is pictured in the other metaphors for worldly clamour – the quest for honour and riches, the cares of those who serve the wills of others, the frequent references to wealth and power, as in the metonymous 'oro' (gold) and 'cetro' (sceptre) of line 60 and the state of those 'abrasando en sed insacïable' (burning with insatiable thirst) for the dangers of government (lines 78–9). The 'vajilla de fino oro labrada' (vessel worked in fine gold) of lines 73–4 is a counterpart to the gilded roof of the second verse, in the sense that both are objects intended to fulfil a proper human need (drinking; shelter) but made in so ornate a fashion that, though intended to enrich those who own them, they become the sign of a deeper, spiritual thirst and poverty.

Balancing these images of worldly clamour are those of the hidden path, itself a metaphor for the good life, influenced perhaps by Matt. vii. 14, 'Because strait is the gate, and narrow is the way, which leadeth unto life, and few there be that find it'. The rejection of fame and wealth because they only increase anxiety and stress is followed in the fifth verse by an evocation of a natural landscape of hill, fountain and river to which the poet flees from the tempestuous sea to find a secret and delightful safety and repose for the soul. His ship has been almost destroyed by the storm; in other words, his rejection of the noise of the world is a result of painful experience, not of seclusion. Unbroken sleep and the freedom of the open skies stand against honour and money (verse 6), birdsong (unlearnt music) against cares (acquired; verse 7). Verses 9–12 describe the garden at the heart of the idyll, a real garden (La Flecha, near Salamanca, 'planted by my hand'), yet also metaphorical, because a sixteenth-century poet does not use the imagery of the *locus amoenus* and the *hortus conclusus* of the Song of Songs (iv. 12-v. 1) without purpose. Through them we see the point of the appeal to the landscape. The garden is planted on the slope of a hill, where a fountain springs and races away to become a gentle stream meandering among the trees and watering the meadow banks and flowers – not unlike the description of the scene at the beginning of the *Nombres*. In it the beautiful flowers of spring anticipate the certain fruit to come (the definition of faith in Hebr. xi. 1 as 'the substance of things hoped for' may have inspired this). The only covetousness here – and again Fray Luis chooses his adjective, *codiciosa*, carefully – is the desire of the fountain to see and to enhance the beauty of the scene. In this garden the breezes blow softly and with fragrant scents – a further development of the imagery of wind – in contrast to the storms which wreck the hopes of treasure-seekers, all noise and darkness (verses 12–13). The competing north and south winds are a direct antithesis of the source (Song iv.16), where they are called on to blow through the garden and awaken its fragrance. The table furnished with peace (lines 71–2) may also have a Biblical origin, in the table of Psalm xxii (xxiii).5, and its simplicity stands in contrast to the golden vessel which may be the reward of those who do not fear the angry seas. The poem ends with a further contrast, between those who burn with an insatiable thirst for power (we recall the previous allusion to the Tantalus myth in the Ode to Felipe Ruiz), and the poet, reclining in the shade, crowned with ivy and laurel, singing and listening to harmonious music. Such music is another example of human art ordered towards the contemplation of the Creator through the created.

There is nothing overtly Christian in this poem, though the Biblical allusions are perhaps more extensive than is generally recognized. But when we begin to understand the conceptual thread which weaves the pattern of metaphor we begin to grasp that this is not just an ode to the simple life but a moral judgement on the folly of those who mistake worldly allure for something of ultimate value, and to see what Fray Luis means when he describes metaphor as a means of contemplation of divine truth. There is a human creativity which is satisfied with simple food and shelter, which makes a garden or performs music, and finds order, peace and beauty in so doing. There is another form of creativity which is restless and acquisitive, which must express itself in the possession of luxurious objects and court disaster in its restless search for treasure. Human desire for worldly wealth and power stems from a moral disorder, the result of which is storm and wreck from which the poet himself has barely escaped, and the loss of the very things from which fulfilment has been sought. The search for peace and spiritual contentment is a search after the God-given order of the universe, in which man co-operates with nature rather than plunders it. That is why the winds blow as sweetly and as gently in the garden to which the hidden path leads as they do wildly and menacingly where worldly clamour sets sail.

The *Cantar de los Cantares*

Not long after he preached his sermon for Augustine, Fray Luis had begun to write a Spanish commentary on the Song of Songs, not intended for publication, for his cousin Isabel Osorio, a nun at the Sancti Spiritus convent in Salamanca. It is the first Biblical commentary he produced, and is the forerunner of two much longer Latin commentaries. It was inspired by a commentary his remarkable contemporary, the erudite Arias Montano (1527–98), had lent him when he passed through Salamanca in 1561, on the condition (never fulfilled) that Fray Luis would translate it into Latin.[24] Instead, he produced his own, and in it we have another early example of his interest in the theology of language, this time the language of divine revelation. If metaphor properly understood could be for Fray Luis a means of ascent towards God, then the language of the Bible and all its figures of speech would show the corresponding process, the divine descent to humanity. By speaking through the words of Scripture God reaches down to the human level and communicates in a manner suited to human limitations. Biblical language is itself a kind of incarnation.

Fray Luis was working within a long and authoritative tradition. The Song of Songs contains some of the most beautiful yet mysterious poetry in the Bible. As he points out, its title translates the Hebrew

superlative, and means 'the best of songs'. The fact that it was ascribed
to Solomon, the wisest man in the ancient world, had helped what was
in fact a wedding-song celebrating physical beauty and erotic love to
gain acceptance into the Biblical canon. This process was also assisted
by the existence already by the first century of an allegorical interpretation of its images. Philo of Alexandria (*c.* 20 BC–*c.* AD 50), a Greek-
speaking Jew living in a Hellenistic culture, and eager to demonstrate
to its finer minds that the Jewish Scriptures were not barbaric and full
of superstition, made allegorical interpretations of some of their more
violent, crude or sensual parts, including the Song. Through such an
approach he could uncover lofty ideas beneath the text, and the most
unpromising passages were made to yield truths which could stand
unashamed in the company of Greek philosophy. On this tradition,
immensely influential until recent times, Fray Luis freely drew. The
Song had become the classical Biblical authority for mystical experience, first from its interpretation as the love-song between God and
his bride Israel or the new Israel (the Church), and then, from St
Bernard of Clairvaux (1090–1153) onwards, more individualistically,
as the love-song between Christ and the soul.

   In the prologue to his commentary Fray Luis makes clear his
incarnational view of the language of the Bible. God, he writes,
created man in his image and likeness, and finally himself assumed
human nature to redeem the human race. But already before the
Incarnation he is revealed in his dealings and conversations with man
throughout the Scriptures, 'en las cuales . . . es cosa maravillosa el
cuidado que pone el Espíritu Santo en conformarse con nuestro estilo,
remedando nuestro lenguaje, e imitando en sí toda la variedad de
nuestro ingenio y condiciones' (i, 70), 'in which the care the Holy
Spirit takes to be conformed to our style by copying our language and
by imitating the whole range of our mind and our condition is a
wonderful thing.' That is to say, the Bible's message comes in a form
and style which is directed towards human needs and recognizes
human limitations. Its style is therefore integral to its purpose: it
reveals the words and images through which the Holy Spirit has
chosen to express the gospel of salvation and therefore requires the
closest scrutiny. That is the basis for what we might call a literary
critical approach to the Bible, since Fray Luis will be concerned to
ensure that the exact meaning of each word and figure is appre-
hended.

   The Song, he explains, is:

. . . la canción suavísima que Salomón, rey y profeta, compuso, en la cual,
debajo de un enamorado razonamiento entre dos, pastor y pastora, más que
en alguna otra Escritura, se muestra Dios herido de nuestros amores con
todas aquellas pasiones y sentimientos, que este afecto suele y puede hacer en
los corazones más blandos y más tiernos . . . Todos aquellos sentimientos que
los apasionados amantes probar suelen, aquí se ven tanto más agudos y
delicados, cuanto más vivo y acendrado es el divino amor que el mundano.

(1, 71)

. . . the sweetest song, which Solomon, king and prophet, composed, in which,
in the guise of an amorous dialogue between a shepherd and a shepherdess,
God shows himself more than in any other Scripture wounded by love for us,
with all those passions and feelings which such a state can and does create in
the softest and tenderest hearts. . . . Here all those feelings which passionate
lovers customarily experience are the more sharply and delicately seen as the
divine love is more intense and purified than worldly love.

Its style employs all the techniques necessary to express hope and fear,
joy and sorrow, ardent sighs and amorous complaints. The Song is
therefore the supreme model for all love poetry, because it is about the
only true kind of love. That, he says, is why it is so difficult, even
dangerous for the young and inexperienced in virtue, 'porque en
ninguna Escritura se explica la pasión del amor con más fuerza y
sentido que en ésta' (1, 72), 'for in no other Scripture is the passion of
love more forcefully and feelingly explained than here.'

Such words might well have introduced a moral or allegorical
exposition, and indeed Fray Luis affirms that under the metaphor of
the love-song 'explica el Espíritu Santo la Encarnación de Cristo y el
entrañable amor que siempre tuvo a su Iglesia', 'the Holy Spirit is
explaining the Incarnation of Christ and the deep love he has always
had for his Church.' There are some twenty passages where this more
spiritual interpretation predominates, and they increase towards the
end of the commentary. These were to stand him in good stead during
his trial, because through them he could answer the accusation that
his commentary was no better than the profane love poetry of
Ovid.[25] But in the prologue he claims that such an approach is outside
his purpose and in any case has been taken many times before. He will
confine himself to expounding the *corteza* (bark, skin, rind, peel) of the
text, its surface meaning, not its hidden message. Of its literary form he
observes:

Este Libro en su primer origen se escribió en metro, y es todo él una égloga
pastoril, donde con palabras y lenguaje de pastores, hablan Salomón y su
Esposa, y algunas veces sus compañeros, como si todos fuesen gente de aldea.

This Book was originally written in verse, and it is all in the form of a pastoral eclogue, in which in the words and language of shepherds Solomon and his Bride, and sometimes their companions, speak as if they were all village folk.

Fray Luis was well read in the classical tradition of bucolic poetry (Theocritus, Virgil, Horace) and had translated examples of it before his trial. He also knew the Italian pastoral writers and the poetry of the first great poet of the Golden Age, Garcilaso de la Vega (1501–36), who had introduced Italian metres and styles into Spanish poetry and profoundly affected its subsequent development. In the final chapter we shall see how Fray Luis adapts some of the conventions of pastoral literature for his own ends. What is important to note about the *Cantar* is that he takes the pastoral mode to be a literary convention, a metaphor as fitting for the Biblical writer as for the expression of human love; indeed, precisely because it is found in the Bible and is therefore inspired by the Holy Spirit, one requiring the most serious attention. In the Song, the language of profane love poetry is the vehicle for the communication of divine love, supremely revealed in the Incarnation.

But, Fray Luis continues, it is a difficult text, for two reasons. First, the passion of love is so strong that 'no alcanza la lengua al corazón', 'the tongue cannot reach the heart' (I, 73). The excess of feeling cannot find outlet in well-ordered expressions and therefore 'van las razones cortadas y desconcertadas', 'the phrases are cut short and disordered'. Mystics habitually claim that language cannot cope with the intensity of their experience, and Fray Luis is anticipating what St John of the Cross was to write of his own verses in the prologue to the *Cántico*, that 'antes parecen dislates que dichos puestas en razón', 'they are more like nonsense than reasonably ordered expressions'.[26] For Fray Luis, lovers human and divine experience the same confusion:

Así que las extrañas cosas que sienten, dicen y hacen los que aman, no se pueden entender ni creer de los libros de amor; de donde será forzoso que muchas cosas de este Libro sean obscuras, así al expositor de él como a los demás que en el divino amor están fríos y tibios; y, por el contrario, será muy claro todo al que ... experimentare en sí la sentencia de esta obra, y ninguna cosa le parecerá imposible ni disparatada.   (I, 105)

Thus the strange things which lovers feel, say and do cannot be understood from books on love; whence many things in this Book will necessarily be obscure, both to its expositor as to others who are cold or lukewarm in divine love; and contrariwise, everything will be very clear to whomever ... has experienced in himself the meaning of this work, and nothing will seem impossible or nonsensical to him.

Recognizing the difficulty of following the thread of the poem, Fray Luis hints at a logical structure supporting this 'broken' language of love. It depends on 'la retórica de los enamorados', 'the rhetoric of lovers', in which 'muchas veces traen lo primero a la postre, y lo último al principio' (I, 200), 'they often put last what comes first, and first, last'. This rhetoric depends on an underlying emotional unity which has produced the text, rather than a superficial literary one:

Y así son todos los lugares de este Libro, donde parece no tener dependencia las unas palabras de las otras, que, si bien se considera el sentido del afecto, la tienen muy grande y muy trabada. Porque estos libros donde se tratan pasiones de amor . . . llevan sus razonamientos o las ligaduras de ellos en el hilo de los afectos, y no en el concierto de las palabras. (I, 111)

And all the passages in this book where one set of words seems not to follow from another are like this, for if the meaning of the emotion is properly considered they are linked, and very closely. For these books which deal with the passions of love . . . carry their meanings and the tying together of their meanings in the thread of the emotions, not in the harmony of the words.

The second reason for the difficulty of the text is that Hebrew is 'lengua de pocas palabras y de cortas razones, y ésas llenas de diversidad de sentidos' (I, 73), 'a language of few words and brief phrases, which are full of different meanings.' This, together with the difference in time and taste between the ancient near east and the present, accounts for the comparisons in the Song which appear 'nuevas, y extrañas, y fuera de todo buen primor', 'new and strange, and beyond all good artifice', though in fact they are 'todo el bien hablar y toda la cortesanía de aquel tiempo entre aquella gente' (I, 74), 'the sum of fine and courtly speech of that time and among those people.' Solomon, after all, was a king, and his upbringing, let alone his wisdom, guaranteed that he spoke his language with greater elegance than anyone else. So for Fray Luis the Song was the ancient oriental equivalent to European pastoral literature, and one moreover divinely inspired and given.

That is why he specifically identifies rhetorical features in his commentary: the metonymy of 'crown' for 'kingdom' (I, 123), the synecdoche of 'seal' for 'ring' (202–3), the apostrophe to the winds (141). He terms the summarizing sentence of vii.6 an *epiphonema*, and the progression of images in vi. 9 (AV vi.10) an 'encarecimiento acrecentado' (171), a 'heightened hyperbole'. He reminds us that the Song is a more exotic blend of eastern imagery than the Renaissance pastoral, and introduces the extraordinary similes at the beginning of chapter iv thus:

En que hay gran dificultad, no tanto por ser la mayor parte sacadas de cosas del campo, que en esto guarda la persona de pastor que representa, cuanto por ser maravillosamente ajenas y extrañas de nuestro común uso y estilo, y algunas de ellas contrarias, al parecer, de todo lo que quieren declarar. Si no es . . . que en aquel tiempo y en aquella lengua estas cosas tenían gran primor, como en cada tiempo y en cada lengua vemos mil cosas recibidas y usadas por buenas, que en otros tiempos o puestas en otras lenguas no se tuvieran por tales. (i, 125–6)

In this there is great difficulty, not so much because they are mostly taken from objects of the countryside, since in this he is keeping to the character of the shepherd which he represents, as because they are wondrously strange and alien to our normal usage and style, and some of them apparently contrary to all they are meant to expound. But . . . at that time and in that language such things were highly prized, as in every time and language we find a thousand things accepted and used as good which at other times or expressed in other languages would not be so considered.

Fray Luis brings the analytical approach of a western mind to the mysterious imagery of the east, so alien to the accepted idiom of his day – hair like a flock of goats, teeth like sheep. Of the first he writes:

Lo que es de maravillar aquí es la comparación, que al parecer es grosera y muy apartada de aquello a que se hace. Fuera acertada si dijera ser como una madeja de oro, o que competía con los rayos del sol en muchedumbre y color, como suelen decir nuestros poetas. (i, 128)

The comparison is to be wondered at, since it seems coarse and very out of keeping with what it is made for. It would have been correct if he had said it was like a strand of gold, or that it competed in quantity and colour with the rays of the sun, as our poets usually do.

But he goes on to explain how the goats feed on mount Gilead, rubbing their old hair off against the bushes of the thickets, so that their coats are made clean and shiny by the resin these exude. That is why the Bride's hair is like the goats of Gilead.

Fray Luis easily resolves an apparent contradiction in v.12 (AV v.11) between a golden head and raven locks. All languages, he says, use gold as an image of perfection, but in oriental cultures dark hair is thought lovelier than fair. His exposition begins to develop a striking conceit, in which gold, the metaphor for excellence, is joined with black, the true colour of the hair, so that both represent the same feature. Only two verses later he reminds us of the commonplace poetic images of his day in a passage most illuminating for his view of the Bible as a literary model:

Los que mucho quieren encarecer una cosa alabándola y declarando sus propiedades, dejan de decir los vocablos llanos y propios, y dicen los nombres de las cosas en que más perfectamente se halla aquella cualidad de lo que loan, lo cual da mayor encarecimiento y mayor gracia a lo que se dice. Como aquel gran poeta toscano que, habiendo de loar los cabellos, los llama *oro*, a los labios *grana*, a los dientes *perlas*, y a los ojos, *luces, lumbres* o *estrellas*; el cual artificio se guarda en la Escritura Sagrada más que en otra del mundo.

(1, 158)

Those who really want to enhance a thing by praising it and expounding its characteristics stop using plain and appropriate words and use the names of things in which that quality they are praising is most perfectly to be found, which gives greater enhancement and grace to what is expressed. Like that great Tuscan poet who, wishing to praise hair calls it *gold*, lips *scarlet*, teeth *pearls* and eyes *lights, fires* or *stars*; a device used in Holy Scripture more than in any other writing in the world.

Petrarch, in other words, is doing what the Bible already and supremely has done, though through very different images.

Fray Luis ends the prologue by outlining his method: a Spanish word-for-word version of the original Hebrew will be followed by a short exposition of the text of some of the obscurer passages. He claims to have made his Spanish version reflect the feel of the Hebrew original:

... no sólo en las sentencias y palabras, sino aun en el concierto y aire dellas, imitando sus figuras y maneras de hablar cuanto es posible a nuestra lengua, que, a la verdad, responde con la hebrea en muchas cosas.   (1, 74)

... not only in the texts and words, but even in their ordering and character, by imitating its figures of speech as far as is possible in our language, which indeed corresponds with Hebrew in many respects.

Fray Luis was certainly among those who felt that Spanish was as fine a vehicle for serious literary expression as Latin and Greek. But here he is bold enough to compare it with Biblical Hebrew. It is a pity he does not go into greater detail about their alleged similarities. He admits that his word-for-word version will be found cryptic and archaic by some. But his intention is to preserve as fully as possible the idiom of the original, and in this he succeeds. This version must be one of the least comprehensible things ever to have appeared in Spanish, largely because of the absence of the copulative verb, the strange juxtapositions of different tenses and the imagery itself. He renders part of vii.5 'El rey atado en las regueras' (1, 175), 'The king tied in the water-channels', while viii.1 reads:

¿Quién te me dará, como hermano mío, que mamases los pechos de mi madre? Hallartehía fuera; besartehía, y también no me despreciarían.

(1, 192)

Who shall give thee to me, as my brother, that thou shouldst suck the breasts of my mother? I would find thee outside; I would kiss thee, and also they would not despise me.

Perhaps this was intended to demonstrate in as vivid a way as possible how difficult Hebrew was to translate into any language – including the Latin of the Vulgate.

Much of the *Cantar* commentary deals with the language and imagery of the Song, the difficulties caused by its vocabulary and dislocated structure, and its depiction of the various states of love. There are a few developed passages, but on the whole it is a plain, fast-moving explanation of the text. There is much discussion of Hebrew words, not as an exercise in pedantry, but because if these are the words God has chosen to veil his meaning in, the critic must do his best to establish their exact significance. Like many of his contemporaries, Fray Luis believed that Hebrew was the language God had given to Adam before the Fall, and in which Adam had named the creatures as God brought them to him (Gen. ii.19–20). To examine Hebrew words and phrases was therefore to gaze more deeply into the mystery of things than any other language permitted, for Hebrew was the only link with the world before the Fall and with the divine mind and its intentions in creation.

From the outset Fray Luis stresses the 'propiedad' (property, intrinsic quality) of Hebrew words, and sometimes the commentary reads like a glossary of the terms behind the Spanish translation. He notes characteristics of Hebrew grammar, like the frequent use of the past tense for the future, as well as constructions like 'son of...' a particular quality to describe a person who embodies it. He sometimes probes nuances of meaning: in ii.9, where the groom is shown peeping through the lattices, he sees a comparison in the Hebrew which is lost in the Spanish. The root of the Hebrew verb means a 'budding flower', peeping out to show just a hint of its beauty. This is how the groom appears, 'mostrando unas veces los ojos y no más y otras veces solos los cabellos' (1, 107), 'now revealing his eyes and now only his hair' to the awaiting bride.

More controversially, as it transpired, he tackles the relationship between the Hebrew original and the Greek and Latin Bibles used by the Church, thus raising the issue of translation to a higher plane. The most curious example, one which was to figure in his trial, occurs in iv.1, where he translates *tsammath* as 'locks', or more precisely, the fringe over the forehead (Spanish *lados*).[27] The verse reads *Tus ojos de paloma, entre tus cabellos* (1, 125), 'your dove's eyes, among your locks', but 'San Jerónimo, no sé por qué fin, entiende por esto la hermosura encubierta, y así traslada: *Tus ojos de paloma, demás de lo que está encubierto*' (i, 127), 'St Jerome, I do not know why, understands this to mean covered beauty, and so translates *Your dove's eyes, apart from what is covered*', clean against the consensus of Hebrew scholars and his own translation of the same word in Isa. xlvii. This implied criticism of the Vulgate text (for much of which Jerome was responsible) was denounced and formed part of the accusations against Fray Luis in his trial. Replying to these from prison, he defends his comments:

Esto dije allí, y no quise descubrir más la llaga porque no era para aquel lugar, ni para la persona a quien se escribía aquel libro; y lo que callé allí, diré aquí, adonde hablo con los hombres buenos y doctos.   (i, 212)

I said that there, and had no wish to uncover the wound further, because it was not for that place nor for the person for whom the book was written; and what I was silent about there I shall now state, where I can speak with good and learned men.

The last remark is doubtless ironical. He claims he is not attacking the Vulgate, merely amending an unimportant detail. Even Jerome, he adds, could not bring himself to translate the word openly and paraphrased what actually means 'the shameful parts of woman'. He still believes Jerome's rendering is faulty. How could such a word, if that is what it means, appear in a work God has dictated for the benefit and health of the soul? How can we believe that if Jerome found it indecent in Latin the Holy Spirit could have put it there in Hebrew? If the woman whose *tsammath* are referred to is a figure of the Church, what is their allegorical significance? And why have they not been introduced into the description of the Bride's thighs and belly, where they might belong, instead of her eyes, where they do not? In a secular love song such a word would be offensive: no Greek or Latin poet ever mentioned such a thing so openly and even Ovid uses a paraphrase. While the Hebrew word *may* have the meaning Jerome ascribed to it, he concludes that it certainly has the meaning 'locks of hair'. Surely in so small a detail the Vulgate can be corrected?

This self-defence, written in December 1573, is a characteristic piece of writing, full of the verve and unanswerable logic which made Fray Luis so formidable an opponent. Its particular delight is to observe how he drives his accusers into an uncomfortable corner. To defend the Vulgate they must defend pornography; to amend it slightly, he becomes the guardian of good taste.

The close attention paid to the language of the Hebrew original makes the *Cantar* an exceptional work of sixteenth-century Spanish literature. But this very attention reveals further aspects of Fray Luis's approach to language. For him, the Bible is the clue rather than one example among many. In it, through human words, God comes close to man, and the study of its words therefore leads man back to God. That study involves both individual words in their grammatical context, and the figures of speech they form. The Biblical poem is a model of literary expression, a source-book and an exemplar of rhetoric because it is divine rhetoric. Fray Luis is not an innovator in this respect. Curtius has shown that long before him Bede, in his *De schematis et tropibus*, 'carried to its logical conclusion the transference of antique rhetoric to the text of the Bible.'[28] The rediscovery of some of the classical rhetoricians in the Renaissance may have spurred on Biblical scholars like Fray Luis to look again at the Bible in this way. But we should be greatly mistaken if we thought that this was some kind of substitute for the study of the Biblical message, 'the Bible designed to be read as literature'. For Fray Luis, form and content were intimately linked; the divinely inspired words were the bearers of the divine message; to study them was to be confronted with it.

Those aspects of the work of Fray Luis we have introduced in this chapter will remain important throughout the book. We have deliberately looked at two early works, a Latin sermon and a Spanish commentary, to show that long before his trial he had acquired a theology of metaphorical language, mature opinions on translation and exegesis, and confidence in handling an obscure text. All of these he was to develop and deepen. We have seen how even these first examples can allow us to read the more familiar parts of his work in a more sensitive way, so that even when he appears to be using conventional images or a stylized setting, these may express conceptual complexities which are easy to pass over. Perhaps, most significantly of all, we have begun to understand how language itself is a theological phenomenon for him. Its metaphors can be a means of ascending towards the truth of God, which in the Bible itself descends covered in human words which are witnesses ultimately to the Word made flesh. Such a lofty view of language suggests that Fray Luis will use it himself with the greatest care, and indeed it influences his own original writings. Those parts of his work we shall go on to study may be less well known, but they will carry us further towards that fuller understanding of his mind and art which is our aim.

2

The strife of tongues

Fray Luis was arrested by an officer of the Spanish Inquisition on the evening of 27 March 1572. He cannot have been unprepared. His friend and colleague Gaspar de Grajal, who had beaten him in the contest for the Chair of Bible in 1560, had been arrested at the beginning of the month, and Martínez de Cantalapiedra, the Professor of Hebrew, the previous day. Between December 1571 and March 1572 a procession of accusers denounced the three Hebraists to the Valladolid Inquisitors, and more denunciations poured in after their arrests.[1]

On 2 December 1571, seventeen propositions allegedly held by the three were presented to the Supreme Council of the Holy Office by Pedro Fernández, the Dominican Prior of Salamanca. Another leading Dominican, Bartolomé de Medina, testified before the Inquisitors on 17 December and 18 February. He told them that in the University there was too much love of 'innovations' (*novedades*) and not enough of the old ways of religion and faith. He accused the three professors of fomenting this: 'Prefieren a Vatablo, Pagnino y sus judíos, a la traslación Vulgata y al sentido de los Santos' (x, 7), 'They prefer Vatable, Pagnini and their Jews to the Vulgate translation and the sense of the Saints'.[2] On 26 December a student denounced Fray Luis's translation of the Song of Songs, copies of which were being circulated. León de Castro, the irascible Professor of Greek, made two declarations, the second on 3 March, in which he expanded upon the accusations about Jewish interpretations of Scripture and referred to examples from meetings of a commission of which he and Fray Luis had been members. Medina's accusation is revealing because it puts in a nutshell the main issues of the trial – the translation and the interpretation of Scripture. Both, as we have seen, were among the earliest concerns of Fray Luis.

Fray Luis had done his best to pre-empt his accusers. Having sought learned opinion about his views on the Vulgate, he lodged a summary of them with the Inquisition on 6 March, doubtless to ensure that it had a correct record of them, not just a garbled version. He also submitted his *Cantar*. He asked for any learned and unbiassed man to examine his submissions and promised to retract anything found to be erroneous. He took the precaution of mentioning his enemies – Dominicans and Jeronymites in general and León de Castro and a fellow-Augustinian called Diego de Zúñiga in particular. But all these measures proved to be in vain.

The trial of Fray Luis and his two colleagues marks one of the most significant crises of Spanish religious and intellectual history in the sixteenth century. Fray Luis was to spend almost five years in prison, Martínez even longer, while the unfortunate Grajal, to the great grief of Fray Luis, was to die in prison before his case was completed. But the outcome represented a victory for moderation and reason over a fanatical adherence to the authority of one Biblical translation, not without parallels in contemporary fundamentalism, and over what can only be described as a form of anti-semitism. It was also a deep personal crisis for Fray Luis, as he struggled with his solitary confinement and with depression, sickness and an outraged sense of justice. But, as he would later recognize, out of the evil came some good. The suffering he endured became a fertile seed-bed in which his ideas about the language of the Bible and the message it conveyed were to mature and begin to produce fruit. When he returned in triumph to Salamanca he had acquired a new stature and was to be a much more powerful presence in the life of the university than he had been when he entered prison.[3]

What prompted this apparently swift reversal in his fortunes? That Fray Luis was one of three university professors from Salamanca arrested in the same month should at least arouse the suspicion that a deliberate campaign had brought this about and that the issues were broader than a straightforward personal attack on him. There were personal antagonisms which motivated some of his accusers, as there were particular controversies at Salamanca in which he had become involved. But the reasons must first be sought in the crisis of authority which had come with the call for religious reform and the shattering of the spiritual unity of Europe in the first half of the sixteenth century.

To Christians of that age, Catholic and Protestant almost without exception, the Bible and its faithful interpretation through the centuries was of paramount authority. It contained the divine will for individuals and society, it was the guarantor of orthodoxy and the source of divine truth. The Old Testament as well as the New was understood as a detailed foretelling of Christ, which accurate methods of interpretation could uncover. The page headings in the Authorized Version show this plainly: the Song is entitled 'The mutual love of Christ and his church.' But its truths were not self-evident. Since its text was often difficult or obscure, it had to be wrestled with. Any challenge to its authority could be seen as a challenge to the Christian faith itself, and that is indeed what has happened since the rise of modern critical study of the Bible. Scholars have recognized how human factors have affected its writing, and its supernatural content and given certainties have been so undermined that for most people in the Christian West the Bible long ago ceased to be the repository of divine revelation.

For centuries the Western Church had used the Latin translation of the Bible begun in the fourth century by St Jerome and known as the Vulgate. But scholars had become increasingly aware of its inadequacies. In the fifteenth century the Italian humanist Lorenzo Valla had described many of his philological and grammatical reservations about the text in his *Adnotationes* (observations) on the New Testament. The renewed interest in ancient literature and the discovery of many old manuscripts of Biblical books especially after the fall of Constantinople stimulated Biblical scholarship of the early sixteenth century and increased doubts about the reliability of the Vulgate. For Erasmus, who had chanced upon a manuscript of Valla's *Adnotationes* at Louvain in 1504 and had become excited about the possibilities of textual criticism of the Bible, the restoration of the Biblical text to its original purity was more than a work of scholarship, it was the necessary foundation for his programme of Christian reform. A renewed Bible would lead to a spiritual and evangelical renewal of the Church. Like many Renaissance scholars, he was powerfully affected by the belief that the return to pure and ancient sources through the stripping away of the accretions of centuries of error could lead to the Golden Age, in this case that of the apostolic devotion and zeal of the first Christian communities. His new editions of the Greek New Testament and of the Fathers grew out of the same concern as his popular satirical writings and his works of inner piety like the *Enchiridion*. In post-Tridentine Spain the Biblical scholarship of Erasmus was still being used, even after many of his other works had been prohibited. Fray Luis often quotes Erasmus in this respect: the second of his *Quaestiones* contains a lengthy examination of Erasmian readings of controversial New Testament texts, during which he both praises and criticizes Erasmus.[4]

Biblical scholarship continued to flourish throughout the troubled period of the early Reformation. The first edition of the Rabbinical Bible – the Hebrew text with paraphrases and Rabbinical commentaries – was printed by Daniel Bomberg in Flanders in 1516–17 and a second edition in Venice in 1524, for which Bomberg consulted a leading Jewish scholar.[5] Attempts continued to establish a better text for the Vulgate. Some scholars corrected it by reference to the Hebrew and Greek originals, as the Lutheran Andreas Osiander did (Nuremberg, 1522 and Cologne, 1527): Fray Luis takes issue with him in the third of the *Quaestiones*.[6] Others preferred to produce a revised text from ancient manuscript evidence, and Robert Estienne, printer to Francis I, brought out a notable series of such Vulgates between 1527 and 1545. Others again made entirely new translations from the originals, and the most important of these was by the Italian Dominican Santes Pagnini, completed around 1518 and published in 1528 with his influential new Latin translation of the Old Testament. His preface 'contained words ominous for conservative minds, "the translation of Jerome is not uncorrupted."'[7]

Estienne's work was especially significant.[8] His 1545 Vulgate appeared with another Latin translation alongside Pagnini's and made use of the annotations of François Vatable, a Christian Hebraist of the first part of the century. These are generally thought to have been brief notes on the Hebrew text copied down by his students in Paris. Estienne also produced portions of the Hebrew Old Testament from 1539–44 and Greek New Testaments in 1546, 1549 and 1550. For his labours he was condemned in 1546 by the University of Louvain and summoned the following year before the Privy Council. His Latin Bibles were also condemned by the University of Paris, and he became a Calvinist after fleeing to Geneva in 1550. Estienne, Pagnini and Vatable are all names that appear frequently in the trial record of Fray Luis and it is clear that he was familiar with their work and prepared to use it where he felt it could be trusted. Other Spaniards, noting that Protestants habitually rejected the authority of the Vulgate and appealed to the originals and to the new editions and versions of the Bible instead, could only see a further undermining of the authority of the Church if Roman Catholic scholars also joined in the attack on the Vulgate.

So contentious had the study of the Biblical text become that the Council of Trent began to debate Holy Scripture and Tradition soon after it was convened at the end of 1545. In its fourth session on 8 April 1546 its decrees on Scripture, Tradition and the Vulgate were ratified. During the debates it had become clear that no single view prevailed within the Roman Church on the nature of the Vulgate's authority or its relationship to the original texts. Opinion in Rome tended towards the liberal, but the Spanish delegation at the Council took a strongly conservative line and Cardinal Pacheco had demanded that every translation of the Bible apart from the Vulgate should be prohibited. The result was a compromise which left the decree open to widely differing interpretations.

The Vulgate decree itself stated that 'haec ipsa vetus et vulgata editio, quae longo tot saeculorum usu in ipsa Ecclesia probata est, in publicis lectionibus, disputationibus et expositionibus pro authentica habeatur, et quod illam nemo rejicere quovis praetextu audeat vel praesumat', 'this ancient and widespread edition, tried by long and various use in the Church, is to be held as authentic in public readings, disputations and expositions, and that no one venture or presume to reject it on any pretext.' By this was meant that it was

... reliable and furnishing dogmatic proofs for practical use in theological lectures and disputations as well as for the ministry of preaching. The basis of this authenticity is not the Vulgate's agreement with the original texts, but the long use made of it by the Church ... It was not the intention of the Council to restrict the study of the original languages of the Bible, still less to stop it.[9]

Although Trent foresaw the need for a revision of the Vulgate it made no plans for this. The decree did not say what 'authentic' meant and was silent about many issues raised during the debates – the existence of copyists' and printers' errors, the correction of the Vulgate by reference to the originals, and the value of other Latin translations. Nor did it pronounce upon the vexed matter of vernacular translations of Scripture. Of the other Latin translations Sutcliffe writes:

It was expressly added that other translations would not thereby be rejected in so far as they helped to the understanding of the one version declared authoritative... The Vulgate was not declared intrinsically superior to other Latin versions nor were these others in any way condemned. As far as they are concerned the decree is purely negative. They are left in exactly the condition in which they were. Only to no other was given the juridical recognition of authority which was accorded to the Vulgate.[10]

That may have been the intention of the decree, but not everyone so understood it. Múñoz Iglesias shows how the decree itself provoked many arguments among post-Tridentine Spanish theologians:

Los que admitían la posibilidad de corregir la Vulgata por otras ediciones, y especialmente por el recurso a los originales, argüían del hecho de que éstos no son rechazados por el decreto. Los que negaban la posibilidad de tal corrección, se aferraban a la letra del decreto . . . y afirmaban que dar una versión distinta a la de la Vulgata era rechazar a ésta.

Those who allowed the possibility of correcting the Vulgate by other editions, and especially by recourse to the originals, argued from the fact that these are not rejected by the decree. Those who denied that such correction was possible clung to the letter of the decree . . . and maintained that to offer a version different from the Vulgate's was tantamount to rejecting it.[11]

Múñoz Iglesias further regards this as a clash between the renascent scholasticism of the middle of the century, with its antagonism towards textual study of the Bible, and the humanist approach which had been practising it for a century. The Dominicans, well represented among the accusers of Fray Luis, regarded themselves as the heirs and defenders of Aquinas, whereas the Augustinians were traditionally more eclectic. Fray Luis and his colleagues were certainly accused of teaching that 'doctrina scholastica nocet ad intelligentiam Sanctarum Scripturarum', 'scholastic doctrine is detrimental to understanding the Holy Scriptures.'[12] The contrast between the two disciplines was often enough made: in his 1579 speech for the Bible Chair Fray Luis took some pleasure in pointing out that when he had stood for the St Thomas and Durandus Chairs his opponents had argued that he knew little about scholastic theology, and now they were saying that he knew plenty about that and not enough about the Bible.[13] But as we shall see, the trial suggests a more complex series of oppositions than a simple clash of scholasticism and Biblical study.

This, then, is the broad background against which Fray Luis began his own critical work on the Bible. But within it there is also a more direct and personal focus to the story of his trial. Although he taught dogmatic theology in his first two chairs, he found during the 1560s that his views on the Bible were coming into increasingly sharp conflict with those of other scholars at Salamanca. Two areas of his work brought matters to a head: his lectures on the authority of Scripture in his *De fide* course of 1567–8, and his membership of a commission of Biblical scholars and theologians at Salamanca which had been convened to recommend whether or not the Estienne Bible with the Vatable annotations should be reprinted. These form the immediate context of his trial and in them Fray Luis was to discover that the unresolved tensions of the Tridentine decree, which themselves grew out of the larger religious controversies of the century, would become part of his own search for scholarly integrity and lead him into great suffering.

Fray Luis began his *De fide* lectures by discussing the nature of Biblical inspiration, but soon turned to more controversial matters as he asked if extant codices contained the pure text of the original authors.[14] He rehearsed the early history of the text as it was commonly understood. The Old Testament was originally written in Hebrew, the first of all languages:[15] some believe that although this text was destroyed after the fall of Jerusalem (586 BC), Ezra the Scribe, who had memorized it, recopied it. The New Testament is in Greek, though many think that Matthew and Hebrews were first written in Hebrew. The history of the New Testament codices is uncertain, as they have perished through negligence and passage of time. The Old Testament was translated into Aramaic (or Chaldee, as the sixteenth century usually called it), and this translation is called the Targum. Fray Luis also describes the various Greek translations and Origen's *Hexapla*, a third-century Polyglot. By Jerome's time a Latin translation from the Septuagint was in circulation (the Vetus Latina), but in many forms and of uncertain authorship. In due course it merged with the Vulgate and this became the normative Bible of the Church.

Jerome used the term 'the Hebrew verity' to indicate that behind his Latin translation lay an original which had to be mastered before translation was possible. Many Christian scholars however believed that the Hebrew text had become too corrupt to be reliable, and some of them that the Jews had deliberately corrupted it, to alter texts Christians used as proofs of the Messiahship of Jesus (*testimonia*). For this reason, Fray Luis tells us, some scholars, like Cano, had preferred the Greek translation of the Old Testament, the Septuagint. What might have been a purely academic dispute was thus bound up with Christian attitudes towards the Jews. For some, to ascribe prior value to the original Hebrew and to presume to correct the Vulgate by this was to declare Judaism superior to Christianity. Fray Luis cannot have been aware of the possible dangers of such an attitude as he lectured, or he might have been more circumspect.

He continues by describing four alleged corruptions of the Hebrew text. Two verses it lacks are present in the Septuagint; five words have been altered; Justin Martyr claimed that the Jews had maliciously corrupted two Messianic texts; while Jewish scholars were said to have introduced changes before the Christian era when they found expressions such as anthropomorphisms which they considered unworthy of the majesty of God – the so-called 'corrections of the wise'. He explains that Hebrew is prone to corrupt readings because so many words are like each other. Their basic pattern is a triconsonantal root and vowels are indicated only by pointing, small signs inserted under, over or between the consonants to show the following vowel. The existence of scribal errors and variant readings is not therefore proof of deliberate tampering where the original reading cannot be ascertained, and he states that no such tampering took place before Jerome because only Justin among all the early Fathers believed that it had. He finds satisfactory explanations for the alleged corruptions: he rejects Justin's accusations and calls the 'corrections of the wise' a Talmudic fable, as Origen and Jerome knew nothing of them and the Jews took infinite care to preserve their sacred text unspoilt. Such differences as there are stem from the problems inherent in the Hebrew itself. Where there are uncertainties about pointing, the Hebrew should be compared with the Greek and Latin and corrected accordingly, after examination of the oldest codices and the earliest citations in the Fathers. Many Old Testament texts Christians use to confirm their beliefs have never been altered, and the Jews could hardly have conspired to do anything, since they were scattered over the face of the earth.

Fray Luis shows himself to be a firm supporter of the 'Hebrew verity'. While allowing that it has problems, he refuses to accept that the Hebrew text has been deliberately distorted by anti-Christian Jews. He is less enthusiastic about the Septuagint. He questions the truth of the legend of its miraculous completion by the seventy-two translators who worked in isolation but produced an identical text. Compared with the Hebrew, it has many additions, omissions, contradictions and obscurities. It omits four important Messianic texts, including the 'names' which most clearly prove the divinity of Christ (Isa. ix.6). It describes the second day of creation as good, whereas the Hebrew and the Latin agree in restricting this to the sixth: two, Fray Luis argues curiously, cannot be good, since the number divides, and the Pythagoreans used it as a symbol of imperfection and corruption. He concludes that the Septuagint cannot have been written with a prophetic spirit (*prophetico spiritu*), a term which becomes increasingly central to the argument of the lectures, otherwise the Church could never have replaced it with the Vulgate.[16] The only comfort he offers its supporters is that it occupies first place among the Greek versions and contains no dangerous errors. Even the fact that the New Testament quotations of the Old habitually follow its text does not impress him, because the New was addressed mainly to Greek-speaking converts.

The material on the Vulgate begins with a discussion of its authorship and why it cannot wholly be ascribed to Jerome. The real problems, however, arise over its authority, and Fray Luis realized this. When he mentions its possible errors and mistranslations and the question of its prophetic inspiration, he adds 'de quo est maxima controversia inter catholicos' (294), 'concerning which there is the greatest controversy among Catholics'. He does not often make such statements.

Trent had taken only very modest steps towards solving long-standing difficulties about the Vulgate. It had established as canonical a number of passages about which there had been doubt for many centuries, and the Vulgate was stated to be the only Latin Bible to be used officially by the Church. In view of what was to happen, Fray Luis's comment that 'the difficulty lies in the meaning of the word authentic' (295) is an understatement. He outlines three characteristic interpretations of what the decree meant. Some say the Vulgate is so inspired that it faithfully represents the original and is to be preferred to the Greek and Hebrew; that is what they understand 'authentic' to mean. Others admit that it contains obscurities but that it alone is to be used as the Biblical basis for definitions of the faith. Yet others believe that though it insufficiently expresses everything pertaining to faith and morals and though it contains obscurities and bad translations and does not wholly give the meaning intended by the Spirit, it is to be preferred to other *Latin* editions and is free of serious error. Where it departs from the Greek and Hebrew it is not to be used against them. This is the view Fray Luis held and tirelessly defended from his prison cell. The record of his trial is to a large extent a commentary on these interpretations of the decree.

Out of them two sharply-contrasted attitudes emerged: that of scholars like Fray Luis, who believed that it contained no error in faith and morals and was more reliable than other Latin versions, and that of those for whom it was quite simply infallible. They stressed that if it were not, the Church would not possess true Scripture and could not therefore refute heresy, especially important since heretics frequently appealed to the Greek and Hebrew over the Latin. They claimed that it had always been used for defining the faith and teaching on morality, that it must either be all true or all false, and that Inquisitors, who might know no Hebrew or Greek, used it in making their judgements. The originals should therefore be correctible by the Vulgate, not vice versa, since the Jews had corrupted the Hebrew and the Greek New Testament contained errors rectified in the Vulgate.

Before answering this fair summary of the conservative interpretation of the decree, Fray Luis states his own position in eight propositions, which were to form the basis of the material he handed to the Inquisitors shortly before his arrest:

(i) The extant Vulgate codices contained variants and corrupt readings, not the original text, so that great care had to be taken to establish an accurate reading. Such variants were shown only too clearly in the great Estienne and Plantin Bibles, and he gives many examples, including one 'ex codice vetustissimo manuscripto, qui apud me est' (300), 'from a very old codex in my possession', revealing himself as something of a collector. He especially notes variants which make better or more elegant sense than the Vulgate readings.

(ii) In the current Vulgate text, some *testimonia* formerly used by Popes and Councils for confirming the faith are missing or have been altered.

(iii) When the Hebrew is equivocal and the Vulgate prefers one reading over other possibilities, this one is not so certain that the others are to be neglected, and sometimes they may prove better. The first example he gives connects with his own work on Genesis towards the end of his life. The Latin of Gen. ii.8 reads 'Plantaverat autem Dominus paradisum voluptatis a principio' (the Lord God had planted a paradise of delight from the beginning). But the Hebrew *qedem*, rendered by 'beginning', refers to time of day as well as place, the time when day begins, that is, the east, as the Septuagint reads. This translation is much more apt, since paradise was traditionally thought to have been created in the East, in Mesopotamia. The Vulgate is therefore misleading.[17]

(iv) Some Hebrew and Greek readings confirm the faith better than those of the Vulgate.

(v) Where there are variant readings and the tradition of the

Church underlines rather than resolves the discrepancies, the Vulgate reading does not have to be received as catholic and certain.

(vi) Some passages in the Vulgate have not been properly translated. Fray Luis realized how contentious this would be, because he lists no fewer than fifteen examples, mostly from the Old Testament.

(vii) The Vulgate translation was not made 'with a prophetic spirit', neither are any or all of its Latin words to be received as if so dictated; nor should it be thought that a better translation is not possible, since the Council did not mean 'authentic' to suggest such a view. This opinion, again highly controversial, is the inevitable conclusion from the foregoing propositions and also proved by the fact that if the Vulgate had been prophetically inspired the Church would not have taken a thousand years to pronounce on its authenticity, and the Doctors of the Church would have been deceived when they consulted the Hebrew or Greek to resolve doubtful passages.

(viii) The Council, he argues, intended the Vulgate to be preferred to the other Latin versions. By this it meant that it was closer to the originals than they were; where they differ among themselves and the tradition of the Church does not resolve the differences, the Vulgate is to be regarded as the most faithful witness; but it should not be assumed that where it differs from the originals it is wrong, since they too have suffered from accidental scribal errors. Authenticity means that it contains no dangerous errors or false meanings, and that generally it expresses the sense of the Holy Spirit more truly than any other Latin version. He proves his interpretation by reference to the comments of those present when the decree was promulgated, notably the Franciscan theologian, Andrés de Vega (1498–1549), and by the conciliar statement putting the decree in its context. If the Council had meant that the Vulgate was verbally inspired it would have appended an anathema, to show that this was *de fide*; and if it had thought it was infallible, it would have stated that every word expressed the Holy Spirit's intention and would have appointed a commission to examine its relationship to the originals to declare it to be truer than they were.

Fray Luis ended his discussion by countering the objections previously raised in favour of the Vulgate's infallibility. Heresy can be refuted from it, since it contains everything necessary for true faith. There is no general rule for judging between the Vulgate and the originals, but he is sure that comparison of texts and sound learning will in each case establish the right conclusion. That the Hebrew codices are needed for this is of no consequence: the Church has always possessed them, as also learned Catholic scholars who can outwit the Rabbis. He supports those who are calling for an official revision of the Vulgate text by such men.

We do not know what the immediate effect of these lectures was at Salamanca, or how quickly their content passed from the lecture hall to a wider and potentially hostile audience. But we do know that before long Fray Luis himself began to circulate the eight propositions among fellow-Augustinians and trusted churchmen, to test their acceptability. One of these was the Archbishop of Granada, to whom a copy was sent via Hernando de Peralta, the Augustinian Prior of Córdoba, and Fray Luis made much of this in his trial. Peralta reports how the Archbishop's fear of certain disturbances at Salamanca led him to refrain from appending his signature to the propositions, and in a letter sent to Fray Luis on the day he was arrested writes that the Archbishop 'solía ser fácil en dar estos pareceres; pero que ya estaba escarmentado, porque se había visto en algunas pesadumbres por ello, especialmente después de que firmó el catecismo del arzobispo de Toledo' (x, 61, 137), 'used to be happy to give such opinions; but he is now on his guard, because he found himself in some difficulties because of it, especially after he signed the Archbishop of Toledo's Catechism'. The reference is a grim one and underlines the change in atmosphere caused by the arrest of Carranza, the Primate of Spain, in 1559, and the placing of his *Catechismo Christiano* on the Index. He was still in prison at this time, his trial dragging on until his death in 1576. Small wonder other churchmen trod warily; at least one of them made an implied connection between Fray Luis's propositions on the Vulgate and the most sensational Inquisition case of the century.

The year following these lectures, Fray Luis became entangled in arguments over related issues with a man who was to become one of his bitterest opponents, León de Castro (c. 1510–85), professor of Greek at Salamanca and an ardent supporter of the Septuagint against all other versions of the Bible. The Estienne Bible with its Vatable annotations obtained a licence for a third edition in Spain in 1569, Fray Luis and Castro both sat on the commission appointed to examine and, where necessary, amend it; and both signed a general judgement (*censura general*) which prefaced it, drawn up by Fray Luis. The Bible was not to be printed until 1584 or available for sale till

1586, and the Index of 1612 required further emendations. Writing in 1570 to Arias Montano about Castro and these meetings Fray Luis made his feelings plain:

Su affición es . . . con los 70 y con los authores griegos y persuádese en sus opiniones así, que lo que desdize dellas ny lo entiende ny piensa que es tolerable y así todo lo que es letra o que tiene cosas de aver nacido de Rabbinos es para él cossa descomulgada. Por esta causa dize mal de Pagnino y de Vatablo . . . y no perdona a S. Ierónimo.

His affection . . . lies with the 70 [the Septuagint] and the Greek authors, and he is so persuaded of his opinions that whatever is said against them he can neither understand nor tolerate; and so everything which is of the literal sense or bears traces of the Rabbis is anathema to him. For this reason he speaks ill of Pagnini and Vatable and . . . does not pardon St Jerome.[18]

The arguments centred at first on the extent to which the literal sense of the Old Testament, explained where necessary with the help of Jewish traditional authorities, was acceptable to Christians in its own right, and did not always need an allegorical interpretation to make it refer to Christ. But the dispute between the two men soon became more personal. Castro had written an enormous commentary on Isaiah, which he showed to Fray Luis. When Fray Luis realized that Castro had mutilated the Hebrew text to make it agree with the Septuagint, on the grounds that the Jews had corrupted the original, he broached the subject with him, privately at first and then in one of the commission meetings. The affair escalated. In February 1570 Castro was summoned to the court about his book and blamed Fray Luis for this. He was extremely angry with him, and, if Fray Luis is to be believed, never forgave him.

I have seen a copy of this rare *Commentaria in Esaiam* at Salamanca, some 1,100 pages long, and crammed full of attacks on Jews and 'judaizers', by which was meant Christians who supported Jewish interpretations of Scripture.[19] The index, for example, contains eight columns of references to Christians and nine to Jews and judaizers. The commentary begins with a treatise defending the Septuagint against recent editions of the Old Testament, in which chapters 47–52 are specifically directed against contemporary judaizers. One of the headings aptly sums up the tone of the whole: 'Quod finis Scripturae Christus est, non David, Solomon, Assyrius, aut aliquid huiusmodi, quod putant Iudaei & Iudaizantes', 'That the end of Scripture is Christ, not David, Solomon, Assyria, or anything of the kind, as Jews and judaizers think.' One of the book's approbations comes from

Francisco Sancho, the Dean of Theology at Salamanca, who, Castro claims, had personally read chapters 29–35 of the commentary. But it is dated 1567–8, just prior to the outbreak of hostilities between Fray Luis and Castro.

But Castro's argument was not with Fray Luis alone. He seems to have taken it upon himself to act as the champion of orthodoxy against those who he thought were selling out to the Jews. He made himself other enemies, too. It is through the activity of Castro that we begin to sense some of the wider links of the trial of Fray Luis with the struggle between an anti-Jewish view of Scripture spearheaded by Castro and a more balanced attitude which was prepared to accept certain Jewish interpretations of the Old Testament where they were of help.

A splendidly intemperate, unpublished attack on Castro's *In Esaiam* can be found among the papers of the distinguished Jesuit historian, Juan de Mariana, in the form of an anonymous letter addressed to Castro.[20] In it, among other things, Castro is accused of being a more pernicious enemy of the Christian faith than Mahomet, because his support of the Septuagint is an implicit attack on the Vulgate, and a man of coarseness and ignorance who from beating boys (*desculando* may carry other, sexual overtones) has passed to persecuting the great men of the realm (f. 12^r). The aim of his commentary is 'repetir a cada passo, los Rabinos, los Judiguelos, los Judai[zan]tes, para atemorizar a España' (ff. 12^{r-v}), 'to repeat at every stage Rabbis, Jew-boys, judaizers, to terrorize Spain'. There are also attacks on his scholarship, or lack of it: he has mistaken marginal verse summaries in the Hebrew Bible for variants, and he should have given an account of the original Septuagint and the Vulgate's authority, as well as have explained why, if the Hebrew is as corrupt as he says, the Pope has approved the *Biblia Regia* and why the Polyglot of the great Cardinal (i.e. the Complutensian) was famed throughout Christendom and published outside Spain by the apostolic see.

The reference to the *Biblia Regia* is significant, because it provides another clue for the context of the trial of the Salamanca Hebraists. Castro was also busy attacking Arias Montano, who was working in Flanders (where the political consequences of questioning established authority had become only too apparent) on the second great Polyglot Bible of the century, under the direct sponsorship of Philip II. Mariana's anonymous letter claims that Castro's only concern is to engender hatred against Arias Montano and the *Biblia Regia*, which he must have perceived as a much more serious example of the attitudes he was trying to combat in scholars like Fray Luis. In another document, also unsigned, Mariana gives cautious support to Montano's enterprise, though he voices several reservations.[21] Montano should have taken greater care in defending the Vulgate's authority and he should not have been so ready to accept the findings of certain heretics (Estienne?) or to include so many quotations from the Kabbalah. Castro's zeal, he comments tartly, may be commendable, but his intelligence (*ingenio*) is not. The main problem with the *Biblia Regia* is that it has been committed to one individual, who, however learned he may be, is bound to make mistakes. It woud have been better and cheaper to have reprinted the Cardinal's Polyglot. He adds that he is not signing his judgement because of the enemies it might make him, further proof of the seriousness of such matters.

The Bible was finished by summer 1571 and awaited the royal *privilegio* and Papal authorization before it could be published. Castro had only succeeded in delaying it. Yet he did not give up easily. In 1575, three years after the Bible was published, Arias Montano was complaining from Rome to the king of Castro's machinations and accusing him of disloyalty:

En todas las naciones . . . no ha habido hombre que abriese su boca a poner la menor excepción en esa obra . . . Solamente en España ha habido un profesor de gramática . . . que se llama el maestro León de Castro en Salamanca, el cual ha levantado a decir mal y poner mal nombre . . . en esta santa obra, movido de un afecto que él dice ser zelo . . . Yo había oído decir muchas cosas de sus bramidos, cuando estaba en Flandes, porque hasta allá sonaron . . . empero nunca creí que se pasaba tan adelante su furia como me decían . . . Procuraba con grande diligencia hacer aquí lo mismo . . . de manera que toda Roma está llena deste ruido de sus bramidos.

In no country . . . has a single man opened his mouth to express the least objection to this work . . . Only in Spain has there been a professor of grammar . . . León de Castro by name, in Salamanca, who has arisen to speak ill of and give a bad name to . . . this holy work, moved by a feeling which he claims is zeal . . . I had heard many things about his roaring when I was in Flanders, because the noise reached even there . . . but I never imagined his fury would reach the pitch I am told it did. He tried with great diligence to do the same here . . . so that the whole of Rome is full of the noise of his roaring.[22]

It is clear from Castro's attacks on Montano that the trial of Fray Luis was part of a more widespread movement against Hebrew scholarship by Castro and his supporters. There is some evidence that he enjoyed considerable influence in some quarters.[23] It is equally clear that, having failed to catch Arias Montano, they were able to move against three professors at Salamanca who represented the approach to the Bible which they detested. That is why the trial of Fray Luis, Grajal and Martínez can be called 'un solo proceso . . . un gran proceso de cultura; 'a single trial, one great trial of culture.'[24]

According to Fray Luis, once Castro's anger over his book had been aroused, he looked around for allies and found a ready one in Bartolomé de Medina, a Dominican theologian in his own right, who was to be elected to the Prime Chair in Theology in succession to Mancio de Corpus Christi in 1575, while Fray Luis was still in prison. Medina had his own, personal grievance against Fray Luis, because he had successfully challenged him in 1566 over a substitution for Mancio during Mancio's illness. Medina could not forget this affront to Dominican prestige. Castro and Medina, Fray Luis claims, summoned a meeting of Dominicans, some Jeronymites 'y otras personas enemigas . . . y repartieron entre sí como en caso de guerra las partes por donde habían de acometer cada uno' (x, 318), 'and other hostile people . . . and allocated, as if at war, the areas which each was to attack'. Many times during the trial Fray Luis was to complain that if Castro and Medina had been as worried then by his views on the Vulgate as they now claimed to be, they would not have waited so long before denouncing him. The delay could be explained only by other, more personal motives, and malice was an improper basis for denunciations, as the Inquisition itself recognized.

We must now follow the course of the trial itself, and see how it relates to the issues we have been looking at. Its most striking feature is not its brutality but its extreme slowness. The Inquisition had a well-developed bureaucracy and its procedures rarely allowed for cases to come quickly to judgement.[25] At his first hearing, on 15 April 1572, Fray Luis was required to give an account of his life and his opinion on why he had been arrested. Three days later, after a hurriedly prepared defence, he expanded on this. He particularly stressed the parts played by Medina and Castro in the scandals which had been spreading among the Salamanca theologians, and went into great detail to remember comments he had made in his lectures, things he had written (like the *Cantar*) and material he had brought to the Inquisitors which might have caused offence. His counsel, Dr Ortiz de Funes, was appointed on 5 May; meanwhile, the prosecutor, Diego de Haedo, had prepared a preliminary set of ten suspect propositions to which Fray Luis began to reply. By 24 July he had agreed with his counsel the questions to be asked of defence witnesses, but on 10

December and 21 January 1573 was complaining that these still had not been sent off. Three further lists were compiled, the last not until August 1574. Even then there were difficulties, since not all the witnesses could be found. Eventually they were examined in two main batches, between January and June 1573 and May and June 1576.

Almost a year after his arrest came a long and eloquent complaint in which Fray Luis listed his principal grievances (7 March 1573; x, 255–8). He had not seen the accusations made against him, so he could not prepare a proper defence. His accusers, he repeated, were his enemies, and the University's honour was at stake while he languished in prison. The accusations must have appeared soon afterwards, since during April and May he began his defence, culminating in a full statement, the *amplia defensa* of 14 May (x, 317–88). His requests for books and papers from his library caused further delays; those made in April and June were only met in the July and November of that year. He first asked for the Vatable Bible and the commission's signed report, for example, in April 1573, but when it finally arrived, in February 1574, it was not the copy he wanted. During 1573 and into early 1574 Fray Luis provided the Inquisitors with a stream of statements, clarifications and complaints, and in March 1574 began to respond in detail to the Vulgate propositions he had submitted and to thirty others extracted from them and other accusations, and covering similar ground (x, 527–32; 537–40).

At the end of that month a new phase began. Neutral and learned judges (*patronos*) were to be appointed to advise the accused about his teachings. Fray Luis's first reaction was to remind the Inquisitors of all those who would not be neutral, and to request a copy of the documents from which the propositions had been extracted, which occasioned correspondence between the Inquisitors and the *Suprema*, the Council of the Inquisition, and brought a negative reply. On 31 March Fray Luis asked for the Archbishop of Granada and three other bishops as *patronos*. After further correspondence with the *Suprema*, the Inquisitors presented him with a short list of names to choose from, none of whom he knew. He appealed to the *Suprema* against its refusal to allow him a *patrono* of his choice and offered to cover the expenses of his new nominee, Dr Sebastián Pérez, out of his own pocket.[26] This seems to have been agreed, but fresh difficulties arose. Pérez's *limpieza de sangre*, his pure Christian descent, had to be proved, and rather than face further delay while a potentially damaging enquiry took place, Fray Luis consented to the appointment of

Mancio de Corpus Christi. Though there is no evidence of personal animosity between the two men, Mancio was a Dominican, and Fray Luis's willingness to accept him suggests that his resistance had been worn down. Mancio arrived on 9 October to begin his work, but by 25 October Fray Luis had dismissed him. He explained why in a paper of 7 December, rather desperate in tone (XI, 38–44). He had now been in prison almost three years, and no real progress had been made with his case. He had only accepted Mancio because it had been so difficult to find anyone the Inquisition would agree to. Mancio had appeared sympathetic at first but had left in a hurry, promising to return early in November, because he had to be in Salamanca for the start of the new academic year. Fray Luis had dismissed him on his lawyer's advice but the reasons had not been communicated to the *Suprema*, and he feared this might further prejudice his case. He now accused Mancio of being in league with Medina and of using Salamanca as a pretext. Nothing happened. On 6 March 1575 he was still waiting – no Mancio. A few days later Mancio wrote to explain that he was unavoidably detained in Salamanca, but by 30 March he was back in Valladolid and the case resumed, after a delay of five months.

Fray Luis then submitted a long justification of his views on the Vulgate (XI, 55–120). Mancio's opinion, which he saw a week later (XI, 126–8), was critical of the implications of these views but not unduly unfavourable, and lacked any suggestion that they might be heretical. But the Inquisitors were not satisfied. They appointed more judges to look at the original propositions on the Vulgate Fray Luis had presented before his arrest. The weeks passed by. By August 1575 Fray Luis was ill, and requested the assistance of a servant, which was granted. Once he had recovered, he began to respond to the new judgements of Dr Cáncer and Fray Nicolás Ramos. Cáncer had picked out five propositions he thought heretical and six others partly so, and he called for their retraction. The Inquisitors could not ignore so serious a conclusion, and further examination was called for. Fray Luis protested vehemently at this further delay: his imprisonment had been hard and cruel, the torment increased by his illness. By November he was sounding deeply depressed, and in a letter to the Inquisitor General pleaded to be moved to a monastery where he could be given the sacraments (withheld throughout the long ordeal) and die among Christians.

Between January and April 1576 there is a long silence in the record, but the pace quickened in the spring. On 5 May a joint judgement of his Vulgate propositions was at last to hand, while judgement on the thirty propositions proceeded. By the end of September the Inquisitors had only one remaining doubt, over which Fray Luis was able to satisfy them. Even so, the procedures required for resolving the case dragged on until December, and it was not until the end of 1576 that he was finally and formally acquitted of every charge against him, though warned to be more cautious and less contentious in the future, and, as was customary, sworn to secrecy about the trial. His return to Salamanca in the new year of 1577 was that of a triumphant hero.[27]

The conservative view of the Vulgate was most clearly stated by Fray Francisco de Arboleda, who declared on 30 July 1572 that

la Vulgata es texto sagrado toda ella, y todas sus partes y partículas por mínimas que sean, y cuanto a todo ello ser auténtica y contener verdad infalible e inviolable . . . entiende haberlo declarado ansí el sancto concilio por aquella palabra *auténtica*, y . . . si alguna vez se hallare el texto griego o hebreo estar de otra manera que en la edición Vulgata . . . será o por estar los dichos textos griego o hebreo corrutos o falsados, o por descuido de impresores, o por malicia de los mismos judíos . . . y ansí no se ha de usar del texto griego o hebreo, sino como de un comento para entender la Vulgata.

(x, 40)

. . . the whole of the Vulgate is a sacred text, in every part and particle, however small . . . and . . . insofar as it is authentic and contains the infallible and inviolable truth . . . this is what the holy Council declared by the word 'authentic'; and . . . if perchance the Greek or Hebrew text be found in a different form from the Vulgate's . . . this will be because the said . . . texts are either corrupt or falsified, or because of printers' errors or the malice of the Jews . . . so that the Greek or Hebrew text is not to be used except as a commentary for understanding the Vulgate.

Dr Cáncer's approach was also strongly conservative. Where Fray Luis argued that the Vulgate was the best available Latin edition, Cáncer said it was the best possible one, true not only in matters of faith and morals, but in every detail: 'Quare idem est authenticum quam authoratum et authoricatum . . . haereticum erit dicere quod Vulgata est minus apta translatio . . . eam authoritatem habet quam illud originale' (xi, 161–3), 'authentic means the same as authoritative . . . and it is heretical to question the accuracy of the Vulgate translation, since . . . it has the same authority as the original'.

Replying to the first set of accusations brought against him, Fray Luis argued on 6 May 1572 that the Council had not stated that every Latin word in the Vulgate had been dictated by the Holy Spirit, but that in it 'no había error ni cosa falsa nenguna, y que era más conforme al primer original que ninguna otra traslación' (x, 214), 'there was no error or false thing, and that it was closer to the first original than any other translation', and alone was to be used in church. Four days later he added that if by falsities were meant scribal and printing errors, words added or omitted, and variant readings of the same text, then 'digo que hay muchas, y así lo dicen todos los hombres doctos y católicos que han escrito' (x, 222), 'I say that there are many, and so do all learned Catholics who have written about this.' But if false things inserted by the translator were meant, there were none which could cause error: 'sino que estaba en ella muy bien trasladado todo lo que era necesario para la fe y las costumbres', 'rather, everything necessary to faith and morals was very well translated.' He agreed that he thought that 'el intérprete algunos lugares no los tradujo tan clara, ni tan cómodamente, ni tan del todo conforme al original', 'the translator did not render some places as clearly or as appropriately or as consistently with the original' as he might have done. The detailed arguments were repeated many times during the trial, supported by authorities ancient and modern, and Fray Luis must have become heartily sick of repeating himself. If the trout are good (the Vulgate) that does not mean the other fish are bad (the originals), he wrote on 25 January 1574. For example, he found three different meanings for Job xx.18, and said that the Vulgate reading was not so catholic that the others had to be rejected. The general rule he advocated was that the Vulgate's meaning was certainly that intended by the Holy Spirit and the others, though not certain, were probable, since the Spirit's words were equivocal in the original. When the Inquisitors raised their final doubt with him it related to the phrase 'hujus editionis', 'of this edition', in the Vulgate propositions. He explained that the 'edition' did not refer to the original of Jerome but to contemporary editions, with all their printing mistakes.

Fray Luis was never to diverge from these views and he lost no opportunity to propagate them after his release in his published Biblical commentaries. But he does seem to have become more guarded in expressing them during the trial. When Mancio returned to continue his examination of the suspect propositions, Fray Luis refined his attitude towards the question of infallibility, perhaps because he had learnt Mancio's opinion, voiced earlier, that he would be acquitted 'con tal que confiesa que la edición Vulgata es de verdad infalible' (xi, 34), 'as long as he confesses that the Vulgate is infallibly true'. On 30 March 1575 Fray Luis declared that this was so, not only in matters of faith and morality, but in everything else, however slight or small, so that its every text (*sentencia*) was true, infallible and *de fide*. He claimed to have a higher view of it than Cano's, explaining that though Catholic doctors have understood 'authentic' in differing ways, Cano had restricted its authenticity to faith and morality. But 'yo afirmo que por *auténtica* determinó que era verdadera y cierta en todas sus sentencias, cuántas en ellas hay, sin exceptar ninguna, o pertenezcan a la definición de la fe o no' (XI, 124), 'I affirm that by authentic it ... determined that it was true and certain in every one of its texts, without exception, whether they pertain to the definition of faith or not'. He added, however, a long justification of his own propositions.

If he did become more careful as the trial dragged on, his vindication was also the vindication of all that he had taught about the Vulgate. One need only consider the amount of detailed Biblical exegesis in his Latin and Spanish works to realize that his intellectual integrity remained unimpaired by the prison experience; indeed, it may have sharpened it. He continued to discuss variant readings and possible mistranslations, and frequently looked back to the original Hebrew to show how the Vulgate had selected one interpretation from among several. He would certainly have echoed the sentiments of his colleague Martínez, who spiritedly retorted to his accusers: 'Que la lengua hebrea sea equívoca, yo no tengo la culpa; pídanlo a Dios que la hiço', 'That the Hebrew language is equivocal is not my fault. Let them blame God – he created it.'[28]

The accusation of judaizing, made repeatedly by León de Castro, was connected with the question of the Vulgate but requires further clarification. Fray Luis and Grajal found themselves in the dangerous position of being of *converso* descent, involved in the study and teaching of Hebrew, and accused of preferring Jewish to Christian interpretations of Scripture. In the minds of the Inquisitors these things must have merged, and the issue itself, the amount of freedom allowed to an exegete and the significance of the original languages in assessing the Vulgate translation, became confused with the more serious suspicion of an intention to return to Jewish origins and practices. The investigation into the Jewish ancestry of Fray Luis which was incorporated into the trial record is part and parcel of this, rather than an isolated example of anti-semitism.[29]

In this context, the letters of the Inquisitor Diego González form a valuable commentary on the trial documents and reveal the thinking of a man who must have been influential in having the cases prosecuted. Forwarding the accusations against the three Hebraists from Salamanca to Valladolid, he wrote that 'por ser Grajal y fray Luis notorios conversos, pienso que no quieren más que oscurecer a nuestra fe católica y boluer a su ley', 'since Grajal and Fray Luis are well-known *conversos*, I believe that they want only to obscure our Catholic faith and return to their law.'[30] Why Fray Luis should have been thought to have wanted to embrace a faith which had not been held in his family for several generations is not clear, except that there was an obsessive fear of subversive activity by minorities, justified to the extent that the *moriscos* had recently risen in Granada.[31] González wrote also to the *Suprema*, expressing the hope that Grajal's imprisonment would be of great effect, because Salamanca was all astir with innovations and a calmer and more orthodox atmosphere needed to prevail. In a third letter (3 September 1572) he claimed that the three had no need of *patronos*, who would only delay things, because they were educated men; and that pressure was building up for quick action because they were public figures and the prisons were full.

Fray Luis was never accused of following Rabbinical commentaries when these contradicted Christian exegesis. The accusation of judaizing concerns Old Testament texts which could be interpreted as prophecies of Christ but which, Fray Luis maintained, also had a perfectly straightforward application to the people and events of the time when they were written – something of broader interest to literary critics as they ponder on the relationship between authorial intention and subsequent interpretation. This reputable and scholarly view was misrepresented by labelling it 'judaizing', and the Inquisition could hardly overlook such an accusation, especially in Spain's foremost university. It may have been no more able than Fray Luis's accusers to distinguish the substantial dispute about hermeneutics from the more sinister insinuations with which it was laced.

A curious incident reported during the trial is symptomatic. Various witnesses recalled having been told how one day at dinner someone had commented on the delay in serving the wine, in such a way that a punning reference to the Messiah might have been intended (Spanish *vino* means wine or 'it/he came'): 'pues si vino ¿por qué no lo recibieron?', 'if it (or he) came, why did they not receive it (or him)?' Fray Luis capped the remark: 'Que es venido necesariamente lo hemos de confesar; aunque podría haber alguna dubda en ello' (x, 78), 'That it (he) has come we are bound to believe and are compelled to, though there is much doubt'. The tale was reported second- or third-hand, as Fray Luis was quick to emphasize, and after much probing to uncover its source the Inquisitors gave up and ignored it. The accusation, however ill-founded, is obvious: Fray Luis had cast doubt on Jesus being the Messiah. Anyone looking for a covert Jewish plot would have pricked up his ears at this. In fact, Fray Luis had merely indulged in some light-hearted repartee, but the inclusion of the incident in the trial documents shows the atmosphere of distrust and the inability of some deponents to distinguish the serious from the trivial.

Martínez, the leading Hebraist of the three, claimed to have made no more than ten references to the Rabbis in as many years, and then only to clarify grammatical points. He pointed out that Rabbinical works were accessible in the University, and that he possessed a few himself, as well as three Arabic mathematical treatises and a passage from the Qur'an copied from the University library for purposes of refutation. But Castro was so obsessed with judaizing that the merest reference to the Hebrew text aroused his passion. It was not that he defended the Vulgate; he stood by the priority of the Septuagint, in which, Fray Luis commented tartly, he believed 'un poco menos que a Dios' (x, 331), 'a little less than he does in God'. He believed the Septuagint translators had used a copy of the Hebrew original uncorrupted by Jews, unlike the Hebrew text on which the Vulgate was based. Fray Luis was not slow to counter-attack: he had seen no Catholic 'que disimuladamente dañe tanto a la auctoridad de la Vulgata como es el dicho maestro León' (x, 298), 'who so covertly damages the authority of the Vulgate as the said master León'. It is astonishing, he continued, that Castro objected when he stated that the Vulgate was sometimes not as accurately translated as it might be, since 'muchos lugares della no tiene por sagrada Escritura, sino por cosas falseadas por los judíos' (x, 240), 'many passages in it he does not hold as sacred Scripture, but as things falsified by the Jews'. A striking feature of his defence record is Fray Luis's ability to turn an accusation against him into one against the accuser.

Castro objected to the Vatable Bible's acceptance of certain Old Testament texts in their historical, Jewish context rather than as prophecies of Christ. Whether his anti-semitism was based on academic convictions or sheer prejudice is hard to assess, but from the character he reveals the latter seems the more probable. Fray Luis responded in customary detail to Castro's attacks on him. In his full defence of 14 May 1573 he gave examples of the kinds of Jewish exegesis Christians could accept, though the same texts might also have spiritual meanings the Jews would have ruled out: 'no todas las exposiciones que dan los judíos en la sagrada Escriptura son malas. Muchas son de sana y católica doctrina, mayormente en los pasos de Escriptura adonde no tenemos pleito con ellas' (x, 328), 'not all the expositions the Jews make of sacred Scripture are bad. Many are of sound, catholic doctrine, especially in those passages . . . where we have no dispute with them'. Such non-controversial items included historical and geographical information and the explanation of Jewish customs. He added an imaginary dialogue between a Jew and a Christian on a passage where Jewish exegesis ran counter to Christian but a literal Jewish and a spiritual Christian exegesis could happily co-exist. He remarked that the Vatable Bible took many of the psalms to refer to the Messiahship of Christ in a way Jewish tradition could not allow, even some which the New Testament had not interpreted in this way. He accused Castro in turn of maintaining, against orthodox belief (e.g. Gal. iv.24), that Scripture only had one sense, and of preferring the Septuagint to the Vulgate where the readings conflicted (x, 410–19).

Fray Luis's judgement on the Vatable Bible had been accepted by his other colleagues. He proposed that when the Fathers and Doctors gave different interpretations of a text and the Church had not chosen between them, Catholics could freely accept them all. If they were in agreement, such an interpretation would become authoritative. Another might be allowed if it was not contradictory or unsound, but it would have a much reduced degree of authority. Castro was displeased by this, but the Vatable text had been amended along these lines, the varying interpretations being retained 'para que cotejándose con los sanctos se viese cuan más altamente declararon ellos la Escriptura, que no estos nuevos intérpretes' (x, 195–6), 'so that by comparing them with the saints it could be seen how they expounded Scripture much more loftily than these new interpreters'. Castro held that an interpretation not found in the saints had to contradict them; for him, *praeter*, other than, meant *contra*, against. Fray Luis attacked this equation, since to expound a passage *praeter* (other than) the saints had done had always been permitted. He cited Isa. liii.8, 'Generationem eius quis enarrabit' ('Who shall declare his generation?'). It could refer to Jesus Christ, his contemporaries or his descendants. If the Spirit had meant it only to refer to Christ, 'nativitatem', birth, would have been used in place of 'generationem'. Castro's insistence that every text had a Messianic significance in its literal sense is best seen in his absurd treatment of Psalm viii.2 ('Out of the mouths of babes and sucklings'). He explained that to celebrate Christ's coming babes were miraculously endowed with the power of speech, a literalism as unacceptable to the rest of the commission as it was to Fray Luis, not because it was Christian, but because it was stupid.

Que bien entiendo que solo este testigo y sus generalidades, con ser mi enemigo, fue el todo de mi prisión: porque lo que deponen los demás, todo se resume en la Vulgata y en los Cantares, lo cual antes de mi prisión manifesté a Vs. Mds.

(x, 342)

Well I understand that this witness alone, with his generalizations, was the whole reason for my imprisonment, since he is my enemy; what the others have testified is all summed up in the Vulgate and the Song of Songs, which I showed you before my imprisonment.

Fray Luis complained to the Inquisitors. He felt that if anyone ought to be on trial it was Castro, whose views were described by another contemporary as 'una ciega opinión nacida de un decreto mal entendido', 'a blind opinion born from an ill-understood decree.'[32]

The translation and commentary Fray Luis had made of the Song is often thought to have been the main reason for his arrest, but the trial record shows that it was secondary to the issues of the Vulgate and judaizing and has to be understood in their context. It is true that the first accusation made by Medina ran: 'Anda en lengua vulgar el libro de los Cánticos de Salomón' (x, 5), 'The book of the songs of Solomon is circulating in the vulgar tongue', but the accusations were not listed in order of importance. The *Cantar* figured in the trial not because a Biblical book had been translated but because of the interpretations given by Fray Luis. Just as his expositions of the literal sense of the Old Testament had angered Castro, so those of the love-song between Solomon and his bride provoked others to denounce him.

On 28 April 1572, Fray Vicente Hernández remembered a priest showing him a copy of the *Cantar* in Granada, and he denounced it to the Inquisition as 'una carta de amores sin ningún espíritu, y casi nada difiere de los amores de Ovidio' (x, 26), 'a love-letter with no spiritual meaning, scarcely differing at all from the love poetry of Ovid'. It was unworthy to be called an exposition, and was erroneous in its criticisms of the Vulgate text: he referred to a specific passage where he accused Fray Luis of following 'por sentido literal la anotación primera de Francisco Vatablo en la Biblia de Roberto Estéphano', 'the first annotation of François Vatable in the Bible of Robert Estienne, in the literal sense', a clear indication of the link between the weightier charges and this one. Other witnesses also denounced the *Cantar* but in general terms. The thoroughness of the investigation is well illustrated by the fact that an Augustinian named Jerónimo Núñez was questioned in Cuzco, Peru, on 10 September 1575, and he told of six quarto notebooks from which he had copied the *Cantar* in the library of the Augustinian house in Quito. It is an impressive testimony to the Inquisition's lines of communication with the New World, and a reminder of how widely manuscript texts could circulate, especially in religious orders, with their long traditions of copying.

Fray Luis's response to Hernández came in his 'Amplia defensa', 'full defence'. His exposition, he said, had not been intended to cover the spiritual sense of the poem but merely its literal meaning, to lay a proper foundation for its principal sense, which in any case was present in his work. If the Holy Spirit considered it appropriate to use the figure of human love for the love of Christ and his Church, why should it be thought unworthy in his exposition? 'Y porque oye allí besos, y en Ovidio también besos, juzga que es carta de amores como las de Ovidio' (x, 364), 'because he hears kisses there and kisses in Ovid too, he judges that it is a love-letter, like Ovid's'. The Inquisitors seem to have been convinced by his argument that the *Cantar* was a necessary, preliminary exercise on which the true significance of the Song could be based, though they were interested enough in the fact that Arias Montano had lent Fray Luis a copy of his own work on the Song to order an investigation into this too (x, 477; 491–3; xi, 18–20; 293–4).

According to Fray Luis, the *Cantar* had been written for Isabel Osorio in 1561–2, and the manuscript had been copied without his knowledge or permission by the friar who looked after his cell. Further copies had been made and circulated. Although many people approved of what he had written, 'a algunos amigos míos . . . les ha parecido tener inconviniente por andar en lengua vulgar; y a mí, por la misma razón, me ha pesado que ande, y si lo pudiera estorbar, lo hubiera estorbado' (x, 98–9), 'it seemed to some of my friends . . . that the fact that it was circulating in the vernacular was not right; and for the same reason I was annoyed. . . . and had I been able to, I would have stopped it'. He had therefore begun work on a Latin version in 1571, which he intended to have examined, approved and published; but illness had intervened, then his arrest.

Vernacular translations of Biblical books had been prohibited at various times in the past, and at Trent the Spaniards Cardinal Pacheco and Alfonso de Castro had called them 'mothers of heresy'.[33] Attitudes elsewhere were less unfavourable, though the Protestant demand for the Bible in the tongue of the people had made the issue an urgent one. All the Council managed to do was to prescribe that all versions should carry annotations and that lectureships should be established in each diocese to promote knowledge and study of the Bible.

When he tried to remember what might have incriminated him, Fray Luis wondered, in his second audience (18 April 1572) whether his brief vernacular expositions of Psalms xli and xii might have offended anyone. But they formed part of the liturgical hours of the Virgin, 'la parte de la sagrada Escritura que anda en romance, nunca se entendió que estaba prohibido declaralla en romance, siendo la declaración buena y católica' (x, 186), 'and it has never been forbidden to expound in the vernacular that part of Scripture which is available in the vernacular, provided the exposition is good and catholic'. Later he pointed out that in any case the nature of the prohibition in the catalogue of forbidden books had been variously interpreted, and the Holy Office had stated that such vernacular commentaries might circulate (x, 430–1). The then Rector of Salamanca had apparently regarded one on Romans as permissible (xi, 272), though in a letter to Fray Luis in July 1571, which shows that Fray Luis had been sounding him out, his attitude towards the *Cantar* was more cautious:

Para publicarse y imprimirse, a mi parecer no conviene que esté en lengua vulgar, porque se pornía en descrimen de impedirse por ser sobre libros de la sagrada Escriptura . . . y en este hay especial razón por los misterios que en él se contienen, por los cuales, como V.P. sabe, ya en la ley vieja no se permitía leer este libro a quienquiera, y pienso que agora se ha de estrechar más la licencia para imprimir libros en romance de cosas de la religión cristiana.

(x, 469)

As far as publishing and printing go, I do not think it proper for this to be in the vernacular, because it would be in danger of being prohibited for being on books of Holy Scripture . . . and in this one there is the special reason of the mysteries it contains, because of which, as you know, in the old law [i.e.

Judaism] it could not be read by anyone who wanted to; and I think that now permission to print books in the vernacular on matters of the Christian religion must become stricter.

Whether the tone of the letter implies that Fray Luis had been thinking of having his *Cantar* published is not clear. But the Index could only legislate about printed books. As long as the *Cantar* remained in manuscript only it was outside its scope.

After his trial, when Fray Luis must have felt much securer, he made his views on the Bible and religious works in the vernacular as plain as he could in the dedication to the first book of the *Nombres de Cristo*. This was begun in prison, or, as he puts it in the dedication with delicate irony, 'no me parece que debo perder la ocasión de este ocio, en que la injuria y mala voluntad de algunas personas me han puesto', 'I do not think I should miss the opportunity of this period of leisure, in which the injustice and ill-will of some have placed me.'[34] It is in effect an apologia for Scripture in the vernacular, and a courageous piece of writing given the times. Scripture, he writes, was given to be a universal remedy for human sin and was therefore written in the language of the people to whom it was addressed, to bring them true knowledge of Christ. In his rather idealized picture of the early centuries of the Church, Scripture acted as a point of unity between people of different education and vocation. This happy state has been altered by 'la condición triste de nuestros siglos y la experiencia de nuestra grande desventura' (1,404), 'the sad condition of our centuries and the experience of our great misfortune.' He is thinking not just of Protestantism but of earlier heresies which had caused vernacular Scripture to be prohibited, like Catharism. So the Church, under pressure of necessity but with mature counsel, has decreed that the Bible should no longer be available in the common tongue. It is ignorance and pride which has brought this about: people have presumed to be their own masters and have fallen into gravest error through reading without proper guidance. Light has turned to darkness. Finding the word of God no longer accessible, they have taken up reading vain books which do not encourage the study and practice of virtue and which foment immorality – Fray Luis is doubtless thinking of chivalric romances and the *Celestina*, which he elsewhere attacks. He has written the *Nombres* to counteract this, 'componiendo en nuestra lengua para el uso común de todos algunas cosas que, o como nacidas de las Sagradas Letras, o como allegadas y conformes a ellas, suplan por ellas . . . sucediendo en su lugar de ellos los libros dañosos y de vanidad' (1, 407), 'by composing in our language, for the common use of all, things which either arise from the sacred letters or are related to them and in conformity with them, and which might stand for them . . . and replace dangerous and vain books.'

Medina and Castro apart, Fray Luis seems to have had one other principal enemy, this time from within his own Order. On 4 November 1572 the Augustinian Diego de Zúñiga made the following deposition:

Estando en Salamanca por huésped, le dijo Fr. Luis de León . . . que había venido a sus manos un libro estrañamente curioso, el cual le había dado Arias Montano, el cual le había dado luz . . . y que el libro era de un italiano habilísimo, . . . hombre de grandísima vida, y que en el principio . . . contaba una revelación que había tenido . . . estando de noche orando, que vió en la oscuridad una luz, y que della . . . salía una voz que dijo: *Quo modo obscuratum est aurum, mutatus est color optimus!*   (x, 68)

While a guest in Salamanca, this witness was told by Fray Luis de León that a strange and curious book had come into his hands, given him by Arias Montano, which had enlightened him [Montano] . . . and that the book was by a very clever Italian, a . . . man of very saintly life, and that at the beginning . . . he recounted a revelation . . . one night at prayer, when he saw a light in the darkness, out of which a voice came saying *Quo modo obscuratum est aurum, mutatus est color optimus.*

The text is from Lamentations iv. 1. Zúñiga was anxious to know if he should denounce this, and having been advised to, asked Fray Luis if Montano was a good Christian. This annoyed Fray Luis, who insisted that the book was sound, though he had not himself read it, and there were a few passages which might have been inserted by someone else. Zúñiga responded, '¡Mas si por dicha lo enjirió el Montano!' (x, 377), 'But what if perhaps Montano did this?' He seemed to want to incriminate the great scholar. More than two years later, on a visit to his widowed mother in Granada in 1562 or 1563, Fray Luis took the precaution of denouncing the book to the Inquisitors there, having, he said, become disturbed by the heresies being discovered in Spain (a reference to the existence of Lutheran and Illuminist cells in certain cities, and perhaps to the Carranza affair). He recalled his conversation that night in his cell with Zúñiga, but admitted he was not entirely sure that Montano had burnt the book, as he had earlier believed.

It seems an insignificant incident. In the trial, Fray Luis himself told the Inquisitors how a student had once shown him a notebook of astrological matter with 'cercos y invocaciones, aunque a la verdad todo ello me parecía que aun en aquella arte era burlería', 'signs and invocations, though truth to tell even for that art it seemed to me a joke'. Nonetheless,

probé un sigillo astrológico, y . . . con un cuchillo pinté no me acuerdo qué rayas, y dije unas palabras que eran sanctas, y protesté que las decía al sentido que en ellas pretendió el Espíritu Santo, acordándome que Cayetano en la Suma cuenta de sí haber probado una cosa semejante con la misma protestación, para ver y mostrar la vanidad della; y así todo aquello pareció vano.   (x, 201)

I tested an astrological sign and . . . with a knife drew some sort of lines and said some sacred words, and protested that I was saying them in the sense the Holy Spirit meant by them, remembering how Cajetan, in his *Summa*, tells how he tried a similar thing with the same protestation, to see and to demonstrate the vanity of it all; and indeed the whole thing appeared vain.

The next day he had intended to test another sign but burnt the book instead. It is a remarkable confession, but the Inquisitors, so watchful for occult practices, did not follow it up. The reference to Cardinal Cajetan was doubtless intended to reassure them by providing an authority for the act. In any case, they may have shared with Fray Luis the characteristically ambiguous attitudes of the age to the different forms of astrology.

Exactly what the Italian book contained we cannot know, only guess that it was something of a speculative or mystical kind, an early example, perhaps, of Montano's interest in such literature. The book apart, Zúñiga also disapproved of the *Cantar*, because Fray Luis applied the verses 'a los amores carnales de Salomón y la hija de Faraón . . . y. dijo que no podía sufrir a leer una cosa como aquella, porque doctores católicos como era Titelman y Nicolao de Lira decían que era cosa escandalosa que se interpretasen [así], y que los mismos judíos lo abominaban' (x, 71–2), 'to the carnal love of Solomon and Pharaoh's daughter . . . and he could not bear to read such a thing, because Catholic doctors like Titelman and Nicholas of Lyra said that it was scandalous for them to be so interpreted, and that the Jews themselves abominated this'. He remembered too how Fray Luis had told him of the growing controversy over the Vulgate at Salamanca in 1568, and of how 'hémosles hecho sufrir', 'we made them suffer' and 'hémosles hecho pasar esta proposición – *Interpretes vulgatus aliquando non attingit mentem Spiritus Sancti*' (x, 68); 'we made them pass this proposition – *the Vulgate sometimes does not grasp the mind of the Holy Spirit.*'

Diego de Zúñiga is chiefly remembered for his openness to Copernican astronomical theory, which he explained, critically but not unfavourably, in his commentary on Job (*In Iob Commentaria*, Toledo, 1584 and Rome, 1591; ix.6). Several decades later Galileo was to praise him as one of the theologians who did not believe that the movement of the earth was contrary to Scripture.[35] As far as the Vulgate and the original texts were concerned, Zúñiga was on the side of Fray Luis. In his exposition of Job xx.17 he wrote:

Non enim Iudaizare putandus est, qui nullum asserit Iudaeorum dogma, qui nihil, quod Catholicae religioni repugnet affirmat . . . His temporibus quidam indocti, & temerarij homines leuiter statim eos Iudaizare clamant, qui non omnia in sacra scriptura exponenda ad sensus anagogicos referant, vel qui facilem, & planam alicuius Hebraei interpretationem sequantur. Quorum inepti clamores adeo formidabiles fuere multis sacrarum litterarum studiosis hominibus, vt eos ab hoc honestissimo, & sanctissimo studio vehementer deterrerent: docti vero homines in sacris litteris vix tuto se versare posse putarent. Quorum propterea stultos clamores deberent Ecclesiae magistratus reprimere, quod impij, quod temerarij, quod sacrarum litterarum studijs infesti, quod pijs hominibus valde contumeliosi sint. Neque aequo animo pati, vt catholici viri Iudaizare dicantur, dum nihil tradunt, quod a pia, & Catholica dissentiat disciplina, sed in vera semper haereant doctrina; licet illam vel ex Hebraeorum, vel ex gentilium libris hauserint.[36]

It is not to be considered as judaizing when someone does not assert Jewish dogma or affirm anything contrary to the Catholic religion . . . In these times certain unlearned and rash men easily and at once cry out that those who do not refer everything to be expounded in Holy Scripture to the mystical senses, or who follow the simple and plain interpretation of a Hebrew [commentator] are judaizing. Their stupid cries have been so formidable to many students of the Holy Scriptures as vehemently to deter them from this most honest and holy study, and men learned in the sacred Scriptures hardly think that they can concern themselves safely with them. Therefore the officials of the Church should curb their foolish cries, because they are impious, rash, injurious to study of the sacred Scriptures, and very offensive to pious men. Nor should they calmly allow Catholic men to be said to be judaizing when they teach nothing contrary to pious Catholic discipline but rather always adhere to true doctrine, whether they derive this from Hebrew or pagan books.

He called for those who make life impossible for scholars to be punished, following this uncompromising statement of the liberal, humanist approach to Scripture, in which the issue of Hebrew studies is linked to the other vexed question of the place of classical wisdom in Christian tradition. The words could almost have come from Fray Luis, the reference to the problems of scholars perhaps have hinted at his trial; though Zúñiga may have had a case nearer home in mind. Alonso de Gudiel, the Augustinian professor of Bible at Osuna, had died in prison in 1573, charged with similar offences to those of the Salamanca Hebraists, and investigations continued posthumously, until 1591.[37]

How, then, can Zúñiga's opposition to Fray Luis be explained? He would certainly not have regarded him as a judaizer, though he prided himself on having reconciled the Latin, Greek and Hebrew verities, rather than having challenged the Vulgate's authority, as he felt Fray Luis had. The answer lies more in the realm of personalities than issues. Scholars had found it hard to accept that a man open to Copernicus could have been so hostile to his fellow-Augustinian, and for some years it was thought that there were two Diegos de Zúñiga.[38] Confusion of names was common enough at the time; the character in the trial is also called Diego Rodríguez, and similar names occur in the Augustinian chronicles. But the true story turns out to be more remarkable.[39] There was only one Diego de Zúñiga, and a sriking character he was. He was born in 1536, probably the illegitimate son of his mother Ana de Arévalo by one of the noble Zúñiga family; she had married one Bartolomé Rodríguez. Diego adopted the Zúñiga name and coat of arms, and Fray Luis's habit of calling him Rodríguez may have been a little unkind. He studied at Salamanca and Alcalá, and was so persuaded of his linguistic, philosophical and theological talents that he had been in correspondence with Cardinal Crivelli in Rome in an attempt to impress the Pope with his intellectual abilities and to gain his patronage. In these letters we hear the voice of the gifted but penniless and underprivileged Spaniard, which we do not often meet, except perhaps in its darker, ironical manifestation, the literature of the *pícaro*; and if it sounds self-satisfied and brash, we must remember that wealthy patronage was essential for such a man if he was ever to fulfil his ambitions. He claims, for example, to have read every book of the Bible at least twelve times in the original, and asks to be allowed to come to Rome to prove his abilities by spending a month or a year (presumably at Rome's expense) expounding any passage of Scripture, demonstrating the falseness of all heresies, and arguing any theological point (or any other subject) with the most learned men of Italy. If the Pope grants his request, as much glory will accrue to him as from the defeat of the Turkish fleet at Lepanto.[40]

Diego de Zúñiga had met Fray Luis as early as 1555, when both were studying at Alcalá. Some years later, at a Provincial Chapter at Dueñas, he was disciplined before the assembled brethren for dissent during the proceedings, a punishment administered by Fray Luis, among others. His own boundless confidence in his gifts was not shared, alas, by Fray Luis. The two men were in dispute at Salamanca on the opinion of Gregory of Rimini on the fate of the heathen, and Fray Luis formed a poor view of Zúñiga's *Manera de aprender todas las ciencias*, offending him by telling him that the subject required fuller treatment and the examples were commonplace. If we add to these personal difficulties the envy and resentment Zúñiga must have felt for the well-connected Fray Luis, who moved with such ease (and free of financial worries) among the great men of the realm, we can begin to understand what motivated Zúñiga to denounce his colleague. At least he had the satisfaction of outliving Fray Luis: the last we hear of him is in Toledo, where his last and most ambitious work, *Philosophiae prima pars* (1597) was published.

Fray Luis may have given a cursory glance to Zúñiga's commentary on Job, though he had begun his own long before Zúñiga's work appeared, and only the last seven chapters of the *Exposición de Job* could have been influenced by it. But apart from some similarities, notably in the introduction (and a common source, Titelman's *Paraphrastica elucidatio in librum D. Iob*, Paris, 1547, probably explains these),[41] the two works are quite different. In any case, if he maintained his earlier opinion, he was not impressed by Zúñiga's scholarship. That was perhaps unfair. That a man scarcely known today wrote commentaries on Job and Zechariah from the Hebrew, Greek and Latin texts, knew the latest in astronomical theory and produced a treatise on almost everything, crammed with all kinds of learning, speaks by itself for the vigour of Spanish intellectual life in the second half of the sixteenth century.

Fray Luis had other enemies too. A defence witness told how the bishop of Zamora held Fray Luis responsible for some scurrilous verse about him which had been published in Salamanca. Fray Luis did not actually deny the charge, though it sounds as if he meant to (XI, 65). He had antagonized the Mother Superior of the Sancti Spiritus convent in Salamanca, where Isabel Osorio was, by supporting the nuns who had resisted her appointment (XI, 337). He had become involved in strife over marriage and inheritances in a family to which he was confessor (XI, 331), and his own family had enemies through the activities of his uncle Antonio, a court lawyer (X, 484; XI, 5–6). He had alienated another Augustinian, Gabriel de Montoya, because in 1569 Fray Luis's insistence on a secret ballot had cost him the position of Provincial, for which he was a candidate and expected to win.[42] But if other enemies took advantage of his discomfiture to add their own denunciations, it was Medina and Castro, with a dangerous combination of personal antagonism and issues which were being hotly contested, who were primarily responsible for the imprisonment of Fray Luis.

The trial documents tell us many other things of interest. They show us the friends of Fray Luis – the solitary Martínez, the blind musician Salinas, to whom Fray Luis dedicated one of his most famous odes and with whom he had spent many hours discussing philosophy, poetry and art (XI, 302), and Grajal, whose death on 19 September 1575 drew from Fray Luis a moving account of the depth of their friendship and Grajal's noble character (X, 326–7).

They also tell us much about Fray Luis's own reading, because from time to time he asked for books and papers from his cell to be brought to him for the preparation of his defence. He possessed a number of Bibles, in Hebrew and Greek, as well as the Aramaic Targums and Hebrew grammars (one of them by Martínez). There were many Biblical commentaries, the standard *Glossa ordinaria* as well as more recent ones by Titelman, Steuch,[43] Lindanus,[44] the converted Jew Sixtus of Siena (1520–69), and Castro's work on Isaiah; among the Fathers and Doctors he asked for copies of works by Augustine, Leo, Hilary, Bernard and Aquinas. Other requests show his wider interests. In his first list he asked for Luis de Granada on prayer (probably the best-selling *Libro de oración y meditación* of 1554); later, for a Greek and Latin Homer, Greek vocabulary and grammar texts (the latter by the Erasmian humanist Vergara), a Greek and Latin Pindar, a Greek Sophocles, works by Horace, Virgil and Aristotle, and also by more recent writers like Bembo and the English humanist Linacre.

In his library too were many manuscripts and notebooks. Some were of his own lectures and commentaries: his early interest in Biblical exposition is evident in the manuscripts of vernacular commentaries on Psalms xli and xii, the beginning of a Latin commentary on the Song, and a paper written when he was eighteen or nineteen on the Septuagint and Vulgate readings of a text from Ezekiel. One notebook contained letters and verses in Latin and Spanish, and it is tempting to speculate that among these may have been some of his original Spanish poems. No trace remains of the works on the Psalms and Ezekiel to which he refers. Other papers included works by his teachers and contemporaries, mostly of the generation of lawyers and theologians at Salamanca who contributed so much to the renewal of these subjects in Spain: Vitoria, Cano, Vega, Sotomayor, Gallo, Guevara, Juan de la Peña, Villalobos, as well as the *Cantares* of Arias Montano and a treatise on ancient Hebrew musical instruments by Cipriano de la Huerga. No doubt he was anxious to exclude from his cause material from the works of others: on one occasion he specifically mentioned some papers of Diego de Zúñiga which were among his own (x, 315).

If his long imprisonment was a time of testing and torture, it did give him an unwilling opportunity to immerse himself in study, reading and writing, and to sharpen his mind as he argued his defence. The enforced 'period of leisure' which saw the genesis of the *Nombres de Cristo* also gave rise to further reflection on the Song and the book of Job, which would grow into his two most ambitious commentaries, and to more translations of classical poets, four of which were actually published while he was in prison. But 'in spite of the temptation to equate Job and León' through the theme of innocent suffering, there is only one prose work in which Fray Luis explicitly linked his prison ordeal to Biblical exposition or indeed made any unambiguous references to his trial, his *In Psalmum vigesimum sextum Explanatio*, published together with the first edition of his Latin commentary on the Song (Salamanca, 1580).[45] It is in many ways a brave and even defiant work, since prisoners of the Inquisition, even when freed, were sworn to secrecy about their trial. Fray Luis does not break his silence in the strict sense, but he does give us a very frank account of his feelings as he meditates on the text of the psalm. We must assume that passages in the present tense remain exactly as he wrote them in prison, and that he deliberately retained them when the text was completed for publication:

An quia jam mensis agitur quadragesimus ex quo inimici mei de me triumphum agere coeperunt et cum apud judices criminando tum apud homines universos detrahendo et obloquendo caput meum oppugnare non cessant, nullaque interim aut levatio malorum ostenditur aut effulget salutis spes, idcirco animum ipse despondeam, et Deum non allaturum innocentiae auxilium putem?

(*Opera* i, 165)

Because it is now forty months since my enemies began to triumph over me, and because they do not cease to compass me about the head by accusing me before the judges and by disparaging and abusing me before all men, and because meanwhile no alleviation of evil is seen nor hope of salvation shines forth, shall I then despair in my soul, and believe that God will bring no succour to innocence?

The reference places the writing of these words in July 1575, shortly before illness and depression overtook him.

The commentary was dedicated to Quiroga, who had become Inquisitor General the winter after the arrest of Fray Luis and who was to be made Cardinal Archbishop of Toledo after his release. Quiroga appears to have been a moderate in Inquisitorial affairs, and Fray Luis attributed to his support his own restoration to liberty:[46]

Nam cum causa lisque mea, saepe cognosci coepta, ejus cognitione variis rationibus intermissa et in aliud tempus dilata, ita produci videretur, nemo ut vires aut animi aut corporis mei tanto oneri suffecturas esse speraret, tu ea ut cognosceretur atque terminaretur aequum esse censuisti, cognovistique eam ipse per te, et ea cognita atque ejus veritate perspecta, et crimine et suspicione criminis exsolutum, libertatique ac dignitati meae pristinae redditum, me tandem meis meosque mihi restituisti. (I, 112–13)

For when the hearing of my case and trial had often begun and for various reasons been interrupted and put off to another time and seemed to be being so protracted that nobody was confident that my powers of mind or body would be equal to such a burden, you decided it would be just for it to be heard and concluded, heard it yourself, and having heard it and discovered the truth about it, absolved me of guilt and suspicion, restored me to my former freedom and position and at last returned me to my friends and my friends to me.

What truth there was in this claim it is hard to say; it is made in the dedication, and dedications of the period were characteristically fulsome. It was a good move, though, for a work which mentioned his trial and imprisonment was bound to be controversial, and he had been warned to avoid controversy.

The psalm (AV xxvii) is one of many which speaks of trust in the protective power of God when enemies are massed around, and it is traditionally ascribed to David fleeing from the wrath of Saul. Fray Luis regarded it as prophetic of Christ, surrounded by enemies in his earthly life, yet vindicated wholly by God, hence its tone of thanksgiving. But he also felt it related to his own situation, as he remembered how he had been arrested:

Tametsi nullo modo is sim qui numerari servis Dei possim, tamen benigne mecum Deo et clementissime agente, expertus in me sum illo meo calamitoso . . . et misero tempore, cum quorumdam hominum artibus in suspicionem laesae fidei criminose vocatus, semotus ab hominum non solum sermone et congressu sed etiam aspectu, per quinque fere annos in carcere et in tenebris jacui. (I, 111–12)

Even though I am in no way a man who can be numbered among the servants of God, nevertheless God acted kindly and mercifully towards me, as I myself experienced during that dreadful and wretched time . . . when, through the wiles of certain men, I was slanderously summoned on suspicion of harming the faith and was kept isolated not only from the words and company but even from the sight of men, and lay for almost five years in prison and in darkness. (112)

But such suffering contained unexpected blessings: 'sed quae mala creduntur maxima, ea expertus sum voluptatibus dulcissimis esse plena', 'those things held to be the greatest evils I have experienced as full of the sweetest delights.' Not only were his own innocence and good conscience a consolation, joy came from beyond him: 'Sed quod me potissimum consolabatur, neque consolabatur solum, sed et laetitia interdum perfundebat tanta, quantam non queo dicere, vis quaedam bonitatis Dei erat immensa et incredibilis' (I, 112), 'But what comforted me most, indeed, not only comforted but filled me sometimes with joy so great that I cannot describe it, was a certain power of the goodness of God, immense and beyond belief.' It was experience of this power which had prompted him to begin the commentary, so that his idleness might bear fruit and his soul be relieved of anxiety through his reading and writing. His one comfort had been to read the Bible and think on divine goodness, and it was the experience of reading this psalm at a time of deep personal distress which had given him that sudden access of joy and confidence he had alluded to:

. . . divinae mihi bonitatis atque providentiae in animo tantum elucet lumen, tantaque excitatur atque existit in me bona spes, ut minime dubitem, quin nostris ille rebus, id est, veritati, cujus nunquam deserit patrocinium, subventurus aliquando tandem sit, et magnum atque praesens auxilium allaturus. (I, 116)

So great a light of divine goodness and providence to me shines out in my soul, and so great and good a hope arises and is awakened, that I doubt not that he will at some time at last come to the help of my cause, that is, of the truth, which he never ceases to advocate, and that he will bring a very present help.

In these passages we glimpse something of the inner strength which sustained him through the darkest moments and reawakened his creativity while others sought his downfall.

There is no direct mention of this religious experience in the trial documents; in them, his chief concern was to protest about the delays and to elicit sympathy and support, not to write a personal journal.

But the exposition becomes an autobiographical confession as well as a Biblical commentary, in which it is quite impossible to disentangle the suffering first person from the cries of David and those of Fray Luis: 'Numquam ego, pater sanctissime, ne si omnia mala irruant in me, aut minus bene de te judicabo, aut oculos meos abs te aut spem dimovebo' (I, 165), 'Never, most holy Father, even if all ills should overwhelm me, shall I either think the less well of you, or remove my eyes or my hope from you'. That is a paraphrase both of David's and Fray Luis's situation. The language he uses is full of Biblical expressions: 'Deliqui, fateor . . . intestinae cupiditates meae, supergressae caput meum, arcem animi hostibus tradiderunt; proditus sum a me ipso' (I, 166), 'I confess that I have sinned . . . the desires of my inward parts, overflowing my head, delivered the ark of my soul to the enemy; I am betrayed by myself'. He deserves condemnation for his lack of gratitude to God, by attributing his successes to his own merits, yet God has treated him indulgently. He has repaid God's kindness by abusing it, and God has allowed him to be punished for his reformation. His present sufferings are not for the crimes he is unjustly accused of but for sins he has indeed committed: 'Falsis aliorum criminationibus vera peccata mea in me punis . . . et aliorum injusta actione juste tu, imo pie et amanter, corrupto vitiis animo meo, ne funditus interirem, ferrum atque ignes adhibes' (I, 167), 'You punish my real sins in me through the false accusations of others, and . . . to my soul, corrupted with vices, you, justly, sweetly and lovingly, through the unjust action of others, bring iron and fire, lest I perish utterly'.

These antitheses ('real . . . false', 'just . . . unjust') are not merely rhetorical flourishes. They express the new understanding Fray Luis reached in the midst of his tribulations, that God could take what in human terms is false and unjust and use it for a just and proper end. The commentary climaxes in a direct appeal to God not to abandon the author in his moment of darkness:

Auxilium tu mihi fuisti a juventute mea; nunc, cum maxime deficit virtus mea, ne derelinquas me. Esto lux densis tenebris malorum oppresso, esto salus de fama et de fortunis omnibus dimicanti, dissipa consilia impia et coelesti immisso lumine detege mendacia atque fraudes, meque his eripe malis, ereptumque meis, id est, tuis famulis redde, et a mortis locis vindica me ad vitae regionem. (I, 167–8)

You have been my succour from my youth; now, when my strength most fails me, leave me not. Be light when I am oppressed with the deep darkness of evil men, be my salvation as I struggle for my reputation and my entire fortune, scatter the counsels of the wicked, and with a ray of heavenly light reveal falsehoods and deceits, deliver me from these ills, and having delivered me, return me to my friends, that is, to your servants, and from the places of death deliver me into the region of life.

When the exposition was published it carried as a frontispiece an emblem chosen by Fray Luis, an axe lopping the branches off a tree and the caption 'Ab ipso ferro'. The words come from the *Odes* of Horace iv.4, in which the Romans are likened to an evergreen oak which is pruned and which draws vigour 'from the same iron' which has cut it down. In the *Exposición de Job* viii.20 Fray Luis remarks that Horace seems to have derived the simile from that passage of Scripture, and he quotes his own translation of the poem.[47] On 20 October 1580 the Valladolid Inquisitors wrote to the *Suprema* to inform them that this emblem had been denounced by one of the judges of the Vulgate propositions in the trial, Ramos:

El prouincial de la Orden de Santo Francisco desta prouincia, fray Nicolás Ramos, a enbiado a este sancto officio el libro que a conpuesto fray Luis de León con la calificaçión que él dél hizo, que embiamos con esta a v.s. para que nos mande lo que en él debamos hazer; y en la enblema del libro berá v.s. quan desacatado es para el sancto officio. Que el libro por andar muy común no le enbiamos.[48]

The Provincial of the Order of St Francis of this Province, Fray Nicolás Ramos, has sent this Holy Office the book written by Fray Luis de León and his opinion of it, which we enclose . . . so that you can tell us what we should do. You will see from the book's emblem how insulting it is to the Holy Office. Since the book is easily obtainable, we have not sent it.

A marginal note of the following day asks Hernando de Castillo to give his views.[49]

Fray Luis chose his emblem deliberately, but Ramos was wrong to think it was an attack on the Inquisition. The Inquisition may have been represented as the axe, but the point was that the suffering Fray Luis had borne had not destroyed him but, as it were, had pruned him and made him bear better fruit. The Inquisitors must have sensed this, since they took no further action, but the episode shows how vulnerable Fray Luis remained for a time after his release. A passage from his discussion of Christian kingship in 'Rey de Dios' in the *Nombres* was denounced on 3 October 1609, long after the death of Fray Luis, on the grounds that it attacked the King of Spain and the Inquisition's policy of excluding descendants of Jews from the religious orders and from ecclesiastical careers: 'Y quiere que sean todos iguales y que puedan entrar en las inquisiciones; i este es lenguaje común de todos a quien toca esta mala raza y se opone todo esto a la nobleza y a la sangre limpia y más a los santos tribunales de la inquisición',[50] 'He wishes all to be equal and eligible to enter the Inquisition, and this is the usual talk of all those touched by this evil race and is totally opposed to nobility and purity of blood and even more to the sacred tribunals of the Inquisition.' Sabino and Juliano have been reflecting in general terms on the need for kings to treat all their subjects equally (*Obras* I, 589–90). An honourable king, Sabino maintains, has no 'vasallos viles y afrentados', 'despised and lowly vassals', and Juliano adds that when kings stain the honour of their subjects they harm their own. The word 'manchar' ('to stain') was often used to describe the dishonour of those who were not descended from pure old Christian stock. Sabino also mentions kings who permit such an affront to pass down through many generations so that it is perpetuated; anything but kings, according to Juliano. There does seem to have been a plea for greater tolerance here, perhaps as a result of Fray Luis's own experience, although the passage is making a broader point about the need for different groups in society to coexist in mutual respect and service. Again, the denunciation was not taken seriously; but again it is interesting to note that it was made at all.

One other, famous passage in the *Nombres* has often been interpreted as a veiled representation of the trial of Fray Luis. As the friends are finishing their conversation on the name 'Hijo de Dios' and evening falls, they catch sight of a small bird on the opposite bank of the river, among the trees. They listen to its sweet song for a moment, then watch with alarm as two large crows attack it. It seeks cover among the branches, but finding no safety, disappears into the water, uttering what sounds like a cry for help. The crows give up the pursuit when all trace of their intended prey vanishes, and fly off in triumph. Sabino is distressed, fearing the bird is drowned, but it suddenly emerges, wet and bedraggled, right by the feet of Marcelo, perched 'sobre una rama baja . . . adonde extendió sus alas, y las sacudió del agua; y después, batiéndolas con presteza, comenzó a levantarse por el aire cantando con una dulzura nueva' (I, 743), 'on a low branch . . . where it stretched out its wings and shook them free of water; and then, beating them quickly, began to ascend heavenwards singing with a new sweetness'. Many other birds fly out from the thickets to accompany it, singing joyfully as they fly out of sight. Sabino is delighted, Marcelo preoccupied, and when asked what he is feeling can only raise his eyes to heaven and sigh 'Al fin, Jesús es Jesús', 'In the end, Jesus is Jesus.'

The incident is puzzling, not so much for the event it describes (I have myself watched red kites hunting over the Escorial *huerto* and the effect on the local bird population is dramatic) as for the reaction of Marcelo. His mysterious words indicate that Fray Luis intends us to grasp some significance from the episode, but what? Is his own pursued innocence the little bird, hunted by the envy and malice of the two black crows, Medina and Castro?

> Cuanto desenlazarse más pretende
> el pájaro captivo, más se enliga . . .[51]

(The more the captive bird tries to free itself, the more it becomes entangled.)

Does he return safe and sound, to the great rejoicing of his friends? The explanation fits, but it has its shortcomings. Would Fray Luis have identified himself with the bird and praised his own renewed singing? Why would he introduce an allusion to his own experience at the climactic point of his exposition, especially when it is followed by Marcelo's enigmatic sigh? Fray Luis constructs his dialogues with great care, and the details are significant. We know from the beginning of the next name, 'Amado', that 'Jesus' was meant to follow 'Hijo de Dios', and 'Jesus is Jesus' would make more sense as an introduction to that name, especially as Fray Luis understands the personal name to encompass all the others. It is possible that the bird is a figure of Christ: the association is an ancient one and has survived into the twentieth century ('The Wind-Hover', by G.M. Hopkins). Christ is persecuted to the death but rises from the waters of death to ascend to his heavenly throne, and to lead from death to resurrection those who pass through the waters of baptism (an image of death and resurrection for St Paul), so that they too may ascend to glory, singing the new song. The allegory does not exactly fit, any more than the more customary explanation; but at least it is integral to the theme of the dialogues.

The prison metaphor is similarly difficult to interpret in the poetry of Fray Luis. It may include reference to his own experience, but it stands for something wider than that. Many of his original poems have been interpreted as arising out of his ordeal, and this is probably correct. Rivers lists nine as poems on prison and deliverance.[52] The famous *décimas* (XXIII) 'Aquí la envidia y mentira / me tuvieron encerrado' ('Here envy and lies / had me confined') are usually held to have been written on his release, and it is not hard to imagine how Fray Luis felt about the envy of a man like Diego de Zúñiga and the false accusations of Castro and Medina. His tercets 'Huid, contentos, de mi triste pecho' ('Flee, pleasures, from my sad breast') are likewise thought to have been written when hopes of his early release had been dashed, and he pictures himself as a captive bird whose plight only worsens as he struggles to break free:

> En mí la culpa ajena se castiga
> y soy del malhechor, ¡ay!, prisionero . . .[53]

(Alien guilt is punished in me/and I, alas! am prisoner of the wrongdoer . . .)

This complaint, that he is the innocent victim of the false accusations of others, is one we have already encountered in the trial documents and the exposition of Psalm xxvi, and becomes the most characteristic way in which he alludes to his imprisonment. The inclusion of a Spanish rendering of the Horatian *ab ipso ferro* emblem in the ode (xii) to Felipe Ruiz (lines 31-5) must also be a consciously intended reference: the poem begins with four verses depicting the folly of material greed, much in the spirit of those images of it we examined in the first chapter, before it passes to praise the happy state of the man who is untouched by the disasters which may befall him. Each of the poems we have just mentioned concludes with a re-working of the Horatian *Beatus ille* theme, which is lifted out of the merely conventional by being associated with a real lawsuit and imprisonment. In the tercets, for example (xv), life in the countryside is shown as free of 'rejas duras', 'strong bars', and free of the hatred, anger and falseness of the world and its tribunals.

The first verse of the moving ode to the Virgin (xxii) also speaks from prison:

> los ojos vuelve al suelo,
> y mira un miserable en cárcel dura,
> cercado de tinieblas y tristeza.[54]

(Turn your eyes to the earth / and see a pitiful man in harsh prison, / beset by darkness and sadness.)

Many of the following verses can be interpreted as a plea for succour in a world in which enmity and injustice abound and in which the poet is attacked and hounded to his downfall. Images of storm and shipwreck – the wind and the abyss bearing down upon one tiny, unprotected boat – dramatically portray his plight (lines 78-88). But here, as in the poems above, Fray Luis is not simply referring to his own troubles. His imprisonment itself becomes a metaphor for all those dark, destructive

forces which imprison the human race and prevent it from seeing truth
and rising to the life of heaven. When the soul is 'desatada/desta
prisión adonde/padece' ('unloosed from this prison where it suffers') it
will find the heavenly Bridegroom (Ode xviii), an answer to the
question which is asked at the beginning of the Ode (x) to Felipe Ruiz:

> ¿Cuándo será que pueda
> libre desta prisión volar al cielo,
> Felipe, y en la rueda,
> que huye más del suelo,
> contemplar la verdad pura sin duelo?[55]

(When shall it be that free from this prison I may fly to heaven, Philip, and in
the sphere most removed from earth, contemplate pure truth without
affliction?)

Whether or not these words were written in the cells of the Inquisition,
they come with all the Platonic overtones of the soul's imprisonment in
the body, a concept which is most poignantly expressed in the ode
(viii) to the night sky:

> Morada de grandeza,
> templo de claridad y hermosura,
> el alma, que a tu alteza
> nació, ¿qué desventura
> la tiene en esta cárcel baja, escura?[56]

(Dwelling-place of grandeur, temple of nobility and beauty, the soul, which
was born for your heights, what misfortune keeps it in this lowly, dark
prison?)

Here, the metaphor of prison is just one part of a conceptual framework which attracts many other metaphors to give it substance – the
earth covered in night and buried in sleep and oblivion (first verse),
mortal folly, the vain shadow, the imagined good (fourth verse), the
whims of this fleeting life (seventh verse), and the anguished question
which follows the evocation of all the harmony, light and treasure of
the heavenly places:

> ¿quién es el que esto mira
> y precia la bajeza de la tierra,
> y no gime y suspira,
> y rompe lo que encierra
> el alma y destos bienes la destierra?[57]

(Who seeing this, and prizing the lowliness of earth, does not groan and sigh,
and break what imprisons the soul and exiles it from these possessions?)

Prison imagery in the poetry of Fray Luis certainly arises out of his own experience, but its significance is not exhausted by locating examples and using them either to date the poems or as commentaries on the poet's life. Its function is the same as that of metaphor in general, to express in as vivid and concrete a way as possible concepts which belong to the realms of philosophy and theology and to the interpretations these disciplines give to the puzzles of human experience. The earthly prison may be a cell in Valladolid or the blindness and folly of unenlightened human desire, but it takes its place in the elaborate scheme of metaphorical antithesis which we have already begun to discern as fundamental to the meaning of the poetry of Fray Luis. Its opposite is not so much the freedom of the lecture theatre at Salamanca as the 'hidden path' Fray Luis so often symbolizes through the idealized setting of the country retreat and through the harmony of music and the contemplation of the night sky, all of which in turn point to the only true freedom he can imagine, that of the life of heaven.

We have spent a while looking at some of the literary reflections Fray Luis made on his trial, and it is fitting to conclude our study of this long interruption of his work at Salamanca with a consideration of three further consequences which it had: the future of the Vulgate, his so-called second trial, and the effect the first trial seems to have had on cases later in the century.

Years after his trial, Fray Luis was invited to assist in the official revision of the Vulgate, which Trent had anticipated but which did not begin in earnest until Sixtus V appointed a commission to oversee its completion in 1586. One of the commission's members, Dr Valverde, approached Fray Luis, now the distinguished Professor of Bible at Salamanca. In his written submission Fray Luis agreed with Arias Montano that restitution of the Vulgate to its original purity was a lost cause, since there were hundreds of places where what Jerome had written could never be known: 'Ansí será posible que, pretendiendo darnos la Vulgata incorrupta, nos la diesen más corrompida que agora anda' (1, 988), 'Thus it is possible that in attempting to give us the Vulgate uncorrupt, a more corrupt one than the one we have will be given us.' This did not greatly matter: in its present form it contained nothing prejudicial to true faith or morality. He could not resist a parting shot at those who, like his former accusers, 'quieren que la Vulgata . . . sea venida del cielo', 'want the Vulgate . . . to have descended from heaven', inspired by the Spirit in its every Latin word. He concluded that the Pope should reaffirm Trent's approbation, and in everything else 'dejar abierta la puerta a la industria y diligencia', 'leave the door open to industry and diligence', since to suppose that the full force of the Hebrew could be appreciated from the Vulgate or any other translation was 'grande engaño, como lo saben los que tienen alguna noticia de aquella lengua y los que han leído en ella los Libros Sagrados', 'a great mistake, as those who have some knowledge of that language and have read the sacred books in it realize.'[58]

The revision was nevertheless completed under Clement VIII in 1592 and is known as the Clementine Vulgate. But the ambiguity of the Tridentine decree was not removed until Pius XII's encyclical *Divino Afflante* of 30 September 1943 stated that Trent had been concerned purely with the Latin Bible in the Western Church. Fray Luis would no doubt have been delighted by this final vindication, if a little puzzled as to why the Church should have taken almost four centuries to decide on what to him seemed so obvious a conclusion.

The 'second trial' of Fray Luis is really a misnomer.[59] He suffered no further imprisonment, and the issues (though not all the personalities) were quite different. Controversy broke out at Salamanca following three disputations held in January 1582 on the subject of the merits of Christ and human predestination. The fullest account comes to us from Fray Luis, who was not an impartial observer. In the first *acto* the Jesuit Prudencio de Montemayor had defended a proposition about the merit Christ earned from his actions. At one point the Dominican Domingo de Guzmán, son of the poet Garcilaso de la Vega, jumped up to complain that Montemayor was heretical to believe that most but not all free human acts were foreordained by God. Fray Luis protested that this was nonsense: many Fathers and modern theologians supported Montemayor's view, and to claim that all our acts were foreordained was Lutheranism, since it assumed that our evil and sinful ones must also be. God foreordained neither these nor 'indifferent' acts like eating and drinking. Guzmán objected that there was no such thing as an indifferent act; Fray Luis retorted that this was a matter of opinion, not faith. Once more, an Augustinian and a Dominican came into conflict.

After the session closed, the manoeuvrings began. The Dominicans were especially active, collecting evidence and presenting it to the Inquisition. The Augustinians were by no means unanimous in their support for Fray Luis, who only five years previously had been warned to steer clear of controversy. In the second *acto* the issue debated was whether one man might be converted and another not if both were in receipt of equal grace from God. Fray Luis again clashed with the Dominicans. He stated that this might be so, since someone might wish to resist converting grace; Domingo Báñez (1528–1604) and the Dominicans held that such grace was intrinsically efficacious. Once again the determination of human freedom came into question. Báñez regarded the view of Fray Luis as Pelagian, making man's salvation dependent on human will, not divine grace, a strange accusation to level at an Augustinian, since Augustine himself had written against the Pelagians and had stressed the limits of the corrupt human will. An open quarrel broke out between Fray Luis and Báñez, in which each accused the other of misreading Augustine.

The third *acto*, in which Fray Luis did not participate, brought matters to a head. It too was concerned with divine grace operating on human free will. Through February and March the interested parties presented their evidence, including several declarations from Fray Luis, some of which name enemies within his own Order. His interventions seem to have been prompted by a desire for justice: 'Una cosa es no tener . . . una opinión, otra cosa es tenella por herética o no opinable', 'It is one thing not to hold . . . an opinion, another to call it heretical and not to be held', he said in the first *acto*.[60] His principal accuser was the Jeronymite Fray Juan de Santa Cruz, who noted in his *censura* that to deny that Christ was free to die, that his death contained no merit, and that God foresaw everything and caused every human act, was Pelagian and heretical. But the *censura* of the Dominican Hernando del Castillo did not altogether support such accusations. On the other hand, he had generally supported Fray Luis in the past and now called some of his propositions 'false, temerarias, y . . . escandalosas', 'false, rash, and . . . scandalous', because they contradicted St Thomas and Augustine. He added, interestingly: 'y más en estos tiempos donde en ninguna universidad de católicos se lee otra doctrina públicamente, y aún en las cátedras que de antiguo están fundadas del Maestro de las Sentencias, Durando, Gabriel, Escoto . . . se quedan . . . con el nombre solo, y la doctrina que se lee es la de estos santos por la gran seguridad que hay en ella',[61] 'and especially in these times, where in no Catholic university is any other doctrine expounded; even in the chairs once founded for the Master of the Sentences, Durandus, Gabriel, Scotus only the name remains and . . . the doctrine expounded in them is of those saints because of the certainty it contains.' In such a comment we sense the victory of Thomism in the sixteenth century over its main medieval rivals. Fray Luis was prepared to challenge this theological hegemony, or at least submit it to critical analysis; his Dominican rivals saw this as an attack on Aquinas.

When the theologians of Alcalá, traditionally envious of Salamanca, were asked to comment on the propositions, they forwarded a mild and balanced opinion to the Inquisitors, effectively saying that it all depended on how they were interpreted. Heresy was not in evidence; only the tenth is called 'rash' because it stated that the doctrine of Augustine and Thomas was Lutheran, an opinion Fray Luis cannot possibly have held. The Inquisitor is reported to have been surprised at the difference from attitudes in Salamanca.[62] Meanwhile, Fray Luis and several Jesuits denounced four propositions of Báñez, mostly on freedom and determination, which received a similarly mild treatment from Alcalá.

From the Inquisitor's letter, it is clear that a cooling-off period was needed for fresh scandal to be avoided at Salamanca. Whether or not the various propositions were false, the participants should be reprimanded for having raised such dangerous issues. Both Montemayor and Fray Luis were censured, the others absolved. In view of his earlier warning to steer clear of controversy, the censure is understandable, though Quiroga must have thought the sentence harsh, since he gave Fray Luis eighteen months to comply with a requirement to expound certain undefined propositions from his chair.[63]

Múñoz Iglesias provides a full account of Fray Luis's teaching on predestination and free will in his survey of the second trial, though in a neo-scholastic manner which is impenetrable to the modern reader and may lead him to suppose that the issues themselves were trivial. They were not; and they are still with us in a more secular form as we discuss the relevance of genetic and environmental factors to moral responsibility for action. The predestination–free will debate is not the creation of theologians with nothing better to do; it is the projection into the Christian faith of a fundamental mystery about human behaviour. Christianity cannot but trace that mystery back to the source from which it understands all existence to arise, God himself. The dilemma arises and must find reconciliation there.

Fray Luis, lecturing on predestination, noted that this took two forms. One was common to good and bad alike: God's foreseeing and ordering of a particular end; the other involved his will in choosing some for blessedness and ensuring that they reached this state with their free wills intact. He tried to solve the problem by using a quasi-temporal language, though he knew well enough that this was inadequate for a God who transcended time. His general principle was that God willed everyone to reach the supernatural end he destined for each, and for this to happen he gave people 'sufficient' means, all that was necessary for that end to be reached. His prescience and omniscience were therefore safeguarded. But since we were created with free will, we could decide whether to accept or reject these means. To reject them, of course, amounted to sin, and in allowing for that eventuality God could be said in some sense to have permitted sin to exist. Next in order, God foresaw original sin and acted to strengthen our chances of reaching his intended purpose for us, now frustrated. He decided to redeem humanity from this bondage by the Incarnation of the Logos. Redemption is thus consequent upon original sin, even though Fray Luis believed that God would have become incarnate even if man had not sinned, in that it now requires a death – the death of the Son – to repair the damage of sin. From the mass of lost humanity God now chose a certain number whom he predestined to glory through Christ. The rest presumably remain doomed to eternal death. His justice is safeguarded, since all deserve to perish; but his grace is revealed, in that some, for reasons entirely consonant with his wisdom but beyond the reach of ours, are saved to enjoy him for ever. It is a position by no means unlike Calvin's though Fray Luis refrains from probing into the fate of the damned.[64]

A division was to emerge between Báñez and his followers, who located the cause of such predestination in the sovereign will of God alone, and Molina and his followers, who believed that there must be a reason why God predestined some to glory and others not. Fray Luis's part in this 'second trial' was marginal and may have attracted more attention than it deserved because of his first. This division grew and in many ways the trial was a preview of the battle between the Jesuit Luis de Molina (1535–1600) and Báñez and a prelude to the *De auxiliis* controversy between Dominicans and Jesuits which was not to be resolved until early in the seventeenth century by Rome.[65] Roman Catholic theologians themselves were divided about matters which are commonly presented as defining the gap between them and Protestants. Fray Luis himself was deeply interested in christological questions, as some of his lectures show. But his involvement in them was not only to engage him in strife, it also yielded the melodious prose of the *Nombres de Cristo*, as we shall in due course see.

The trial of the Salamanca Hebraists had resonances through the rest of the century. The Augustinian General, Tadeo de Perusa, wrote to the Spanish Provincial to express his distress at the imprisonment of Fray Luis and to exhort him to assist in his release.[66] Otherwise, leading figures maintained a notable silence, the result more of caution than of approval of the principal accusers.[67] Other Augustinians were watched. Lorenzo de Villavicencio (c. 1520–83), himself a secret agent of the Inquisition and a scholar with firm views on the authority of the Vulgate and the original texts, had his file examined by the Seville Inquisitors, but they could find nothing to incriminate him.[68] Diego de Zúñiga was thought to have been accused of similar offences to those of the Hebraists, but the Valladolid Inquisition could find no record of this in 1572 and the following year he was cleared of a charge for which he must have been denounced. By 1584 he was given permission to keep and read Hebrew and Aramaic Bibles at Toledo.[69] A Salamanca student from the Andalusian Province was imprisoned in 1580 for holding an unspecified opinion about the Vulgate which he claimed to have learnt from his teachers, and in 1590 a copy of the trial record of Fray Luis was sent to Seville to be compared with this. Right at the end of his life, therefore, Fray Luis's trial was remembered and used when another Augustinian was in trouble, and his name continued to appear in the records of the Seville Inquisition at least until 1594.[70]

But the most fascinating example comes not from the Augustinians but from José de Sigüenza (1544–1606), the Jeronymite librarian of the Escorial, whose trial record has only recently been published.[71] Sigüenza, like Fray Luis, was denounced through malice, envy and ignorance, but unlike him escaped lightly: he was confined for a while to a nearby monastery, and cleared of all charges within a few months (1592–3), charges which included 'hebraizing' and 'judaizing'. His accusers were also trying to attack Arias Montano indirectly. Montano had been giving Hebrew classes to selected members of the Escorial community from the beginning of 1592, and the resentment of those left out was wrapped up in theological grievances. Several deponents denounced Sigüenza for teaching that the study of Hebrew was harmful to scholastic theology, just as the Salamanca Hebraists had been accused of damaging such theology through preferring Biblical studies. He was also accused of maintaining that he had profited more from Montano's expositions than from those of the saints and Doctors, and of propagating a story which seems to have grown out of a remark by Fray Luis, that all Montano's Biblical knowledge had been infused in a single night.[72]

Sigüenza was also denounced for Lutheranism, which seems to refer to his belief that Scripture alone, rather than devotional treatises, was the best nourishment for the spiritual life, a belief twisted into a pseudo-Lutheran statement about Scripture as the sole authority in the Church.[73] In his trial as in Fray Luis's, one cannot help forming the impression that some witnesses really did not know what they were talking about. Fortunately for Sigüenza, the Inquisitors were better informed. One of the judgements on the propositions on which he was tried read: 'Se pueden explicar en buen sentido y en malo; y serán verdaderas o falsas, conforme a la limitación que se les pusiere',[74] 'They can be explained in a good sense or a bad one, and they will be true or false according to the limitation put on them', a verdict which shows a refreshing sense of balance in an age of such extremes. It is reminiscent of one of the more admirable statements of Fray Luis: 'Y de los libros de Lutero se puede decir con verdad que declara algunas cosas muy bien, aunque en sus errores yerra mucho' (x, 519), 'Of the books of Luther it can truthfully be said that he explains some things very well, though where he errs, he errs greatly'.

Sigüenza was the favourite court preacher of Philip II at the time of his trial, but such patronage had not prevented other high-ranking men of the realm from falling into disgrace. Yet the fact that Sigüenza suffered so lightly suggests that by the 1590s the conservative view of the Vulgate's authority no longer presented the same dangers as it had twenty years before. Part of the reason for that must be that it had received a decisive defeat when Fray Luis was restored to liberty. For the conservatives, to challenge the infallibility of the Vulgate was to undermine the foundations on which the teaching authority of the Church rested, already seriously damaged by Protestantism. Likewise, to give credence to any Jewish interpretation of the Hebrew Scriptures was for some of them tantamount to declaring that Judaism was superior to Christianity, and this awakened all the old fears of a Jewish plot to destroy the Church from within. Scholars like the Salamanca Hebraists took a more open attitude towards religious truth, and if dogmatic and predetermined positions had to be questioned in the light of advancing knowledge, then they happily questioned them. Their acquittal vindicated the liberal interpretation of the Tridentine decree and ensured that the door would not be shut to scholarly investigation of the Greek and Hebrew originals. For this, Fray Luis and Martínez each spent five years in solitary confinement, and for this Gaspar de Grajal died.

3

The language of revelation

During his long imprisonment, Fray Luis found his understanding of the language of Scripture both tested and deepened. His election to the Bible Chair at Salamanca in 1579, itself marked by further controversy,[1] enabled him to concentrate on the subject dearest to him with the official blessing of his University and with the kind of personal authority which belongs uniquely to those who have suffered for their beliefs and received public recognition of their integrity. The result was a series of Biblical commentaries which are central to his work and which established him as the leading Spanish exegete of his age. It was as an interpreter of the language of the Bible that Fray Luis was to do some of his most creative writing.

Over many centuries of Biblical exposition, it had become customary to discern four 'senses' or levels of meaning in Scripture. A piece of doggerel still often quoted in the sixteenth century defined them:

> Littera gesta docet,
> quid credas allegoria,
> Moralis quid agas,
> quo tendas anagogia.

(The literal sense teaches you the events, allegory what you should believe, the moral sense what you should do, the anagogical sense whither you are bound.)

To expound Scripture, therefore, involved more than explaining the surface meaning of the text; it meant probing beneath it, for more hidden levels of significance. This was already evident from the New Testament, which itself resorted to allegory (Gal. iv.22–6), and which consistently interpreted Old Testament texts as finding their fulfilment in Jesus Christ the Messiah. The Western classification of the four senses into the literal (or historical), the allegorical, the moral (or tropological) and the anagogical (or mystical) had originated with Augustine and John Cassian (c. 360–435), but was not fixed, many exegetes being content simply to distinguish between a literal and non-literal interpretation, and some following much more complex schemes.[2]

The rediscovery of Aristotelian philosophy and the rise of scholasticism in the later Middle Ages had caused a shift away from the near-equality of the four senses towards the primacy of the literal, and, consequently, the increased importance of the Greek and Hebrew originals, on which alone the literal sense could be established. The exact relationship between the literal and non-literal senses, however, remained controversial, as the trial record of Fray Luis abundantly demonstrates. Fray Luis has left us no systematic treatment of his views on this subject, but his most pertinent comments come in a series of lectures he gave in 1581, published only thirty years ago, as a *Tractatus de sensibus sacrae Scripturae*.[3] Before we pass to the commentaries themselves, it is worth pausing over this.

Fray Luis begins by affirming the literal sense of Scripture, which the Bible shares with other forms of literature. But Scripture also contains a mystical or spiritual sense, much harder to grasp, yet in some way latent in the literal. He defines the literal sense as the primary meaning of the words in their grammatical setting, but observes that this also includes figures of speech characteristic of a particular language – what in his commentaries he often calls 'the habitual manner of expression' of the Bible. As a skilled linguist, he knew that language was a complex phenomenon and that more than a thorough knowledge of grammar was needed if another language was to be mastered – especially Hebrew, with its alien structure and idiom. The literal sense he sees as fundamental to any other and it must always be expounded first. It alone is capable of furnishing texts and arguments on which the dogmas of the faith can be established. He therefore aligns himself with Antiochene and later scholastic tradition, against those (like León de Castro) who were prepared to violate the literal sense in their desire to wrest Christian truth from any and every text.

Fray Luis also believes that one text can have several literal meanings. One of his examples helps us to see how his exegetical work relates to the very conception of the *Nombres de Cristo*. Psalm ii.7 reads 'Thou art my son; this day have I begotten thee.' The literal reference is to Christ. Prophecy is not necessarily allegorical or mystical: here the first meaning is Messianic, since it is God who is speaking. It refers to Christ's birth in time, but equally to his eternal generation from the

Father and to his day of resurrection.[4] He agrees with Augustine on why many meanings can cohere in the literal sense. Nature and philosophy testify that God is infinite, and his wisdom and liberality are evinced in the fact that his words have many meanings, beyond even the knowledge of the human author through whom they were revealed. Only one argument challenges this view, that it is harder to argue against heretics if one text does not have one clear literal meaning. But if the many meanings are all equally true, as in this example, there can be no danger of being led astray, and Fray Luis insists that the straightforward verbal sense of a text must never be bypassed, even if it contains a trope or a grammatical absurdity or means a number of things all at once.

Next Fray Luis clarifies how allegory works, both in the literal and mystical senses, for it has two distinct usages. One, according to its rhetorical definition as extended metaphor, belongs to the literal sense; the other, to the mystical. When Nathan tells David the story of the rich man who stole a poor man's ewe (II Sam. xii) he is in fact referring to David's seduction of Bathsheba and the plot to get rid of her husband. This is the kind of allegory 'qua saepe utuntur rhetores et . . . poetae' (310), 'which rhetoricians . . . and poets often employ'. The parables of Jesus are the classic New Testament example: the literal meaning lies not in the actual words Jesus used but in what he said they meant. Allegory in the moral sense of Scripture also belongs to the literal sense: the story of Lot teaches us to avoid drunkenness, the story of David and Saul, that we should love our enemies. The moral is applied directly from the story to our lives, with no hidden meaning. The literal sense therefore includes stylistic devices which convey a plain meaning. The mystical sense, on the other hand, may be found where the language itself appears simple but is hiding a deeper truth.

In order to clarify this, Fray Luis takes Augustine's distinction between 'allegoria sermonis' and 'allegoria facti', which may be termed rhetorical allegory and allegory of event – allegory as a literary device, and as a means of indicating concealed events, facts, truths. Rhetorical allegory uses metaphor, hyperbole, proverbs, parables, paradox, 'omnesque tropos et figuras oratorum, et poetarum' (319), 'all the tropes and figures of orators and poets', 'quando aliud praetenditur verbis, aliud significatur in sensu' (318), 'when the words suggest one thing and the meaning is another'. The mountains and hills of Psalm cxiii. 4 did not skip like rams and lambs; the words

describe the rejoicing of Israel at the Exodus. The leech's two daughters who cry 'Give, give' (Prov. xxx.15) probably signify lust and
avarice, the two daughters of sin and the devil. This is the kind of
allegory – metaphor to us – common in other literature, especially
poetry, and Fray Luis calls the classical poets, with their tales, 'veluti
theologi gentilium', 'like the theologians of the pagans'. Some of the
early Fathers had been able to reconcile their love of classical literature with their Christian faith on the grounds that Christian truth
could be discovered in it by means of allegory. In the Renaissance, as
more of classical antiquity became known and loved, a similar problem about the use of pagan literature in a Christian culture arose. Fray
Luis, here and elsewhere, takes his place with those who believed that
God had revealed himself to those who lived and wrote before Christ
in the pagan world, and through them had prepared it for his final
revelation. Hence his mention of the *prisci theologi* and his belief in a
continuous, if secret theological tradition from ancient times. It is one
of the places where his classical learning and his Christian faith most
fruitfully coincide.

But allegory of event is quite different. It is the foundation of the
mystical sense of the Bible and is unique to the Bible, because God
alone can inspire it. It occurs 'quando id quod verbis significatur,
gestum est revera, sed res gestae et significatae per voces alias significant et figurant' (319), 'when what the words signify happened in
reality, but the things which happened and are signified by the words
stand for and signify other things'. The murder of Abel, Noah's ark,
Ishmael and Isaac, the rivalry of Jacob and Esau, the Exodus and the
wilderness wanderings, the sacrificial law given to Moses at Sinai – all
these stories happened as recorded, but their true reference is to the
story of our redemption in Christ: 'Haec et alia similia . . . Christus
Dominus per se . . . docuit secundum allegorias et figuras mysticarum
rerum esse dicta et facta ad praefiguranda mysteria redemptionis
nostrae' (326), 'these and other like things . . . Christ the Lord himself
. . . taught to be sayings and acts which prefigured the mysteries of our
redemption by allegories and figures of mystical things'. We shall
never understand Fray Luis's approach to the Old Testament, or that
of any other expositor until comparatively recent times, unless we
recognize this strong conviction that its stories, while true in themselves, pointed to Christ, and carried a meaning mysteriously present
in their telling which explained the story of his coming to those who
interpreted them correctly. Allegory of event was therefore an essen-

tial part of the task of the Old Testament exegete, and its virtual absence from the *Cantar* helps to explain the discomfort felt by some of those who read it. But in order to establish this spiritual sense, the literal was not to be violated: the allegory had to derive from the text itself, not be imposed upon it to accommodate any desired meaning.

Fray Luis discusses briefly how typology fits into this scheme. He sees it as a particular kind of allegory of event, which foreshadows in the Old Testament the history of Christ and his Church in the New. If the story of David's killing of Goliath is interpreted as Christ's struggle with Satan and victory over him on the Cross, it counts as typology and thus *allegoria facti*; but if it is seen more generally as the struggle between flesh and spirit in the Christian life, it is *allegoria sermonis* in the literal sense, a moral directly applied to our lives from a story. Both literal and spiritual meanings can coexist within the same text: the exile of Hagar and Ishmael (Gen. xxi) and the prohibition on break- ing the bones of the Passover lamb (Exod. xii.46) can either be interpreted literally as part of the stories of Abraham or the Exodus, or spiritually, as the casting out of the old law at the coming of the new and the sacrifice of the unblemished Lamb of God.

In the treatise there is relatively little attention given to the mystical sense in general. Fray Luis's aim is to clarify the different kinds of allegory which are found in the Bible. In the final two sections he deals with the limitations and dangers of allegory, and with the importance of establishing dogmatic truth from the literal sense alone. Excessive reliance on allegorical interpretation could easily lead away from revealed truth and make Scripture mean anything you wanted it to. Heretics ancient and modern – the Priscillianists of old, the Anabap- tists of the sixteenth century – evaded the truth of texts used against them by insisting that they were to be understood allegorically. Allegory could make plain texts obscure, and challenge the Biblical basis of doctrinal statements. But Fray Luis knew well enough how difficult it was to be certain when allegory was appropriate and when not: 'Oportet itaque ut allegorias tum sobrie, tum etiam apte et concinne figuremus. Et quamvis haec res non comparetur praeceptis, sed spiritualis hominis mens et exercitatio et bonorum auctorum lectio dux ac magistra in hac arte sit' (326), 'It is necessary for us to make allegories soberly, aptly and suitably. However, this is not a matter of rules; let the mind and reflection of a spiritual man and the reading of good authors be both guide and teacher in this art'. With Augustine, Fray Luis believes that allegorical exegesis must serve to increase love of God and neighbour, and that it is a help in turning stories about evil men into edifying pointers towards good things yet to come.

As a guideline, Fray Luis states succinctly which parts of the Bible are most likely to benefit from allegorical exegesis:

In libro Proverbiorum, in Ecclesiastico, in Sapientia, in Ecclesiaste, in Epistolis Apostolorum, in his Evangeliorum locis, ubi dogmata fidei et praecepta atque consilia traduntur vitae agendae, non est recedendum a litterali sensu; nec vero tute fit ab eo digressio, quoniam ab antiquis temporibus haereticorum evasio fuit intelligere spiritualiter, quae ad litteram erant accipienda.   (328)

In the book of Proverbs, in Ecclesiasticus, Wisdom, Ecclesiastes, the Epistles, and in those passages of the Gospels where the dogmas of the faith and precepts and counsels for behaviour are given, the literal sense is not to be departed from; nor can it be departed from safely, since from earliest times the refuge of heretics was always to understand spiritually what was to be accepted literally.   (328)

But allegory is certainly to be used in expounding the Pentateuch, especially Leviticus, with its rites and ceremonies, and the other historical books of the Old Testament. He says nothing about the corpus of prophetic writings, but repeats his warning: 'Iterum autem admoneo ut non quavis occasione sumpta confugiamus ad allegorias, sed assuescamus eis uti raro et maturo consilio, et fugiamus imperitos quosdam homines, qui quovis testimonio proposito statim suam adiungunt interpretationem allegoricam', 'I advise that we should not have recourse to allegories on any and every occasion, but become accustomed to using them rarely and with mature deliberation, and avoid certain ignorant men who at once add their own allegorical interpretation to whatever text is proposed.' He no doubt had León de Castro in mind. Though these issues were not prominent in the trial, there are hints that Martínez and Grajal similarly attacked excesses in this direction and angered their opponents.[5] 'Solus sensus litteralis est efficax ad probanda et stabilienda dogmata fidei et ad destruendas haereses' (329), 'The literal sense alone is capable of proving and establishing the dogmas of faith and of destroying heresies', Fray Luis continues. Such a view was of more than peripheral concern after the polemical literature engendered by the birth of Protestantism and the restatement of the Roman Catholic position at Trent. Many controversies had been fought over the exact meaning of disputed passages. Fray Luis musters an impressive list of supporting authorities, from Augustine and Jerome, to Aquinas and the Catholic polemicist Alfonso de Castro (1495–1558), in order to show that allegory is unsuitable for proving dogma because it stems 'ex similitudine unius rei cum aliis, et una atque eadem res plures et diversas referre possit', 'from the likeness of one thing to others, and one and the same thing can mean many different things' – even to the extent of being mutually contradictory. The lion of Rev. v.5 is Christ; the lion of I Pet. v.8 is the devil.

Only where the apostles used the mystical sense (allegory of event) may we safely use their authority to establish dogma from it. The examples of Hagar and the bones of the Passover lamb are repeated, with their Christian interpretations. Though these arise from the mystical sense, the apostles used them to refer explicitly and literally to Christian truth. Of the first example, he says: 'Ego non dico quod efficit ut ille sensus mysticus esset litteralis, manet enim mysticus, sed . . . quod sensus mysticus eius eiectionis est abrogatio legis; et quia hoc Apostolus dixit secundum litterae suae sensum . . . sensus ille mysticus est infallibilis auctoritatis' (331), 'I do not mean that this makes their mystical sense literal, for it remains mystical; but . . . that it states literally that the mystical sense of her expulsion is the abrogation of the Law; and since the apostle expressed it in this literal sense . . . this mystical sense is of infallible authority'.

Towards the end, Fray Luis deals with the superiority of one sense over any other. In the Old Testament, the spiritual sense is superior, because Paul taught that the Law was the shadow of things to come, and that Christ was the true measure and end of the Law. But he is more cautious about the New, because the spiritual sense of the Old tends to become the literal sense in the New: 'Cum in pluribus partibus novi Testamenti non sit requirendus sensus spiritualis distinctus a sensu litterae, non possumus dicere quod spiritualis praestet litterali; nam litteralis ipse est qui continet spiritualem' (333), 'As in many parts of the New Testament there is no need for a spiritual sense distinct from the literal, we cannot say that the spiritual excels the literal, for the literal contains the spiritual'.

In a few places, like the cursing of the fig tree (Mark xi) and (according to Augustine) the raising of the widow of Nain's son (Luke vii. 11–17), the spiritual sense is to be preferred, since it comes closer to Christ's intended meaning.

In the *Tractatus* we learn that there are clear differences of approach in interpreting the two Testaments. The fact that Fray Luis published more commentaries on the Old suggests that he was not only committed to the study of Hebrew but also to the challenge of interpreting a body of sacred literature in which, as he believed, the whole story of salvation through Jesus Christ lay submerged but accessible. But the place all expositors had to begin was the literal sense, not just the grammar and idiom, but also the rhetorical techniques. The words and images themselves were divinely inspired, and close attention had therefore to be paid to the style of Scripture, since it expressed the will of God. The exegete was both a student of language and all its complexities and a searcher after those truths veiled in the text of the Old Testament which pointed to Christ. It is for such reasons that the *Tractatus* lays for us a good foundation on which to build our appreciation of the Biblical commentaries of Fray Luis.

We tend to forget how much modern literary criticism owes to the long history of Biblical interpretation, even though words like 'exegesis' and 'hermeneutics' come directly from it. George Steiner has written:

The modern 'practical critic', the present-day interpreter of poetry, drama or fiction, is direct heir to the long and ancient tradition of scriptural commentary. The very concept of a serious text and of the techniques of understanding and transmission which keep it alive in education, in sensibility, in culture at large, are, in the West, inseparable from the Bible.[6]

Modern critics are also to a degree heirs of the critics of classical antiquity, and these ancient writers are themselves present in the history of Biblical exegesis, since so many Fathers, Doctors and Renaissance Biblical scholars were indebted also to classical antecedents. Although it may seem that contemporary Biblical scholarship has come down decisively in favour of the literal sense, there have been significant reworkings of Biblical stories in twentieth-century fiction, while the emphasis has shifted from the language of the Bible to the interpretation of theological statements, and from allegory to myth. The controversy surrounding *The Myth of God Incarnate*, for example, shows parallels with the old division between 'literalists' and 'allegorizers'. The former use linguistic, historical and contextual criticism to interpret the Christian faith to our own age; the latter claim that its whole manner of speaking cannot be understood in an age which has read the new trinity of Marx, Freud and Darwin, and which lives between the holocaust of the Second World War and the threat of nuclear annihilation. It is perhaps because this older tradition of exegesis, in which the literal, allegorical and spiritual coexisted, has been almost entirely forgotten that people find it hard to see how one text (or one dogmatic statement) can carry a multiplicity of meanings which are not exclusive but complementary. The *Tractatus*, like all the Biblical writings of Fray Luis, comes from just such a vanished world.

The commentary *In Abdiam*: the nature of prophecy

In 1589, Fray Luis published a volume of Latin commentaries on Obadiah, II Thessalonians, Galatians and the Song of Songs (in its final threefold exposition) which represent the summit of his achievements as a Biblical scholar. The commentary on Obadiah (*In Abdiam*) provides a good illustration of some of the theories of the *Tractatus*, for the book raises daunting questions about the nature of Biblical prophecy and its exegesis, even though it is only twenty-one verses long.[7]

In the dedication to Pedro Portocarrero, Fray Luis explains what moved him to prepare for publication lecture notes which as they stood were insufficiently polished:

Itaque non eo commotus sum, quod aliorum nomina mea ederentur: sed quod varie corrupta, et multa contaminata ederentur modis, eo sum inductus, ut mea, talia qualia sunt, a me edi integra, quam ab his corrupta mallem. Nam plagiarii isti, ut plagium celent, quae edunt, ea invertunt: quae autem invertunt, deteriora reddunt.   (*Opera* III, 6)

So I was not troubled by the fact that my works were being published under the name of others; but because they were being published with various corruptions and spoiled in many ways, I came to prefer to publish my works as a whole, just as they are, rather than corrupted by others. For in order to hide their borrowings, those plagiarists alter what they publish, and in doing so they make it worse.

The comment is an interesting one, since it reveals a concern for authorship which would have surprised the great medieval commentators.[8] A Biblical commentary was likely to be a compilation of what had gone before, rather than a work of original scholarship. Fray Luis must have had a sense of doing something new, but also – and understandably, in view of his earlier troubles – of wariness in case the misunderstandings of others twisted the meaning he intended and provoked renewed controversy.

The prophecy itself he calls difficult, 'tum propter earum rerum, quas scribit, magnitudinem: tum propter scribienda rationem obscuram et involutam' (7), 'both on account of the magnitude of the things the prophet wrote, and the manner in which it is written, obscure and convoluted'. It is directed against Edom, but, surveying both Jewish and Christian expositions, he could find no agreement on

Edom's true identity: the Hebrew doctors, for example, thought it referred to the Romans (they believed Aeneas came from Idumaea) because of their oppression of the Jews, while the converted Jew, Paul of Burgos (1350–1435), believed it foretold Jewish persecution of the young Church. But such explanations do not fit. Edom cannot mean the historical Idumaeans, because the future Obadiah predicted never happened – they did not assist in the capture of Jerusalem, nor were they wiped out. Fray Luis therefore inclines towards a figurative interpretation, often found in prophecy. Israel and Jacob stand for those who honour true religion, including the new Israel, those who have faith in Christ (23). Babylon may refer to that city, to Rome, or to the impious in general (24). Other Biblical references to Edom have to be examined, and Fray Luis finds that almost all the Fathers interpret its appearance in Isa. lxiii.1 as 'omnes orbis nationes verae religioni inimicas' (25), 'all the nations of the world hostile to true religion', a view he confirms through etymology. 'Edom' comes from a Hebrew word meaning 'red', the colour of blood, of sin and shame. Thus Israel and Jacob on the one hand, and Edom and Esau on the other, represent humanity in Obadiah, the faithful constantly at war against the faithless.

Throughout the commentary, the nature of prophetic language and its obscurity preoccupies Fray Luis, and he develops an unusual theory of double prophetic inspiration. As they foretell the future, so prophets may be illuminated to perceive spiritual truths of a higher order, which become woven into their utterances: 'Misceantque ea inter se ad eum modum, ut difficile distingui atque discerni possint, ex quo obscuritas existit maxima in eorum scriptis' (30), 'they intermingle them in such a way that it is difficult to distinguish or discern them, for which reason the greatest obscurity exists in their writings'. The emphasis on obscurity is worth noting, because this provides the expositor with his real challenge. It is not an obscurity which merely tickles the intellect; it contains the fundamental mysteries of salvation. What does Fray Luis mean?

He gives an example from Isa. xlv, which begins with a prophecy about Cyrus. But, 'lumine majore illustratus, in media oratione se ad Christum convertens, in has voces prorupit: "Rorate coeli . . ."' (31), 'illumined by a greater light and turning in the midst of his words towards Christ, he bursts forth "Drop down, ye heavens" . . .' – a Messianic prophecy which cannot therefore refer to Cyrus. This text was often used by Christians disputing with Jews about Messianic prophecy in the Old Testament, and is a favourite of Fray Luis in the *Nombres*. In this passage, as more generally in Daniel, whose prophecies begin historically but go on to introduce material beyond such a frame of reference, the expositor's task is therefore to differentiate accurately between the historical references and the wider applications. But both forms of prophetic inspiration he sees as belonging to the historical sense: 'Allegoria enim haec in nomine est, non in re ipsa, estque ea ab historia, historicoque sensu non aliena: nam historia verbis, cum propriis, tum translatis conscribitur' (36), 'This allegory lies in the word, not in the thing itself and is not foreign to history and to the historical sense: for the history is written in words which have a proper and a transferred meaning'. Obadiah's prophecy thus has both a historical reference, looking towards a predicted future, and a figurative one, latent in the literal sense of the text, and it moves constantly between them. Fray Luis defends this opinion with considerable rhetorical powers, as though it were controversial. Obadiah, he concludes, begins with the punishment of the historical Idumaeans, then gradually shifts towards that of the figurative ones (the faithless) and towards the final triumph of the Christian Church over all such enemies of God.

Prophetic imagery creates its own set of problems, too. In Obad. 4 the eagle is a simile of exaltation and impending downfall, and since this bird belonged to the Roman standard some have taken the verse to prophesy the fall of Rome. But Fray Luis points out the 'eagle' has many Biblical meanings: it can indicate the strength and youth of kings, or the heavenward ascent of the spiritual man. In Rev. xii there is a hard vision to interpret, in which a dragon persecutes a young woman and her child, and she escapes on eagles' wings to the wilderness. Fray Luis believes this must be an allegory of the Church as it existed from the first just man to the end of time (76), foreseen in Psalm ii and here related to the birth and death of Christ, the defeat of the dragon and his return to earth being the second age of Roman persecution of the Church, which ended with Constantine the Great, when the dragon's power was no more. The two wings represent the empires of Rome and Byzantium, and the prophecy signifies all those calamities which the Turks have inflicted on the Church (78). So it is that the 'eagle' image enables Fray Luis to carry the scope of prophecy into his own lifetime, during which the Spaniards and Turks continued to dispute the mastery of the Mediterranean, through the standard exegetical practice of expounding one text (or image) by another.

Indeed, the most interesting passage of the Obadiah commentary ranges far beyond the text of the book and makes this same connection between Biblical prophecy and contemporary affairs. Since Fray Luis believes that included in the literal sense of Obadiah is a foretelling of Christ and the Church, he attacks Jerome's exegesis of verse 17 ('But upon mount Zion shall be deliverance') as referring to the Jews' return from the Babylonian captivity to Jerusalem during the reign of Cyrus. He blames this misinterpretation on Jewish scholars, such as the rabbi Jerome consulted on this passage, and David Kimhi[9]. Controversy again calls forth a rhetorical style:

Sed abeamus ab hostibus: nostri[s?] quid obsecro? sive illi veteres, qui heroicis temporibus Ecclesiae vixerunt, sive iis [ii?], qui aetate nostra, aut avorum nostrorum scriptis floruerunt, Lyranus, Vatablus, Montanus, nonne omnes Christum, in his scriptis proprie contineri cognoscunt? At opponitur nobis Hieronymus. At Hieronymus, si, qui ejus auctoritate abutuntur, attente ejus scripta legerunt, timide et diffidenter id asserit.   (135)

But let us leave our enemies. What appeal can I make to our own people? Those of old, who lived in the heroic ages of the Church, or those in our own time or the times of our forefathers, who were eminent in their writings, Lyra, Vatable, Montano – do they not all recognize Christ to be contained in the strict sense in these passages? But Jerome is quoted against us. If they would read his writings carefully, whose authority they abuse, they would see that Jerome himself, diffidently and timidly, makes the same claim.

The rhetoric continues (with a good example of *occupatio*) for another page, as Fray Luis pours scorn on the opposing view and insists that the verse contains hidden mysteries of Christ and his Church, because the prophecy was not historically fulfilled (the Idumaeans were wiped out in many battles, not one, and the northern kingdom of Israel was never recovered after the Exile). The 'house of Jacob' (verse 18) thus means the apostles and faithful Christians of the early Church, the 'house of Joseph' its Gentile converts and the 'house of Esau' the impious. The 'flames' are the fires of the Gospel, destroying idolatry and spreading the light of its truth rapidly. Fray Luis renews his rhetorical tone with an attack on Josephus's beliefs about what happened to the ten lost tribes of Israel,[10] and explains the final verse, 'and the kingdom shall be the Lord's', as the advance of the Gospel into the four corners of the earth.

It is here that Fray Luis discovers a prophecy fulfilled in his own times. He believes that the three invitations to the wedding-feast in the parable of Matt. xxii come to the servants (the Jews), the other servants (the Romans) and the rest, those converted 'ultimo mundi tempore' (155–6), 'in the last age of the world.' This, to which

Obadiah's last verse points, is, he insists at length (156–74), his own, in which the New World has been discovered and the Gospel proclaimed to its heathen inhabitants.

The tremendous impact of the discovery of the New World on the European imagination in the sixteenth century is hard for us to appreciate half a millennium later, when North America and Latin America are present to us daily in terms of power and wealth, strife and poverty. Its effect on many aspects of Spanish life – currency inflation, the creation of a great overseas Empire, debates about whether the American Indians were human and whether they should be converted to Christianity by force or not – is well enough known. What is more surprising is to find it reflected in the pages of an Old Testament commentary by a Spanish professor. Yet the discovery of the New World 'posed a challenge to the authority of the Bible', because the Bible, the repository of divine revelation, appeared to know nothing of it.[11] How could its authority be maintained if so significant a thing were missing from its pages?

It was not long before explorers were describing the lands they discovered in Biblical terms. Scholars had often wondered whether the Garden of Eden had survived intact in some remote part of the world, and these discoveries rekindled their hopes of locating it. They were, of course, to be disappointed. Fray Luis supported the view that it had been swept away by the Flood, and specifically cited the failure of so many voyages to unknown places to discover it as the reason why belief in its continued existence could no longer be sustained.[12]

The cultural and spiritual inheritance of Europe was also pressed into service to help digest the significance of the New World. Eden had long been associated with the classical Elysian Fields, and both these with the pervasive myth of a long-lost Golden Age, when life was peaceful and harmonious, innocent and fruitful, a time eloquently evoked by Don Quixote.[13] Some idealists even tried to found their own utopian societies in the new lands: myth can have a real creative power on the human mind.[14] Others thought the Indians lived an almost Edenic life, uncorrupted by the vices of wealth and power – the origin of Rousseau's noble savage. Montaigne reflects this in his characteristically subversive essay on cannibals. Who are the real cannibals – the savages of the New World, or the savages of the Old, murdering each other in the French religious wars? Eden was also associated with the 'garden enclosed' (*hortus conclusus*) of Song iv. 12, and this in turn with the topos of the 'pleasant place' (*locus amoenus*) of

Renaissance pastoral literature. This network of interrelated symbols demonstrates the Renaissance genius for finding relationships between things in a way strange to us; and of that, the linking of Biblical prophecy to contemporary history is an important part.[15]

Fray Luis had adumbrated this in his Spanish commentary on Job xxviii, almost certainly written before *In Abdiam*. His own translation of the obscure fourth verse reads 'Divide arroyo de pueblo peregrino', 'The stream divides from a strange people', and he remarks that 'señala . . . el descubrimiento del Nuevo Mundo, que en la edad de nuestros padres se hizo, y es profecía manifiesta dél' (*Obras* II, 441), 'it signals . . . the discovery of the New World made in the time of our fathers and is a clear prophecy of it'. He argues that 'stream' is a rhetorical understatement for 'ocean'; thus the Atlantic divides these inhabitants from a strange people, the Spaniards, 'que entre todas las naciones se señalan en peregrinar, navegando muy lejos de sus tierras y casas, tanto que con sus navegaciones rodearon el mundo' (442), 'who among all the nations are noted for travelling, sailing very far from their lands and homes, to the extent that they have sailed around the world'. 'Fire below' (xxviii.5) means volcanoes, many of which have been found in America; its remoteness is described in verses 7–8; while subsequent references to mining lead him to allude to the huge quantities of precious metal extracted between 1545 and 1585 from Potosí in Peru (444).

It is verse 20 of Obadiah which prompts a more theological consideration of this theme: 'And the captivity (Vulgate *transmigratio*) of Jerusalem, which is in Sepharad (Vulgate *in Bosphoro*), shall possess the cities of the south.' Fray Luis expresses wonder at the vastness of the territories discovered, the multitudes of their inhabitants who have hitherto dwelt in darkness, and the achievements of those Spaniards who have undertaken perilous journeys over a greater area than the Romans ever covered. The Gospel, it was thought, had been preached to all mankind, yet here are peoples who have never heard even a whisper of it (156–7). With perhaps more idealism than accuracy, he adds: 'Mirum denique post tot saecula ad eos esse delatam [doctrinam Evangelii], et . . . a maxima eorum parte susceptam, ejus ut suasu, a majoribus acceptas religiones desererent, et fera corda cultu pietatis mitigari sinerent, seque totos incredibili studio ad Christianae vitae mores traducerent' (157), 'Wondrous it is that after so many centuries it [the Gospel] should be brought to them, and . . . be accepted by the greatest part of them, so that through its persuasion they should abandon their ancestral faiths and allow the wildness of their hearts to be tamed by pious worship and all pass over to the leading of a Christian life with unbelievable zeal'.

His answer to Scripture's silence is to deny it. So remarkable an event could not have been ignored by the prophets, and chief among its witnesses is Isaiah, especially his eighteenth chapter, which had baffled generations of commentators. Only Paul of Burgos had approached the truth, suggesting it predicted the conversion of those not yet Christian; but he had no idea who these might be. Fray Luis claims that his explanation of these prophecies as referring to the discovery of America is original, and he derives it from a close attention to their language. The 'land shadowing with wings' (Isa. xviii.1) is a land abounding in ships – Spain, for *cymbalo alarum* is a metaphor for boats. The opening 'Woe' foresees the tribulations and hazards faced by the audacious and skilful Spanish sailors around the globe. The land 'beyond the rivers of Ethiopia' can be the New World and the 'vessels of bulrushes' are again the explorers' ships. God now sends his 'swift messengers' (the Spaniards) to proclaim the Gospel to 'a nation scattered and peeled', scattered because of their distance and alien customs and religion, peeled (Vulgate *dilaceratum*) because the Indians are smooth-skinned. They are 'a people terrible' because they are cannibals, sacrifice human blood, paint themselves horribly for war, cannot tell justice from injustice and are sexually depraved. They are a nation 'meted out' (Vulgate *exspectantem*) not because they were looking for salvation, but because it came, and 'trodden down' because of their natural servitude, or because their lands lie at the antipodes of Palestine. The spoiling of their land by rivers (verse 2) is related to Plato's myth of Atlantis, which Fray Luis seems to accept.

Expounding verses 3–6, he stresses the eschatological significance of the rapid spread of the Gospel over vast tracts of land, prompted by the image of the harvest, which is so often a Biblical image of judgement. His eschatology is Pauline: the Gospel is preached to all nations before the Jews are finally brought in and the End comes (Rom. ix–xi). He describes briefly the slaughter, famine and disease the Spaniards inflicted on the Indians, but quickly passes to the amazing rapidity with which they accepted the Gospel, even though they have borne only the flowers rather than the fruit of virtue, as verse 5 indicates. The metaphor of the pruning-hook in the second part of the verse shows that arms, not reason, had to be used to convert them, while the drowning and killing of many Spaniards is foreseen from the

Hebrew word behind the Vulgate *derelicta*, meaning 'the longest branches', suggesting the Spaniards, who have reached the farthest extremities of the globe. The grim picture of birds of prey and wild beasts feasting upon the dead (verse 6) depicts Indians and Spaniards who died unburied in the fighting, and the final verse repeats how the Spaniards have brought the Gospel to the New World.

Having thus prepared the way, Fray Luis can now return to Obadiah 20's 'transmigratio Ierusalem, quae in Bosphoro est.' He knows that behind 'Bosphoro' lies the Hebrew *sepharad*, the name for Spain, and launches a fierce attack on an unnamed contemporary who refused to accept this, with many Rabbinical and Patristic authorities and a sentence from Arias Montano to prove his point. The exile to Sepharad was to Spain, since that is where the Jews were sent. Spain is a metaphorical Bosphorus because of the Straits of Gibraltar. 'Non sine arcano Dei consilio in Hispaniam confluxit Judaeorum nobilitatis pars maxima' (172), 'Not without the secret counsel of God was the greatest part of the Jewish nobility brought together into Spain'. Fray Luis says nothing about the expulsion of the Jews from Spain in the very year the New World was discovered, and concludes that the last verse of Obadiah looks to the third, final extension of the Gospel before the End, and to the Day of Judgement, presided over by apostles and saints.

We have described Fray Luis's exegesis of Obadiah and related texts in some detail, because within a relatively short compass it tells us much about his approach to Biblical language. All the meaning he finds comes out of the literal, historical sense, within which figurative language belongs. The literal sense of Scripture has much wider and richer scope for him than its name might suggest to us. What is so disconcerting to a twentieth-century reader is the mixture of the fanciful and the arbitrary on the one hand, and the step-by-step internal logic of his method on the other. When he is describing the voyages to the New World and the nature of its inhabitants he is matter-of-fact and is reflecting what he has read and heard. The way he relates this to words and images in the Biblical text, though in each case he makes his train of thought clear, is alien to us. We can admire his ingenuity, but we cannot share his presuppositions. Nonetheless, it is important to grasp that though some of his exegesis may have been original, he was working within well-defined traditions and was used to making connections between words and concepts, language and thought, which will elude us.

In *II Ad Thessalonicenses*: language and eschatology

A further development in the thought of Fray Luis takes place in his commentary on II Thessalonians, written by St Paul to a community of Christians who were expecting the imminent second coming of the Lord, in order to persuade them to conform their behaviour to such a belief instead of becoming embroiled in fruitless speculation about the exact moment.[16] Fray Luis, who himself believed in a literal second coming, treats the subject not by expounding obscure images and phrases but by another of his common techniques, the scholastic *quaestio*: 'Utrum . . . sciri possit ex Sancta Scriptura, et auctoritate sanctorum, quo tempore Christi adventus futurus sit?' (474), 'Can it be ascertained . . . from Scripture and the authority of the saints when the second coming of Christ will take place?' First come the arguments in favour of this thesis. According to the *domus Eliae* (a prophecy attributed to Elijah and used by the Christian Kabbalists Galatinus and Pico and in the Talmud), the world is to last six thousand years. Nine Doctors of the Church support this theory. A date of 1656 for the end of the world is favoured 'secundum veram computationem Hebraeorum et Vulgatae editionis' (476), 'according to the accurate reckoning of the Hebrews and the Vulgate'. Other proofs are subsidiary, and curious: pagan seers, like the Sybils, all set a fixed duration for the world; the creation took six days, one day is as a thousand with God (Psalm lxxxix.4); in Gen. i.1 there are six *alephs* (the first letter of the Hebrew alphabet) and *aleph* has a numerical value of a thousand in Hebrew; our first six parents, from Adam to Jared, all died, but the seventh, Enoch, was taken directly to heaven, therefore death reigns for six thousand years and the seventh millennium ushers in the End, with the reward of eternal life for the blessed. These are not the views of Fray Luis; merely his selection of the strongest arguments, and at the end of his discussion he rejects them, showing that the *domus Eliae* is no more than a Rabbinical gloss, that the Fathers never affirm as certain the view attributed to them, and that other interpretations of the evidence are more probable.

Meanwhile, he defines the nature of the enquiry. It is one thing to ask if God has established the time of the End, another to know whether that time is so set forth in Scripture that it is accessible to us. Origen, for example, taught that although God had fixed a time, it was not for us to know it. Fray Luis's own views are given in a series of propositions. First, the time of the End is indeed fixed by God from all eternity; his immutability demands this. In his human nature, Christ may have known it, though Fray Luis is reluctant to commit himself to this view. Second, no date can be ascertained from Scripture or Tradition 'sine temeritate ingenti' (478), 'without enormous rashness'; that is, without coming dangerously close to heresy. Third, Scripture expressly predicts that certain things must happen before the End: the proclamation of the Gospel throughout the earth, the conversion of the Jews, the return of Elijah and Enoch, apostasy and the revelation of the Antichrist. Signs may be seen; times may not be known. The commentary remains unfinished at this point. Fray Luis was called away to Valladolid on business concerning his Chair, as a marginal note records (481).

Some have misread this passage and claimed that Fray Luis believed the world would end in 1656, whereas he rejected any such certainty or even the attempt to do more than read the signs.[17] We know that one of these, the preaching of the Gospel in the New World, he observed with particular attention, and believed he had found prophetically foretold in Scripture. This example from *II Ad Thessalonicenses*, apart from its intrinsic interest in showing us something of Fray Luis's eschatological teaching, also introduces a significant feature of his expository technique. Sometimes a particular theological question will be raised in the middle of a commentary, and he is able to deal with it at greater length than with an image. This marks not only his Biblical commentaries but his Spanish prose works, and the detailed examination of an image or word followed by a more general discourse on a theological topic is a characteristic pattern in both. In such discourses, the reader cannot help but feel distant from the Biblical text which appears to have engendered them, even where, as here, they are germane to the underlying argument of a passage. Nevertheless, Fray Luis is following tradition, both in introducing wider issues and in treating them in the form of a *quaestio*; and the pattern is familiar enough today, when exegetes will expound the precise meaning of words and images and give a broader theological account of the sense of a passage or a book. For a fuller understanding of the movement from image to concept, from apparently random images to a sequence of ideas in which they find coherence, there is no better example than Fray Luis's longest Latin work, the threefold commentary on the Song of Songs.

In Canticum Canticorum: language as mystery and allegory

In his preface to the reader, Fray Luis reveals the origin of *In Canticum Canticorum Triplex explanatio*.[18] He recalls his earlier Spanish commentary, written not to probe the mysteries of the poem but to establish an accurate understanding of its obscure text. He recounts how it was copied and circulated without his knowledge, the struggles he had to clear his name, and his eventual restitution to honour and dignity. This preface was written for the first edition (1580), when memory of his ordeal was uncomfortably close. Though he has been vindicated, 'multi me hortati sunt, ut latine verterem eum librum, ipsumque . . . ederem' (II, 12), 'many have urged me to translate that book into Latin, and to . . . publish it'; hence he has added a commentary on the true, hidden meaning of the poem and a fuller exposition of the text. The commentary is also prefaced with a *censura* by Sebastián Pérez, whose old Christian ancestry had been questioned when Fray Luis asked for him as a *patrono*; and by original Latin poems addressed to two friends, Felipe Ruiz and Juan de Grial, to whom he dedicated some of his most famous Spanish odes. He did not forget his friends.

Each chapter in turn receives a literal, mystical and allegorical interpretation. The first (*prima explanatio*) deals with textual criticism, language and imagery, the second (*altera explanatio*) with the growth of the Christian in the spiritual life, and the third (*tertia explanatio*), added to the definitive 1589 edition, with the history of the people of God from Creation to the End. This last is allegory in the rhetorical sense, requiring an image-by-image account for which an accurate understanding of the text is fundamental.

The literal exposition is not of such interest as the others, because on the whole it expands the material sketched out in the Spanish commentary; but one addition is worth noting, because Fray Luis explains in the second chapter why the imagery of physical love is appropriate as a picture for the divine. Solomon's excellence as a poet, he says, is above that of all others, including the poets of classical antiquity:

Affirmo . . . in hac . . . mutui amoris expositione, Salomonem reliquos omnium linguarum, atque gentium poetas, et oratores omnes, tam longe, tamque multum superasse, ut si, quae illi scripserunt cum ejus scriptis conferantur, statuendum sit, in illorum litteris amoris quidem inesse umbram quandam pertenuem: solidam autem, et expressam, atque adeo vivam, et spirantem, atque agentem imaginem contineri in his Salomonis scriptis.

(145)

I affirm that in this story of mutual love . . . Solomon has so far and so greatly surpassed the other poets of all languages and peoples and all orators, that if their writings are compared with his, it must be established that while some tenuous shadow of love is found in their works, in his is its entire, clear, living, breathing and active image.

The tenuous shadow (*umbram pertenuem*) of classical poetry contrasts with the complete image of love in the Bible (*solidam . . . expressam . . . vivam, et spirantem, atque agentem imaginem*), closer to love's reality than the shadows of it in all other poetry. Human love is a fitting image of divine love because it too is a shadow of that ultimate reality, its closest likeness. Its ardour and passion participate in the spiritual yearning which characterizes divine love. The language of human love is not mere decoration; it is ontologically linked with its nobler partner, it is, one might say, its sacrament. That is why the other expositions are needed to complete the sense of the poem.

This contrast between the 'shadow' and the reality of love stems from Christian Platonism, but here Fray Luis applies it to the relationship between the surface meaning of the text and its deeper significance. The words and images of human love thus become symbols which participate in the nature of that which they symbolize, and the commentator who comes to them must show how the reader can move from symbolic statement to the truth contained therein, without departing from the language of the text and without straining credibility by creating artificial links between sign and signified. 'Oportet . . . ut allegorias tum sobrie, tum etiam apte et concinne figuremus', 'It is necessary for allegories to be used soberly, aptly and suitably': *In Canticum Canticorum* provides another working model for the theories of the *Tractatus*, and helps us to see exactly what Fray Luis meant by these qualities of aptness, sobriety and suitability. To guide him was an authoritative tradition which had already grappled with the Song and provided detailed interpretations of all its images. Before we pass too hasty a judgement on an exegetical method which makes assumptions we may not share, let us bear in mind that Fray Luis approached the language of Scripture as the word of God and that he was supported by a continuous tradition of such exegesis and let us first approach his commentary on his own terms.

The second exposition raises a question often asked about the religious poetry of Fray Luis: is it mystical? Critics have formed very different opinions.[19] A convincing answer is hardly possible. Much depends on the definition offered of mysticism. While he writes of experiences which are mystical in the sense that they relate to the life of prayer and to God's raising of the soul beyond its natural powers, it is difficult to tell if this reflects personal experience or is derived from his thorough reading of spiritual classics. The commentary shows close familiarity with traditional Christian teaching: Fray Luis divides the Song into stages which correspond to the threefold way of purgation, illumination and union, and explains the imagery accordingly. Purgation (for beginners) lasts from i.1 to ii.7, where the second calling of the Beloved marks the transition to illumination (for proficients), ii.8 to v.2a. Thereafter comes the unitive way (for the perfect). He observes that commentators have differed on whether the love symbolized in the poem is God's love for the Church or for the individual – the two major strands of interpretation through the Christian era. He believes it refers to both, the singular being the image of the universal; and that is another reason for his adding a third commentary.

This exact division is made because some, mistakenly, he thinks, have found the Song incoherent, merely a collection of short, unrelated poems. His division also matches the three eulogies of the Bride's beauty; one occurs in each stage, each intenser than the last. But the Song does not stand alone. It is itself part of a progression. Proverbs and Ecclesiastes, which precede it, have taught the way of God through counsels in human behaviour and wisdom. Now comes the best way of all, love. Belief in the common authorship of these books by Solomon becomes a unifying principle for the great disparity of material they contain.

The exposition of the images in the mystical sense shows the same disconcerting tendencies we have earlier alluded to. The soul's love for God begins impure and needs the blandishments of the first verse – kisses and breasts. The savour and ointment of the next are metaphors for the presence of God, seen in the dramatic beauty of the heavens but also in the lower creation. Three of the king's chambers (i.3) are open to the soul in this life – consideration of the natural order, knowledge of it, Christian contemplation of it. The famous 'I am black but comely' refers to the beauty of the soul's new life and the ugliness of what remains of the old.

With the state of ecstasy signified by the wine-cellar (AV 'banqueting-house', ii.4), the way of the proficients begins. Here God 'partim apparet, partim occultatur' (165), 'partly appears and partly is hidden'. Fray Luis distinguishes two forms of ecstasy: one when the mind is continually filled with the light of the divine presence and, 'sublimium rerum cognitionibus occupata, aciem suam ad externa haec et sensibilia referre non potest' (161), 'occupied with the knowledge of great and sublime matters cannot look upon the external things of the senses'; the other, though of a lesser kind, intense, and foreshadowed here. This he calls an 'illapsus', the soft and exceedingly sweet speech of God with the soul, which catches it up as a fire and converts it wholly to him. He seems to be amplifying St Bernard's comment that the two forms of ecstasy are of intellect, enlightenment and knowledge on the one hand, and will, fervour and devotion on the other (*On the Song of Songs*, Sermon 49.4).[20] Again following Bernard, he finds the springtime imagery of ii. 10–13 especially appropriate for a state in which the skies of the soul are clearing and the seed of Christ growing. Bernard's 'voice of the turtle' calls souls 'in our land' (the exile of earth) to the heavenly homeland; so too for Fray Luis, souls 'ardereque incipiunt desiderio coelestis patriae, suspirantque ad illam crebro, sonatque in ipsorum cordibus turturea Spiritus Sancti vox gemitibus inenarrabilibus' (166), 'begin to burn with desire for the heavenly homeland, they sigh for it frequently, and the voice of the dove of the Holy Spirit sounds in their hearts with unspeakable groanings' (compare Sermon 59.3–5). The soul is to be dove-like (ii.10) in fidelity, doves being a traditional symbol for this (Bernard stresses chastity instead), in its love of the quiet and solitude of the country away from the clamour of the city (earthly concerns) and in its acceptance of suffering, borne patiently and in hope, for the sake of constancy of love.

The dove and her haunts provides us with a good example both of Fray Luis's indebtedness to a Christian tradition which had assimilated profane themes and of his critical distance from the conventions of secular poetry of his own age. The extolling of the countryside as a place for spiritual solitude reflects that idealized view of nature which gathers up the lost innocence of Eden and the myth of the Golden Age and which enjoyed a great popularity in Renaissance pastoral literature. Whereas Fray Luis writes of the countryside in general, Bernard's dove avoids green boughs and haunts inaccessible regions – tree-tops and mountain ridges (Sermon 59.7). But both reject any erotic overtones, any connotation with the 'bird of Venus', so characteristic of European love poetry and so sensually evoked, for example, by Góngora (*Polifemo* 40–2).

Even at this stage, trials and tribulations await the soul. The little foxes (ii.15) are the insignificant sins which sap the will (Bernard refers them to subtle temptations but also to contemporary heretics, Sermons 62–6). But the night-time wanderings of the Bride in search of her Beloved (iii.1–3) introduce a more sombre note. Night represents times of trouble and bitterness in Scripture, for though God is present in everything, he sometimes seems withdrawn, and the light of grace vanishes before thick darkness. Three times in the Song – once in each of the three ways of prayer – the Bride cries out: at the beginning, to lament the Bridegroom's absence; here, to seek but not at first to find him; and finally (v.7) when she is wounded by the watchmen. God permits such suffering to purge us of self-love or of too easy a reliance on the blessings we have hitherto received. This theme of purgative suffering is developed at some length (193–200). The soul's faithfulness will not go unrewarded if she perseveres in love to seek God through the darkness.

The theme surfaces again in chapter five, when the soul enters the way of the perfect. Here, Fray Luis writes, it sometimes happens that the soul most keenly experiences the absence of God, and the torment is great. But once again God is moving her to love him better: 'Tunc enim subtrahere se a nostro conspectu solet, neque jam amplius dulciter et jucunde in nos illabitur: quinimo adversi aliquid, vel nobis immittit ipse, vel ab aliis inferri permittit, quasi virtutem nostram isto modo . . . probare velit' (299), 'For then he is wont to withdraw from our sight, and he no longer sweetly and pleasantly enters us; rather he puts into us something adverse or allows it to be put in by others, as if in this manner he desired to test our virtue'. Moreover, God wills the soul to assist others on the path, and if this is done reluctantly he withdraws and tranquillity is forfeited. But if it places the salvation of others above its own inner peace, he restores his presence. Thus Fray Luis teaches an active, outward-looking spirituality, and insists that a private road to God is bound in the end to be self-centred and to bring its own dark night of suffering, which will depart only when apostolic labours are renewed.

This is a different voice from Bernard's, for whom night is interpreted as ignorance, faithlessness and perversity, as well as immoral behaviour (Sermon 75.10). But anyone familiar with the sixteenth-century Carmelite mystics of Spain will be struck by this insistence on suffering as the road towards union unfolds. Like St John of the Cross, Fray Luis teaches that the higher you progress, the harsher such suffering will prove. Unlike him, he creates no theological system out of these 'dark nights' and neither probes so relentlessly the innermost recesses of the soul nor insists on a passive waiting in the darkness till God please to grant his light again. Nevertheless, it is remarkable to find Fray Luis writing in these terms in 1580, before he can have read anything of St John, if he ever did. His own description of a dark night of the soul, which, like so much of St John's poetry grows out of the imagery of the Song, has been largely ignored by those who have written about his mysticism. He was not as well read in spiritual literature as in the Bible, and if his teaching is as derivative as some believe, no exact source for this dark night theology is readily identifiable. One cannot therefore help thinking back to his personal confession in the commentary on Psalm xxvi. Indeed, release from this 'night of tribulation' seems to remind him of his prison experience, though the reference is more guarded than in that work: 'Nam quotiescumque, aut videmus ipsi, aut ab aliis audimus, aliquem praesertim bonum et modestum virum a carcere, ab ignominia, ab inimicorum manu, a morbo, a captivitate, a similibus permultis . . . statim nobis occurrit revereri, et admirari providentiam Dei' (203–4), 'For whenever we see or hear from others that some especially good and modest man is freed from prison, disgrace, from the hand of his enemies, from sickness, captivity and many such things . . . it at once happens that we honour and wonder at the providence of God'.

Returning to the sequence of the exposition, the strange imagery at the start of the fourth chapter causes him no difficulty. From this point he cannot have been helped by St Bernard, whose sermons were never completed and do not pass beyond the third chapter of the Song. For Fray Luis, the hair represents the thoughts of the mind. Previously used of beginners, it here refers to proficients, who can control vain distractions more successfully. The hills and valleys pictured in iv.1–2 are images of man as microcosm, in whom lofty reason is born to rule over the lowly faculties of anger and concupiscence. The neck (iv.4), where we eat and breathe, is prayer, by which we are nourished and through which we are joined to Christ our head through his Church. Prayer, he says, is insufficiently heeded by philosophers, who learn the life of blessedness from books rather than experience – an echo of the conventional distinction between scholastic and mystical theology which at first sight is surprising from the pen of a scholar who held a University chair. The defences of the neck are the strength prayer brings to resist evil, while the breasts (iv.5) stand for the growth of the proficients. In this section, where the distance between image and explanation seems at its greatest, we find clear examples of what Fray Luis meant by an apt, sober and suitable use of allegory, because in each case he identifies the moral or spiritual quality and the element in the image which responds to it – hair which can blow about, like distractions; the neck, which is a place of joining; the height and depth of reason and sensuality read from the height and depth of hill and valley.

The 'garden inclosed' (iv.12), the *hortus conclusus*, 'in quo non modo nulla pars inculta sit . . . qui totus peregrinis et aromaticis abundet arboribus' (258), 'in which no part is uncultivated . . . and which all abounds with strange and fragrant trees' is perhaps the most influential of all the Song's images in European literature.[21] Fray Luis will later expound it traditionally, as the Church; here, concerned with moral and spiritual growth, he explains that it represents the just and the fruit they bring forth. The fruit of good works at once reminds him that certain foolish persons in his own time – by which he means the Protestants – have denied that these can please God, and so it is that religious polemic of the sixteenth century works its way into the exegesis, just as it had from a twelfth-century context when St Bernard preached about the little foxes. Though all sin in this life, many good works are done free of sin by the just. All good works come first from God by the merits of Christ, whose righteousness is impressed upon the soul of the just man and bears fruit in his actions. The more we exert ourselves in good works, the more abundantly Christ communicates to us his merits and makes us like him. In a series of antitheses Fray Luis contrasts 'vos' heretics with 'nos' faithful: 'Vos quidem fontem omnium bonorum Christum esse fatemini, sed fontem, qui intra sese contineat aquas suas: nos ex eo fonte, quem item inexhaustum et Oceano majorem esse fatemur, largos bonorum omnium rivos derivari, et ad singulos justos pervenire affirmamus' (262), 'you indeed confess Christ as the fount of all good things, but one which contains its waters within itself; we affirm that from that fount, which we confess to be inexhaustible and greater than the ocean, there flow copious streams of all good things which reach every just man'. The awakening of the north wind (iv.16) is interpreted as the blowing away of these 'pestilential doctrines'.

What Fray Luis claims here represents the stalemate which had been reached between Catholics and Protestants after Trent, though his use of an image (the fountain) to contrast the two positions is perhaps easier for us to respond to than theological expositions of justification by faith alone by either side. Yet the symbol of the *hortus conclusus* as a place of moral and spiritual growth in the Church was so pervasive that the great English Congregationalist hymn-writer Isaac Watts (1674–1748), who stood on the other side of the theological divide, could quite naturally turn to the same passage in the Song to evoke the same kind of 'fragrance' of Christian living in one of his Eucharistic poems:

> Like Trees of Myrrh and Spice we stand,
> Planted by God the Father's Hand;
> And all his Springs in Sion flow
> To make the young Plantation grow.
>
> Awake, O heavenly Wind, and come,
> Blow on this garden of Perfume;
> Spirit Divine, descend and breathe
> A gracious Gale on Plants beneath.
>
> Make our best Spices flow abroad
> To entertain our Saviour-God:
> And faith, and Love, and Joy appear,
> And every Grace be active here.[22]

Both men shared a common exegetical tradition of the Song; Catholics and Protestants alike today have lost it.

The soul now enters upon the way of the perfect (v.2b); it sleeps to the senses and awakens to God and his gifts. The image which gives Fray Luis his clue is 'sleep'. The ecstasy beyond words of the unitive way is so called because God requires the soul to be covered in silence and to be hidden. The very brevity of the description implies profundity of meaning. That is how he explains the fact that this vital transition is indicated by just six words, 'Ego dormio, et cor meum vigilat', 'I sleep, but my heart waketh'. In Scripture, whenever God alludes to such mysteries, 'summa parcitate verborum utatur; rem notet uno, cum altero verbo, atque ejusmodi significationis verbo, ut facile intelligatur, quod verbo subest arcanum esse aliquid, et ineffabile, et quod verbis, quamvis multis non posit dici' (292), 'he uses words most sparingly; he indicates one thing through one word or another, and through a word of such significance that it may easily be understood that something hidden and ineffable lies under it, which cannot be stated in words, even in many words'. In this 'sleep' God is calling the soul more urgently than before. He both enters it and is hidden within it; he enters both by inspiring it to devotion and good works and by a clearer infusion of divine joy. The watchmen who find and wound the soul (v.7) are unworthy bishops and pastors, examples of which, Fray Luis adds, are to be found in his own time. Most of the rest of this chapter consists of the Bride's praise of Christ, beginning with his physical beauty but moving quickly to his nature. The 'white and ruddy' colours (v.10), for example, mean the mixing of the divine and human in Christ; while the hair which is both gold and black receives an enormously complex treatment.

The inward peace God grants the soul, seen in the Beloved's feeding in the garden (vi.1) is something the Jews have never understood, in their search for Messianic peace of an earthly kind (a theme to the fore, as we shall see, in 'Braço de Dios').[23] Though the highest degree of virtue possible in this life has now been reached, the end of the journey is distant yet, and the soul must not relax from effort. The end comes with the beatific vision, beyond physical death, in which God will be enjoyed for ever (362). In the seventh chapter Christ praises the soul in a sequence of images working from feet to head, reversing the conventional head-to-feet progression of European love poetry, earlier used in the Song too. Fray Luis explains: whereas before the virtues of the soul were themselves perceived, now it is the effect of those virtues, the 'feet' which carry out good works. The true greatness of the Christian life is its humility, he continues, a paradox derived from Christ's joining of his sublime divinity to lowly human nature, which he unravels as he stresses more and more the total rule of Christ in the life of the soul.

In the final chapter the soul, desiring to love God openly, seeks solitude with him. Though he is present in the whole creation, to know him through what he has made is to know him but imperfectly and to risk adhering to love of the creature, not the Creator. Thus the perfect seek God 'without' (vii.1), to see him as he is and to be transformed in his image. When they pass from this life, they enter the blessedness of immortality, but meanwhile the soul must continue to care for those not yet saved – the little sister who has no breasts of viii.8 – and to cultivate the study of divine love, the vineyard secured by its walls and towers (viii.10–12) against the devil. Only one thing then remains: to await the second coming of Christ, which the Bride urges the Beloved to hasten in the final verse ('Make haste, my beloved'), so that the wedding of Christ and his Church may complete the espousals already begun.

This second exposition of the Song has covered the journey of the soul from its beginnings in the love of God to the beatific vision, and the apparently random images gain coherent meaning from their allegorical relationship with the steps of this journey. Fray Luis is at pains to demonstrate exactly where the points of contact between the imagery and the theology come. The third exposition unfolds the Song as an allegory of the history of the Church, and in a long preface to this new material he explains why it has been added (82–114).

The allegory has been judged unsuitable for various reasons. The speakers do not behave as lovers should, women do not take the initiative or go out to search for their lovers into the city at night, and divine love should not be contaminated with sensuality. To answer these objections, Fray Luis argues that there is in fact consistency between the imagery used and the meaning intended. God declares his love for the Church in these terms because we respond more readily to human love, which belongs to our experience, than to divine, which does not. The pastoral imagery is entirely appropriate: Christ calls himself a shepherd; marriage is one of the figures the Bible uses for his union with the Church, alongside the shepherd and his flock and the vine (John x, xv). The poem must also be approached as a drama, with scenes, time changes and chorus, like the chorus of classical tragedy.

How then does Fray Luis derive a love-song between Christ and his Church from these verses? The answer is again that the images themselves contain the clues, and the structure of the poem, in the three clear divisions he has previously applied to the spiritual life, corresponds to the traditional three ages of the Church: from the Fall to the giving of the Law at Sinai, from the Church of Israel (Moses) to Christ, from the Church of the New Israel (beginning at the Incarnation) till the End. The three descriptions of the Bride's beauty in the poem, as an infant, a child and a nubile maid, reinforce this pattern.

The first verse, 'Let him kiss me with the kisses of his mouth', expresses the desire of the ancient people of God for the Word to be made incarnate. The Word made flesh is the divine 'kissing' of humanity, and kisses are better than wine because at the Incarnation the Church beholds on earth joys beforehand only known in heaven. Here Fray Luis follows closely in the steps of St Bernard, who in a beautiful passage tells of our ancestors' desire for this 'sacrosanct kiss, that is, the mystery of the incarnate Word' (Sermon 2.7–9), and out of many Biblical texts builds up an impression of the meaning of this kiss which carries great imaginative and artistic power.[24] The savour (i.2) is the fragrance of the promise of the Messiah, and the virgins, this infant Church, as it responds in discipleship ('Draw me', i.3). The Bride's dark colouring naturally becomes sin, introduced by the Fall, and the unkept vineyard (i.5) the loss of paradise. Less obviously, perhaps, the strife of 'my mother's children' is the war in heaven between Lucifer and St Michael, the heavenly analogue of the Fall. When Christ and the Church praise each other's beauty (i.14–15), the adornments of the Bride signify the external splendour of the cult before Sinai: 'Illius enim aetatis homines Deum colebant, magis externis ritibus magnifice, quam spiritus interiori veritate perfecte. Nam quamvis in Ecclesia semper interior Dei cultus fuerit . . . tamen interior Dei cultus perfectus proprius est Ecclesiae Evangeliae' (130–1), 'for at that time men worshipped God more splendidly in outward rites than perfectly in the inward truth of the spirit. For although inward worship of God has always existed in the Church . . . the perfect inward worship of God is more appropriate to the Church of the Gospel' – a comment Erasmus would have thoroughly approved of.

Just as in i.7 the 'egredere' (AV i.8, 'Go thy way forth') signals Abram's departure from Ur for a nomadic life (Gen. xii), in which God's promise to him is to be fulfilled, so 'leaping upon the mountains' (ii.8) points to Moses descending from mount Sinai with the tables of the Law. This introduces the second period of the Church's history. When the Beloved calls to the Bride 'Rise up' (ii.10) he is summoning the Church of Israel out of slavery in Egypt, and the 'little foxes' become the Egyptians who attempt to prevent the Exodus. The hurried departure from Egypt is seen in the swiftness of the 'hart upon the mountains' (ii.17), while the whole of the third chapter, with its common theme of searching and wandering, describes the Exodus and the forty years in the wilderness. Moses and Aaron are the 'watchmen' (iii.3) who part the Red Sea so that the people reach the safety of 'my mother's house' (iii.4), the promised land. The Chorus (iii.6–11) expresses the wonder of those who beheld the Church in the wilderness. Solomon's bed is the Ark of the Covenant, Solomon here being a figure of Christ; and the sixty warriors about it are the six hundred thousand men recorded as having left Egypt (Exod. xii.37).

In the fourth chapter the Church reaches the promised land, and her youthful perfection is praised in the portrait of a young and beautiful woman. Though he says that each image does not necessarily have to correspond to a particular aspect of the perfection of this Church, Fray Luis maintains that this can be done, and apportions the images of hair, teeth, headbands, cheeks, pomegranates, neck and breasts among the twelve tribes, in another of those passages where the modern reader feels most keenly the distance between his world and that of Fray Luis. But the exposition soon becomes more approachable. The mountain and hill (iv.6) stand by synecdoche for the hilly country of Palestine, rich in myrrh and incense; while the honey and milk (iv.11) is the teaching of the Church, honey for its sweetness and milk because its members are as yet but beginners. The 'garden inclosed' and 'fountain sealed' of iv.12 are images of the holiness of the Church of Israel when many fruits grew on its trees and much water flowed from its fountain – an idealized picture of the beginnings of Israel which Fray Luis has no doubt acquired from the prophetic contrasts between original faithfulness and present corruption (e.g. Jer. ii.2–3, Hos. ix.1–2, Amos v.25). Again, the power and influence of this symbol may be seen in the same poem of Isaac Watts, which begins with a picture of the Church of English Dissent as a 'garden wall'd around', safe from the snares and compromises of the world:

> We are a Garden wall'd around
> Chosen and made peculiar Ground;
> A little Spot inclos'd by Grace
> Out of the World's wide Wilderness.[25]

As the allegory of the garden is revealed, so too is the final stage of the Church's history. The Beloved comes in his Advent and Incarnation, as he reaches the Bride's house: 'Open to me, my sister, my love' (v.2). He comes cold and wet, thus showing his humanity; the putting off of his coat ('Expoliavi me tunica mea', with its echoes of the Passion) signifies persecution at the hands of his own people. But he persists in calling, and those who hear, repent (the myrrh of v.5). His followers are themselves persecuted (v.7, the watchmen who wound), but proclaim him even in adversity (v.8). The Church has now progressed sufficiently to offer her first hymn of praise to Christ (v.10–16). 'White and ruddy', he is, as before, divine and human. His head represents his birth, his hair, his youth and maturity, his eyes, the light of his teaching and his holiness, his belly, his tomb and cross, his marble and gold legs, his victorious resurrection and so on.

Hidden in Christ's description, Fray Luis also discovers the history of the Church Militant, initiated with his death and continuing till the End. His hair ('sicut elatae palmarum', v.11) suggests martyrs, virgins and saints, because palms are the martyr's symbol; gold, the splendour of the Church from Constantine to Gregory, turning to ivory as charity declines though piety remains; while the first monks shine like sapphires. More recently and grievously, nations have abandoned the Church and only the marble is left, firm and white but cold and hard. The Renaissance myth of the Golden Age is applied to Church history: 'priscos illos homines vere fuisse aureos, nos autem marmoreos' (318), 'those ancient men truly were of gold, but we, of marble', born of stone, like Deucalion and Pyrrha of classical mythology. Whereas before the Gospel was preached with simplicity and gentleness, now it is imposed by violence, 'per homines ferro succinctos, auri magis rapiendi, quam verae religionis in aliorum animos inserendae cupidos, infinita edita strage hominum, totisque non modo populis, sed gentibus etiam ad internecionem deletis' (318–19), 'by men girded with iron, more desirous of plundering gold than of bringing the souls of others to true religion, with an unlimited slaughter of men, so that not only whole peoples but even nations have been massacred'. This sombre reference could be to the carnage of contemporary European history but in this context seems more likely to represent Fray Luis's horror at the slaughter of Indians in the New World in the name of Christianity.

In the last days of the Church, when men will study virtue and reform their lives, and when God will again pour out his gifts on it, as in days of old, it will nonetheless face grave perils. Antichrist will come; but it will overcome him. The Jews, who for so long have resisted the true Messiah, will be received into its fold. Chapter six describes the spread of the Gospel into the whole world, to make its desert a garden. Christ now praises the beauty of his Church in its future apostolic zeal (vi.4–9): 'Prius pulchram ipsam esse dicebat, nunc praeterea suavem et decorem, et florentissimae ac sanctissimae urbi similem, et militum aciei instructae omnino parem, in quo . . . et illius eximia significatur sanctitas, et animi invicta fortitudo, et egregia erga Deum pietas declaratur' (371), 'Previously he called her beautiful, but now as well sweet and comely, like a most flourishing and holy City and to an army drawn up in battle . . . which signifies her outstanding sanctity and unconquered strength of soul, and reveals her illustrious piety towards God' (371). Again the exegesis becomes involved: the contrast between the 'threescore queens and fourscore concubines, and virgins without number' and 'my dove . . . is but one' (vi.8–9) is between the multiplicity of Jewish sacrifices and the one sacrifice of Christ. Since the text expresses an antithesis between the many and the one, Fray Luis has looked for a correspond-

ing theological one, forgetting perhaps that Christ himself is address-
ing the Church when he speaks of the one dove.

The strange figure of Amminadib now enters, with his chariots
(vi.11), the source of the mysterious and haunting ending of the *Cántico
espiritual* of St John of the Cross:

> Que nadie lo miraba . . .
> Aminadab tampoco parecía
> y el cerco sosegaba,
> y la caballería
> a vista de las aguas descendía.

> With none our peace offending,
> Aminadab has vanished with his slaughters:
> And now the siege had ending,
> The cavalcades descending
> Were seen within the precinct of the water.[26]

St John makes Amminadib represent the devil, and the horsemen the
bodily senses, no longer able to distract the soul now that she has
entered the sanctuary of the spiritual marriage. As a Hebrew scholar,
Fray Luis knows this cannot be correct, because in the literal sense the
word is not a proper noun but means 'my people, a prince'. We recall
that in the *Tractatus* he insists that the literal sense must not be violated
in order to expound the other senses. So for him, Amminadib means
the princes of Rome, ruling the world and the Church. God sent the
apostles first to the Jews, then among the Roman 'chariots', and made
his Church in Rome the 'prince' of all the Churches. His conclusion is
quite the opposite from St John's: Amminadib is not the devil, but the
Roman Church, which will no doubt comfort those who have always
held the two to be identical.

The Church is praised again in vii.1–9, by the Chorus and the
Bridegroom. Her feet are beautiful (vii.1) because the Gospel was first
preached to lowly and humble men, and feet are the lowliest part of
the body. The two breasts (vii.3) show how the exegetical tradition
contained many possibilities: they are king and Pope, the two Testaments, Scripture and Tradition, Peter and Paul, sacraments and
doctrines – any appropriate pair, one is tempted to add. The neck
(vii.4) is by common consent, however, the Fathers and pastors of the
Church, also called towers, by virtue of their strength. Eyes are the
prophets, noses those who guard the Church from heresy, hair the
martyrs and purple their blood or burning charity. The origins of
monasticism are seen in 'go forth into the field' (vii.11), which means

to search for solitude and to cultivate the desert places, an idea prompted by Jerome's description, which is quoted: 'O desertum, Christi floribus vernans', 'O desert, springing with the flowers of Christ'(406). The garden in the wilderness is another example of the pervasive theme of Eden: the outward reality of the desert is the locus for an inward, unseen flowering of the spirit.

The opening verses of the final chapter continue with the themes of the dethronement of idols, the splendour of the Christian Desert, the rejection of the Jews and the calling of the Gentiles. The Church is then exhorted to remain faithful and some decline from virtue is predicted (viii.6–7). 'What shall we do for our sister?' (viii.8) introduces the favourite theme of the spread of the Gospel into the New World, the inhabitants of which are 'little' in knowing the right and using reason, and very hard to convert. They may be beautiful, but they conceal their true nature, aptly described in the metaphors of 'wall' and 'door', the first representing their wildness and resistence to moral improvement, the second their gullibility. The military metaphors here also have a sinister ring: 'Postremo in istarum gentium ad Christum conversione vis quaedam est adhibita; non enim evangelium illis annuntiatum est, ut olim annuntiabatur per inermes homines, sed armati, aut . . . ii, quibus armati homines praesidio erant, pietatis doctrinam ipsis tradiderunt' (452), 'Some force was finally applied in the conversion to Christ of these peoples; for the Gospel was not preached to them as once it was, by defenceless men, but armed men or . . . those defended by armed men delivered to them the teaching of holiness' – a comment which implies disapproval.

The present age is reached with this universal preaching (viii.10). The return of the Jews is foreseen in the allegory of the vineyard (viii.11–12; compare Isa. v.1–7). The 'companions' (viii.13) are false friends, whose lives are unworthy of their vocation and who have infiltrated the Church. This gives Fray Luis a last opportunity to write as so many moralists have about their own times. Since true piety is all but extinguished, and morality and discipline all but forgotten, and since evil lodges in the very bosom of the Church, the only hope is to pray for the return of Christ the Judge. The evil he has in mind is caused by the enemies of Christendom, be they Turks or Protestants: 'Nos inter nos collidimur intestinis dissidiis: de religionis doctrina orta dissensio, a parvis primum ducta initiis, ita crevit paulatim, ut innumerabiles populos, atque nationes ab Ecclesiae corpore dividens, in errores induxerit perniciosos et impios' (461), 'We clash with one another in internal dissensions; disagreement arose about the doctrine of religion, and from small beginnings has slowly grown so that, separating numberless peoples and nations from the body of the Church, it has led to pernicious and impious errors'. A thick night of sin has spread throughout the Church, and only Christ's hastening (viii.14) to return can dispel it.

Fray Luis's attempt to derive teaching about prayer or the history of old and new Israel from a poem which seems to have nothing to do with such things can hardly convince the modern reader. His commentary may be admired for the loftiness of its conception, the ingenuity of its exposition, and the beauty of its style. We can appreciate the need to establish the correct text to understand what the words mean, but we cannot imagine that the author of the Song meant these other things. We may be moved by the rich and alien imagery of the poem, even in translation, and wonder how it managed to be included in the Biblical canon, but we become suspicious that in the tradition Fray Luis was working in, a text could mean anything at all. We are taught to believe that somewhere, if only we can find it, lies the goal of a true meaning and a correct interpretation.

Yet we find no unanimity about the interpretation of literature in our own day. The same text may be interpreted in radically differing ways. Our approach, as much as that of Fray Luis, depends on presuppositions; only ours are secular theories, his a religious conviction. A critical theory of a number of senses through which the sacred text could be understood may not be so far removed from theories which have long since moved away from restricting literary criticism to the elucidation of the author's intended meaning, and which commonly recognize the social, cultural and psychological factors which contribute to the making of a work of art and are therefore present in it.

Are there, therefore, any factors which encourage us to revalue the hermeneutical approach of Fray Luis? First, of course, it was as natural to him as our approaches are to us. But it rested on two foundations which we are much less likely to share: his belief in the divine inspiration of Scripture, which invested every syllable of its text with the potential of revelation, and his confidence in the authority of past commentators, like St Bernard, whose influence we have seen at several points. If we judge his approach wrong, then we must, how-ever regretfully, dismiss fifteen centuries of allegorical and mystical exegesis as misguided. Second, although some of his explanations seem arbitrary, especially in the long sequences of images which describe the protagonists, in most cases Fray Luis develops them on the basis of something inherent in the image – a quality, even some-times its etymology – which points him in the direction of his account of its significance. He ranges freely through Scripture to find support-ing examples. Honey and milk (iv.11), for instance, he rightly per-ceives as Biblical symbols for the word of God, and can thus quite naturally associate them with the teaching of the Church (e.g. AV Psalm cxix.103, Ezek. iii.3, I Cor. iii.2). He is not expounding the Song's images as an isolated phenomenon, but in the total context of Scripture. Since the Biblical writers themselves constantly refer back to the events and images of the history of salvation, not only in the New but also in the Old Testament, Fray Luis's sense of the unity of Biblical language is by no means misplaced. Who now can tell what poetic tradition the author of the Song was following and what resonances his chosen words carried which we no longer hear?

We work from the premise that a literary text is a complex phenom-enon. We have developed critical theories which allow us to read out of the text meanings which seem as arbitrary as those derived from allegorical exegesis of Scripture, and certainly as dependent on pre-supposition. We have learned to read a text, for example, as it bolsters the oppressive structures of society or subverts society's conventions. Fray Luis also saw the complexity, but, believing his text to be divinely inspired, assumed that it was as it was for a purpose, one which was part of God's revelation.

In one important sense he was right. The Song of Songs does contain an implied theology and spirituality, or it could never have hymned human love through the imagery of the natural creation. In his profound study of the poem, Francis Landy, working from the details of the Hebrew text, has articulated the nature of this theology:

The theme of the book is the process of fusion and differentiation, the paradise that only exists in the world through being inaccessible to it, or is only accessible outside its limits, through imaginative transcendence. The union of lovers, and that of the Self in the poem, is accomplished by the poem that parts them . . . The human paradox is that the source of our existence is elsewhere (respectively in the mother, God, nature, non-life), and we both need to make contact with it, to integrate our origins, and to free ourselves from them.[27]

It is rooted in Biblical symbolism:

The story of the garden of Eden is a mirror-image of the Song; each is reflected, sees itself as well as its antithesis in the other. Each finds its identity in the other; the garden of Eden is the mythical prototype of that of the Song ... Paradise formulates the paradox that our identity is founded in difference. We leave what we love in order to live.[28]

If the love of Bride and Bridegroom can be portrayed in the cosmic terms of animate and inanimate nature, then the lovers in a sense become everything in creation, by attracting all these metaphors to themselves, and the intertwining of the images is the embrace of the lovers. We are not as far as we thought from Fray Luis, who believed that God was the greatest begetter of metaphor, and that consequently such an outpouring of it as he found in the Song must be traceable back to him.

The *Exposición del libro de Job*: Scripture and the vernacular

The development of the English language has been profoundly influenced and enriched by the King James Bible. Spanish had no such equivalent, and that is one of the reasons why Fray Luis is so unusual among Spanish writers in his confident and pervasive use of the language of Scripture in his own tongue. Milton, for example, though outstanding, is not alone. In England, as in Germany, a magnificent vernacular Bible became the common possession of the people, and the idioms of a Semitic tongue were introduced into the currency of everyday speech and mingled there with others from very different sources. The Arabic influence on Spanish, though still recognizable, does not seem to have encouraged acceptance of its Hebrew cousin, for reasons which will become clearer in due course.

It is plain that Fray Luis regretted the almost total ban on vernacular versions of Scripture. Both his incarnational view of its language and his defence of its translation in the prologue to the first book of the *Nombres* underline his preoccupation with making Scripture accessible to those who could not read Latin. The *Exposición de Job* represents his longest and most ambitious attempt to remedy the deficiency.

Begun in prison, the first thirty-five chapters of *Job* were completed by the end of 1580. Fray Luis resumed work on it ten years later and finished it just before his death.[29] Though it expounds a long and difficult Hebrew text in Spanish, it is nevertheless as scholarly and as

complex as if it had been intended for a Latin readership of professional theologians. Whether or not it was the first major vernacular
commentary of Catholic Spain is uncertain, since it was not published
until 1779; but its conception and execution are remarkable in any
case. Fray Luis must have known that its chances of publication were
small, yet he persevered because of his conviction that ordinary people
needed to be confronted by the Biblical message directly.

A restored, partly autograph manuscript of *Job* is today among the
treasures of the University Library of Salamanca.[30] Its pages bear the
rubric of the Inquisitorial censor Juan Alvárez de Mármol, who
examined it in 1594. This probably represents the attempt made by
Fray Basilio Ponce de León soon after the death of Fray Luis, to have
the works of his distinguished forebear published. We cannot be sure
why he failed – probably a combination of difficulties with the Spanish
commentaries on the Bible and lack of personal enthusiasm.[31] The
censura composed by Fray Luis's successor in the Bible Chair, Juan
Alonso de Curiel, probably in 1593, has also survived.[32] Curiel
thought highly of *Job* and believed it should be more widely available.
However, as it was in Spanish it would need a licence from the Council
of the Inquisition, which ought to be granted. The book could instruct
those who knew no Latin: Job 'es uno de los [libros] que se entiende
que podrían andar sin peligro en lengua vulgar, por contener historia
llana y dottrina moral', 'is one of the books which it is understood
could circulate in the vulgar tongue without danger, since it contains
plain history and moral teaching' – in other words, no dangerous
mysteries. Such licences, he added, were normally granted for the
Epistles and Gospels, and even those who insisted most on banning all
vernacular Scripture had sometimes excepted Job. It contained no
doctrinal problems, but the text was very difficult and the Church
would greatly benefit from so full and good an exposition as this. Fresh
attempts early in the seventeenth century also failed to have *Job*
published, and when the process began again in the 1770s two of those
consulted were still expressing concern about Scripture becoming
available in the vernacular. But the defence won the day, and *Job* at
last appeared in print.

Fray Luis dedicated his work to the remarkable Mother Ana de
Jesús, a Discalced Carmelite nun who took the Carmelite Reform into
France and the Low Countries early in the seventeenth century, and
to whom St John of the Cross dedicated his *Cántico espiritual*.[33] Fray
Luis had come to know her towards the end of his life, when he became

involved both in preparing the first edition of the works of St Teresa of Avila, and in defending the privileges of the Discalced nuns against proposed changes in the Teresan constitutions.[34]

In his dedication, Fray Luis explains that Job is not only history but also doctrine and prophecy (*Obras* II, 27). It tells the story of Job's patience and suffering but also corrects our behaviour and prophesies future mysteries. It is written in verse and dialogue, so that it can be more enjoyable and more firmly imprinted upon us. Because it is very obscure in many places, through its poetic style and the great antiquity of its language, he provides three approaches to it. First, as with the *Cantar*, comes a word-for-word version of the Hebrew text in Spanish, 'conservando, cuanto es posible . . . el sentido latino y el aire hebreo, que tiene su cierta majestad' (28), 'preserving as far as possible . . . the Latin sense and the Hebrew air, which has its own particular majesty'; next, the commentary proper; and finally a rendering in Spanish verse, following, he says, the example of many writers and saints of old, in order to increase the love of Holy Scripture. We know from the trial documents (x, 186–7) that he had prepared a Spanish version of the book in prison, and we may assume that this was the foundation on which he built the rest.

In his prose translation, Fray Luis makes few concessions to Spanish grammar and syntax, and conserves the Hebrew word order and idiom, with its abrupt switches of tense and highly condensed sentences. A literal English translation of the passage immortalized in Handel's *Messiah* and beginning in the Authorized Version 'I know that my Redeemer liveth' runs thus, according to Fray Luis's Spanish text:

Yo conozco que mi Redentor vive, y que a la postre sobre polvo me levantaré. Y tornará a cercarme mi cuero, y en mi carne veré a Dios. Al cual yo veré por mí, y mis ojos le verán, y no extraño esta esperanza reposa en mi seno. Pues ¿por qué decís: Persigámosle, hallemos contra él raíz de palabra? Temed a vosotros de la faz de la espada, porque vengador de delictos espada, y sabed que hay juicio. (319)

I know that my Redeemer lives, and that at the last upon dust I shall raise myself. And my skin will once more surround me, and in my flesh I shall see God. Whom I shall see for myself, and my eyes will see him, and not strange this hope rests in my bosom. For why do you say: let us persecute him, let us find against him root of word? Fear yourselves the face of the sword, because avenger of wrongs sword, and know that there is judgement.

This is much less clear even than the Vulgate translation, which agrees with Fray Luis in several places where the King James translators do not. The result is a version as disconcerting and often as incomprehensible as his Spanish translation of the Song, only on a much grander scale. As there, he adds archaisms, to increase the majesty of the work – *fambre* for *hambre* (hunger, v.22), *fiucia* (hope, viii.14), *escuchedes* for *escuchad* (hearken, xiii.6). That language should be thought of as more awesome when it was archaic is in itself an interesting point; but the intentions of Fray Luis went beyond a concern with the feel of the text. He was not so much translating it into Spanish as showing how extraordinarily difficult the Hebrew was when so translated. He was implying that the Vulgate masked these difficulties, and that only a full commentary on the Hebrew text could allow a reader to make sense of it. A vernacular version, far from making Scripture plain, only intensifies the obscurity of its original meaning.

Fray Luis's own experience of unjust suffering has quite naturally led critics to suppose that he must have been drawn to Job and to wonder how closely the exposition relates to his own feelings. One writes of being able to reconstruct 'the intimate biography of the poet and to follow the path of his spiritual state' through the commentary, though this rather ignores the gulf between the unpleasant ordeal of Fray Luis and the appalling calamities which befell Job.[35] Baruzi, perhaps more sensitively, regards Job as leading Fray Luis to a self-deepening in painful experience, one 'which need not be limited to the prison ordeal.'[36] In Scripture, God reveals himself in a language adjusted to human experience. Fray Luis often returns to this. But there is a third element which he sometimes implies, but which more frequently we can only guess at: the particular, personal experience of the commentator, which may (as we have seen in the exposition of Psalm xxvi) be related back to the Biblical text or itself become a mediator, if at one remove from the original, of the revelation contained in that text for the reader.

Some passages in *Job* do stress the importance of personal experience for understanding suffering: 'Y si los que esquivan la adversidad entendiesen el bien que en ella se encierra (como algunos que han hecho de ello experiencia lo entienden)' (60), 'If those who avoid adversity could only understand the good which lies within it (as some of those who have experienced it do)'. But we have to be cautious about assuming a straightforwardly autobiographical connection between Biblical text and exposition. It is more subtle than that. Take, for example, xvi.22: 'Aunque yo no hable, hablará mi inocencia, porque aunque calle, puesto en silencio su muerte, la inocencia tiene

su lengua y su vida . . . El tiempo . . . al fin trae a luz la verdad . . . El
Juez, que engañar no se puede . . . testificará mi inocencia' (295),
'Though I say nothing, my innocence will speak, for though I am
silent, in the silence of death innocence has its own tongue and life . . .
Time . . . in the end brings the truth to light. . . the Judge, who cannot
be deceived . . . will testify to my innocence.' It could so easily be Fray
Luis speaking. But it is only an expository paraphrase of Job's words in
that verse. A more promising case is xxxii.3:

Es propio de gente a quien la pasión ciega faltarles los ojos y el discurso de la
razón para ver las razones que hay para condenar lo que oyen, y perseverar
. . . en . . . condenallo, sin saber decir la causa porque lo condenan; como
testificando contra sí mismos que condenan, porque desean condenar, y no
porque hallan causa que lo merezca.   (503)

It is characteristic of people blinded by passion to lose the use of their eyes and
the discourse of reason in order to see what reasons there are to condemn what
they hear and to persevere . . . in condemning it, without being able to say
why they are condemning it; as if testifying against themselves that they are
condemning because they want to condemn, not because they have found
just cause for this.

León de Castro was one such, and Fray Luis perhaps had him in mind.
What is surprising, though, is not that possible references to personal
experience can be found, but that there are few of them in *Job* and
none which makes that direct link between the Bible and the author of
the commentary evident in the exposition of the twenty-sixth psalm.

As a piece of prose-writing, *Job* inevitably suffers in comparison
with the *Nombres*, as a verse-by-verse exegesis must in comparison with
the sustained flow of a devotional treatise. Dozens, perhaps hundreds
of times Fray Luis stops to unravel some complex detail in the text,
using expressions like 'the original literally reads' and 'this can also be
expounded differently'. To establish the literal sense he explains the
problems of understanding and translating the original, which is often
extremely compressed in style, or omits words or changes their order
so that the meaning has to be inferred: 'Es gentileza propria de aquella
lengua trocar ansí las palabras, y suplir de la primera parte del verso lo
que falta a la segunda, y de la segunda lo que en la primera faltó'
(510), 'it is a quirk of that language to change the words round, and to
add from the first part of the verse what is lacking in the second, and
from the second what was lacking from the first'. Hebrew words are
discussed. Job's 'boils' come from an illness the name of which we do
not know (56); *shalom*, peace, does not have the sense of the absence

of evil but rather the presence of 'todos los bienes' (290), 'all good things' – an interpretation that has become popular in the twentieth century. Translations, he points out, often differ because of the obscurity of the original and the structural similarity of so many Hebrew words. Hence the Vulgate can translate 'rest' in xxiv.11 (401) where other versions have 'press oil': the Hebrew originals for both seem to come from the same root.

Fray Luis also pays attention to the literary features of Job, and some of his remarks bear more widely on how the Bible is to be read. What, he asks, is Satan doing in the heavenly court (i.6), when he is supposed to have rebelled against God long before, and to have been thrust out of it? Why does the Bible here speak of Satan as among the sons of God? Either, he answers, because in the courts of human monarchs good and bad men both serve and the Bible is adapting its language to the level of human understanding; or the prophet who wrote Job was recording a vision he had had, as Isaiah, Daniel and Ezekiel record theirs. Prophets may see such 'figures' in their imaginations or with their eyes, 'y son ellas imágenes que tienen su ser, pero no el mismo que representan, ni son ello mismo, sino figuras suyas hechas por Dios y que, en lo que significan, son conformes al hecho de la verdad, y en la manera como lo significan se ajustan . . . con nuestro entender' (42), 'and they are images which have their being, but are not identical with what they represent, nor are they that thing itself, but figures of it made by God, which conform to the truth in what they signify and are . . . conformed to our understanding in the manner of signifying this'. Biblical images are not to be understood literally but as pictures of some profounder truth – a point which loses nothing today in the face of a resurgence of crude literalism and a loss of sensitivity to the purpose and power of Biblical poetry.[37]

Many times Fray Luis shows his grasp of the figurative language of the Scriptures. 'Porque *camino* en la Sagrada Escritura es lo que uno hace y lo que dice . . . el blanco adonde tira y el estilo de vivir' (78), 'For *way* in the Bible is what a person does and says . . . the goal he aims for and his style of living'; '*corazón* . . . por figura significa *entendimiento* y *saber*' (543), '*heart* . . . means figuratively *understanding* and *knowledge*'; '*sangre* . . . todo aquello en que se mezcla violencia e injuria' (293), '*blood* . . . everything involving violence and injury'. Sometimes he gives a reason: darkness means trials and tribulations, because these 'escurecen' (372), 'darken' the soul with sadness and prevent activity. Even when the meaning of the image is unexpected, it is accurately perceived: table is a Biblical word for happiness (584), as English-speaking readers may recall from our twenty-third psalm.

The art of sacred rhetoric in the Bible is further explored. Fray Luis frequently praises the elegance and appositeness of Job's figures of speech, and identifies particular devices. Hyperbaton he finds in xxiv.5, 'A él pan para sus hijos' (399), 'to him bread for his sons; there are examples of metonymy and synecdoche; of litotes, when the ocean is called a stream (xxviii.4); and of *conformatio* (personification), when the abyss is made to speak (xxviii.14). Given the forensic setting of the book, he also indicates where the rhetoric of the law-courts is being used. Job's case begins in earnest (xiii) as Job calls on God to produce the evidence against him, if there is any, while in xx.5 Job 'pregunta, y aunque pregunta, no duda, mas antes afirma, porque esta manera de dudar es afirmar con más fuerza' (337), 'asks, and although he is asking, has no doubts, but rather affirms, because this manner of doubting is to affirm the more forcefully'. He cries out for the written indictment against him (xxxi.35), and finally God does appear, alone able to pass sentence and to vindicate his servant. Fray Luis especially likes the vividness of style of the book, in the descriptions of an angry man (xvi.9) and the horse (xxxix.22) – indeed, Virgil himself is said to have borrowed the latter in the *Georgics*, and Fray Luis includes his own translation of the passage in question (651).[38]

As for the moral sense of the book, Fray Luis finds it straightforward enough. The story of Job is the story of Everyman: 'Y no está la buena dicha del hombre en ser próspero; la adversidad es la que de ordinario le hace feliz' (59), 'The good fortune of man lies not in being prosperous; adversity is what normally makes him happy'. We are taught that riches and success are not the road to freedom and contentment. Job's hunger (iii.23) is the hunger of those who serve their own desires, which is itself a torment: 'sospiran antes de la riqueza por alcanzarla, y, alcanzada, gimen y laceran con ella' (81), 'they sigh before wealth to gain it, and once gained, they groan and suffer by it'. So too with honour and pleasure. But the moral application is not to the individual only, but also to society. Fray Luis points to the Old Testament emphasis on justice and mercy, and on the harm usury does to the poor (368). Adultery is condemned as an evil which destroys social unity and the common peace (482). He has harsh words for masters who ill-treat their servants, refuse to pay them their wages and terrify them with threats when they ask for them (483). He attacks the materialism of his own age: whoever has gold appears to have everything and to be strong, wise and powerful; but to trust gold is to put faith in wind (489).

Job was a favourite book of those attracted by the ethics of neo-Stoicism in the seventeenth century.[39] But Fray Luis did not so regard it: 'Porque el sufrimiento no está en no sentir, que eso es de los que no tienen sentido, ni en no mostrar lo que duele y se siente . . . Que el sentir natural es a la carne, que no es de bronce' (66), 'For suffering does not lie in feeling nothing, for that belongs to those who have no feeling; nor in not showing pain and feeling . . . Feeling is natural to the flesh, which is not of bronze'. It is therefore natural to complain as Job did. He may, through his patience in adversity, seem a model of Stoic virtues, but he is nothing of the kind. He does not overcome suffering by indifference; he is overwhelmed by it, obsessed by it. But he did not sin. Therein lies the exemplary quality of the man, as Fray Luis so well perceived.

Theodicy is thus central to the book's message: how can a God who permits such suffering to fall upon an innocent man be just? Fray Luis does not tackle the question systematically; indeed, the nature of the commentary precludes that. But it is a constant preoccupation throughout it. Divine providence is read supremely in the Old Testament from the splendours of creation (xxvi). God's universe is an ordered, harmonic structure. The Fall introduces the dissonance which all but wrecks it, and human attempts at justice can never succeed: 'Porque si los príncipes y regidores del mundo son en sus oficios muchas veces injustos, es porque les es advenedizo y como extraño el oficio, porque ninguno por su naturaleza es rey, y todos lo son, o por voluntad de los hombres o por su violencia' (546–7), 'For if princes and rulers of the world are often unjust in their offices, this is because their office is accidental and as alien to them, for none is a king by nature, and all are so either by the will or through the violence of men'. God alone is justice by nature and essence (660). The unjust will be punished after death (223), though even on earth punishment may be meted out to those who wrong and oppress others (93). The good and the just are punished, however, for their own improvement. The book's message is summed up in the last chapter, which reveals the supreme power, wisdom and justice of God. God was satisfied with Job and could find no fault in him. But he hates inhumanity and deceit, 'aunque se vista de celo sancto' (685), 'even if . . . clothed in holy zeal', as with Job's comforters. He takes care in the perfecting of his saints, he loves mankind and desires its salvation, he ordains all things for the good. If Job could be faulted at all – and it was a slight and forgivable fault, Fray Luis adds – it was that he was a little excessive in his complaining and in his wanting to know the reason for his affliction. When more is restored to him than he had lost, Fray Luis sees the image of Christian justice, replacing that of the old law with the perfect love and justice of God in Christ (688).

In the Hebrew division of the Old Testament, Job belongs with Proverbs, Psalms and five shorter books among the Writings, most of which are regarded by modern scholars as belonging to the genre of Wisdom literature. But Fray Luis, following long tradition, calls it prophecy. It requires an overlay of Christian interpretation to turn a book which grapples with the problems of human existence into prophetic literature. Fray Luis, who read the Old Testament through the New, believed that prophecy was integral to the intended sense of the book. The Hebrew text of xix.25 is obscure, and scholars are now more hesitant to affirm that it is an early example of an emerging belief in life beyond death. But Fray Luis is confident. Job 'sabe que hay Redentor, en que profesa y profetiza la venida de Cristo, y sus dos naturalezas, humana y divina. Porque en decir que vivía entonces, cuando nacido no había, dice que es Dios que vive siempre; y en llamarle Redentor suyo, dice que ha de nacer hecho hombre' (327), 'knows that there is a Redeemer and thereby professes and prophesies the coming of Christ and his two natures, human and divine. For in stating that he was then living who was not yet born, he says that he is everlasting God, and in calling him his Redeemer, he says he is to be born as man'. He sees Christ's humanity contained in the mystery of the Hebrew word *gaal*, 'redeemer', the one who takes another's debt upon himself. This hope in the coming Messiah becomes Job's consolation through his sufferings. Christ's resurrection ('he shall stand . . .') and second coming ('in my flesh I shall see God'; xix.26) are likewise foretold. So Job becomes a christocentric book, and Job's hope, the Messiah, rather than the unfathomable majesty and power of God who speaks from the whirlwind.

But also hidden within the book is something more akin to the *altera explanatio* of *In Canticum Canticorum*. Increasingly in the last chapters of his exposition Fray Luis gives the spiritual sense. These, written at the end of his life and after his editing of the works of St Teresa and his encounters with the Carmelite Reform, demonstrate a growing concern for personal spirituality. The picture of peace in old age (v.23ff) represents the taming of the 'alimañas fieras de nuestros sentidos y sus inclinaciones y aficiones bestiales' (122), 'wild animals of our senses and their bestial inclinations and affections', which sounds much more like St John of the Cross, while thunder and lightning (xxxvii.4) come from heaven to refresh the sterile soul with rain so that it can bring forth fruit. 'Songs in the night' (xxxv.10) are heard when God grants the soul repose in the darkness of adversity (568). Several passages confirm that Fray Luis has his own understanding of the dark night of the soul. Commenting on xxx.20, he writes of souls who can bear travail if God's light is present but who are in pain if he withdraws:

Entonces [el alma] siente de veras su calamidad y trabajo, o por decir verdad, todo su trabajo es menor en comparación de que Dios se le asconda. Porque demás de la soledad y desamparo que siente grandísimo, la parte del sentido flaca envía imaginaciones aborrecibles a la alma, que le son de increíble tormento, unas veces desesperando de Dios y otras teniéndose por olvidado de El. (469)

Then [the soul] truly experiences its calamity and travail, or rather, all its travail is small in comparison with the fact that God is hidden from it. For apart from the solitude and abandonment it feels most acutely, its weak, sensual part sends loathsome imaginings into the soul, which are an unbelievable torment to it, so that sometimes it despairs of God and at other times believes itself forgotten by him.

The parallel with St John is not exact: the torment here comes from the residual power of the senses, rather than from the absence of God in the centre of the soul which has overcome their domination, and Fray Luis does not seem to regard this dark night as a divinely ordained period of preparation, to be borne patiently and in faith, for the consummation of the spiritual marriage.

We have seen how Fray Luis approached the problems of translation of a difficult Hebrew text into Spanish and how from it he was able to comment both on the language and the theology of Job. His personal experience of suffering, though present in the exposition, is less easy to identify there. But the effect of working with Scripture in these ways has more significant results on Fray Luis than the autobiographical or the scholarly elements we have been examining. Scripture itself made Fray Luis into an artist with words, and this natural consequence of his exegetical labours is most clearly evident in *Job*. For he went on to make his own poetic version of the Biblical book, and to expound some of its passages in a Spanish prose style of great richness and beauty. Here is the bridge between the scholar and the artist, between the language of the Bible and the original works of Fray Luis.

He did not complete his poetic version: parts of chapters xxiv, xxvii–xxviii, and xxx–xxxi were supplied, with great success, by the eighteenth-century editor and poet Diego González. Quevedo included thirteen of these verse renderings in the first edition (1631) of the poetry of Fray Luis. The fact that the original of Job is almost all in poetic form must have made Fray Luis feel justified in adding a Spanish verse translation, and he may have done the same for the Song.[40] It is a considerable *tour de force*. Beyond doubt he was inspired by the superb poetry of the Hebrew text, but the Spanish version is not and could not be more than a free rendering of the original which clarifies many of its ambiguities. It stands thus in sharp contrast to the Spanish prose translation of Job. What is not immediately apparent is how much the Spanish verse depends on the exposition. Where Fray Luis has offered a number of possible interpretations for a text, he conserves only the most probable in his verse. Read by itself, this bears no trace of the intense exegetical labours which had first to be undertaken, because it smooths out all the obscurities and makes plain what the exposition has taken great pains to establish. This is particularly so when Fray Luis perceives a prophetic sense. The reference to the coming of the Redeemer is made quite explicit (xix.25–6):

> Bien sé que hay Redentor para mi vida,
> que el suelo hollará el siglo postrero.
> (332)

(Well I know that there is a Redeemer for my life, who will tread the earth on the last day.)

So too is the discovery of the New World, by adding a reference to 'us' which is missing in the original:

> Que a luz vendrá por tiempo aquella gente,
> que la mar de nosotros dividía. (449)

(In time will come to light that people, which the sea divided from us.)

The versifying of the prose chapters presented major difficulties, not least the introduction into the rigid form of the Spanish tercet of Eliphaz the Temanite, Bildad the Shuhite and Zophar the Naamathite (62).[41] Fray Luis solves this ingeniously, with some slight alterations to the names. His commonest technique is to expand some of the original images and to omit others. He develops Job's cursing of the

night of his birth, 'Lo, let that night be solitary, let no joyful voice
come therein' (iii.7), into something more Spanish-sounding:

> Fue noche solitaria y desastrada,
> ni canto sonó en ella ni alegría,
> ni música de amor dulce, acordada.
>
> (83)
>
> It was a solitary and hapless night,
> nor song sounded in it, nor joy,
> nor music of love, sweet and tuneful.

Serenades of love on warm nights grow from the 'joyful voice' and
solitary night of the original, while the placing of the two adjectives at
the end of the line is characteristic of Fray Luis, especially when the
second is longer and carries forward the meaning. Compare, for
example, the 'cárcel baja, escura' (lowly, dark prison) at the end of the
third stanza of the 'Noche serena' ode (VIII). Another feature of his
poetry which has often been noted is his splitting of adverbs across
lines. There is an example in the verse rendering of xvii, 'soberana-/
mente' (305); compare the 'miserable-/mente' of the penultimate
verse of the first ode.[42]

Fray Luis creates some memorable and beautiful lines, as in his
version of xxix.23, 'And they waited for me as for the rain; and they
opened their mouth wide as for the latter rain':

> . . . mi habla descendía
> cual lluvia en sus oídos deseosos,
> como en sediento suelo agua tardía.
>
> (461)
>
> My speech descended
> like rain upon their longing ears,
> as upon thirsty ground the late-come water.

The last two lines form a doublet, an equivalent to the parallelism of
the Hebrew poem, the 'rain' and the 'late-come water' descending on
'longing ears' which become, metaphorically, 'thirsty ground'. The
adjective 'tardía', placed at the end of the line, underlines the sense of
delay, while the 's' alliteration may suggest the sound of the falling
rain. It is in such passages that we can appreciate the art of Fray Luis
as a poet translating poetry, with his sensitivity to the nuances of the
original and his marrying of style to content.

In the more developed passages of the prose exposition itself that
same marriage can be seen as Fray Luis brings out the significance of

the images in the original. He uses many formal rhetorical devices himself. There are examples of *rogatio* (60), *occupatio* (482–3), *sermonicatio* (133), *adnominatio* (202, 361), *anaphora* (326), *transitio* (352, 367), *acervatio* (387, 389) and *alliteratio* (367).[43] Mere enumeration would, however, be tedious. It is not surprising that a Biblical book which he regarded as an exemplar of sacred rhetoric should have led him to employ similar techniques in his exposition of it. What is less expected is the great care he takes in the construction of his prose, where we observe what he meant when, in the dedication to the third book of the *Nombres*, he explained how he counted and measured the syllables in his writing to achieve his aims of clarity, harmony and sweetness (*Obras* 1, 688). In the following case, his sentence, like a musical phrase, rises in a crescendo of three verbal constructions, each longer than the last, before dying away again into the 'perpetual oblivion' which is the theme:

Y ansí dice que la muerte será su sepultura, porque se hará señora de
ellos enteramente y del todo,
quitándoles la vida
y escureciéndoles la honra
y sumiéndoles en perpetuo olvido la memoria y el nombre. (432)

And so he states that death will be their sepulchre, because she will
become their mistress wholly and completely,
by robbing them of their life
and by darkening their honour
and by burying in perpetual oblivion their memory and name.

Death, the destroyer, is the subject and active agent; the destroyer 'wholly and completely' (a doublet to reinforce the meaning) of tyrants, the mistress of those who lord it over others (hence the word *señora*). Its action is threefold, taking life, obscuring honour and burying memory and name (a further doublet, the rhetorical figure of *interpretatio*); but by disrupting the pattern of participle followed by object in the two inset expressions, 'in perpetual oblivion' forces itself into a position of syntactical prominence which lends weight to the theme of the annihilating power of death.

In the first chapter, we identified some of the chains of metaphor in the poetry of Fray Luis, and the abstract concepts of which they are the visible representation. Even in the heart of a Biblical commentary we find them worked into the exposition, as Fray Luis creates his own images in order to reflect on the significance of those in the Biblical text. Images of greed and avarice are suggested by xxiv.21. Hypocrites who prey on widows, whose houses they are devouring under the pretence of religious devotion, are portrayed as birds and bloodsuckers, in a vivid picture anticipating Molière's Tartuffe:

Acuden luego estas aves, y coloreando con largas devociones y oraciones su entrada, negocian su interés y regalo, y llegándose a ellas, allegan sus riquezas a sí, y pareciendo que las santiguan, las chupan dulcemente la sangre.

(406)

Then these birds arrive, and dressing their entrance up in lengthy devotions and prayers, they negotiate their own interest and desire, and when they come up to them [the widows] they get their riches for themselves, and while seeming to bless them, sweeetly suck their blood.

The oppression of poor peasants arouses the anger and compassion of Fray Luis, in a memorable description of the greed which causes it:

Porque sin duda es mal grandísimo al pobre labrador, que con el sudor suyo y de su familia ha lacerado todo un año, volviendo y revolviendo la tierra, pasando malos días y no descansando las noches, madrugando y ayunando, al calor y al hielo, en la cultura del campo, y . . . confiando de las aradas ese poco trigo en que estaba su sustento y su vida; el señor del suelo donde sembró, ocioso y descansando y durmiendo, al fin de su trabajo, despojarle de todo el fructo dél y comer el ocioso y vicioso tantos sudores ajenos, y alegrarse él con lo que el miserable llora y sospira.   (xxxi.39; 496–7)

For this indeed is the greatest evil for the poor labourer, who by the sweat of his and his family's brow has exhausted himself for a whole year, turning and turning over again the ground, spending evil days and not sleeping at night, rising early and going hungry, in heat and frost, to cultivate the land, and . . . trusting that the furrows would yield that pittance of wheat which was his sustenance and his life; for the master of the land he sowed, idle, resting and sleeping, to rob him at the end of his labours of the whole of their fruit, and for the idle and wicked man to eat the sweat of so many others, and for him to rejoice over what the poor man weeps and sighs for!

The antithesis is startling. The seven present participles describing the labourer's toil prolong the sense of his agony as he wrests a handful of grain from the earth, only to have it consumed by luxury and privilege. The curse of work as Fray Luis pictures it has clear links with the story of Adam's fall (Gen. iii.17–19), and it is not accidental that the idle rich landowner is in active partnership with what can only be the work of Satan. His greed is powerfully expressed in a double metaphor: he is seen as eating (rather than drinking) the sweat of his labourers, the sweat itself being a metaphor for their miserable toil.

The antithesis of light and darkness is as old as figurative language, but Fray Luis still finds original ways of treating it. His paraphrase of xxiv.13 describes those who have abandoned righteousness for power and oppression:

Ellos huyen de la luz, y son claros; son enemigos de la claridad, y viéneseles a casa lo que es ilustre en el mundo; aman las tinieblas del error, y andan ricos, resplandecientes, ilustres; caminan a escuras, y no tropiezan en desastre; andan sin estrella de guía, y nunca yerran el camino de la buena dicha; su trato es de la noche, y sucédenles las cosas como si las negociasen de día.

(402)

They flee the light, and are bright; they are enemies of brightness, all that is illustrious in the world comes to visit them; they love the darkness of error, and go rich, resplendent, illustrious; they travel in the dark and meet with no disaster; they go without a guiding star, and never miss the path of good fortune; their behaviour is of the night, and things turn out for them as if they were dealing with them by day.

Through the contrasting images he manages to convey a complex series of ideas. Light has two faces, the light of goodness, which the evil run from, and the light they appear to have because of their riches and status. This ironical light is in fact the same as the darkness of error which they love, and in it they prosper on their journeys. The whole passage is about life, for which the language of journeying is a metaphor, and about a moral and an immoral way in which to lead it, envisaged as true light and a false light which must be understood to be darkness.

The metaphor of the tempest is often used by Fray Luis for a similar purpose: to attack the folly of trust in material gain.[44] There are several examples in *Job* (e.g. ix.18, where the description of the storm has close parallels with that in Ode x, 'A Felipe Ruiz'). The most interesting of them ends with a recapitulation of images characteristic of the elaborate style of the seventeenth-century dramatist Calderón:

Y trae a comparación el aire solano, que es violento y furioso . . . Y porque hizo mención de las aguas y de la tempestad y turbión nocturno, dice bien, en consecuencia de aquello, del viento y del torbellino, que todo suele andar junto. Y en juntar esto dice que la lluvia los cerca, y la noche y la tempestad los espanta, y el viento los arrebata, y el torbellino los arranca de su lugar; y las aguas y la tempestad de la noche y el torbellino y el viento son la muerte cuando los sobreviene, que los trata en el alma y en el cuerpo, y que hace estrago en sus cosas, como el viento, el torbellino, la tempestad y la noche.

(434)

And for comparison he introduces the westerly wind, which is violent and furious . . . And because he mentioned the waters, the storm and the squall at night, he therefore speaks appropriately of the wind and the whirlwind, for they all usually come together. And in joining them he says that the rain surrounds them, and the night and the storm terrifies them, and the wind beats against them, and the whirlwind uproots them from their place; and the waters and the storm at night and the whirlwind and the wind are death when it comes upon them, and affects them in body and soul, and wreaks havoc on their possessions, like the wind, the whirlwind, the storm and the night.

Night, which in these last two quotations has symbolized error and death, is also typically for Fray Luis an image of rest and refreshment. Commenting on iv. 13, he gives a beautiful description of its restorative powers:

Y con ser ansí que la noche es reparo de los miembros cansados y que con el sueño de ella lava el corazón sus tristezas; y con ser ansí que templa el aire encendido, y que con su templada y saludable humedad los árboles y las plantas se rehacen del día, y que su rocío baña y fertiliza las yerbas, ni las plantas, ni los arboles, ni los animales y cuerpos se reparan ansí con la noche cuanto las tinieblas della acarrean mejoramiento y salud al alma que en ellas vela. Porque la tiemplan los afectos que la encendían en fuego, y la olvidan de lo que entre día hace afán y trabajo, y la renuevan y la fortalecen y la bañan con el rocío del bien, que mezclado con gozos dulcísimos sobre ella desciende; con que no solamente se alienta y esfuerza, mas también se empreña y hace fértil para mil partos bienaventurados, que saca a luz a su tiempo.   (97)

And since night is the restorer of tired limbs and in her sleep the heart washes itself of its sorrows; since it tempers the fiery air and by its tempered, healing moisture trees and plants recover from the day, and its dew bathes and fertilizes the grasses; yet neither plants nor trees nor animals and bodies are as much restored by night as her darkness brings recovery and health to the soul which watches through her. For darkness tempers the affections which inflamed the soul, and blots out what was tiresome and laborious during the day, and it renews and fortifies and bathes it with the dew of goodness, which falls upon it mixed with the sweetest joys; so that not only is it encouraged and strengthened, but also impregnated and made fertile for a thousand blessed births, which it brings to light in their season.

The soul's refreshment at night is even deeper than that of the natural creation. Images of heat and cooling, fire and dew, activity and rest express the theme both in the physical and spiritual realms.

But, as supremely in his 'Noche serena' ode (VIII), night is the time to contemplate the splendours of the heavens and draw from them their lesson: 'Nadie alza los ojos en una noche serena y ve el cielo estrellado, que no alabe luego a Dios, o con la boca o . . . con el espíritu' (569), 'No one lifts up his eyes on a calm night and sees the starry sky who does not at once praise God, with the lips or . . . with the spirit'. Fray Luis's greatest prose exposition of this theme comes at the beginning of 'Príncipe de la paz', in the second book of the *Nombres*, but it appears too in *Job*:

Y llama *música de cielos* a las noches puras; porque con el callar en ellas los bullicios del día, y con la pausa que entonces todas las cosas hacen, se echa claramente de ver, y en una cierta manera se oye su concierto y armonía admirable, y no sé en qué modo suena en lo secreto del corazón su concierto que le compone y sosiega. (635)

And he calls pure nights *heavenly music*, because in the silencing of the tumults of the day, and in the pause which all things make, one clearly sees and in a certain manner hears their wondrous concert and harmony, which sounds I know not how in the secret place of the heart and composes and calms it.

The clear vision begins with the physical sight of the heavens, but it is the spiritual harmony they represent which is heard in the soul and brings peace.

One of the finest passages in the whole commentary describes the growth of the Gospel (xxvi.14), a theme we know to have been dear to Fray Luis. Its first sentence is one of those enormously long Golden Age constructions, but so carefully crafted that the sense is never lost. The cumulative effect of clause upon clause represents how the Gospel spread from 'a few poor men' throughout the known world; the second, which brings the passage to its climax, is of a directness and brevity in complete contrast:

Y oir los hombres, que nació Hombre Dios, y que se puso en la cruz por los hombres, y que resucitó inmortal de los muertos, y que vive Señor de todo lo criado en el cielo, y ver la osadía con que unos pocos y pobres decían a voces que erraba en sus religiones el mundo, y cómo se oponía a los sabios y a los reyes de él una humildad tan desnuda, y cómo muriendo vencía, y derramando su sangre hacía gente, y ver tanta virtud en una palabra tan simple, que llegada al oído, penetrase luego a lo secreto del alma y, entrada en ella, la desnudase de sí y de sus más asiduos deseos, y la sacase del ser de la tierra, y le diese espíritu, ingenio y semblante divinos, y hollando sobre cuanto se precia viviese moradora del cielo; maravilló extrañamente sin duda a los que lo oyeron, puso a los que lo vieron en espanto grandísimo, crió admiración de Dios, y de contino la cría en los que la experimentan en sí. Grande es en todo Dios, pero en este hecho es grandísimo. (424–5)

And for men to hear that God was born Man, and was put on the cross by men, and that he rose immortal from the dead, and lives Lord of all creation in heaven, for them to see the boldness with which a few poor men cried aloud that the world was mistaken in its religions, and how so naked a humility stood against its wise men and its monarchs, and how by dying he conquered and by shedding his blood formed a people, and for them to see so great a

power in a word so simple that when it was heard it should penetrate to the
secret part of the soul, and once lodged there, divest it of itself and its most
sought-after desires, and take it from being of the earth and give it a divine
spirit, mind and semblance, and by trampling down all that is esteemed
should live dwelling in heaven; doubtless this greatly astonished those who
heard it, and put those who saw it in the greatest awe, engendered wonder at
God, and continually engenders it in those who themselves experience it.
Great in everything is God, but in this deed greatest of all.

Surely Fray Luis is expounding the secret of the 'senda escondida', the
hidden path which, as his first ode '¡Qué descansada vida!' tells us, is
known only to 'los pocos sabios que en el mundo han sido' ('the few
wise men there have been in the world'). A few poor men, a naked
humility, a simple word have the power to confound the errors of the
world, dethrone its idols and clothe earthbound humanity in the spirit
of divinity.

The language of Scripture spoke to Fray Luis with a unique
authority and out of a living tradition of exegesis. Its authority meant
that its words were the visible signs of divine revelation, often hidden
beneath apparently simple images. The tradition gave him an understanding of the multiplicity of meanings inherent in the text, beginning with the literal sense, for which his knowledge of Greek and
Hebrew stood him in good stead and distinguished him from the great
majority of commentators in Golden Age Spain. Then, especially in
Old Testament prophecy and poetry, the exegete could build the
deeper, spiritual senses on the foundations he had laid. In both
Obadiah and Job Fray Luis found future events foretold and something of the mystery of Christ veiled in obscure passages. In II
Thessalonians he could move from the text into a more general
discussion of eschatological issues. But it is with the Latin commentary
on the Song, with its three expositions of the one Hebrew text, that we
encounter the fullest example of Fray Luis's method, one which raises
a whole series of questions about the link between text and interpretation and text and personal experience.

Yet surely the Spanish exposition of Job is his most extraordinary
achievement, if only because Fray Luis was working directly from
Hebrew into Spanish, with only the most cursory glance at the
Vulgate or the Septuagint. That alone, in the context of the age and of
his trial, speaks volumes. His prose translation and poetic version of
the Hebrew text attempt to show the two extremes he so much wanted
to bring together: the obscurity of the original, lest anyone make the
Bible too easy, and the beauty of its poetry, so that everyone might

enjoy it and be attracted to its message. He knew he could not combine the two and remain faithful to the genius of both. Between them stands the exposition, which mostly works at the literal level. But, even as he wrestled with the images of Job, Fray Luis was creating his own, weaving into new patterns images which run through his own poetry, yet which carry the same meaning as those he found in Scripture. With such an approach to language in mind, we must not allow the clarity of Fray Luis's diction to mask from us the profundity of his thought.

4

The language of mystery

No part of European history has been as cruel and bloody as the recurrent persecution of the Jews. Their expulsion from Spain in 1492 is one of the capital moments in this terrible story, and theologians, historians and literary critics are still debating its consequences. In recent years there has been a sustained attempt to reassess the work of Fray Luis in the light of his Jewish family background, as part of a more general trend towards reaching a fresh appreciation of Golden Age Spain by looking back to that older Spain of three faiths and cultures which had been severely damaged by the late fourteenth-century pogroms and dealt a terminal blow by the expulsion. 'The setting up of the Inquisition in 1478 marked the official transition from a pluralistic and heterodox society to a rigid and closed society bent on enforcing orthodoxy.'[1] The effect of this on Golden Age religious, intellectual and artistic life remains a matter of controversy. How and in what forms may Judaism have survived till the time of Fray Luis? Did descent from a *converso* family affect his attitudes and beliefs? To what extent did his study of Hebrew language and thought influence his own literary output, and are there any signs in this of a particular attachment to Jewish traditions?

To answer such questions, we need a wider perspective than six-teenth-century Spain provides. Without it, conclusions may be reached which are unbalanced and misleading.

The study of Hebrew in the Church

Should Christians study Hebrew at all? The question had been a matter of long and grave dispute, and answers often followed the ebb and flow of Jewish–Christian relationships. As early as the fourth century, St Jerome had spent considerable sums of money 'persuading Jewish scholars . . . to help him unravel obscure texts like the book of

Job' as he prepared his translation of the Old Testament into Latin – the beginning of the Vulgate.[2] Until around 1300, the Church had generally been open to Hebrew scholarship, and Andrew of St Victor (d. 1175) was strongly influenced by his contacts with Jewish sources, notably the school of exegesis which had been founded in northern France by the great scholar Rashi (1040–1105).[3]

But from Jerome until the Renaissance neo-Platonist Pico della Mirandola (1463–94), such Hebrew scholarship as there was in the Church came mostly from converts from Judaism, and Spain could boast of a long succession of these, especially in the fourteenth and fifteenth centuries. The most distinguished was Pablo de Santa María, or Paul of Burgos (d. 1345), often cited as 'Burgensis' or 'Paulus Hebraeus' by Fray Luis. He became Bishop of Burgos and was the author of the *Additiones* to the *Postilla* of Nicholas of Lyra (c. 1270–1340), the standard supplement to the most influential exegetical work of the later Middle Ages.[4] Lyra himself had insultingly been nicknamed 'Rashi's ape' by his detractors, because of his use of Rabbinical material. Alongside a genuine desire to understand the Hebrew Scriptures better ran that darker current which turned so easily from attacking Christians who used Hebrew scholarship into naked anti-semitism. The trial of Fray Luis is only one of many examples.

In its more enlightened periods, the Church believed that the best way to convince Jews of their errors was to master their tongue and their holy books, and to confute them from the evidence they themselves revered. The mystic and philosopher Ramón Llull (c. 1233–1315) persuaded the Council of Vienne (1311–12) to set up centres for the study of oriental languages in five universities, to forward the conversion of Jews and Muslims. The Trilingual College at Alcalá was founded with a similar aim. The study of Hebrew there was not simply one aspect of the humanist revival of learning, but also evangelistic, to equip Christians with the necessary skills to preach and teach more effectively among other faiths.[5] Cardinal Cisneros acquired many ancient manuscripts, at considerable cost, for his Polyglot, and employed three Jewish converts on it, who brought with them a knowledge of Hebrew from the inside and a zeal for their new faith which contradicts the often-drawn picture of an outward conformity masking an inward devotion to old beliefs and practices.[6] Meanwhile, Jews had enthusiastically taken up the new techniques of printing, especially in northern Italy, where a number of Hebrew Bibles appeared towards the end of the fifteenth century. The most famous of these was the Soncino Bible of 1488, and it did not pass unnoticed by Christian scholars.[7]

The disagreements provoked by Christian use of Hebrew scholarship are best seen outside Spain, in one of the most celebrated intellectual battles of the pre-Reformation period.[8] In 1506 Johannes Reuchlin (1455–1522), the first great Christian Hebraist of the Renaissance, had his Hebrew grammar *De rudimentis hebraicis* published. This inspired many successors, among them the grammars written by Cipriano de la Huerga, Fray Luis's teacher, and later by Martínez and Arias Montano, his friends and colleagues. Reuchlin's *De arte cabalistica* (1517) brought non-canonical Jewish literature into the foreground of European thought. But he was bitterly attacked by the converted Jew Johann Pfefferkorn who, with the support of the Dominican friars of Cologne, attempted to have all Jewish books destroyed. The controversy lasted some years. 'A monk of Freiburg (where Reuchlin studied) said plainly in 1521, "Those who speak this tongue are made Jews".'[9] The Reformers' insistence on the priority of the originals over the Vulgate brought a new dimension to the argument: Catholic scholars who agreed with this might be attacked not only as crypto-Jews but also as crypto-Protestants.

If the study of Biblical Hebrew was dangerous to defend, study of the Talmud, a compilation of the Mishnah (oral teaching) and Rabbinical discussions of this, which was authoritative within Judaism and which yielded important information about the background to both Testaments, was even more so. It had been subject to expurgation and prohibition, and appeared on the Spanish Index of 1559.[10] Scholars like the Flemish layman Andreas Masius (1515–73), so highly regarded by Arias Montano, believed that attacks on the Talmud were damaging to the Christian faith, because Jews could be converted from the correctly interpreted evidence of their own most precious traditions. Others came to distinguish the 'fables of the Rabbis' (as Fray Luis often calls them) from a true Talmud, an outer shell of falsification from a divinely inspired inner core.

Spain experienced these tensions sharply, in spite (or because) of the expulsion or forced conversion of its Jewish population. Until 1492 it had been 'the home of the best Hebrew manuscripts and of Jewish scholars and commentators.'[11] The growth of the Inquisition after 1480 was an ominous sign. It dealt with converted Jews suspected of having lapsed back to their ancestral faith and relied on a large body of local informers. There were many denunciations, trials and sentences. Yet the ambivalent attitude, the *sic* and the *non*, towards Judaism as towards so much else, is evident from the fact that at the same time Cisneros was founding his College at Alcalá and relying on the scholarship of *conversos*.[12] Similarly, a rabidly anti-semitic professor like León de Castro could campaign with considerable success against the Salamanca Hebraists and Arias Montano at the same time as Montano was combing the booksellers of Flanders for ancient manuscripts, many in Hebrew, at the command of his master, Philip II, in order to enrich the royal library of El Escorial.[13]

It might be thought that with such royal patronage, scholars would have enjoyed relatively unhindered access to Hebrew and Aramaic manuscripts. A hitherto unpublished paper by the Jesuit Juan Mariana (1536–1623), entitled 'De libros de Rabinos', 'On Rabbinical books', shows that this was not the case.[14] Mariana is complaining (to whom is unclear) of the obstacles scholars are encountering in obtaining Hebrew works, following what he considers too severe an application of the catalogue of prohibited books.[15] He argues that the study of Hebrew has always been favoured in the Church and taught in the universities. The only works on Old Testament Hebrew are by Rabbis and they should be made available just as Homer is for a better understanding of New Testament Greek and Virgil and Horace for the Latin Bible (not the most convincing of comparisons). He points out that very few people in Spain can actually read Hebrew books – 'por ventura en toda ella no son treinta' (f.5y), 'perchance not thirty in the whole country'. Unless matters improve, there will be even fewer; the study of languages should be encouraged in Spain, where it is needed. Further, Rabbinical sources, disapproval notwithstanding, have been used by the greatest Biblical commentators, Jerome, Lyra, El Tostado and (especially) Vatable. Since so few scholars read Hebrew, far more of them become familiar with Rabbinical material in the Latin works of such men. Those who oppose Hebrew books can neither read nor use them, and there are some in Spain, he adds, who despise what they are incapable of grasping (including more than a superficial interest in classical literature). Moreover, no one has ever 'judaized' through reading these books, while other dangerous works have been available to Jesuits and done no harm either. He mentions in this respect among others Erasmus and Vives:

Jamás en estos libros se ha hecho preuención ninguna, y que los he visto puestos en nuestras librerías de Roma, Paris, Louayna, Alcalá antes que el dicho catálogo saliesse, y . . . siendo el Talmud vedado tan expresamente se hallara en nuestras librerías de Roma y de París por concessión de los summos Pontífices, que semejantes libros y en lengua tan peregrina nunca se ha tenido por inconveniente que gente como los de la Compañía los tenga y se aprueche dellos.   (f. 6ᵛ)

There has never been any prohibition of these books, and I have seen them in our public bookshops in Rome, Paris, Louvain and Alcalá before the said catalogue appeared. . . . And . . . the Talmud, which is so expressly forbidden, can be found in our Rome and Paris bookshops by concession of the supreme Pontiffs, for it has never been thought improper for such books . . . to belong to and be used by people like those of the Company.

He recalls that an anonymous Jesuit of contrary opinion was reprimanded in Rome and Spain. Finally, previous attempts to ban these books have failed, and Spain, with its new laws, is out of step with the rest of the Church. The laws should be used with all possible moderation and the books made available not only to scholars 'pero aun a qualquier mediano theólogo que quisiese estudiar la dicha lengua', 'but even to any average theologian who might want to study the said language', as was originally intended.

Mariana adds several other points. Greek and Latin writers, who can be widely read, contain many attacks on Christianity, while there are Christian writers, like Galatinus, who counter Rabbinical objections to the faith. Learned men will be deprived of a singular aid in disputes with the Jews if they cannot convince them out of their own holy texts. He agrees that some Christian scholars have given too much weight to the literal sense of the Old Testament and have neglected the Fathers and Doctors; but he praises the use Pagnini makes of them, and comments that to build the mystical sense on the literal 'no es de reprehénder, antes es de singular prouecho' (f.7ᵛ), 'is not to be reprehended but rather is of singular benefit'. The Targums, full of Jewish 'superstition', are not prohibited and are even available in Latin translation. Parts are in the Complutensian Polyglot and all of them in the *Biblia Regia*. Always and everywhere the Church has read these books, and caution must be exercised 'para que este demasiado zelo no cunda con la autoridad de santo officio' (f.8ᵛ), 'lest this excessive zeal spread with the authority of the Holy Office' – or Greek books will suffer next.

This is a significant document, the more so for being contemporary with the issues contested in the trial of Fray Luis. Mariana's is the voice of serious scholarship, protesting against over-rigorous censorship and the Inquisition usurping the Church's responsibilities. His later comments on how Indexes should be prepared (ff. 24ʳ–38ʳ) show that his liberal attitude extended to the whole question of censorship (except where obscenity was concerned). Though he holds up as an example the Tridentine Index (Rome, 1564), with its tolerant approach to Latin literature, he was not quite as open-minded as some of his contemporaries.[16]

The 'Jewish' Fray Luis: a critical history

In 1955, Millás Vallicrosa suggested that there was a closer link between Fray Luis and Hebrew Spanish poetry than had previously been accepted.[17] He perceived that the syncretic neo-Platonism which influenced Fray Luis contained Arabic, Jewish and Kabbalistic strands, and he proposed that Hebrew Spanish poetry had exercised a general influence on that of Fray Luis, where he sensed, especially in the ode to Felipe Ruiz (x), a spiritual quality it contained but Augustinian and Neoplatonic sources did not. He defined this as a lyrical approach to a cosmological mysticism, expressed in contemporary Neoplatonic terms, based on contemplation in ascending order of the creation, which awakened the soul to moral values. He could not find any decisive examples of verbal parallels and went no further than to suggest that some expressions used by Fray Luis were analogous to those of the Hebrew poets of Spain. The imagery from the Song in the ode 'Morada del cielo' (xviii) particularly struck him, as he could find no earlier Christian poems which so dwelt on the sweetness of mystical experience and the marriage union.

Millás left many questions unanswered. He seemed to disregard the long history of the interpretation of the Song in Christian tradition and he did not ask how, and from which texts, Fray Luis might have known the works of medieval Jewish poets. To refer to Jewish culture persisting in Spain after 1492 and to the likelihood of its transmission into the time of Fray Luis is to pose rather than to answer the question. It certainly does not follow that because he used Rabbinical sources in his Biblical commentaries (easily accessible through earlier Latin exegetes) he was familiar with other forms of Hebrew literature.[18]

Nonetheless, this stimulated further research into the possibility that Hebrew sources might have influenced Fray Luis more explicitly than had been thought. Habib Arkin, acknowledging his debt to Millás, aimed to show that Fray Luis and the other Hebraists 'estaban directa e íntimamente vinculados a una tradición escriturística española, que, a su vez, debía mucho a la influencia e impulso de la hermenéutica hebrea', 'were directly and intimately linked to a

Spanish Scriptural tradition, which, in turn, owed much to the influence and impulse of Hebrew hermeneutics' and that Fray Luis could be considered as 'la culminación de esta tradición jamás interrumpida y continuamente evolutiva', 'the culmination of this uninterrupted, continuously evolving tradition.'[19] He based his claim on the *Cantar* and *Job* but did not consult the Latin cómmentaries, which are more fully representative of the Biblical scholarship of Fray Luis and which were prepared for publication by him. He described the flourishing of Hebrew exegesis in twelfth-century Spain, but gave only a superficial account of medieval Christian developments. He cited parallels between Fray Luis and Rabbinical authors, without entertaining the possibility that Fray Luis knew them through intermediate sources, which, from the evidence of the authors he actually refers to, is more likely. Fray Luis in fact possessed or used little Rabbinical material, in comparison with Arias Montano, a point made long ago by Entwistle, who, with Gutiérrez, has been the only challenger of the increasingly accepted 'Jewish' Fray Luis.[20]

Kottman's *Law and Apocalypse* took this a stage further. Fray Luis is not only a Christian Hebraist, but his 'philosophical views are cast in an Hebraic tradition, not in an Hellenic one as supposed by nearly every other commentator', while 'cabbalism is the basis of his moral thought.'[21] His understanding of the law, the Incarnation, the role of the Jews in salvation history and the discovery of the New World are all deeply marked by his Christian Kabbalism, and 'the Jewish cultural tradition may be considered an exclusive source of his own doctrine on mysticism' (p. 86). Kottman's is the most serious attempt yet to establish the 'Jewish' Fray Luis, though his thesis has not been without its critics.[22]

The most alarming consequences of too ready an acceptance of this view can be seen in the most recent contribution, in Noreña's *Studies in Spanish Renaissance Thought*, which abounds in inaccurate judgements.[23] His translation of *converso* as 'converted Jew' and his application of this term to Fray Luis is especially misleading. The term tends to be used loosely, both of actual converts and of anyone who happened to have some Jewish blood in their ancestry, as many sixteenth-century Spaniards did. The two uses need carefully to be distinguished. We know well enough from twentieth-century experience how within three or four generations from emigration, resettlement or conversion the characteristics of the former culture can be all but effaced and people lose their awareness of having once belonged to an alien race. *Converso* ought to describe only those who were themselves

converted from Judaism to Christianity; otherwise, one may legiti-
mately speak only of a *converso* inheritance. Fray Luis certainly came
from *converso* stock, but that does not make him or his grandparents
Spanish Jews or mean that he enjoyed private access to Jewish
writings and traditions. For these reasons, we must examine afresh the
facts and then seek to establish the true nature of the relationship
between Fray Luis and the Jewish faith.

The family background

We possess an unusually full record of the ancestry of Fray Luis
because during his trial the records of members of his family who had
been accused and in some cases found guilty of lapsing back to
Judaism after their supposed conversion were fetched out of the
archives (x, 146–73). The mood of the times is well captured by two
letters I came across while leafing through a manuscript in Madrid.[24]
They purport to be copies of an original correspondence, though I
suspect that they belong to the same pernicious kind of manufactured
evidence as the so-called *Protocols of the Elders of Zion*. The first, from
'la sinagoga y Judíos de Spagna a la sinagoga y Judíos de
Constantinopla', 'the Synagogue and Jews of Spain to the Synagogue
and Jews of Constantinople', asks what is to be done in times of such
persecution and with an order to convert or leave the country within
four months. It is clearly meant to have been written in 1492. The
reply includes the following advice:

El mejor y postrer remedio . . . es el baptizar los cuerpos quedando los ánimos
firmes en lo que se deue a nuestra ley, i con esto os podréis vengar de todos los
agrauios que os han hecho, porque si os an profanado vuestras sinogas [*sic*]
hazed vuestros hijos clérigos y prophanaréis sus Iglesias, si os si os [*sic*] an
Muerto vuestros hijos haced vuestros hijos médicos imitaréis los suyos, si os an
tomado vuestras haciendas tratantes [?sois] trataldes de manera que presto
sean vuestras las suyas, y haciendo esto vengaréis . . .

(ff.73^{r-v})

The best and final remedy . . . is to have your bodies baptized but to remain
firm in what is due to our law, and by this means you will be able to avenge all
the wrongs they have done you. For if they have profaned your synagogues,
then make your sons clerics and they will profane their churches; if they have
killed your sons, then make your sons doctors and be like theirs; if they have
by their dealing taken away your estates, deal with them in such a way that
theirs will soon be yours; and by doing this you will be avenged.

The advice is too conventional for the letters to have been authentic,
but that hardly matters. Forged or genuine, they represented the fears

which motivated the many denunciations of *conversos* and *judaizantes*, fears which were still alive when Fray Luis and Grajal were described by the Inquisitorial prosecutor as well-known *conversos* who desired only to return to their old law. They also help to explain the Spanish obsession with *limpieza de sangre*. It was as if Judaism was a contagion which tainted those unfortunate enough to have been born with it in their blood and which inclined them towards apostasy and rebellion.[25]

Not even the dead were allowed to rest in peace. Posthumous condemnation could bring further suffering and material hardship to their descendants, and that is why the trial of Fernán Sánchez de Villanueva Avivelo of Quintanar, a great-great-great grandfather of Fray Luis, was not a matter of indifference to his family at the end of the fifteenth century. If the dates given by his grandson Pedro de Villanueva and his daughter-in-law Juana de la Serna are conflated (x, 147, 149) he must have lived from about 1380 to 1460. In 1491, with his deceased wife Elvira Sánchez, he was posthumously tried for heresy and apostasy. Juana, the now remarried widow of one of his sons, Gonzalo de Quintanar, testified that some thirty years previously, when they had been living with the old man (almost at the end of his life), she had seen him 'haciendo gestos e abtos que los judíos hacen cuando leen' (x, 147), 'making gestures and actions the Jews make when they are reading', and also observing the dietary laws. Though housebound, 'en todo facía vida de judío' (x, 150), 'he lived the life of a Jew in every respect.' She further claimed that his wife knelt when the Torah passed by in street processions. His grandson testified in his defence that he had become a model Christian after his conversion, at about the age of forty, and in fact 'por le llamar Davihuelo después de ser cristiano, hobo mucho escándalo y muertes de hombres en la dicha villa' (x, 149), 'through his being called *Davihuelo* [an insulting form of David] after becoming a Christian, there was much scandal and men died in the said town'. But it was to no avail. The poor old man and his wife were condemned as heretics and schismatics, exhumed from consecrated ground, their bones burned and their goods confiscated from their descendants (Cuenca, 29 June 1492). Their son, Juana's dead first husband, was more fortunate: he was posthumously absolved (23 March 1499) and his 'memory and fame' were restored. He was defended by his grandson, Graviel de Villanueva, of El Toboso, whose own father had been posthumously condemned, exhumed and burned (1491; x, 162).

A second batch of trials took place between 1510 and 1512. A daughter of Pero Rodríguez (and therefore an aunt of Graviel) had married Lope de León in Belmonte. She was Leonor de Villanueva, a great-grandmother of Fray Luis, and with her younger sister Juana was accused of Jewish practices. According to a maid, they had already been accused in 1491 and reconciled (unlike Leonor's husband, who died around 1485). On 18 April 1512, in Cuenca, the Inquisitors sentenced her, but again she abjured and was reconciled. Her sister, aged about 70 in 1510, was reconciled 'con confiscación de bienes y cárcel perpetua' (x, 159), 'with confiscation of goods and life imprisonment' (8 July 1511), an expression which rarely meant what it said.[26] Both women were condemned to the 'perpetual habit' (x, 161), a reference to the *sambenito*, a yellow penitential garment worn as a public sign of shame and hung up in the local parish church after the death of the condemned so that their family might be reminded of their infamy. The *sambenitos* of these unfortunate women were exhibited in Cuenca cathedral until 1529, and their families struggled unsuccessfully thereafter to keep them out of the parish churches in Belmonte and Quintanar (x, 166–9). Leonor's was consequently displayed in Belmonte on 9 November 1548, and thus the shame of the forebears was visited upon the children and made visible before the whole community.

There had also been trouble on the other side of the family. The paternal grandfather of Fray Luis, Gómez Fernández de León, appeared before the Inquisitors on 15 March 1529, claiming to be a hundred years old. His parents and grandparents were reputed to have been *conversos*, though they had a clean sheet with the Inquisition. One witness, interviewed during the trial of Fray Luis, seemed to remember that the old man's wife or mother or mother-in-law had been imprisoned, and Fray Luis's uncle Juan, a canon of Belmonte, was questioned about this. On 27 August 1529 Gómez was condemned 'a que saliese en penitencia a la iglesia colegial de Belmonte, y en cierta pena pecuniaria por haber dicho palabras contra el honor y autoridad del Santo Oficio y oficiales dél' (x, 165), 'to come forth in penitence to the Collegiate Church of Belmonte, and to a certain monetary fine for having spoken words against the honour and authority of the Holy Office and its officials'. So the old man, who in 1576 was still remembered as a gentleman who used to ride out on a white horse to visit his vineyards, was lightly punished for disrespect towards the Inquisition, not for anything connected with Judaism.

How much Fray Luis knew of his *converso* background is a matter for speculation; he never saw these papers. But something of it had reached him, because when questioned about his ancestry in his first audience with the Valladolid Inquisitors (15 April 1572; x, 180–1), he claimed that he did not have a full knowledge of his lineage, but that in 'ciertos contrarios que tuvo su padre, le pusieron en su hidalguía que venía de casta de conversos', 'certain problems his father had, they put on his pedigree that he came from *converso* stock.' As his father was a lawyer, this was no doubt intended as a slur on him and his career, and is presumably what started the enquiries into the family history.

Not until late November 1576, just before Fray Luis was released, was any witness called to answer questions about his ancestry, and nothing was mentioned about Jewish blood. The silence of the Inquisition on this matter was an effective response to the insinuations of some of his enemies. That there was Jewish blood in his ancestry cannot be denied, and he must have known about the *sambenitos* of his great-grandmother and her sister, for members of his family still lived in Belmonte even if his parents had left it when he was a small child. This part of the 'Jewish' Fray Luis is not in dispute. But he was brought up and educated as a member of a distinguished Christian family. It is the implication that his Jewish inheritance is somehow consciously present in his work which needs to be looked at more closely, and to test that we must turn first to the nature of Kabbalism and to the survival of Jewish scholarship in sixteenth-century Europe.

Kabbalism

We are indebted to Gershom Scholem for the definitive account of the history of Jewish mysticism.[27] *Kabbalah* means 'tradition' and 'is not the name of a certain dogma or system, but rather the general term applied to a whole religious movement.'[28] The oldest Kabbalistic text, the *Bahir*, was edited in Provence during the twelfth century and influenced by speculative currents of thought within Jewish forms of Gnosticism. The movement developed and changed over several centuries and should not therefore be thought of as a single, undifferentiated phenomenon which can easily be subject to generalizations. The common modern use of the term, by which it comes to mean secret, occult knowledge, is misleading.

Early Jewish mysticism centred on two Biblical passages, the creation of the world in Gen. i and the vision of the glory of God in Ezek. i.

In Spain, Kabbalism enjoyed its Golden Age around the year 1300. Abraham Abulafia, born in Zaragoza in 1240, is regarded as the founder of the school of 'prophetic Kabbalism', which taught a way of ecstasy for the elect in the so-called Path of the Names. It is here that we begin to encounter a view of language, and especially of Hebrew, in which words themselves become the means towards this ecstatic contemplation: 'Basing himself upon the abstract and non-corporeal nature of script, he develops a theory of the mystical contemplation of letters and their configurations, as the constituents of God's name' (pp. 132–3). Since God has created all that is, everything participates in him. He has himself revealed his Name in a series of letters: 'There is a language which expressess the pure thought of God and the letters of this spiritual language are the elements both of the most fundamental spiritual reality and of the profoundest understanding and knowledge. Abulafia's mysticism is a course in this divine language' (p. 133). Hebrew words are something like musical harmonies, only instead of the notes of the scale are their letters, which can be combined in different patterns and acquire their own inner meaning, even where the sequence of letters appears meaningless. Since every language is derived from the original, Hebrew, each can be approached in such a way, and Abulafia gave Greek, Latin and Italian examples too. 'For in the last resort, every spoken word consists of sacred letters, and the combination, separation and reunion of letters reveal profound mysteries to the Kabbalist, and unravel to him the secret of the relation of all languages to the holy tongue' (p. 135). Since Hebrew consonants also carry numerical value, whole new areas of meaning can become accessible through them. Words are thus seen as coded messages from the creator of language, and divine significance is to be found in them even when their constituent letters are jumbled up.

The 'rabbinical Kabbalah' represents a second strand, which stands alongside the prophetic to form the whole. It is based on the Path of the Sefiroth, 'various phases in the manifestation of the Divinity which proceed from and succeed each other' (p. 209). The names of these 'phases' become fixed – the 'supreme crown', the 'wisdom', the 'intelligence' of God and so on. The greatest Kabbalistic work of all is the *Sefer Ha-Zohar*, *The Book of Splendour*, which 'alone among the whole of post-Talmudic rabbinical literature . . . became a canonical text, which for a period of several centuries actually ranked with the Bible and the Talmud' (p. 156). Scholem describes it as a mystical novel set in an imagined landscape: the author's 'descriptions of the mountains of Palestine . . . are of the most romantic kind and accord far better with the reality of Castile than with that of Galilee' (p. 169). It appears to have been written around 1280 in Guadalajara by Moses de León, who spent his last years in Ávila and died at Arévalo. A five-volume collection of different sorts of writings, it draws inspiration from the Kabbalists of Gerona, 'who between . . . 1230 and 1260 did more than any other group to unify and consolidate what was pregnant and living in the Kabbalism of Spain' (p. 173).

The *Zohar* speaks of two worlds, of *En-Sof*, God in himself, and of his attributes. The ten fundamental of these are the *sefiroth*, 'the creative names which God called into the world, the names which He gave to himself' and which belong to 'the hidden world of language, the world of the divine names' (pp. 215–16). In contrast to most other expositions of the first verse of the Bible, the *Zohar* describes speech itself as having been separated from *En-Sof* at the beginning, explaining that the 'hidden Nothing' is the subject of the verb 'created', and that what was created was 'God', that is, the name of God. God-in-Himself spoke his Name, and that Name becomes the point of access for humans into the divine mystery. In place of the ecstatic experience sought by prophetic Kabbalism comes *devekuth*, 'the continuous attachment or adhesion to God . . . a contemplative value . . . not predicated upon special or abnormal modes of consciousness' (p. 233).

Such a distinction between God and his attributes is not unique to this form of Kabbalism, since it is present in the mystical theology of the pseudo-Dionysius and later of Meister Eckhart. Likewise, *devekuth* is described in terms which might apply to St John of the Cross. The importance of Spain in the development of Kabbalism, and the significance Kabbalism attached to words, are facts beyond dispute. They do not necessarily mean that Fray Luis's own sense of names as revelation originated there; still less that he was trying to smuggle the essence of Jewish mystical theology into Christianity.

In fact, by the fifteenth century Jewish mystical speculation was already in decline. But the expulsion from Spain wrought a profound change in its direction. 'A catastrophe of this dimension, which uprooted one of the main branches of the Jewish people, could hardly take place without affecting every sphere of Jewish life and feeling' (p. 244). Whereas earlier Kabbalism had concentrated its attention on the beginnings of the world rather than Messianic hopes, it now turned towards the End, to a promised redemption out of suffering and exile, and was transformed 'from an esoteric into a popular doctrine' (p. 244). Catastrophe had changed the direction of Hebrew theology before: the fall of Jerusalem in 586 BC and the subsequent exile in Babylon had forced it to come to terms with national disaster, while the desecration of the temple by Antiochus Epiphanes in the second century BC found its theological explanation in the book of Daniel and the rise of apocalyptic expectation. Bitter experience in the present once more reawakened hope of future vindication after 1492:

> To summon up and to release all the forces capable of hastening the 'End', became once more the chief aim of the mystics . . . The birthpangs of the Messianic era, with which history is to 'end' or (as the apocalyptics would have it) to 'collapse', were therefore assumed to have set in with the Expulsion. (p. 247)

Similarly in our own century cynical Jews have identified the Holocaust with the coming of the Messiah. Paul Tillich delivered a famous sermon in which he told how a man who had hidden in a Jewish graveyard during the war witnessed the birth of a baby in a grave and heard the old gravedigger who assisted the mother cry out: 'Great God, hast Thou finally sent the Messiah to us? For who else than the Messiah Himself can be born in a grave?'[29]

Some forty years after the expulsion, the town of Safed in Upper Galilee became the centre of the new Kabbalism, and from here it spread throughout the Jewish world, through teachers like Isaac Luria (1534–72), who believed that the End would come in 1575. Nevertheless, his influence increased, and from around 1630 Lurianic Kabbalism was to become 'something like the true *theologia mystica* of Judaism' (p. 284). That lies outside our story. Those who have called Fray Luis a Kabbalist must mean that he was familiar at least with some of what we have been examining, and be able to show that it influenced his own thinking – unless it is to be presumed that the greatest proof of his indebtedness is its failure to appear in any of his works. The argument from silence is never strong and in any case is unnecessary. Fray Luis acquired such knowledge as he had of the Kabbalah, as of every other aspect of his Hebrew scholarship, from two principal sources, the movement known as 'Christian Kabbalism' and his studies at Alcalá. More convoluted explanations are redundant.

Christian Kabbalism and the transmission of Jewish traditions

Christian Kabbalism was largely a phenomenon of the Renaissance, though it continued to influence European thought until the end of the seventeenth century. The Prologue to the Complutensian Polyglot, addressed to Pope Leo X, strikes a note which will become very familiar:[30]

Certainly since there can be no word, no combination of letters, from which there does not arise, and as it were spring forth, the most concealed senses of the heavenly wisdom; and since the most learned interpreter cannot explain more than one of these, it is unavoidable that after translation the Scripture yet remains pregnant and filled with both various and sublime insights which cannot become known from any other sources than from the very fountain of the original language.

No translator can adequately convey the full mystery of the sacred text. The phrase 'combination of letters' appears to owe something to the techniques of Kabbalism, yet centuries before this, St Jerome had stated that every word, syllable, sign and point of the Hebrew Old Testament contained significance, and the essence of his *Quaestiones hebraice in Genesim,* in which for example he commented on the meaning of the change of names of Abram and Sarai, passed into the standard textbooks of medieval and Renaissance exegesis.[31]

The varied group of scholars called Christian Kabbalists revived interest in the hidden mysteries of the Hebrew text in the late fifteenth and early sixteenth centuries.[32] They were concerned to understand as much as they could about the Hebrew language and became interested in non-canonical texts. But this academic interest was linked to a wider exploration of the *prisci theologi,* the first theologians, whose secret knowledge from the age of man's innocence in Eden, or at least from closer to that age than the present, was believed to have been handed down continuously but orally and to be accessible beneath the text of any number of obscure works. The Florentine Academy made much of this, and saw connections between different traditions of wisdom in the ancient world: Pico, following Origen, believed that the secret doctrine God gave Moses on Sinai had been given to the seventy elders he appointed, and had eventually formed the Kabbalah.[33] Egyptian, Hermetic, Jewish and Greek wisdom was originally one, and witnessed to knowledge once possessed by man but now fragmented and all but forfeited. To regain it – a goal for which scholarly endeavour was the essential tool – was to find the key to a long-locked gate. Who could tell what garden might not lie on the other side? Such a search for revelation through hidden knowledge has remained a characteristic of esoteric groups: witness, for example, the history and the role of the Book of Mormon as an addition to the Christian Scriptures.

But these scholars also regarded Rabbinical and Kabbalistic works as a rich new quarry from which Christian truths could be mined as from the very heart of Judaism. Polemic between Jews and Christians over the interpretation of Old Testament texts went right back into the New Testament itself. By the late Middle Ages the Bible had been so exhaustively combed that it was difficult to find fresh arguments in this long and bitter struggle. Several anti-Jewish tracts written by *conversos* included material from Kabbalistic writings, while Renaissance scholars like Ficino and Lefèvre d'Etaples sought eagerly in them for demonstrations of Christian truths. The doctrine of the Trinity and the divinity of Christ, in which Christianity diverged sharply from Judaism, was found to have mysterious proofs in works the Jews cherished as their own.

The most significant figure in the development of Christian Kabbalism was Paul of Heredia, a Spanish Jew converted in his old age, who lived probably in Sicily. His two surviving works, *The Epistle of Secrets* and *The Crown of the King*, influenced both Reuchlin and Galatinus. Reuchlin's *De arte cabalistica* linked Kabbalism with the Pythagorean mysteries and provided a bibliography of Kabbalistic works, later revised by Masius. As Secret himself suggests, it resembles the *Nombres de Cristo* in its form, a conversation between three people in three books. Typical of its subject-matter is the discussion of the relationship between the divine name YHWH and the Hebrew form of the name Jesus, YHSWS. The addition of the consonant *shin* to the name of God, composed of vowels and therefore unpronounceable, renders it pronounceable and shows that the Son is the Word of the Father, the Uncreated become Incarnate, the Unknown made known. Reuchlin also explains some Kabbalistic techniques: *gematria*, calculating the numerical value of the consonants of one word and replacing it by those of another or equivalent value; *notariacon*, using the letters of one word as the initial letters of other words; and *themourah*, the use of permutations of letters. He also expounds the powers of the seventy-two names of Jesus the Messiah, with many references to Biblical texts, e.g. Isa. ix.6, so fundamental to the *Nombres*.

But the most widely circulating work was by the Italian Franciscan Galatinus (Pietro Columna, *c.* 1460–1540), whose *De arcanis catholicae veritatis* was published in 1518. It drew heavily on the earlier material and became the common point of reference for proponents and opponents of use of the Kabbalah, which it not only examined, it turned against the Jews. The idea that Christian Kabbalism was 'an attempt to develop an interpretation of Scripture upon which both Christians and Jews could agree' could hardly be further from the truth, though the suggestion that Fray Luis used Galatinus in the *Nombres* merits consideration.[34] Egidio de Viterbo (1465–1532), the General of the Augustinians from 1506–18, researched into the *Zohar* and left many manuscripts on Christian Kabbalistic themes, though his works remained unedited. Secret regards these as the most remarkable of all the humanist attempts to assimilate the Kabbalah into Christianity. Seripando shared this interest, but lacked the linguistic expertise. But both men brought Christian Kabbalism into the forefront of Augustinian scholarship. In France and England scholars took up its ideas avidly, although not until Robert Fludd (1574–1637) did they reach their greatest spread in England.

In Spain, as elsewhere, Christian use of the Kabbalah was both defended and attacked. Alfonso de Zamora (*c.* 1474–*c.* 1544), while attacking it as such, was prepared to use its techniques to demonstrate Christian truths. Antonio de Guevara (*c.* 1480–1535) repeated the widespread view in one of his Epistles, addressed to the Jews of Naples, that God had given two laws to Moses on Sinai, one written on tablets of stone, the other communicated by word of mouth. This latter became the Talmud. Such a distinction was applied to the Kabbalah by, among others, the converted Jew Sixtus of Siena (1520–69), whose *Bibliotheca Sancta* was among the books in Fray Luis's library. The author contrasted the true Kabbalah, akin to the mystical sense of Scripture among Christians, with the false one, linked with necromancy and relying on juggling letters and numbers to manipulate the occult powers inherent in them.

Others were less happy with its use. Pedro Sánchez de Ciruelo (d. 1554), a colleague of Zamora's, attacked the whole basis of Kabbalistic thought in his *Paradoxae quaestiones decem* (Salamanca, 1538), on the grounds that it was a vain and diabolical superstition. With its techniques, any conclusion could be drawn from any text.[35] A similar criticism was made by Miguel de Medina (1489–1578), one of Philip II's theologians at Trent, who wrote in his *Christianae Paraenesis* (Venice, 1564; f. 2ᵛ) that by these techniques the Antichrist may as well be derived as the Trinity from the same words.[36]

The other main source for Fray Luis's understanding of Jewish theology was his period of study under Cipriano de la Huerga at Alcalá, which had become the main centre for transmission of Jewish learning through *conversos* like Zamora. Zamora himself translated and copied commentaries by Jewish exegetes, notably David Kimhi (1160–1235), some of whose works survive in the library of El Escorial, including one in the hand of Arias Montano.[37] The study of Biblical Hebrew required knowledge of extra-Biblical Hebrew literature, and we may be sure that at the very least Fray Luis knew some Rabbinical writings and had heard of the Kabbalah. Exactly what he understood by it is, as we shall see, another matter; what is important is that through the intermediate sources we have identified he had access to some of these Jewish traditions, often already studied by Christians to provide unexpected confirmations of Christian doctrine, and that there is no need to posit any secret contacts or hidden sources to explain his familiarity with them.

Fray Luis and Kabbalistic thought

Fray Luis was fundamentally a Hebrew scholar fascinated by textual and linguistic detail, not for its own sake, but as the basis on which accurate interpretations of Scripture could be made and Christians have their knowledge of the Bible enriched. He mentions Rabbinical authors and occasionally uses material which seems Kabbalistic in inspiration, but he does not share the main preoccupations of Reuchlin and Galatinus. We must now assess the nature of his debt to this tradition and his understanding of the role of the Jewish people in the history of salvation.

One of his most sustained contributions to Jewish–Christian polemic comes in the first of the *Quaestiones*, which asks if the Scriptures the Jews accept prove both that the Messiah has come and that the Lord Jesus is he.[38] Fray Luis explains that the Jews exclude the Apocrypha from their Canon, and will only acept the evidence of the Hebrew and Septuagint texts, thus ruling the Vulgate out and giving them the advantage. Nonetheless he will fight on their terms. The first text studied had a long history of exegesis – Gen. xlix.10.[39] The Vulgate, rejected by Jewish exegetes, makes its Messianic meaning explicit: 'The sceptre shall not depart from Judah *donec veniat qui mittendus est*' (*till he who is sent shall come*). The Hebrew reads simply *shiloh*, the Old Testament site where Samuel was to anoint Saul as king over Israel; the AV preserves this, with its 'until Shiloh come'. Fray Luis therefore has to prove that *shiloh* is a Messianic name, against those (like Samuel ben Meir, a grandson of the famous Rashi) who argued that it referred only to the historical place or those who believed that a Jewish kingdom still survived somewhere beyond the mountains, a view on which Fray Luis pours scorn. He argues, following Kimhi, that *shiloh* has Messianic significance. He connects it with the pool of Siloam, a symbol of future kingship, as shown by the miracle Jesus performed there(John ix). But he draws his evidence mostly from another text, Haggai ii. 7–8, which Jewish and Talmudic scholars accepted as Messianic. He attacks the notion that the Messiah has come but remains hidden; he applies the shaking of the earth in the text to the wars and civil wars of the age into which Jesus was born; and he contrasts the fact that the Jews have lost homeland, temple and ruler and been forced into misery and exile with the Christian inheritance of the promises they once possessed. The argument is complex and refers to many other Biblical passages. It has no Kabbalistic features, however, depending rather on a thorough knowledge of Jewish and Christian exegetical traditions. The vagueness of the references to the former – 'the Jews', 'Talmudists' – suggests intermediate sources rather than specific authors or works, and there is no speculation or Kabbalistic juggling with letters.

A further example comes from Fray Luis's last set of lectures, on Genesis.[40] This is of particular interest, given that so much early Kabbalistic speculation was about creation and origins. The first word of the Hebrew Bible, *bereshith*, 'in the beginning', had engendered a Kabbalistic tradition all of its own. It was in the story of Adam, the first man, the first theologian, the one who had dwelt in paradise until the Fall and who had named all the creatures, that the secrets hidden in the Genesis text were most likely to be found. Here, if anywhere, we might expect to find Kabbalistic influences at work on Fray Luis. He refers in the lectures often enough to the 'Hebrew doctors', but his main source is unquestionably St Augustine's *De Genesi ad litteram*. The precise meaning of Hebrew words concerns him greatly: *bara*, 'created', in the first verse implies, he says, a doctrine of creation *ex nihilo*, in contrast to *asah*, used for the 'making' of the six days (f. 9r). One Jewish opinion he examines concerns the season at which the world was created. According to the Hebrew doctors it was the autumnal equinox, because plants and fruits were already there for animals and people (created on the fifth and sixth days) to eat. Christians had long since accepted this view, and, as Fray Luis observes, it found support in El Tostado and Lyra. We would surely not accuse John Donne of being a crypto-Kabbalist when in one of his sermons he gives a spiritualized version of it: 'In paradise, the fruits were ripe, the first minute, and in heaven it is alwaies Autumn, his mercies are ever in their maturity'.[41] Fray Luis also mentions Christian exegetes who follow the alternative theory that creation occurred at the spring equinox, which he supports as more probable, since spring is the start of new life and growth. But this view had also been expressed by some Jewish scholars, so that his exegesis is simply a choice between traditional explanations.

Elsewhere in his Genesis lectures he mentions both Ficino and Pico, proving that he knew and used the works of the Florentine Academy, the first main centre of Christian Kabbalism. But the most convincing evidence comes from the passage discussing the Garden of Eden. Fray Luis believes this to have been an actual historical place and complains that 'hebraei Cabalistae omnia haec, quae de paradyso dicuntur, non solum alegorice interpraetantur sed etiam senset [sic] nullo alio modo interpraetari posse: quorum sententia Princeps vere fuisse Phylo Iudeus in libello de mundi aedifitio et in libro de plantatione' (f. 39[r]), 'the Hebrew Kabbalists not only interpret allegorically all these things . . . concerning paradise, but also believe that this cannot be interpreted otherwise; Philo the Jew is the first of their opinion in his book on the creation of the world and in his book on the planting' (presumably of paradise, Gen. ii.8). Origen followed his view, which Fray Luis calls erroneous. It is one of the very few places where he actually refers to Kabbalists, and he does so only to condemn their allegorizing of the story of Eden. By tracing this tradition back to Philo of Alexandria, he seems to imply that Philo himself was a Kabbalist, whereas he antedates Kabbalism by many centuries. The passage can mean only one thing: the Kabbalists to whom Fray Luis refers are those who press the allegorical exposition of Scripture too far, at the expense of the literal; those, in other words, who break the cardinal rules given in the *Tractatus*. Fray Luis is using the term 'Kabbalism' in an imprecise way and had little idea who the real Kabbalists were or what was distinctive about their teaching. In this respect he is entirely at one with his contemporaries.

The last work Fray Luis had published in his lifetime is a dense treatise on the exact timing of the death of Jesus and its relationship with the Passover.[42] In the Synoptic Gospels, the Last Supper is a Passover meal, but in John Jesus dies on the eve of the feast, when the Passover lambs were being slain in preparation. Fray Luis reconciles the two accounts by an intricate chain of argument which shows a complete mastery of the sources and especially of the very complex sacrificial procedures laid down in Leviticus. His solution depends on a correct understanding of the Jewish method of calculating when each day begins. The treatise contains many examples of what he described in his trial as forms of Jewish exegesis acceptable to Christians, in this case information about customs and rituals. He makes no attempt to find hidden meanings in the sacrificial regulations of the Pentateuch, preferring to explain that there is a typological link, as John already saw, between the slaughtering of the Passover lambs and the death of the Lamb of God. This use of Jewish sources is entirely characteristic of Fray Luis.

In the second book of the *Nombres* (Braço de Dios) Fray Luis turns to examine the errors of Jewish exegesis of the Hebrew Scriptures, and once again we find him pressing his scholarship into the service of his Christian faith. Juliano asks Marcelo, the principal speaker, if he thinks that the Jews accept Isa. lii.10 and liii.1 as Messianic texts. He replies:

– No lo darán ellos . . . porque están ciegos; pero dánoslo la misma verdad. Y como hacen los malos enfermos, que huyen más de lo que les da más salud, así estos perdidos en este lugar, el cual sólo bastaba para traerlos a luz, derraman con más estudio las tinieblas de su error para obscurecerle . . . Porque si no habla de Cristo Isaías allí . . . ¿de quién habla?
– Ya sabéis lo que dicen – respondió Juliano. – Ya sé – dijo Marcelo, que lo declaran de sí mismos, y de su pueblo en el estado de ahora. Pero, ¿paréceos a vos que hay necesidad de razones para convencer un desatino tan claro?

(*Obras* I, 545)

'They will not . . . because they are blind; but truth itself tells us so. Just like bad patients, shunning the more what improves their health, they go astray in this passage, which alone is sufficient to bring them to the light, and the more they study it they pour out the darkness of their error to obscure it . . . For if Isaiah is not speaking of Christ there, of whom . . . does he speak?'
'You know what they say', replied Juliano.
'I do', said Marcelo. 'They apply it to themselves and to the present state of their people; but do you think reasons are needed to confound so obvious a folly?'

Fray Luis then expounds the Messianic expectation of the Old Testament, especially in these two chapters from Isaiah. World empires have come and gone, yet after many prophecies and three thousand years of history, no military Messiah of the kind the Jews look for has appeared. God's promises are never quite as man expects, and the militaristic imagery of some Messianic texts requires a spiritual exegesis to reach its heart. The Christ is to preach peace, not war. God hides his meaning because his mind is unfathomable; the metaphorical language reveals the need to probe beneath the surface for the true sense. Since the Jews failed to understand 'material' miracles like the Exodus, how could they be expected to understand a spiritual revelation like the Incarnation? Scripture itself – here we return to the theme first expounded in the prologue to the *Cantar* – speaks to us 'como hombre a otros hombres, y nos dice sus bienes espirituales y altos con palabras y figuras de cosas corporales, que les son semejantes, y para que los amemos los enmiela con esta miel nuestra, digo, con lo que El sabe que tenemos por miel' (1,556), 'as a man to other men, and it communicates its lofty, spiritual gifts through words and figures of corporeal things which resemble them, sweetening them with this our honey (I mean what He knows we take as honey), so that we love them'. The 'arm of the Lord' acts secretly and invisibly, and God's Messiah is a humble, suffering servant.

Christ's coming is shown in two main Old Testament figures. Agricultural metaphors allude to his grace, military metaphors to his victory over Satan on the Cross. Such language enables good people to penetrate its true meaning, whereas the evil stumble before it. Sabino, who has been trying to interrupt Marcelo, asks if some great sin has caused the Jews to be so blind. Marcelo responds that their first error lay in the adoration of the golden calf, an act of idolatry which led to their subsequent denial and rejection of Christ. Having disposed of the errors of Jewish exegesis in this way, Fray Luis is free to expound the true nature of the 'arm' or government of God, and of the power of Christ's victory over Satan, which is carried forward by the poverty, simplicity and weakness of the first Christians, yet which has spread throughout the world and is even now dethroning idols and subjecting all peoples to Christ. The final sign of the error of the Jews is therefore that favourite theme of Fray Luis, the spread of the Gospel into the New World and the conversion of its inhabitants.

What, then, of the introduction to the name 'Jesús', in the third book of the *Nombres*, which appears to show evidence of Kabbalistic influences? Jesus is the name of Christ proper to his humanity, and is not given by analogy. The name of his divinity is 'Word', and its Hebrew form *dabar* has three consonants, d, b and r, as its root. Fray Luis examines the significance of each of these, of both syllables in the word, and of the whole, 'porque *Dabar* no dice una cosa sola, sino una muchedumbre de cosas . . . o junto a todo él, o a sus partes cada uno por sí' (1,769), 'because *dabar* does not state only one thing, but a multitude of things . . . either as a whole or in each of its parts'. The *d* has the force of an article, and since the office of the article is to indicate distinctiveness and to add to the excellence of the noun it accompanies, it well suits Christ, who gave being to everything and guides and exalts all. The *b*, according to Jerome, stands for building, and this too is a property of Christ, the 'edificio original . . . la traza de todas las cosas', 'original building . . . the pattern of all things'; hence another of his Scriptural names, 'tabernacle'. All that was to be created dwelt eternally in Christ, so that all might dwell in him when created, an idea Fray Luis develops from Gregory of Nyssa and associates with a verse from Ezek. i, one of the most important sources of Kabbalistic speculation, in his own translation: 'and the wheel is in the midst of the wheel, and the animals in the wheels, and the wheels in the animals.' Both 'wheels' are in Christ, 'porque en el está la divinidad del Verbo y la humanidad de su carne, que contiene en sí la universidad de todas las criaturas ayuntadas y hechas una' (1, 770), 'because in him is the divinity of the Word and the humanity of his flesh, for he contains in himself the universality of all the creatures united and made one'.

Again, following Jerome, he says that *r* means head or beginning, and Christ is the beginning and head of all creation, the source and fount of life, governor of all, the first-begotten of the dead, King of kings and High Priest of priests. *R* also signifies spirit, and though this applies to each Person of the Trinity and is proper to the Holy Spirit, it is given to Christ for good reason. The Word is the bridegroom of the soul, and the soul is spirit, so that Christ becomes soul of the soul and spirit of the spirit. In this union with the human soul, Christ the spirit works as spirit, coming and going we know not whence or how. There follows, appropriately enough, a long quotation from one of the seminal works of this tradition, St Bernard on the Song (1, 771–2).

The syllables declare other properties of Christ. *Da* and *bar* as two consecutive words mean 'this is the Son', words God spoke to the three disciples on the Mount of Transfiguration. Of all the possible words for 'son', *bar* has the special meaning of 'bring to light', 'create' (as in Gen. i.1), and this is a Son who brings many sons to birth (cf. Hebr. ii.10). With the letters reversed, *rab*, there is set forth the bringing of many excellent things into one, and Christ is the fulness of humanity and divinity. *Dabar* as a whole has various meanings. As the word formed in the mouth, 'imagen de lo que el ánimo esconde' (1, 773), 'the image of what the soul conceals', Christ is the image of the Father, hidden within him, and he is our image, representing the Father to us, the image which brings him to light and imprints him on every created being. As law, reason, duty, *dabar* shows that Christ is the principle of reason for the creatures, the law by which they are judged and the duty towards which they must look if they do not want to be eternally lost. As an act proceeding from another person, Christ is the loftiest of all that proceeds from God, 'la grandísima hazaña, y la única hazaña del Padre, preñada de todas las demás grandezas que el Padre hace, porque todas las hace por El' (I, 773–4), 'the greatest deed and the only deed of the Father, pregnant with all the other great things the Father does, for he does them all through him'. Thus Christ is light from light, fountain of all light, wisdom born of wisdom, the abyss of all that is great and excellent and noble. Finally, as being itself, reality, *dabar* shows Christ as the source from which the life of every being flows.

This is an exceptional way of exegeting a Hebrew word for Fray Luis, justified only because *dabar* is of exceptional significance. Even so, his analysis follows Jerome's, and each detail revealed in its letters is applied to Christ, the divine name of Jesus of Nazareth – Christ the source of all creation, through whom all things were made, and Christ their goal, to whom they all tend. Many of the Biblical texts in this exposition come from Paul, and that is no accident, for the Christ of Fray Luis is very much the Pauline Christ; not some occult power to be revealed through juggling letters, but the power from which everything originates and whose being is stamped upon language itself, so that it too may testify to the glory of the Word. This christocentric universe is not that of the Kabbalist. Indeed, the treatment Fray Luis gives the name 'Jesus' shows how far he is in spirit from the world of the Christian Kabbalists:

Y no diré del número de las letras que tiene este nombre, ni de la propiedad de cada una de ellas por sí, ni de la significación singular de cada uno, ni de lo que vale en razón de aritmética, ni del número que resulta de todas, ni del poder, ni de la fuerza que tiene este número, que son cosas que las consideran algunos y sacan misterios de ellas, que yo no condeno; mas déjolas, porque muchos las dicen y porque son cosas menudas, y que se pintan mejor que se dicen. (I, 774)

And I shall say nothing of the number of letters this name has, nor of the property each has in itself, nor of the particular significance of each one, nor of its arithmetical value, nor of the sum of them all, nor of the power and force of this number, which are matters some consider and from which they derive mysteries, which I do not condemn; but I omit these things, because many explain them and because they are trivial matters, better described than explained.

He prefers to note that as Christ is the proper name of his divinity and contains many other names together, so Jesus, the name of his humanity, represents his work and his office better than any other name. He must be thinking of Christian Kabbalists like Galatinus when he remarks that some have considered these mysteries, but he finds their work unimportant in comparison with what he wants to say.

The one thing he does mention we have already encountered in such writers. In Hebrew, the name 'Jesus' contains the four letters of the name of God and two others. The name of God cannot be pronounced, because it is entirely composed of vowels, or because no one knows how it should sound, or out of respect for God.[43] Fray Luis suggests that it is like the sound made by a dumb person, a rough, unformed interjection, which teaches us our own dumbness before God, who cannot be contained within our intellect or expressed by our tongue. Each time we wish to name him we can only stammer, fall silent. The addition of the two consonants in the Hebrew name Jesus means that God has a 'pronunciación clara y sonido formado y significación entendida . . . la *palabra* divina, que no se leía, junta con estas dos letras se lee, y sale a luz lo escondido hecho conversable y visible' (1, 775), 'clear pronunciation, a formed sound and an understood significance . . . the divine *word*, which was not read, with these two letters is read, and what was hidden comes to light, made conversable and visible'.

This passage does not prove that Fray Luis was dependent on some secret source, it merely picks up one of the commonplaces of Christian Kabbalist literature. Fray Luis goes on to expound the name in the spirit of what he has already established about *dabar*. Jesus, as the angel of the Annunciation said, means salvation, health, healing, and in a fine passage Fray Luis contrasts the misery of the sick human condition with the remedy of Christ. Man's condition is unstable and he is inconstant, a sickness partly inherited from Adam and partly the result of the perverse inclination of his own free will. It is not so much one sickness as 'una suma sin número de todo lo que es doloroso y enfermo' (1, 776), 'an infinite sum of all that is painful and sick'. The offices and names of Christ bring healing to the many aspects of this pervasive sickness; 'Jesus' is the whole, the other names each contribute to the healing. 'Jesus' is thus all the names expounded in the *Nombres* and all those which are not:

De arte que, diciendo que se llama Cristo *Jesús*, decimos que es *Esposo* y *Rey* y *Príncipe de paz* y *Brazo* y *Monte* y *Padre* y *Camino* y *Pimpollo*; y es llamarle, como también la Escritura le llama, *Pastor* y *Oveja, Hostia* y *Sacerdote, León* y *Cordero, Vid, Puerta, Médico, Luz, Verdad* y *Sol de justicia*, y otros *nombres* así.

(I, 777)

By stating that Christ is called Jesus, we state that he is Bridegroom and King and Prince of Peace and Arm and Mountain and Father and Way and Shoot; and this is to call him, as Scripture also does, Shepherd and Sheep, Victim and Priest, Lion and Lamb, Vine, Gate, Doctor, Light, Truth and Sun of Righteousness, and other such names.

A more accurate measure of the relationship between Fray Luis, Kabbalism and Jewish tradition is best obtained from assessing his debt to the most popular of the Christian Kabbalists, Galatinus and his *De arcanis catholicae veritatis*. This work, cast in the form of a dialogue between three people in twelve books, makes much use of Rabbinical and Kabbalistic material, and is intended to prove from it the truth of Christian beliefs about Christ and God. From his description of the Kabbalah in I.vi, it is clear that Galatinus had no understanding of its development as modern scholarship knows it. Like his contemporaries, he perceives it as an oral transmission of teaching from earliest times which has only relatively recently been written down by the Jewish doctors so that it may be preserved. The Fathers ignored it because though Catholic truths might be discerned in it, seekers might be misled by other matters it contained. But later writers – and Galatinus praises Paul of Burgos, Pico and Egidio de Viterbo – have all written on the subject. Like Galatinus, they are not concerned with the Kabbalah in itself, but with how it may be useful to Christians, and they do not distinguish the spiritualizing exegesis of the early period from the speculative use of numbers and letters which developed later. Galatinus devotes two chapters to a defence of the Christian use of the Talmud and its value as a source for correcting errors in the Christian Greek and Latin Bibles is stressed, for it has older and better readings of some texts.

In II.x Galatinus studies the divine name, the tetragrammaton. He claims that YHWH distinctly expresses the mystery of the Trinity, and he derives it first from a twelve- and then a forty-two-letter name which mean 'Father, Son and Holy Spirit' and 'The Father is God, the Son is God, the Holy Spirit is God, Trinity in Unity and Unity in Trinity'. This, he says, was incomprehensible until the Messiah came. His method does not matter; what is important is the complex meaning Christian Kabbalists were prepared to derive from combinations of Hebrew letters. He continues by stating that the three consonants found in the four letters express the three hypostases of the Trinity: the *yod*, which has no origins, reveals the Eternal Father; the *he*, which means to be and to live, the Son; and the copulative *wau*, the Spirit. Capnio, one of the interlocutors, asks why in old codices the divine name was written as three *yods*, one on top, two beneath. Galatinus replies that among other reasons, the three identical letters represent the three hypostases of the Trinity, the equality of the three Persons, and the fullness of God which belongs equally to each. The three letters *y*, *h* and *w* also signify the past, present and future aspects of the Hebrew verb, and therefore demonstrate the eternal changelessness of God, the same yesterday, today and tomorrow.

There are certainly similarities between this and the general discussion of names which opens the *Nombres* dialogues. Fray Luis there notes that Hebrew adds and subtracts letters from words to suggest degrees of good or bad fortune, or masculinity and femininity, while letters can change place and make words chameleon-like. But again, he calls these 'cosas menudas' (1, 420), 'trivial matters', easy to observe, obscure in speech. The tetragrammaton is different, though. Since it is all vowels, it signifies one who is all life and spirit, pure, uncompounded being (1, 421). Each letter can be put in the other's place, and often is, so that each represents all and all are in each. This is an image of the simplicity of God, of his containing all perfections within his one perfection. Thus, his perfect wisdom is identical with his infinite mercy, and his knowledge, power and love are all contained within each other.

Marcelo then stoops forward, and in a gesture reminiscent of Christ's (John viii. 6), writes in the sand with a stick. He draws the Aramaic form of the divine name, the three *yods*, and gives the exposition of this from Galatinus in an abbreviated form – the equality, unity and single essence which the letters represent. The whole episode is a model of the way Fray Luis uses Christian Kabbalistic material. He is familiar with it, but offers his readers only a bare outline. Absent are the complexities of linguistic analysis, the proofs that letters are ciphers, the long quotations from the Rabbis and the long series of letters which open out into Trinitarian doctrine. These are the things he regards as interesting, but trivial. They are not worth communicating to a more general audience. What he selects is simply the core, the evidence that the divine name in Hebrew and Aramaic contains an image of the Trinity – probably the most commonplace idea out of this whole tradition.

The third book of the *De arcanis* is another likely source for the

Nombres. In III.iii–vi Galatinus attempts to show that the Bible itself, as well as some ancient Hebrew doctors, proves the divinity of the Messiah, and he looks at the title 'verbum Dei', 'Word of God', so prominent in Fray Luis's exposition of 'Jesus'. In III.vii–viii he expounds 'filius Dei', 'Son of God', the first name in the third book of the *Nombres*. But the correspondence goes no further than that. Galatinus uses Rabbinical sources to confirm Christian doctrine on the sonship of Christ; Fray Luis, in a much longer, more theologically searching study, quotes from the Gospels and Epistles and from Virgil and St Basil as he meditates upon the five 'births' of Christ he has discovered. The strange incident of the persecuted bird in any case stamps it unmistakably with the author's originality.[44]

Other names Fray Luis uses are also present here. Galatinus entitles III.xii 'Quod Messias est facies Dei', 'That the Messiah is the face of God', but again his entire interest lies in showing that the Biblical texts which use this metaphor are Messianic. Fray Luis assumes that, and though he makes considerable use of one of the texts Galatinus introduces (Psalm lxxix. 20), his real concern is with the meaning, not the pedigree, of the image. There are greater similarities between 'germen' ('shoot'; III.xvi) and 'Pimpollo', the first of the *Nombres*: several texts are common to both (e.g. Isa. iv.2, Jer. xxxiii.15), and the exegesis Fray Luis gives of Zech. vi.12 may be based on Rabbinical material, as he refers to 'some' who make it into a purely historical reference to the building of the temple by Zerubbabel. Galatinus ignores this, in favour of those authors who make 'germen' an exclusively Messianic name.

Galatinus devotes a separate study to the name 'ros', 'dew' (III.xvii), which Fray Luis does not, though he certainly uses the fundamental text for it (Isa. xlv.8) in 'Pimpollo'. As this is one of the commonest texts Christians traditionally interpreted as Messianic it may not be all that significant in terms of the influence of Galatinus on the *Nombres*. But his treatment of it provides at least one point of literary interest. Explaining how fertile the nightly dewfall is, he writes:

Ita uirtus diuina nocturno tempore beatissimam virginem foecundauit. Nam quemadmodum ostrea nocte & uerno tempore rorem recipiens, in interioribus suis margaritam gemmam preciosissimam generat: Ita gloriosa uirgo spiritu sancto superueniente filium Dei concipiens, Messiam preciosam margaritam generauit. (p. 147)

Thus the divine power made the Blessed Virgin fertile in the night-time. For as the oyster receives dew on spring nights and generates in itself the pearl, the gem of great price, so the glorious Virgin by the overshadowing of the Holy

Spirit conceived the Son of God and generated the Messiah, the pearl of great price.

In Góngora's *Polifemo*, a poetic recreation of the story of Acis and Galatea, the monstrous giant calls out in his beautiful love-song to the nymph who spurns him:[45]

> Pisa la arena, que en la arena adoro
> cuantas el blanco pie conchas platea,
> cuyo bello contacto puede hacerlas,
> sin concebir rocío, parir perlas.

> Walk on the beach, that I may there admire
> How shells beneath your feet to silver turn,
> From which, made fruitful by your shining tread,
> Without conceiving dewdrops, pearls are bred.

As far as we know, Góngora owed nothing to Galatinus or to Kabbalism, and the idea that the dew could beget pearls in oysters goes back to the natural historians of the ancient world. His is a profane and erotic poem; Galatinus takes the legend and applies it to Mary and Christ, as he takes Rabbinical material and uses it for the same ends.

Other names, like 'Eternal Father' and 'Prince of Peace', Galatinus passes over quickly, and only 'Jesus' (III.xx) need concern us further. He finds this name foreseen in several texts Fray Luis does not cite, as well as in pre-Christian and Rabbinical writings: he treats the Erythraean Sibyl as he does the Kabbalists, since a verse attributed to her yields the meaning 'Jesus Christ, Son of God, Saviour, Cross' from its first letters. Since Jesus became the saviour of the Gentiles, it was appropriate for his name to have been revealed to Gentile as well as Hebrew prophets. Though Galatinus distinguishes between a five- and a four-letter form of the name in Hebrew, the latter belonging to Jesus of Nazareth, he does briefly make two points Fray Luis was to use: that Jesus alone is the complete name of our salvation, its beginning, middle and end; and that it contains all the letters of the tetragrammaton, not only in Hebrew but also in Aramaic and Greek, a refinement of the argument Fray Luis did not pursue.

It is easy to jump to quick but wrong conclusions about the attitude of Fray Luis towards the Jews, given his own family history, his views on the role of the Jewish people in history and his use of Hebrew scholarship and Rabbinical material. In apparently favouring the Jews, he is not showing *converso* sympathies but simply expounding Pauline theology. We saw in the previous chapter how he rejected the view that the world was to end in 1656 and how he regarded the preaching of the Gospel in the New World as ushering in the closing stages of human history, as the Bible itself taught: 'the gospel must first be published among all nations' (Mark xiii.10). Next would come the conversion of the Jews and their return to Christ, the reappearance of Elijah and Elisha and a time of apostasy and of the disclosing of the Antichrist. The Jews, having rejected the Messiah, fell into error and sin, and in their place the Gentiles were called. The misery of their scattered condition is the divine judgement on them. But this is not the end of their story. Fray Luis envisages a time, a necessary prelude to the End, when they will be saved. This could be interpreted – indeed, Kottman strongly suggests this – as Fray Luis giving his ancestors another chance to repent. But it is not. It is the traditional theological resolution of the problem posed by the fact that the omnipotent God, having in the first place chosen the Jews, cannot entirely cast them aside. They retained a special place within the divine dispensation. At some future stage, when the rest of the world had accepted Christ, they would acknowledge the Christian Messiah and be reincorporated into the people of God. The classic exposition of this is Paul's, in Rom. ix–xi: 'a hardening has come upon part of Israel, until the full number of the Gentiles come in, and so all Israel will be saved' (xi.25–6). Since there is good Old Testament warrant for the faithfulness of Israel being maintained by a tiny remnant while the majority lapses into apostasy, and since it speaks both of a 'hardening' of human hearts by God so that his purposes can be achieved through their apparent resistance, and of the mission of Israel as that of a light to the Gentiles, Paul's thesis itself is grounded in Scripture.[46] This view has remained normative within Christian theology, and unless the whole of history is to be understood as a conspiracy theory, it is more helpful to see Fray Luis as a Christian greatly indebted to St Paul than as a crypto-Jew. To suggest the latter contradicts the evidence, and does justice neither to Christianity nor to Judaism.

There is evidence that Fray Luis used Christian Kabbalistic sources, and notably Galatinus. But whereas the *De arcanis* is a work of polemic, the *Nombres* is a literary and artistic masterpiece expounding the centrality and universality of Christ. Fray Luis seems to have used Galatinus to locate texts supporting exegesis of a Messianic name, but there is no discernible pattern to this and we cannot be sure that the parallels noted do not have a more general source, since they are commonplaces of Christian–Jewish debate.

That is symptomatic of the whole issue of Fray Luis and Judaism. It is undeniable that he wanted Christians to understand more fully their Old Testament inheritance, because this could confirm and deepen their faith. But his *converso* ancestry is less significant than the fact that he participated in the world of sixteenth-century scholarship, which loved to probe difficult texts for hidden meanings, and which found in extra-canonical Jewish literature an endlessly fascinating source for this. At least some of the evidence suggests that what modern critics have called Kabbalistic influences stem in fact from Jerome and Patristic sources; while what appears to be a remarkably favourable attitude towards the destiny of the Jewish people is a very solid exposition of St Paul.

We must therefore question whether there is much value at all in the approach to Fray Luis which starts with Fray Luis the *converso*. Apart from the ambiguity of the word, can it really be helpful, when the consensus seems to be that *converso* literature is marked by its cynicism and despair (the prime example being *La Celestina*)? Of much more interest is the attention Fray Luis pays to the Hebrew language and to the structure of its words. Once again, he approaches language as revelation, as the visible sign of the wisdom and love of God communicated to the eyes and ears and hearts of his people. The prose and poetry of Fray Luis radiate a confidence and an optimism which knows only too well the power of the darkness, but which is shot through with a yearning for glories as yet unperceived, but soon to be known beyond the prison of the body, and with a serene faith in Christ, the Alpha and Omega of all creation. That faith receives its outstanding expression in the *Nombres de Cristo*, to which we now turn, in which the images of Scripture are opened out and themselves beget new images from the inspired imagination of Fray Luis.[47]

5

The names of the Word

From its beginning, Christian theology has approached the person and work of Christ through the names and titles given him in Scripture. These visible yet mysterious signs in the sacred text indicated where true knowledge of God's revelation through his Son was to be found. But they were not self-explanatory. Some, like 'shepherd' and 'way', Christ applied to himself; others, especially those in the Hebrew Scriptures, required great exegetical skill to fathom.

This long tradition, which still survives in a few popular hymns, has been extremely influential in Christian writing.[1] As early as the second century, one of the Greek Apologists, Justin Martyr, defended Christ's divinity with particular reference to the names 'Christ' and 'Jesus' in his *Dialogus cum Tryphone Judaeo*, and established names as significant in polemic with the Jews.[2] A century later, Origen distinguished between those pertaining to Christ's divine and human natures, and expounded several – way, good shepherd, son of God, king, lamb, rod and flower.[3] Among the early Latin writers, St Cyprian of Carthage (d. 258), also in controversy with the Jews, considered Christ as arm of the Lord, mountain, spouse, judge and king.[4] St Augustine wrote: 'By similitude Christ is many things he is not by property', thus underlining the theological significance of Biblical metaphor: figuratively he is a rock, door, corner stone, lion and lamb; but in his true being he is the Word.[5] St Isidore of Seville (*c.* 560–636) listed some sixty Scriptural names of Christ, eight of which are among the *Nombres*, in his widely-read *Etymologiae*.[6]

This Patristic tradition developed through the Middle Ages and into the sixteenth century.[7] St Bernard of Clairvaux treats the theme in two of his sermons, on the Circumcision (the feast of the name of Jesus) and the names of the Saviour. Scholastic theologians, however, were more concerned with names for God. In the *Summa*, for example, Aquinas asks whether God can be named at all, and what relationship exists between names used of him and also applied to the creatures.[8]

It is clear, therefore, that in writing a treatise on the names of Christ, Fray Luis could draw on a venerable inheritance. But he approached his task in an unusual way. By writing in Spanish, he meant to make the Bible and Christian doctrine accessible to the many who were excluded from reading them because they knew no Latin, as he made plain in his prefatory remarks to the first and third books of the *Nombres*. Unlike most theological treatises, it was written with deliberate attention to style, so that its readers might not only learn but also enjoy what it taught through the harmony and sweetness of its language (*Obras* 1, 688). In the *Nombres*, Fray Luis united all those concerns we have hitherto found in separation, blending his skills as a Biblical exegete with his interest in the workings of language, and his abilities as a theologian with his desire to deepen the devotion of ordinary people to Christ. The result is a work which shows as nothing else he wrote does the essential and intimate bond he sees between word and meaning, style and content, image and concept, the written word and the Word made flesh.

In the end, Fray Luis wove his creation around fourteen names in three books. The first two books of the *Nombres* appeared together in 1583. The first contains 'Pimpollo' (Branch, Shoot, Rod, Bud), 'Fazes de Dios' (Face of God), 'Camino' (Way), 'Pastor' (Shepherd), 'Monte' (Mountain) and 'Padre del siglo futuro' (Everlasting Father, Father of the Age to Come); the second, 'Braço de Dios' (Arm of the Lord), 'Rey de Dios' (King of God), 'Príncipe de la paz' (Prince of Peace) and 'Esposo' (Husband). The third book (1585) added 'Hijo de Dios' (Son of God), 'Amado' (Beloved), and Jesus, and was completed by 'Cordero' (Lamb), which appeared posthumously, in 1595. These names are the material from which, through a wide range of exegetical and theological tradition, and in his incomparable prose, Fray Luis wove his christological masterpiece.

The Incarnation

Though the centrality and universality of Christ, the true subject of the *Nombres*, arises directly out of Scripture, it is also supported by a foundation of incarnational theology not nearly so apparent in the text. The fundamental thought of Fray Luis about the person and work of Christ is found in his *De incarnatione tractatus*, the text of lectures he gave as early as 1566–7.[9] Later lecture series as well as the *Nombres* refine his ideas, but here we find the core of his christological thinking. The lectures expound one of the great set texts of medieval theology, the *Commentary on the Sentences of Peter Lombard* by the scholastic (but not necessarily Thomist) theologian Durandus (*c.* 1275–1334). That this was itself a commentary on an earlier work should not lead us to suppose that it was merely slavish paraphrase. Material accumulated in layers, and did not prevent one theologian from questioning the views of his predecessors. New opinions, unless judged heretical or dangerous, were added to existing tradition, so that a later commentator, like Fray Luis, approached it not as an undifferentiated mass but a collection of opinions some of which existed in a state of mutual tension. This was certainly so where theological questions had received no binding answer.

This is evident in the third question of the first 'Distinction' of Durandus. What was the principal reason for God assuming human flesh? Was it for his own glory, to bring creation into communion with himself, to make satisfaction for human sin, to reveal the truth or to give us laws that justice might be enthroned among us? For all these reasons and more, answers Fray Luis: 'Et ita, nobis fuit Christus redemptor et sanctificator, doctor et legislator, et denique auctor omnis bone atque felicitatis; unde Isaias, c. ix, tribuit Christo varia et multa nomina, propter multitudinem rerum a se gerendarum' (*Opera* IV, 30), 'And thus, Christ was for us redeemer and sanctifier, doctor and law-giver, and in short the author of every good and favourable thing; whence Isaiah, ch. ix, attributed many and varied names to Christ, on account of the many things achieved by him'. The names of Christ are thus a means towards understanding the fullness of the salvation he brings, and Fray Luis was considering them in this formal way long before he conceived the *Nombres*.

Two of these reasons emerge as the most probable ones for the Incarnation. Christ either came to redeem the human race from sin or to reveal his glory and bring the universe to perfection. Fray Luis arranges his discussion around a single question. If man had not sinned, would God, immortal, impassible, abounding in glory, have become man? Tradition gave him two answers. Duns Scotus held that God became man because this was the highest and most excellent of all his works; Aquinas, on the other hand, because man needed to be redeemed from sin, though he did not discount the Scotist view, which came to be associated with Franciscan theologians.[10]

Before expounding his own opinion, which follows Scotus, Fray

Luis looks at objections to it through many Biblical texts and Patristic references which explicitly connect Incarnation with Redemption. Two arguments are singled out: the Incarnation, as the highest of all God's works, must have been for an urgent and pressing need, and if made consequent upon human sin reveals the extent of God's love for humanity in a manner impossible to grasp if the link between redemption and sin is broken. But for Fray Luis such objections carry little weight. He takes the Scotist view as more probable and demonstrates it by a critical analysis of Aquinas and by a full exposition of his own conclusions. He maintains that the Thomist account is deficient, since it requires God to have foreseen from all eternity that man would sin, and thus for God in some sense to be the cause of human sin. It also requires man's predestination to precede rather than to follow the Incarnation in the foreknowledge of God. Sin then appears to have priority over Incarnation, human folly over eternal wisdom and self-disclosure. But what really troubles him is that the New Testament consistently speaks of the election of the faithful on account of Christ, never of his predestination on account of their sin.

Although God knows all things simultaneously, he does not know them in the same way. Some he knows as future, others as merely possible. Theologians have therefore distinguished God's 'simple intelligence', which sees all that might possibly be, from his 'vision' of future things. His simple intelligence is prior to his vision: the potentiality of something must necessarily precede its actuality, and the act of willing must precede the act of seeing. Fray Luis's argument here is difficult, but from it he establishes an ordering of God's knowledge which enables him to proceed with his incarnational theology. First, God understands all that might be possible; then, out of this, he wills particular things to be; and finally, he foresees what he has willed into being. The sequence is logical, not temporal, though temporal language cannot be avoided. All that God, the infinite ultimate Cause of all, creates has a likeness to his being, and he can create an infinite number of beings, some more, some less perfect in relation to their divine origin and perfection. But he only creates by likeness; no creature can actually participate in his divine substance. Though Fray Luis does not say so here, there is an evident link in his mind between this creation by 'likeness' and metaphorical language, which implies a likeness between two different objects, and, as we may recall, can use all things as metaphors for God, because God has made them all in his image and likeness.[11]

The loftiest form of God's self-communication is to unite himself to a creature in hypostatic union, a technical term from early Greek theology which means the union of substance, *hypostasis*, between the divine and human natures in Christ. But in his simple intelligence God could not have foreseen Christ before man, nor man before man's spiritual and corporeal nature, nor this before its constituent elements (air, fire, earth, water). God knew principles before effects, parts before the whole, things in their natural being before their existence by grace or in hypostatic union. Knowledge of this last presupposes knowledge of all the preceding. Therefore, everything that God created leads up to his greatest act, the Incarnation; and the communication of his goodness and perfection to the creatures issues in the highest gift he could bestow on creation, the Incarnate Word, in whom his glory is made manifest. Whether Adam sinned or not, God's purpose would have remained: to reveal his glory and to bring the universe to perfection through Christ.

Fray Luis finds this amply confirmed in Scripture, notably in Prov. viii and Col. i. But the Scriptural metaphor 'germen', or 'fructus', is further evidence, for the whole tree is contained in the fruit and seed, as Christ is the seed and fruit of the whole universe, by whom and for whom it exists (IV, 48). Galatinus provides a different, but complementary argument from Christian Kabbalism: some Hebrew scholars believed God to have created the world out of love for the Messiah. This is precisely the metaphor translated 'Pimpollo', the first of the names to be expounded in the *Nombres*. There, as we shall see, Fray Luis will explore the same christological theme but with much greater attention to Biblical imagery than to scholastic theology.

It follows that even if Adam had not sinned, Christ would have come. His Incarnation is not dependent on human sin, but on the divine purpose for the whole creation; to make it so dependent is repugnant to the Christian faith. The Incarnation adds an 'incredibilis quaedam et immensa dignitas' (IV, 53), 'a certain incredible and immense dignity' to humanity, far greater than that of man's state before the Fall and therefore still to be given him whether he sinned or not. Fall or no Fall, humanity is brought to its divinely appointed glory by the Incarnation. One reason, but only one, for it is to cancel the sin which enters creation after the Fall. This accounts for the manner of Christ's coming and the necessity of his Passion and sacrificial death. Fray Luis can only speculate about how Christ would have come if man had not sinned; but it is a Christ who is both passible and mortal who secures our redemption. Thus the Incarnation is primarily undertaken for the glorification of God, the communication of his goodness, the perfecting of the universe and the deification of humanity.

Fray Luis's anxiety to share with the readers of the *Nombres* the full teaching of Scripture is tempered by his caution in wishing to spare them the intricacies of scholastic theology. He will go into considerable exegetical detail but only rarely (and then in the form of a *quaestio*, built into the dialogue) offer a comparable density of doctrinal exposition. Concentration on images, metaphors, 'names', provides an alternative theological method.

For Fray Luis, then, Christ is the key which unlocks the whole mystery of human existence and the meaning of the universe. He is the final and greatest act of God's communication of his glory to his creation, and the hypostatic union reveals the destiny which awaits every creature. His theology is a salutary and attractive counterbalance to one which begins with human sinfulness rather than divine purpose. It has found an eloquent if equally difficult exponent in our own century, in the writings of Teilhard de Chardin, and there are clear echoes of it in C.S. Lewis's *Perelandra*. It does, however, appear seriously to weaken the dominant teaching that Christ came to this world as the divinely given means of rescuing lost humanity from the curse of sin and death, and to make the Passion and the Cross less than the pivotal events of human history. Whether that judgement can be sustained only the *Nombres* can tell us.

On names in general

Such is the title of the introductory chapter of the *Nombres*. It brings us back to Fray Luis's understanding of language and of the relationship between words and what they signify, especially (but not exclusively) in Scripture. Most of us regard words as sets of letters which have arrived at their current form through processes we can more or less identify, and think of them as having only an accidental relationship with the meaning they represent. Fray Luis would not have thought so. He believed that the reality of the object participated in the word by which it was named, and that the form and sound of a name or word were related to the significance it was intended to convey. To know the name of something was in some sense to understand its being, even to master it, as with the demonic 'Legion' in the Gospels, who is forced to tell Christ who he is. Since the language of Scripture was divinely inspired, its works could be expected to be closer than others to this ideal union of word and meaning.

Fray Luis's theory of names has been fully studied by Alain Guy, but we must at least outline it.[12] The name, or noun, 'es una palabra breve, que se substituye por aquello de quien se dice y se toma por ello mismo' (*Obras* I, 414), 'is a short word which is substituted for the thing of which it is spoken and is taken to be the thing itself'. It represents the object's being in our mind and our speech. Fray Luis defines perfection as diversity comprehended within a governing unity, man himself being an example, a microcosm, whose being exists in all other beings as theirs do in his, reduced out of their diversities into a unity. This is the ground of the relationship between the creatures and God, 'de quien mana, que en tres personas es una esencia, y en infinito número de excelencias no comprensibles, una sola perfecta y sencilla excelencia' (I, 415), 'from whom there flows, who in three Persons is one essence, and in an infinite number of excellent things beyond comprehension, one single perfect and simple excellence'. Language allows this truth to find expression. Through words, the reality of many things enters the mind of one person, which can contain a multiplicity of objects freed from their physical bounds. Thus the word is a spiritual reality, which enables the individual to participate in all the variety of creation, and it in him. The mind refines objects having solid, physical reality in the external world into ones 'espirituales y delicadas' (416), 'spiritual and delicate', into images in both mind and mouth of the truth of their being. Words which exist in our soul or mind he calls images by nature, since there is a natural likeness between the external object and its internal representation. But spoken words are images by art, created by us to express their reality. In the *Nombres* he will be more concerned with images by nature, and therefore with the relationship between the image and what it represents. He further distinguishes proper from common nouns, explaining that the former are so called because they signify a particular property, an idea which will become important to him.

Hebrew, he continues, as the first language, the language of Eden, maintains a closer connection between the meaning and the sound, shape and origin of the word than other languages.[13] This is shown in the Bible when God brings all the creatures to Adam to be named: 'and whatsoever Adam called every living creature, that was the name thereof' (Gen. ii.19). These names, predating the Fall, were those which most appropriately represented the being of creatures within the human mind and expressed it through the human voice. In his search for 'likeness' and 'conformity' between meaning and form, he examines the root of *corregidor* (a local royal official; from *corregir*, to correct) and *casamentero* (a marriage-broker, from the one whose job is to mention, *mentar*, the marriage), before passing to discuss the change in names of certain Biblical characters, like Peter. He then moves on to the sound of words, at which point he introduces the tetragrammaton, the ineffable, unpronounceable name of God, which is composed entirely of vowels, to signify pure spiritual Being.[14]

The theological direction of the argument becomes evident when we reach the climax of the exposition of names, the Incarnation. Now God enters the world of human speech, and the ineffable name is spoken, the name of the unbegotten Son, the uncreated Word: 'Y como Dios tenía ordenado de hacerse hombre después, luego que salió a luz el hombre quiso humanarse, nombrándose' (424), 'And as God had ordained that he would in time become man, once man came into the light he willed to become man by giving himself a name'. Since God is 'un abismo de ser y de perfección infinita', 'an abyss of being and of infinite perfection', no one name can possibly be an adequate image of this. Therefore in Scripture Christ is given many names, to represent 'su mucha grandeza y los tesoros de sus perfecciones riquísimas, y juntamente la muchedumbre de sus oficios y de los demás bienes que nacen de él y se derraman sobre nosotros', 'his very greatness and the treasures of his richest perfections, together with the multitude of his offices and of all the other benefits which are born from him and poured out on us.' Because our capacity is so limited, we can recieve them but little by little, as water decanted into a jar through a long and narrow neck. Because the names are so many, Fray Luis has chosen ten (in the first instance) 'como más substanciales' (425), 'as more substantial', which have been written down on a piece of paper, the point of departure for the exposition proper.[15] Among the names he mentions several, like lion, sacrifice and stone, are not treated in themselves but play important parts in the exposition of others. Some refer only to the divine nature of Christ, others are common to the Trinity, but 'los *Nombres de Cristo* que decimos ahora, son aquellos solos que convienen a Cristo en cuanto hombre', 'the *Names of Christ* which concern us now are those which alone are proper to Christ as man' – the names of the Incarnate Word.

The *Nombres de Cristo*: the first book

The first name Sabino reads out is 'Pimpollo', which he gives also in its Hebrew and Latin forms, and with four texts, two from Zechariah and one each from Isaiah and Jeremiah. The role of Sabino and Juliano, the third and youngest speaker, is generally to ask questions, interpolate comments, and break the long flow of Marcelo's exposition into more manageable portions. By using his three speakers in these varied ways, Fray Luis injects life and vigour into the debates.

Marcelo begins by explaining how appropriate a name this is to study first, since it deals with the new and wondrous birth of Christ, and by reviewing the four texts to prove that it is one of his names. The reader is at once faced with some daunting Old Testament exegesis. The first text (Isa. iv.2) refers to 'the branch of the Lord', and only in the Aramaic Targum does this become 'the Lord's Messiah'. Arguing against Jewish exegetes, he attacks those who interpret the text to refer to the restoration of Jerusalem and the rebuilding of the temple under Zerubbabel. The 'branch of justice' in the second text (Jer. xxxiii.15) confirms his christological interpretation, because only Christ is the bringer of true justice (a point proved by evidence from a secondary text in Psalm lxxii). The third text (Zech. iii.8) is understood messianically by the Jews in any case, and Marcelo so interprets the fourth (vi.12). Sensing that the reader needs guidance, he pauses at this point to summarize the argument, that this is indeed the first of the names of Christ; and adds that it is related to other similar Scriptural names, like branch, flower and root. Thus the name 'Pimpollo' belongs to a cluster of Scriptural metaphors, all of which indicate particular qualities of Christ.

Juliano declares that Marcelo's proofs have aroused their hunger for such a fruit. Marcelo, in return, calls it the sweetest of fruit, but only regrets, in a conventional disclaimer, that the poverty of his words will not do it justice. Then he suddenly changes the direction of the argument, because, turning to Sabino, he asks if the beauty of the earth and sky around them, and the greater beauty of the invisible world, has existed from all eternity, created itself, or was brought to light by God. The reader's attention is kept by this abrupt switch, which seems to have no connection with what has just been established. But in fact the question introduces the theological foundation of the dialogue itself.

Marcelo and Sabino move with a studied spontaneity towards the answer. God created the world of his free will, so that he could bestow gifts on his creatures. These gifts belong to three distinct orders of union: union of nature, by which all are made according to the likeness of the Creator; union of grace, given only to creatures with understanding (i.e. humans) to communicate God's supernatural gifts, so that they can be brought closer to him; and union of persons – hypostatic union – the joining of God and man, seen only in Christ. Since this is the highest kind of union, the others are preparatory:

Dios, a fin de hacer esta unión bienaventurada y maravillosa, crió todo cuanto se parece y se esconde; que es decir que el fin para que fue fabricada toda la variedad y belleza del mundo fue por sacar a luz este compuesto de Dios y hombre, o, por mejor decir, este juntamente Dios y hombre, que es Jesucristo.   (433–4)

God created all that is, seen and unseen, in order to make this blessed and wondrous union, which means that the purpose for which all the variety and beauty of the world was formed was to bring to light this compound of God and man, or rather, this one who is God and man together, Jesus Christ.

The conclusion is the same as in *De Incarnatione*, though reached by a different, simpler route. For now the metaphor, the name, comes into its own, and begins to dominate the exposition.

Just as in a tree neither root, trunk, branches, leaves nor flowers exist for themselves but all are ordered towards the producing of the fruit, the true purpose of their being, so too the heavens, the stars, earth with its flowers and waters and fish, and animals and people, have been brought into being for the Son of God to take human flesh and to produce the single divine Fruit which is Christ. And, as the fruit contains within itself all the potential of the tree, trunk, flowers and leaves, so Christ contains within himself the whole created order: 'De la grandeza y hermosura y cualidad de los medios, argüimos la excelencia sin medida del fin' (435), 'From the greatness, beauty and quality of the means, we argue the measureless excellence of the end'. Marcelo illustrates this with a further simile. A great palace, with its walls, towers, chambers, courtyards, galleries and porticoes, all its finery, decorations and treasures, and all its staff witness to one who is greater than them all, the king for whom it is built. So it is with all the beauties of the temple of creation: incomparably greater than them all is the One for whose birth they were ordained and to whom in the end they will be subjected. Then comes the Scriptural proof, from Col. i.15–19: Christ is the image of the invisible God, through whom and for whom all is created. He is the Fruit Isaiah longed for (xlv.8), a text interpreted messianically by the Church from the Patristic period onwards.

The metaphor of fruit produces further consequences. 'Todo aquello que es verdadero fruto en los hombres, digo fruto que merezca parecer ante Dios . . . no sólo nace en ellos por virtud de este *Fruto*, que es Jesucristo, sino en cierta manera también es el mismo Jesús' (436), 'All that is true fruit among men, I mean fruit worthy to appear before God . . . not only is born in them by virtue of this *Fruit* which is Jesus Christ, but is in a certain manner also Jesus Himself'. Marcelo extends the metaphor to include the Christian life itself, for this derives from Christ, who pours down justice and holiness upon the faithful so that their ensuing good and holy works are 'como una imagen y retrato vivo de Jesucristo', 'as an image and living portrait of Jesus Christ'. Paul indeed calls them Christ, individually and corporately, and four Pauline texts are cited in evidence.

Juliano breaks in to remind Marcelo, who thinks he has finished and is asking Sabino for the next name, that he has not yet spoken of the conception of Christ, as he had originally promised. Marcelo obliges, first returning to the Hebrew word for 'shoot' or 'fruit', which means a fruit which grows of its own accord, without need of cultivation. This teaches two lessons: that nothing in the world was of sufficient merit or value to deserve the fruit of the Incarnation; and that the power of God alone brought about Christ's birth from the Virgin's womb. Juliano is delighted to discover that the virginal conception is proved by ancient prophecy. Five texts are given, the dominant one being the dew which descends from heaven in Isa. xlv.8. Meanwhile, Marcelo speaks of his own devotion to her, in words reminiscent of the Ode to the Virgin (xxii) Fray Luis wrote, probably from his prison cell: 'Aunque lo es [Abogada y Señora] generalmente de todos, mas atrévome yo a llamarla *mía* en particular, porque desde mi niñez me ofrecí todo a su amparo' (438), 'Though she is generally [the Advocate and Lady] of all, yet I dare to call her *mine* in particular, because I offered myself from childhood wholly to her protection'. The exposition ends as it had begun, with further exegesis (of Psalm cix and Isa. liii), related now to Christ's conception and birth of Mary.

Much we have seen in 'Pimpollo' characterizes the *Nombres* as a whole. Scholastic theological exposition and Biblical exegesis, with reference back to the Hebrew underlie it and sometimes come to the surface. But what dominates and unites the piece is the metaphor of fruit and its satellite metaphors, developed out of Scripture and not merely illustrating but becoming the substantial theme. The metaphor of Christ as the universal Fruit becomes a vivid and persuasive way of communicating complex, abstract truths – that creation exists through and for Christ, that his glory would have been made manifest even if Adam had not sinned, that growth in the Christian life is growth from and in Christ, and that his virginal conception and birth are God's chosen means to this end. It enables Fray Luis to give lyrical expression to his themes and to draw the reader into them by the sweetness of the style, just as he intended.

The second name, 'Fazes de Dios', is brief but complex. Seven texts introduce it; the fifth and seventh (from Psalm lxxix and Numb. vi) are discussed at some length and in them we can hear Fray Luis arguing for a properly christocentric understanding of the Hebrew Scriptures, as opposed to the exegetical travesties of such as León de Castro. The meaning of the name is summed up in the thesis that Christ reveals most clearly and perfectly in his soul and his body the nature of God. Marcelo maintains that in his human nature Christ displayed perfect physical beauty without arousing any kind of sexual desire. He praises and describes it as he finds it portrayed in Song v.10–16, where the Bride hymns the beauty of the Beloved, a theme taken up later in 'Cordero'.[16] The Platonic overtones are evident from the exhortation: 'Pues pongamos los ojos en esta acabada beldad, y contemplémosla bien, y conoceremos que todo lo que puede caber de Dios en un cuerpo . . . resplandece en aquéste; y . . . es como un retrato vivo y perfecto [de Dios]' (449), 'Let us fix our gaze on that perfect beauty and contemplate it well, and we shall know that everything of God which can be contained within a body . . . shines in this one, and . . . is a living and perfect portrait [of God]'.

What, then, of Christ's soul? Closer to the being of God than all else save the Word, it sees all that was and is and shall be, knows all arts and sciences, and is the fount of good being, as God is of Being itself, for from it flows all the grace which makes men just and good and perfect. It 'recría y repara y defiende . . . a todo el género humano' (451), 'recreates, repairs and defends . . . the whole human race'; as befits a soul in unbroken communion with God, its power and knowledge is scarcely less than his. Marcelo imagines a series of mirrors reflecting a beautiful face, the first of which – the soul of Christ – most fully displays the original. It is a picture previously used in the general introduction (415), as a way of explaining how many things can exist simultaneously within our mind.

Whereas in 'Pimpollo' Marcelo was concerned with the universal Christ, in 'Fazes de Dios' he turns to his person, and to the paradoxes inherent in one whose human body and soul are joined to the divine being; inherent, that is, in orthodox christology. Just as theology and metaphor were intertwined there, so here paradox and antithesis give stylistic representation to the underlying christological paradox. The Christ of perfect humility in his humanity is Lord of men and angels and all creation, adored by them and united with God. The Christ whose meekness bore the enormity of our sins also brings us the greatness of divine forgiveness. The loftiness and majesty of Christ foreseen by Job (xi.8–9) is one with his compassion for all creatures, birds, ants, flowers, even the vilest worm. The intensity of Christ's love for us is expressed in a passage of fine devotional writing which introduces imagery of fire, so often associated with love, human or divine, and in this case, both:

Porque no padezcamos infierno y porque gocemos nosotros del cielo, padece prisiones y azotes y afrentosa y dolorosa muerte. Y Dios, por el mismo fin, ya que no era posible padecerla en su misma naturaleza, buscó y halló orden para padecerla por su misma persona. Y aquella voluntad ardiente y encendida, que la naturaleza humana de Cristo tuvo de morir por los hombres, no fue sino como una llama que se prendió del fuego de amor y deseo, que ardían en la voluntad de Dios, de hacerse hombre para morir por ellos. (453)

So that we should not suffer hell and so that we should enjoy heaven, he suffers chains and whippings and a shameful and painful death. And God, since he could not suffer this in his own nature, for the same end sought and found a way to suffer it in his own person. And that bright and burning will in Christ's human nature to die for men was but a flame kindled from the fire of love and desire burning in the will of God to become man and to die for men.

At once the imagery changes: 'No tiene fin este cuento; y cuanto más desplego las velas, tanto hallo mayor camino que andar, y se me descubren nuevos mares cuanto más navego', 'This story has no end, and the more I unfurl the sails, the further I find I have to journey, and the more I sail onwards, the more new seas open out before me.' The more Marcelo looks on the Face of God, the more there is revealed the perfection and the very being of God. The exalted note on which 'Fazes de Dios' ends is far removed from the exegetical labours of its beginning, yet it could not have been reached without them.

In contrast, 'Camino' needs no Biblical proofs because it is a name Christ uses of himself. Marcelo is thus free to concentrate on its significance. But he does not forget Scripture. Rather, as Fray Luis so often does in his commentaries, he makes a more general statement about imagery of the Bible, where 'way' has four principal meanings: character or behaviour; aim and profession in life; deeds; or the Law. He points to the road which they can see, the way to the court and the king, to illustrate the theme he now introduces – that Christ is the way to heaven and heaven can only be reached if we walk upon him. The setting of the dialogue once more becomes an image of its content. Marcelo next uses an image from everyday life, the way in which mothers hold their toddlers' arms with theirs and become both their ground and their guides. The idea of mothers' arms as 'ground' seems fanciful, but Marcelo means us to understand that without such support little children could not walk at all. That is how the Lord helps our weakness and our smallness to walk in his way and rise to heaven.

Christ is the true and universal way, a way free of obstacles for the weak, narrower and harder for the strong. Isaiah's description of the way of the Lord (xxxv.8–10) provides Marcelo with a Biblical picture he proceeds to expound. It is a high road of virtue, above the love of earthly things; it is also a level or plain road, without stumbling-block. Those who travel a different way will find obstacles at every step; those who seek riches lose their life, those who look for honour find their shame; those who travel for pleasure meet pain. Because Marcelo uses the word 'senda' ('path') as well as 'camino', we are forcibly reminded of the 'senda escondida', the hidden path in Fray Luis's famous Ode to the solitary life (1); and indeed the moral is the same, as our earlier study of his poetic imagery has shown.[17] Greed for riches and the quest for fame and honour can never deliver the fulfilment they claim to offer. Their alluring voices are the way towards destruction.

The poetry cannot have the theological or Biblical profundity of Fray Luis's prose expositions. The fact, for example, that 'camino' occurs three times in the Isaiah text leads Marcelo to speak of Christ as the way for three kinds of people, beginners, proficients and the perfect, the traditional terminology of the Western mystical tradition. He finds these ways prefigured in the architecture of Solomon's temple, its portico, palace and sanctuary.[18] What the poetry may imply can here be treated more comprehensively, though still with stylistic power. Marcelo dwells on the need for cleanliness on this way. A double *polyptoton* on 'andar' and 'mover' ('to walk' and 'to move') describes our redemption: 'Cristo es el *Camino nuestro*, y el que anda también el camino; porque anda El andando nosotros o, por mejor decir, andamos nosotros porque anda El y porque su movimiento nos mueve' (461), 'Christ is *our Way* and he who also walks the way; for as we walk, he walks, or rather we walk because he walks and because his moving moves us'. But we can only so walk once we have been redeemed:

Que no somos redimidos por haber caminado primero, ni por los buenos pasos que dimos, ni venimos a la justicia por nuestros pies . . . Así que no nace nuestra redención de nuestro camino y merecimiento, sino, redimidos una vez, podemos caminar y merecer después alentados con la virtud de aquel bien.   (462)

For we are not redeemed because first we walked, nor by the good steps we took, nor do we reach justice on our own feet . . . so that our redemption does not come from our way and merit, but, once redeemed, we can travel and find merit thereafter, nourished by the virtue of that good.

Marcelo explains the metaphor of redemption, repaying debt and buying back from captivity, a more telling one in the sixteenth century, used to such dealings between Christians and Moors, than for us today. He finds the eventual conversion of the Jews prophesied by Isaiah, and tells of God's love for his chosen people of old in a striking horticultural image: 'Tiene en el pecho de Dios muy hondas raíces aqueste querer, pues cortado y al parecer seco, torna a brotar con tanta fuerza' (464), 'That love has deep roots in the heart of God, since though severed and apparently withered, it buds again with such vigour'.

Marcelo's understanding of redemption, that we do not earn it by our good works, but that first Christ redeems us and then we are able to please God to the extent that we follow Christ's way, does not sound very different from Luther's. It is an important statement on justification from a moderate Catholic position, a far cry from Protestant and Catholic caricatures of each other's views. Perhaps because the metaphor of the way, with the concentration of meaning and paradox which the use of *polyptoton* creates, is never far from the surface, the bitter debates of the century seem to find some resolution here. Likewise, the picture of God's deeply rooted love for the Jews, miraculously alive in his heart though apparently dead from the human side, expresses in vivid imagery and in a manner far removed from the strident anti-semitism of some of his contemporaries Fray Luis's very Pauline understanding of the history of the Jewish people in salvation. At moments such as these, his christocentric vision of the universe, of which human history is but a part, touches the painful wounds of his own age and brings to them a word of healing. For Christ is the way through whom each person finds right behaviour, a true aim, good works and the will to follow his law; in sum, he fulfils all that the Bible means by 'way'.

'Monte' is one of the most complex and impenetrable names for the modern reader, because of the extraordinary series of associations made between a number of Biblical texts referring to mountains and mountains in general. The main reason why Christ is given this name is 'por la abundancia, o . . . por la preñez riquísima de bienes diferentes que atesora y comprende en sí mismo' (486), 'for the abundance or . . . for the very rich impregnation of different gifts which he treasures and comprehends within himself'. The Hebrew for 'mountain' is equivalent to the Castilian 'pregnant', and appropriately so, thinks Marcelo, because mountains swell above the earth and conceive and bring forth many of earth's treasures − trees for timber and fruit, herbs with secret powers, fountains and riverheads, precious and common metals and stones. Mountains are thus like wombs pregnant with riches; so Christ, in his humanity, encloses all that is good and beneficial and delightful and glorious:

En El está el remedio del mundo y la destrucción del pecado y la victoria contra el demonio; y las fuentes y mineros de toda la gracia y virtudes que se derraman por nuestras almas y pechos, y los hacen fértiles, en El tienen su abundante principio; en El tienen sus raíces, y de El nacen y crecen con su virtud . . . El mismo es el sacerdote y el sacrificio, el pastor y el pasto, el doctor y la doctrina, el abogado y el juez, el premio y el que da el premio; la guía y el camino, el médico, la medicina, la riqueza, la luz, la defensa y el consuelo es El mismo, y sólo El. En El tenemos la alegría en las tristezas, el consejo en los casos dudosos, y en los peligrosos y desesperados el amparo y la salud.

(487)

In him lies the remedy against the world and the destruction of sin and the victory over the devil, and the fountains and mines of all grace and virtues which are poured into our souls and breasts and make them fertile have their abundant principle in him; in him are their roots and from him they arise and grow by his power . . . He himself is priest and victim, pastor and pasture, doctor and doctrine, advocate and judge, prize and prize-giver; guide and way, doctor, medicine, wealth, light, defence and consolation, he and he alone. In him we have joy in times of sadness, counsel in doubtful cases, and in dangerous and desperate ones, protection and healing.

Here indeed is an *amontamiento*, a 'heaping up', a congeries in which the rhetoric matches and illustrates the content, the wealth of virtues and names contained in this mountain which is Christ.

Marcelo leaves for a while this series of connections between mountains, pregnancy and Christ, to return to the first of his texts, Nebuchadnezzar's dream of the stone 'cut without hands' which smote the image of the statue, turned it to dust, and itself became a great mountain which filled the earth (Dan. ii.34–5). This stone is Christ, so named because of strength combined with smallness, qualities proper to stones. Christ refuses to use his omnipotent power to destroy the tyranny of the devil, but chooses rather to be small, and to allow himself to suffer a most cruel death:

Y esta pequeñez y flaqueza fue fortaleza dura, y toda la soberbia del infierno y su monarquía quedó rendida a la muerte de Cristo. Por manera que primero fue piedra, y después de piedra *Monte*. Primero se humilló, y, humilde, venció; y después, vencedor glorioso, descubrió su claridad y ocupó la tierra y el cielo con la virtud de su nombre.   (489)

And this smallness and weakness was hard strength, and all the pride and dominion of hell lay vanquished before the death of Christ. Thus first he was a stone, and after a stone, a *Mountain*. First he humbled himself, and, humble, conquered; and then, glorious conqueror, he revealed his brightness and filled heaven and earth with the power of his name.

Marcelo sets this vision of the stone which became a mountain alongside the classic exposition of the *kenosis*, or self-emptying of Christ, from Phil. ii, where Christ abandons divine majesty to humble himself, assume humanity, and die, in order to be raised victorious by God and receive universal homage. His very humility becomes his glory. Marcelo sees that precisely what was weak and despised in Christ – his Passion and his death – is in fact hard as stone, because it shatters all the proud power of the world, as if it were fragile glass. The stone struck the feet of the statue in the vision and brought it down. Such a blow cannot of itself be mortal; yet in the Gospel's first striking against worldly vanity, God chose what was lowly and despised to begin his work, until this 'stone' becomes a mountain and fills the earth.

Returning to the Psalm text, Marcelo applies the 'high hill of Bashan' to the abundance of Christ, since Bashan stands for the deep, well-watered soils of fertile mountains, from which rich harvests are produced. But the harvest imagery suggests another Messianic psalm (lxxi), which is expounded in terms of spiritual fruits. Part of it is given in a Spanish translation by Fray Luis, which leads Juliano to interrupt with a question about the right use of poetry and prompts Marcelo's comments on this.[19] The exposition centres on three qualities of the corn which 'shall shake like Lebanon' (lxxi.16). Corn gives life, whereas trees produce a show of leaves rather than much fruit, and represent the ancient philosophers and others who strove after virtue by their own efforts. This corn grows taller than cedars, just as the Christian saints surpass in fame and honour the great and wise men of the world. Finally, it begins tiny yet rises quickly to an incomparable greatness. So the ancient philosophers, for all the beauty and sweetness of their words, cannot compare with Christ, who with one dead corn of wheat (John xii.24) and twelve lowly men, and by a teaching hard and bitter in men's eyes, filled the world with virtue beyond compare.

We begin to see the exegetical and stylistic links. Daniel and both Psalm texts are drawn together by the theme of smallness which becomes greatness, weakness which becomes power which will fill the earth. The life-giving corn of the psalm becomes the corn of wheat which dies in the ground, only to sprout with new life. Marcelo goes on to allude to other Biblical passages which illustrate the same process – the grain of mustard seed, the pearl of great price, the leaven in the lump, and the example of St Paul himself, whose feast day they are celebrating. Just as one image may contain many meanings, so one concept can be expressed through many images. When we understand that, much of the strangeness of older traditions of Biblical exegesis disappears.

Marcelo, having woven this second elaborate pattern of images and ideas – corn, trees, ancient philosophy and Christ – next applies it to personal life. One word sown in the soul can by its hidden power utterly change a life; the immoral, the greedy, the cruel, like dry branches fit only for burning in hell, grow in virtue and good and become an 'árbol verde y hermoso, lleno de fruto y de flor' (495), a 'beautiful green tree, full of fruit and flower'. Now the tree, which has just been used as a symbol of relative unfruitfulness, becomes a symbol of the fruitful Christian life. Similarly, burning wood, here suggestive of hellfire, will be used in 'Esposo' as a simile for the soul on fire with love for God.[20] One image may yield contradictory meanings; we must not assume that it will always represent similar ones.

'Monte' ends with Marcelo returning to the Psalm text he had begun with (lxviii) before his excursus into Psalm lxxi, and to a further exposition of the theme of fertility, this time based on variant interpretations of the Hebrew for the 'hill of Bashan' – a 'mount of cheeses' or 'of swellings'. He is undaunted by the apparent incongruity. The 'mount of cheeses' he adapts to the theme of fertility and pasture: it is a metonymy, the effect (cheese) standing for the cause (rich grazing). The 'mount of swellings' introduces a grander concept. Christ is not a mountain which rises directly to a single summit, but a '*Monte* hecho de montes, y una grandeza llena de diversas e incomparables grandezas' (496), a 'mountain made of mountains, and a greatness filled with diverse and incomparable great things'. He is a mountain envied by others and chosen above all others by God. From the mention of envy, supported by further texts (Luke ii.34; Psalm ii.1–2), he shows that opposition and persecution are inherent in the Christian life, from the sufferings of Christ onwards. Indeed, long before the Incarnation Lucifer envied Christ and rebelled against God. Satan is thus the father of all persecutions, ever hostile to Christ and to his people. But his labours are in vain: they can only increase the triumph and the glory of Christ. On this more sober note, 'Monte' ends. It is a theme which is developed much further in the final name of the first book of the *Nombres*, and grows to dominate much of the rest of the work. Here, for the first time, the true significance of the Passion in Fray Luis's theology begins to emerge.

'Padre del siglo futuro' is prefaced with only one text (Isa. ix.6), but also with an allusion to the story of Nicodemus, which, as it demonstrates men's need to be reborn, assumes great importance in the exposition. This begins where 'Monte' left off and prepares the way for the fullest treatment of the theme of birth and rebirth, in 'Hijo de Dios'. Marcelo first reminds his friends of God's purpose in creating human beings, that before creation he had determined to elevate human nature and bring it to share in the highest of his gifts, as ruler of every creature. So far the dialogue has concentrated on this purpose, and the place of Christ in achieving it. But now sin is introduced; sin not as a human failing, but as a spiritual power opposed to the divine purpose, personified in Lucifer and originating in the fire of envy which possessed him when he discovered God's intentions.

Lucifer's plan was to damage the human body and soul, to make it unfit for heavenly things, even before Adam and Eve appear in Eden.[21] When they do, he menacingly observes that the fruit of one tree alone is forbidden to them, and determines so to poison it that not only they but the entire race of their descendants will suffer the curse. In the Fall, therefore, he sows the poisonous seeds of future pride, ambition and greed, born from his own nature and infecting all who eat. As he conceived his plan, so he acted. Man fell, God's purposes took a tumble. Marcelo thus sees original sin working not in a crude or mechanical way, but as a poison which spreads from generation to generation and which, once in the system, cannot be eradicated. All are born 'culpados y aborrecibles a Dios, e inclinados a continuas y nuevas culpas, e inútiles todos para ser lo que Dios había ordenado que fuesen' (503), 'guilty and hateful to God, and inclined to continual and new acts of guilt, and unfit all of them for what God had ordained that they should be'.

God's justice now finds itself opposed to his merciful and loving purposes, in an irreconcilable dilemma:

Porque se contradecían y como hacían guerra entre sí dos decretos y sentencias divinas . . . Porque, por una parte, había decretado Dios de ensalzar al hombre sobre todas las cosas, y, por otra parte, había firmado que, si pecase, le quitaría la vida del alma y del cuerpo; y había pecado . . . No podía Dios . . . no cumplir su palabra; porque no es mudable Dios en lo que una vez dice, ni puede nadie poner estorbo a lo que El ordena que sea.

(503)

For two divine decrees and sentences were in contradiction and as if at war with one another . . . For on the one hand, God had decreed than man would be exalted above all things and on the other had affirmed that if he sinned he would take away the life of his soul and body; and man had sinned . . . [But] God . . . could not fail to fulfil his word; for God is not changeable in what he once says, nor can anyone hinder what he ordains must be.

A rebirth of humanity is the only way in which both promise and penalty could be fulfilled:

Y el medio y la salida fue no criar otro nuevo linaje de hombres, sino dar orden cómo aquellos mismos ya criados, y por orden de descendencia nacidos, naciesen de nuevo otra vez, y para que ellos mismos y unos mismos, según el primer nacimiento muriesen, y viviesen según el segundo; y en lo uno ejecutase Dios la pena ordenada, y la gracia y la grandeza prometida cumpliese Dios en lo otro.

(504)

And the means and the solution was not to create a new line of men, but to ordain how those already created and born in order of descent might be born again a second time, so that one and all might die according to their first birth and live according to their second; and in the first respect God would carry out the penalty he had ordained, and in the second fulfil the grace and greatness he had promised.

This solution of the divine dilemma is well grounded in the traditional language of Christian theology and devotion; both Wesley and Newman, for example, popularized it in their hymns.[22]

Human beings, inheriting Adam's sin, are born with a body and soul which bear the image and likeness of God, but also:

un espíritu y una infección infernal, que se extiende y derrama por todas las partes del hombre, y se enseñorea de todas y las daña y destruye. Porque en el entendimiento es tinieblas, y en la memoria olvido, y en la voluntad culpa y desorden de las leyes de Dios, y en los apetitos fuego y desenfrenamiento, y en los sentidos engaño, y en las obras pecado y maldad, y en todo el cuerpo desatamiento y flaqueza y penalidad, y, finalmente, muerte y corrupción.

a spirit and an infection from hell, which extends and spreads through all the parts of man, and possesses, damages and destroys them all. For it is darkness in the understanding, oblivion in the memory, guilt and disorder of laws of God in the will, unbridled fire in the appetites, deceit in the senses, sin and evil in works, a falling apart and weakness and affliction in the whole body, and, in the end, death and corruption.

This is a graphic picture of the human condition, infected by the archetypal, inherited sin of Adam; a heavy doctrine of the Fall, as Augustine's. But it is not exactly Platonic. The soul is not a pure heavenly spirit imprisoned in a physical body from which its seeks release, but a poisoned thing in itself. Sin is spiritual, located in the faculties of the soul, memory, understanding and will. We must remember this when we read the poetry of Fray Luis, in which the soul's imprisonment and oblivion is so often lamented. In the Ode to Salinas (III), for example, the soul is aroused to memory of its forgotten, bright origin by the blind musician's art, but that does not itself bring salvation. It has to free itself, as it reaches self-knowledge, of its wrongful attachment to 'la belleza caduca engañadora', 'deceitful, fleeting beauty'. Though the poem's imagery is largely positive, because the poet is imagining the harmony and sweetness of heaven, it begins from the same experience, the darkness and error of human desires, and ends there too, only with the difference that the vision the music has given is carried back to the world of the senses, to be treasured there.

Marcelo explains that in his first birth man could freely choose good or evil, but lacked a governing principle to incline him towards the good. God had formed man physically perfect and added to him his own life, so that man was 'una imagen suya sobrenatural y muy cercana a su semejanza' (506), 'a supernatural image of him and very close to his likeness'. This perfection was forfeited in the Fall, and in its place came the image and likeness of Satan, the spirit of evil. Marcelo uses two metaphors to expound this, poison and fire, the first predominating, the second suggested perhaps by the fire of hell, from which it proceeds and to which it is bound. Since we are all born in Adam's line, we all inherit this poison which strikes at the root of our common origin and at each one of us when we are born. The substance of our body and soul is good, since it is from God. The evil spirit of Satan is received freely and therefore culpably by us. It affects us in two ways, 'virtually' (we might say 'potentially') before we are born, through our ancestry in Adam, and 'formally' ('actually') at our birth. The distinction is scholastic, so Marcelo uses a horticultural analogy earlier applied in 'Pimpollo' to Christ as the fruit of the universe. Its application here to evil shows that the universe now contains two conflicting powers, Christ's and Satan's, competing for human allegiance. The peach stone contains root, trunk, leaves, flowers and fruit. If some foreign colour or taste were injected into it, the stone would not show it and the result would not be visible until the tree grew. So the evil spirit is found within us through the wrong choice of our first father; but we grow in conformity with its promptings and become responsible for our sins. Its poison leads to perdition. The stronger it becomes, the weaker we are; like the woodworm in the wood, it gnaws at and all but consumes our nature, and brings disorder in every part. The old Adam, corrupt in body and soul, must die.

Only the rebirth of our nature by a new spirit has the power to overcome this death. This 'new man' or 'new Adam' (the expression is classically Pauline) lives in direct opposition to the old, and Marcelo expresses this in a reversal of the picture he has just drawn to emphasize the destructive power of the Fall. With the new man comes:

luz en el ánimo y acuerdo de Dios en la memoria, y justicia en la voluntad, y templanza en los deseos, y en los sentidos guía, y en las manos y en las obras provechoso mérito y fruto, y, finalmente, vida y paz general de todo el hombre, e imagen verdadera de Dios, y que hace a los hombres sus hijos.
(510–11)

light in the soul and remembrance of God in the memory, and justice in the will, and moderation in the desires, and in the senses a guide, and in hands and works a profitable merit and fruit, and, in the end, life and a general peace in the whole man, and the true image of God, which makes of men his sons.

There follows a clearly autobiographical insertion. Juliano praises Marcelo for weaving together so many strands of Christian doctrine and for expounding accurately the relationship between faith and works, inward disposition and outward acts. The works we do as we are moved by this new spirit become themselves the cause of our growth, since they nourish it. Marcelo accepts that this provides the basis for a thorough refutation of Lutheran error, which he would undertake had he the time. But 'no está todo en mi poder, ni soy mío en todos los tiempos. Porque ya véis cuántas son mis ocupaciones y la flaqueza grande de mi salud' (513), 'not everything is in my power, nor am I my own master at all times. For you can see how many duties I have and how poor my health is' – characteristic complaints of Fray Luis. There were pressures from Rome for an adequate Catholic counterblast to Protestant polemical writings such as the *Centuries of Magdeburg*.[23] Perhaps it had been mooted that Fray Luis should offer a Catholic reply to Luther on justification by faith, and Fray Luis was here explaining how impossible this would be for him. If this were so, it would be further evidence for the increased personal stature of Fray Luis in the years following his release.

But Juliano and Sabino are unconvinced. In spite of this, they say, you still have time to produce '¡ . . . otras escrituras que no son menos trabajosas que ésa, y son de mucho menos utilidad!', 'other writings no less laborious than this and much less useful!' That, Marcelo replies, is because each of these is in itself brief, whereas such a refutation would be a very complex and serious matter, not to be begun if it could not be finished. All he desires is an end to lawsuits and fights in the University, so that he can be free to think and write.[24] We can only speculate what these 'other writings' might be – his original poems and translations, well enough known to his circle of friends and admirers during the 1580s, or even each of the *Nombres*, which generally eschew polemic in favour of a gentle, eirenic tone. Whatever the reference, Fray Luis is using not only Marcelo but Juliano and Sabino to reflect his own frustrated priorities and divided loyalties, alongside the technique of interruption to break up a long theological exposition.

The principal argument resumes with the form God takes to ensure man's second birth, Christ's becoming man so that we might be reborn in him. For this, man required a new father. Here we come to the puzzle at the heart of this name, for it appears to confuse the Persons of the Trinity by ascribing fatherhood to the Son. So Marcelo carefully explains what kind of father the incarnate Son was to become: 'Porque lo primero, porque había de ser *Padre* de hombres, ordenó que fuese hombre; y porque había de ser *Padre* de hombres ya nacidos, para que tornasen a renacer, ordenó que fuese del mismo linaje y metal de ellos' (514), 'For first, since he was to be the *Father* of men, he ordained that he should become man; and because he was to be the *Father* of men already born, so that they could be born again, he ordained him to be of the same lineage and condition as them'. For this purpose, Christ had to assume flesh, but in such a way that it was not human flesh corrupted by the Fall. The consummate wisdom of God shines forth in enabling this second father to be descended from the first but without his sin. Christ was born not of the will of the flesh, which transmits sin, but by the will and power of God in the womb of the Virgin Mary, herself a descendant of Adam. By the virginal conception, therefore, God resolves this further difficulty, and Christ both conserves our humanity and preserves it from original sin.

Marcelo returns to the analogy of the seed which contains the coming flower and fruit, and to the image of fire, to illustrate the nature of our rebirth. In the Incarnation, God encloses as in a seed all who are to flower and fruit as his members, in this life and the next, just as earlier the seed of evil planted in Adam infected us all. This new birth will lead to our deification, when 'seremos unos en espíritu, así entre nosotros como con Jesucristo, o por hablar con más propiedad, seremos todos un Cristo' (515), 'we shall be one in spirit, among ourselves as with Jesus Christ, or to put it more appropriately, we shall all be one Christ'. The Incarnation not only restores the damage done by our first birth in Adam, but also leads us to a better state than his in Paradise: we are all contained within Christ embryonically, just as fire is the fountain and source of all that burns, before any particular burning comes to be. Marcelo's argument, as so often, is fundamentally Pauline (Rom. v). All that has the potential for rebirth in Christ is placed in him by God in a hidden, spiritual way. When Christ dies on the Cross, we die; the 'old man' of our unredeemed humanity is crucified. When Christ rises, we are raised to new life like his, beyond the power of death:

De manera que hizo Dios a Cristo *Padre* de este nuevo linaje de hombres; y para hacerle *Padre* puso en El todo lo que al ser *Padre* se debe: la naturaleza conforme a los que de El han de nacer y los bienes todos que han de tener los que en esta manera nacieren; y, sobre todo, a ellos mismos los que así nacerán, encerrados en El y unidos con El como en virtud y origen.   (517)

Thus God made Christ *Father* of this new lineage of men and to make a *Father* of him endowed him with everything being a *Father* involves: his nature like those who are to be born from him, and all the gifts those so born are to have; and especially like those to be so born, enclosed in him and united with him in potential and origin.

How does this father engender us? We are born and grow under the influence of the serpent's poison and inherit the spirit of sin and disorder from Adam. In Christ lies both the potentiality and the actuality of our rebirth, but first the poison must be removed by the appointed means, the suffering and death of Christ:

Procedió Cristo a esta muerte y sacrificio aceptísimo que se hizo de sí, no como
una persona particular, sino como en persona de todo el linaje humano y de
toda la vejez de él, y señaladamente de todos aquellos a quienes de hecho
había de tocar el nacimiento segundo, los cuales por secreta unión del espíritu
había puesto en sí y como sobre sus hombros; y así, lo que hizo entonces en sí,
cuanto es de su parte, quedó hecho en todos nosotros.   (520)

Christ went to this death and most acceptable sacrifice which he made of
himself, not as an individual but as in the person of the whole human race and
its old self, and notably of all those whom this second birth was indeed to
touch, who by a secret spiritual union he had placed within himself and upon
his shoulders; and thus what he did then in his person, all that was his to do,
was done in all our persons.

The Sacrament of his Body reveals this. His true body, sacrificed on
the Cross and embracing there all humanity, appears beneath the
species of the bread and wine, the bread itself formed of many separate
grains united in the one loaf. Marcelo finds the words of consecration
prefigured in the sacrifice of Isaac, where the dry wood, in the
'lenguaje secreto' (521), 'secret language' of Scripture, means the
sinner; in the scapegoat ritual of Leviticus; and in the robe of the high
priest, representing before God 'la universidad de las cosas', 'the
universality of things', for which before God he pleads.

In his divine nature, Christ is not subject to death, nor does he
inherit it in his human nature, because he is born free of the penalty of
Adam's sin. But he does inherit from his Mother passibility and
mortality, so that in his human nature he can suffer and die. In his
resurrection, which Scripture also calls 'birth' and 'generation' (an
idea more fully developed in 'Hijo de Dios'), he comes forth from the
hand of God not only free of all sin but also of passibility and death,
and endowed with glory. His resurrection becomes the means of
rebirth of all who are found in Christ even before they are first born, a
rebirth into a life of growing justice until they reach the same immortality and freedom from sin as Christ himself possesses.

With the challenge of Protestant theology in mind, Marcelo stresses
that this is but the beginning of a lengthy process by returning to the
imagery of natural growth, contrasted with the 'fuego ponzoñoso',
'poisonous fire' brought to our flesh by the serpent in Eden. Just as by
our sin we become more and more infected with the spirit of poison
and death active within us by virtue of our birth in Adam, so by our
rebirth in Christ the seed and first roots of the fruit of justice and
immortality are brought to us, and can begin to grow. What is done
for us in the person of Christ does not of itself make us just and saved, as

Marcelo believes the Lutherans teach, but requires to be taken into our lives. The corn needs water and sun for it to sprout from the grain; 'asimismo . . . no comenzaremos a ser en nosotros cuales en Cristo somos, hasta que de hecho nazcamos de Cristo' (524), 'likewise . . . we shall not begin to be in ourselves what we are in Christ, until indeed we are born of Christ'. Then, in place of the 'poisonous fire' comes a 'simiente de vida, . . . un grano de su espíritu y gracia que, encerrado en nuestra alma y siendo cultivado como es razón, vaya después creciendo . . . hasta llegar a la medida . . . de *varón perfecto*', 'seed of life . . . a grain of his spirit and grace which, enclosed in our soul and duly cultivated, then begins to grow . . . till it attains the measure of *perfect man*' (Eph. iv.13).

But are all reborn in Christ? Marcelo raises the question of divine predestination, by no means an exclusively Calvinistic concern. Only those who are baptized are reborn in Christ, for baptism is the sacrament of this generation: 'Tocando al cuerpo el agua visible, y obrando en lo secreto la virtud de Cristo invisible, nace el nuevo *Adán*, quedando muerto y sepultado el antiguo' (525), 'When the visible water touches the body and the invisible power of Christ acts in secret, the new *Adam* is born, and the old one lies dead and buried'. Marcelo illustrates this in a particularly telling way, because he turns to a simile which is based on the exact antithesis of water, namely fire. As wood is set alight by being brought into contact with the flame, so in baptism we are reborn into the death and resurrection of Christ – a characteristically Pauline doctrine. In the sacrament outward and inward truths, 'representation' and 'truth', are joined: an outward representation of Christ's death and resurrection in the life of the Christian, and the inward truth of the 'verdadera vida de gracias y verdadera muerte de culpa' (526), 'true life of grace and the true death of sin'. Though water and fire are opposites, Marcelo finds in Cyprian the reason why water is the sign of this rebirth. The guilt of our old life is poison, as a serpent's venom; water renders this harmless. The pattern of images expresses the interrelatedness of different points in the exposition. The poison or poisonous fire of original sin and its consequences in human life is neutralized by the water of baptism, which is the outward sign of the inward regeneration in Christ. This regeneration is likened to a sprouting seed rather than to the final fruit, to show the relationship between Christ's work and ours; while what happens in baptism is further explained by the analogy of wood being set alight. Each of the images may be simple and commonplace, but, exactly as in the poems of Fray Luis, it is the pattern he weaves with them which reveals his artistry.

Because this has been so closely argued a piece, Marcelo recapitulates at length. One clarification takes us to the heart of the theological controversies of the century. Protestants and Catholics might agree that the beginning of our rebirth is entirely unmerited by us. But Marcelo, and through him Fray Luis, believes that once Christ is received we may grow in conformity with him and that our good works become meritorious – that is, they count towards our salvation – if they derive from Christ's life within us. Inherited original sin became our moral responsibility once we engaged in evil deeds arising from its poisonous hold on us; the infused spirit of Christ, freely bestowed on us, needs our active co-operation so that the good works we do in union with him make us more acceptable in the sight of God. It is not, as Protestants feared, that good works performed in separation from Christ could somehow persuade God to save us. Here again, Marcelo's is a moderate statement of the Catholic position, and had Fray Luis written his refutation of Protestant heresy his opponents might have been surprised by his argument. His christocentric approach and his Pauline theology would have attracted them and perhaps have become a fruitful point of dialogue. Perhaps because this is devotional rather than controversial literature, and certainly because it uses images and metaphors to articulate its theology, it speaks with the voice of the reconciler and in a manner which brings pictures from ordinary experience into the preserve of theological polemics.

Marcelo ends his exposition by returning to Isa. ix.6, and the idea of the Father of the 'siglo futuro', the 'age to come' (not apparent from the AV's 'everlasting'). The first age began with Adam and ends with those who die in descent from him; the second age began with Abel and lasts for ever. Abel is chosen presumably because his innocent death is a type of Christ's offering of himself on the Cross. These two ages coexist in human history, the first visible and old, the second invisible and new. Marcelo finds them pictured in Psalm ciii, and he expounds it accordingly. The natural world, with its clouds, storms, thunder and lightning, is the old world, contrasting with the new world of the Church, in which apostles, doctors and saints rain down true doctrine and the Spirit of God blows upon his people. Guided and protected through nights of violence and bitterness, the Church is being brought to a perfection in which all base metal is melted away and it shines forth in all purity. Then the faithful will live in God and he in them, and they will be kings who serve the king of kings in a life of unimaginable sweetness and delight. Sabino reads out a verse translation of the Psalm by Marcelo's 'friend' – Fray Luis; Sabino, who is described as a young man with a pleasing voice, beautiful in body and soul. Such details are not accidental; they are a way of revealing the Christ within, who has been the subject of the discourse. Marcelo now calls the friends to rest. The sun is strong, and they will resume later, at Sabino's suggestion on an island thicket in the middle of the river.

The second book

The second book of the *Nombres* begins with 'Braço de Dios', which we have already studied.[25] There is considerable continuity of theme between the names, and perhaps because of it, the texts for 'Rey de Dios', 'Príncipe de la paz' and 'Esposo' are given together in the introduction to the first (Psalm ii.6, Zech. xiv.14; Isa. ix.6; John iii.29, Matt. ix.15).

'Rey de Dios' focusses on the qualities Christ possesses for his rule, the condition of the subjects over whom he reigns and the way in which he governs them. The difference between human kingdoms and Christ's is seen in further texts from Daniel's visions. The contrast suggests that there are principles here which Christian rulers and their subjects ought to take to heart, and Marcelo says as much.

First among Christ's kingly qualities are his humility and gentleness, which human kings should imitate. Since God is ruler of all, earthly rulers should follow his example of caring for the lowliest worm and the beauty of fields and flowers which we so carelessly trample underfoot. Next comes Christ's schooling in human suffering, which is expanded into a memorable statement linking his childhood, ministry and death:

Porque, ¿qué quedó de probar? Padecen algunos pobreza: Cristo la padeció más que otro ninguno. Otros nacen de padres bajos y obscuros, por donde son tenidos por menos: el padre de Cristo, a la opinión de los hombres, fue un oficial de carpintero. El destierro y el huir a tierra ajena fuera de su natural, es trabajo: y la niñez de aqueste Señor huye su natural y se esconde en Egipto. Apenas ha nacido la luz, y ya el mal la persigue . . .

Mas vengamos a la edad de varón. ¿Qué lengua podrá decir los trabajos y dolores que Cristo puso sobre sus hombros, el no oído sufrimiento y fortaleza con que los llevó, las invenciones y los ingenios de nuevos males, que El mismo ordenó como saboreándose en ellos; cuán dulce le fue el padecer, cuánto se preció de señalarse sobre todos en esto, cómo quiso que con su grandeza

compitiese en El su humildad y paciencia? Sufrió hambre, padeció frío, vivió
en extremada pobreza, cansóse y desvelóse, y anduvo muchos caminos, sólo a
fin de hacer bienes de incomparable bien a los hombres.   (578)

For what did he not experience? Some suffer poverty; Christ, more than any
other. Others are born of lowly and obscure parents, and are held for this to
be of little account: the father of Christ in the opinion of men was a carpenter
by trade. Exile and flight from one's own country to a strange land is a
hardship and the childhood of this Lord flees from his own country and hides
in Egypt. Scarcely is the light born and already evil is persecuting it . . .
But let us come to the age of his manhood. What tongue can tell the pains
and sorrows Christ placed upon his shoulders, the unheard-of suffering and
fortitude by which he bore them, the findings of and the faculties for fresh
evils, which he himself ordained as if delighting in them; how sweet suffering
was to him, how much he prized himself to rise above all others in it, how he
desired his humility and patience to compete in himself with his greatness? He
suffered hunger, endured cold, lived in extreme poverty, grew weary and lay
sleepless, and travelled many roads, solely to bring gifts of incomparable
goodness to men.

The tightness of style and the accompanying conceits have the feel of a
Donne sermon about them – 'childhood' flees, 'light' is born. They
express above all the universality of Christ's sufferings, undergone in
his person on behalf of all children, to overcome all darkness. There is
no nostalgia about the Christmas story or his childhood; they are the
beginning of the story of his sufferings, continued during his ministry
and climaxing on Calvary. Marcelo takes us on into Passiontide, Palm
Sunday, the Last Supper and the agony in Gethsemane, so acutely
experienced that 'lo que la misma muerte . . . no pudo hacer sin
ayudarse de las espinas y el hierro, en la imaginación . . . sin armas
ningunas lo hizo' (580–1), 'what death itself . . . could not achieve
without the aid of thorns and iron, it achieved . . . unarmed in his
imagination'.
The horror grows.

También sintió la pena que es ser vendido y traído a muerte por sus mismos
amigos, como El lo fue en aquella noche de Judas; el ser desamaparado en su
trabajo de los que le debían tanto amor y cuidado; el dolor de trocarse los
amigos con la fortuna; el verse no solamente negado de quien tanto le amaba,
mas entregado del todo en las manos de quien le desamaba tan mortalmente;
la calumnia de los acusadores, la falsedad de los testigos, la injusticia misma, y
la sed de la sangre inocente asentada en el soberano tribunal por juez; males
que sólo quien los ha probado los siente.   (582–3)

He felt also the pain of being betrayed and given up to death by his own
friends, as he was on that night of Judas; of being abandoned in his travail by

those who owed him so much love and care; the sorrow of friends who change
with fortune; of finding himself not only denied by one who loved him so
much, but of being wholly delivered into the hands of one who hated him so
mortally; the calumny of accusers, the falseness of witnesses, injustice itself,
and thirst for innocent blood seated as judge on the sovereign tribunal; evils
which he alone who has experienced them can feel.   (583)

The last clause suggests Fray Luis, speaking through Marcelo, is
claiming some understanding of some of Christ's sufferings through
his own prison ordeal. Satan, not Pilate, is directing the events. When
Christ appears before Pilate and the crowd disowns him, the King
becomes a sacrificial lamb, anticipating a name yet to be expounded.
So Marcelo leads us on, inexorably, to the Cross, in a passage full of
Johannine echoes:

Subió este nuestro *Rey* en la cruz. Y levantada en alto la salud del mundo, y
llevando al mundo sobre sus hombros, y padeciendo El solo la pena que
merecía padecer el mundo por sus delitos, padeció lo que decir no se puede.
                                                                    (584–5)

This our *King* ascended the Cross. And when the salvation of the world was
lifted up on high, bearing the world on his shoulders and suffering alone all
the penalty the world deserved to suffer for its crimes, he suffered beyond all
telling.

There, all his senses were possessed by pain – his eyes gazed on his
stricken mother, his ears rang with the taunts of his enemies, his taste
sipped gall and vinegar, his touch found only bitter wounds. And at
last, he knew the one thing left to him to know – the iciness of death.

    This passage calls forth some of the finest and most sustained prose
writing of Fray Luis, drawing no doubt on centuries of Christian
devotional writing on the Passion. The parallelisms and antitheses,
the personification of abstract qualities, the Biblical and classical
allusions (Christ, for example, as a new Atlas), the rhetorical questions
and the vivid focussing on the characters, scenes and events of the last
week of Christ's life result in a meditation on the Passion which is
emotive yet restrained and beautiful. Its beauty is perhaps its most
unexpected feature. But like the beauty of a crucifix which does not
dwell on the physical torment but reveals instead Christ's inner
desolation, it is a composed and a controlled beauty, for though it
represents the limits of human endurance it is also pointing to the even
greater power of God's love, which is to work its greatest miracle in the
depths of human pain.

    This, Sabino observes to Juliano, is a new road for a king, and he wonders if any ancient writers on the education of princes understood it, since contemporary kings evidently do not. But the possibility of Gentile prophecy is here discounted; some writers recommended bodily travails, but never those of the spirit. Contemporary monarchs rule for their own self-aggrandizement and will inflict merciless laws and burdens, whereas Christ rules for the sake of his subjects. They never know the affliction and poverty of those they govern: Christ does.[26] No Christian prince has that perfect knowledge which right judgement requires: that is Christ's alone. His subjects, reborn in him as his children, are brothers and sisters of one another, freemen, not vassals, for there are no slaves in the kingdom of God. Earthly kings must make and enforce laws to punish vice, and Sabino feels for them in this, because in God's kingdom all are noble and good through the goodness which created them and with which they are endowed. God rescues us from the death of sin incurred in Adam, and ceaselessly tries to find a way for his love to penetrate our ingratitude, like someone trying to gain entry into a fortified castle by testing all its doors – a simile linked with the picture of the bridegroom covered in dew who seeks to enter the bride's chamber (Song v.2). The effects of such love in the truly Christian soul far outshine the finest virtues of antiquity: 'Y la virtud más heroica, que la filosofía de los estoicos antiguamente . . . soñó . . . comparada con la que Cristo asienta con su gracia en el alma, es una poquedad y bajeza' (592), 'And the most heroic virtue Stoic philosophy ever dreamed of. . . is mean and low compared with that which Christ by his grace establishes in the soul'. That is because Christ has conquered every vain ambition, embraced suffering and death and freed himself from attachment to anything less than heaven.

The study of Christ's kingship concludes with the nature of his new law. Again, Marcelo distinguishes worldly rule from Christ's. Human laws, however well-intentioned, tend to make us want to do what is forbidden, just because it is. Without expounding Paul's detailed criticism of the Mosaic Law, he goes to its heart: the Law was given to make people better, but only compounded their sin. With Paul and most Christian tradition, he understands the root of sin to lie in a disorder of the will. Laws can either teach us or move our will, either consist of rules and regulations, or aim to heal the will and restore right judgement. The Fall so darkened the mind that it no longer knew how to behave, and so destroyed the will that it lost almost its entire capacity to love the good. The law of rules gives the mind correct information, but by failing to affect human motivation leaves man in a worse situation than before; he knows what he ought to do, but cannot find the strength of will to do it. This is the law which commands and forbids, the law of the Old Covenant, bitter and burdensome.

With Christ's perfect and delightful law of grace and love comes the remedy, for we are now enabled to love what is commanded. The difference between these two kinds of law is emphasized by Biblical contrasts – slavery and sonship, a temporary and an eternal law, the letter and the spirit. Christ, by uniting his power and spirit with the human will, achieves the growth and sanctification Mosaic law could not; indeed, its limitations were clearly prophesied (Jer. xxxi.31–4). Christ is therefore truly the king of (i.e. from) God, since all other kingships are partial and perishable and his is eternal. No tyranny or violence by kings or their subjects will last for ever, and they are as alien to Christ, who has compassion on suffering and has himself been the victim of violence, as they are to his subjects, united in a bond of perpetual peace and nobly born of a common Father.

Juliano intervenes to remind Marcelo that he has not yet explained how Scripture distinguishes the kingdoms of this world from the rule of Christ. Marcelo's starting-point is Biblical imagery: winds and wild beasts signify human power; mountains, divine. But he concentrates on Dan. vii and Zech. vi, generally understood as prophesying the four empires of Chaldaea, Persia, Greece and Rome. Where, then, do the Moors and Turks fit in? Sabino asks, raising the question of the relevance of Biblical prophecy to contemporary events. Marcelo explains that some scholars – probably friends and colleagues of Fray Luis, because he is at pains to stress that they are people 'a quien todos amamos y preciamos mucho por la excelencia de sus virtudes y letras' (601), 'whom we all love and greatly esteem for the excellence of their virtues and learning' – regard them as offshoots of the Roman Empire. He disagrees: the Turkish Empire has peoples, laws and government distinct from Rome's. Indeed, if that argument is pressed, there can only ever have been one empire, since one inevitably supersedes another. He is inclined to believe that the Old Testament prophesies the course of history only until the coming of Christ, and that the Turkish Empire, though clearly foreseen in the beast with seven heads and ten horns in the New (Rev. xiii), is therefore not foretold in it. Marcelo cannot here be speaking with the voice of Fray Luis, whom we know believed the Old Testament to have contained prophecies of the New World.[27]

Sabino had asked a second question. Why, if Christ's rule is gentle and pacific, is it foreseen in Psalm ii as a breaking and dashing in pieces of the nations? Marcelo answers by returning to the vision of the statue which crumbled away in Daniel ii, thereby completing the exposition he had begun in 'Monte'. Neither text implies an immediate, literal destruction of the enemies of God. The stone which struck the feet of the statue at the Incarnation began a process which is continued through the preaching and spread of the Gospel until Satan's kingdom is brought down. This exegesis of one text by another demonstrates Fray Luis's christocentric view of history. History moves around the work of Christ and has meaning through him alone. History before his Incarnation, witnessed to notably in the Old Testament, points towards his coming. History afterwards is the working out of what he began, until its consummation.

Marcelo goes on to describe the two complementary manifestations of Christ's kingdom, the personal or individual, and the public or political. In each, conflict and war struggle with peace and victory. Within the believer, the appetites of the flesh rise to attack the indwelling kingdom of Christ, but little by little he conquers, till he reigns in splendour on the throne of the soul. Only at the last resurrection, though, will the struggle cease and the triumphs of peace begin. Then the soul will rule over the body and its faculties be possessed by grace, which 'le dará ser de Dios y la transformará cuasi en Dios' (606), 'will give her the being of God and will transform her almost into God'. The language is a reminder that Fray Luis knew the Christian mystical tradition well; but whereas St John of the Cross will write of transformation in God without qualification, the theologian in Fray Luis, anxious to avoid any suggestion that the individuality of the soul may be swallowed up after death, inserts the cautionary word 'cuasi', 'almost'.[28]

The public manifestation of the kingdom of Christ is envisaged in now familiar terms – idols are dethroned and the Gospel embraces new worlds. If some pagan kingdoms appear to flourish for a while (Marcelo is surely thinking again of the Turks) this is only to perfect the stones of which the Church is built and to provide new tests of faith and opportunities for victory until all is subject to Christ. Then war will yield to life and glory and God will be all in all; humanity will live in obedience to him, and he will provide for their every need. The divine King now assumes another of his names, for he becomes a shepherd who feeds, guides, heals and refreshes his flock. There are many names but only one Christ, and those names which at a human level might appear to belong to different categories, like king and shepherd, are united in him. Marcelo finds pictures of the heavenly kingdom in Isa. lx and lxv and falls silent, only to remark that much else could be said about this name. Then he is silent again with his friends under the starry sky.

Towards the end of 'Braço de Dios' Sabino had referred to the great theatre under which they were sitting and which provided their audience. As 'Rey de Dios' began, Marcelo was moved to respond to this by confessing that he was accustomed 'a hablar en los oídos de las estrellas, con las cuales comunico mis cuidados y mis ansias las más de las noches' (574), 'to speak into the ears of the stars, with whom most nights I communicate my cares and anxieties'; though he believed them to be deaf. There is therefore a gradual build-up to the opening of 'Príncipe de la paz', which evokes the night sky as 'una imagen perfecta de la paz' (613), 'a perfect image of peace'. In his 'Noche serena' ode (VIII) Fray Luis contrasts the truth of heaven seen in the darkness of the sky at night with the folly and blindness of human bondage on earth and calls on mortals to look upward:

> ¡Oh, despertad, mortales!
> ¡mirad con atención en vuestro daño!
> las almas inmortales,
> hechas a bien tamaño,
> ¿podrán vivir de sombras y de engaño?

> Awaken, every mortal!
> Look on the damage done you with reflection!
> Shall souls which are immortal,
> made for such high perfection,
> find sustenance from shadows and deception?

There, everything earthly and material recedes into insignificance in the peace, joy and eternal light of heaven.

This poem needs to be read alongside the beginning of 'Príncipe de la paz', which moves far beyond conventional statements about the beauty, silence or vastness of the night sky, though it is certainly coloured by Pythagorean and neo-Platonic tones. For Marcelo it is a visible representation of the theme he is to explore. Peace (he quotes Augustine) is 'una orden sosegada', 'a tranquil ordering'. In the night sky each star has its exact place in relation to its greater and lesser companions and the whole forms 'una pacífica unidad de virtud', 'a peaceful unity of power'. Its beauty is therefore not simply aesthetic, but moral and spiritual. It is a 'voz . . . sin ruido', 'voice . . . without noise', an undoubted echo of the wordless proclamation by the heavens of the glory of God in Psalm xviii.3. This silent voice passes deep into our souls and begins to order and pacify their confusions, so that they are calmed. As our passions and affections are quieted, reason once more assumes its rightful place as ruler of the soul and remembers its 'primer origen', 'first origin' till it 'pone todo lo que es vil y bajo en su parte, y huella sobre ello' (614), 'puts everything vile and low in its place and tramples it underfoot'. The elements themselves and the brute beasts grow calm and rest after sunset, and every noise is stilled. Peace is the universal good of all things and wherever it is seen it is loved. Our whole life's endeavour is to reach it, though many go astray and choose mistaken goals.[29]

Marcelo's exposition proposes a far-reaching meaning to a word we usually understand negatively as an absence of conflict. He sees peace as a universal striving after fulfilment, inherent in the entire creation; it is a way of describing our whole manner of living; and its image is in the night sky. It is a concept deeply influenced by Fray Luis's reading of the Hebrew Old Testament and its concept of *shalom*. Marcelo's thesis is that the only true source of peace is Jesus Christ, its author and prince.

At Sabino's prompting, he reminds his friends that peace is composed of two essential elements: repose and order. Order requires each element of human society, and indeed of creation, to play its divinely appointed part and to fulfil its particular obligations. The high and the lowly must occupy their given places and perform their distinctive 'offices'. Everything therefore exists in a state of mutual obligation and is bound together. Order without repose does not bring peace, for all struggle to break free of their bounds and everything becomes chaotic and disordered, an idea powerfully dramatized by Calderón in his *autos sacramentales*, *La vida es sueño*, in which the four elements, air, fire, earth and water, are seen fighting among themselves for mastery before creation, and *El gran teatro del mundo*, where some of the characters refuse to accept their lot or else misuse what they have been given.[30] Similarly, repose without order brings complacency and tends towards evil.

Peace, as the summary of the Law which Christ gives makes clear, affects relationships with the self, the neighbour and God. For peace in the soul, reason must command the senses, not reluctantly, but gladly. For peace with neighbours, the rights of others must be respected and duties performed; this would end strife and war in human communities and the domination of passion and desire in the self. This merits a longer reflection in praise of reason governing our inconstant appetites, for which the favourite metaphor of the stormy sea is used. Peace with God is vital, since the Bible describes only too clearly the consequences of his anger. One of the examples of this comes from our 'common friend', the author, whose verse translation of Job xix.8–11 is quoted in illustration. These three aspects of peace are interrelated and lead to a life of harmony with God and friendship with all people.

Marcelo now passes to Christ's work as the true author of peace and introduces a critique of the claims of other philosophies and religions. Their basic mistake is to assume that our disorder is the result of ignorance, and that if only we had the correct knowledge all would be well. The ancient philosophers and the Old Testament both fell into this error. Others, like Indian and pagan philosophers, thought that the answer lay in a correct diet, because they believed that violent movements of the flesh and blood caused human disorder – a view by no means unknown today. But neither the right food nor the correct knowledge is sufficient to bring peace to the soul. Marcelo, interestingly, argues for the truth of Christianity not from specific Biblical texts but because of its analysis of the human condition, and he passes beyond the conventional bounds of contemporary discussion by introducing Hinduism into the argument.

He is certain that Christianity offers the true diagnosis and cure of human disorder. The Fall damaged both body and soul. The soul is the seat of the will as well as of reason; and it is the damage done to our will which is at the root of all subsequent evil. Adam sinned not through sensual disorder or ignorance but because once the door of his will was opened the spirit of the Devil took up residence there and brought disorder to his senses and blindness to his reason. Thus to attend solely to reason or the body is to misunderstand the disease and propose remedies which fall far short of our true health, Christ, whose grace can cure the sickness of the will. Otherwise, the problems only worsen: the Law reveals sin but fails to cure it, and Plato himself taught that ignorance was often better than knowledge for a damaged will.

Marcelo turns to the setting again to show the nature and work of grace as the bringer of inward and outward peace. He points to the reflection of the night sky in the calm water before them which bears a clear image of the heavens yet retains its own substance. When we receive grace it is in such a way. Grace is 'una como figura viva del mismo Cristo, que puesta en el alma, se lanza en ella y la deifica, y . . . es el alma del alma' (628), 'as a living figure of Christ himself, which, having entered our soul penetrates and deifies it and is . . . the soul of our soul'. The soul can now reach her true stature and become more and more like God, till we pass from being creatures to adoption as his children. The first work of grace in the soul is to incline the will towards loving the good, so that at last the desired fruit of peace is tasted. It puts an end to the fear of God's anger and thus brings peace with him; it reconciles reason and will and so calms the turmoil of the senses; it assures us of God's favour; and it brings joy. This last fruit of peace Marcelo derives from a long passage of St John Chrysostom's exposition of the fourth psalm, introduced with the words 'si bien me acuerdo' (633), 'if I remember well'. Fray Luis hoped to familiarize his readers with the Fathers as well as Scripture; but because this is supposed to be a dialogue certain conventions must be obeyed. He has to pretend that Marcelo is recalling what in a theological treatise could simply be quoted, just as he has to pretend many other things to make the artificiality of the form appear more natural.

But Juliano is not yet satisfied. He wants to add that only with Christ can we possess peace, and engages in a lively and fast-moving dialogue with Sabino, which centres on the true nature of happiness. The love we direct towards our desired end can issue in happiness or misery, depending on the nature of that end. Love is wrongly used if it is directed towards what is mutable; hence Christ alone is worthy of our love, because he never changes and never breaks the unity of love which binds him to his own. He is the only true and fertile ground of love and only from him do good fruits come. Not even when the flower of Sabino's youth fades and old age and weakness afflict him will Christ's love for him weaken or grow old, and at the end he will be renewed as the eagle, clothed in immortality and divine gifts and completely united with Christ his true spouse (the cue for the next name). Marcelo, in mock humility, suggests that Juliano should expound this as he has already begun, but turns instead to kneel on the ground in silent invocation as he prepares to continue.

He announces at once the threefold structure of 'Esposo': the intimate union between Christ and his Church, its sweet and delightful effects, and the way in which it occurs. The name is a sign of the marvellous tenderness with which Christ treats us, for it signifies the closest of all ties, in comparison with which even the physical union of husband and wife is cold, because it joins only bodies, not spirits.

First, the soul of the just person becomes one with the soul and divinity of Christ, who imprints upon it his likeness, human and divine, so that it seems to be another Christ – similar language to that used in the previous name about the deification of the human soul. The image Marcelo uses for this imprinting of Christ's likeness is that of a fire, the flames of which reach up to heaven; for such is his power working within us. It is appropriate, because it is the Holy Spirit, the Pentecostal flame, which brings about this union. Second, this intimate union brings the historical miracle of the Incarnation into Christian experience through the Mass:

Porque, demás de que tomó nuestra carne en la naturaleza de su humanidad, y la ayuntó con su persona divina con ayuntamiento tan firme que no será suelto jamás, el cual ayuntamiento es . . . un matrimonio indisoluble, celebrado entre nuestra carne y el Verbo, y el tálamo donde se celebró fue . . . el vientre purísimo, así . . . también esta misma carne y cuerpo suyo, que tomó de nosotros, lo ayunta con el cuerpo de su Iglesia y con todos los miembros de ella, que debidamente le reciben en el Sacramento del altar, allegando su carne a la carne de ellos, y haciéndola, cuanto es posible, con la suya una misma.   (651–2)

For apart from having taken our flesh in the nature of his humanity and united it with his divine person with a bond so firm that it will never be broken, a bond which is . . . an indissoluble marriage celebrated between our flesh and the Word, the marriage bed where it was celebrated being . . . the purest womb, so . . . also he joins his very flesh and body, taken from us, to the body of his Church and all its members who duly receive him in the Sacrament of the altar, by bringing his flesh to theirs and making it as far as possible one with his.

Marcelo and Juliano give a long list of Patristic authorities to support this view, and one can only presume that it was controversial; more, perhaps, to do with the fact that the meaning of the sacrament and the doctrine of transubstantiation was being expounded in Spanish than with the need to challenge Protestant theology. For Marcelo also provides an unusual number of similes to illustrate this union. The first is a commonplace of mystical literature, the others are rather more unusual. Iron put into fire becomes fire, not because it is fire by substance, but because it becomes so by assuming the qualities of fire; we are reminded of the earlier image of the night sky reflected in the water, which similarly retains its substance. So our bodies remain our own but take on qualities Christ gives them. A republic unites a vast diversity of people by one law and the protection of one wall; how much more appropriate to speak of the union of Christ's flesh and ours, which are much more closely related. A perfumed glove leaves its fragrance on the hand that wears it even briefly; so Christ's body communicates his power to our flesh. The cool breeze which now refreshes them had not long before blown with the heat of the day.

For a moment, Marcelo returns to the forbidden fruit which, once tasted, brought poison to the human race ('Padre del siglo futuro'), to show how the eating of Christ's body is the medicine which brings healing and life: 'Aquel fruto atoxicó nuestro cuerpo, con que viene a la muerte; esta carne, comida, enriquézcanos así con su gracia, que aun descienda su tesoro a la carne' (656), 'That fruit poisoned our body, so that it comes to die; let this flesh, once eaten, so enrich us with its grace that its treasure descend still to the flesh'. Again, Patristic quotations reinforce the argument. Marcelo continues with the work of love in causing unity. The higher the love, the greater the union; our union in Christ's body and soul is the highest and greatest of all. A cloud through which the sun is shining becomes penetrated by light; and so Christ bursts forth through the eyes and mouth and senses of the faithful soul, so that its every act is his. This is a bond closer than nature or art can make; and in a series of lyrical antitheses Marcelo contrasts the union of physical marriage with the incomparably greater union with Christ, which brings deification of body and soul and identity of willing and loving.

We pass to the delights this union brings. The proof of its immeasurable greatness is that it is beyond the power of human words. The tongue falls silent; all the soul's strength is employed in enjoying it; all physical activity is suspended, as if in a swoon. In this delight, everything we will or do is free of obstacles and conforms to the nature and desire of the particular faculty. Its cause is 'la presencia, y . . . el abrazo del bien deseado' (661–2), 'the presence and . . . the embrace of the desired good', and its sources are fourfold – knowing and feeling in the mind, action by which the desired end is obtained, the good in itself, and the permanent indwelling of God in the soul. Through each of these, Marcelo develops a contrast between desire for things earthly and heavenly. For example, in a passage reminiscent of Augustine's famous 'Our hearts are restless till they find their rest in thee', he argues that since the true end of man is the vision of God, nothing less will bring him what he seeks: 'Sois el deseo del alma, el único paradero de nuestra vida, el propio y solo bien nuestro, para cuya posesión somos criados, y en quien sólo hallamos descanso, y a quien, aun sin conoceros, buscamos en todo cuanto hacemos' (664), 'You are our soul's desire, the only resting-place of our life, our true and only good, for whose possession we are created, and in whom alone we find rest, and whom we seek, even without knowing you, in all that we do'. Unlike bodily delights, those which God gives are not subject to diminution and impurity. They are not like water in a glass, limited and enclosed, but like the waters of a river, constantly replenished from their source.

When God so embraces our soul, 'penetra por ella todo, y se lanza a sí mismo por todos sus apartados secretos hasta ayuntarse con su más íntimo ser' (666), 'he completely penetrates it and himself passes through all its secret hidden places till he joins himself to its most intimate being'. This happens suddenly, without the foreplay of human love, and because it cannot be expressed directly, Scripture has many images for it – hidden manna, wine-cellar, breasts, table and banquet, sleep, white stone, intoxication, swoon, ecstasy. Its effects are described in similarly mystical terms, like the oxymoron of 'violencia dulce'(668), 'sweet violence', but also more practically, in the lives of martyrs and hermits. One simile, however, is worked out at greater length, the ancient one of green timber set on fire, producing first smoke and cracklings until all the dampness is expelled and the fire transforms the wood into itself:

Y acontécele. . . al alma con Dios, como al madero no bien seco, cuando se le avecina el fuego, le aviene. El cual, así como se va calentando del fuego y recibiendo en sí su calor, así se va haciendo sujeto apto y dispuesto para recibir más calor, y lo recibe de hecho. Con el cual calentado, comienza primero a despedir humo de sí, y a dar cuando en cuando algún estallido; y corren algunas veces gotas de agua por él; y procediendo en esta contienda y tomando por momentos el fuego en él mayor fuerza, el humo que salía se enciende de improviso en llama que luego se acaba; y dende a poco se torna a encender otra vez, y a apagarse también; y así hace la tercera y la cuarta, hasta que al fin el fuego, ya lanzado en lo íntimo del madero y hecho señor de todo él, sale todo junto y por todas partes afuera levantando sus llamas, las cuales, prestas y poderosas y a la redonda bullendo, hacen parecer un fuego el madero.   (669–70)

And it happens . . . to the soul with God as to timber not quite dry when it is brought to the fire. As it grows hotter from the fire and receives its heat into itself, it becomes the fitter and the readier to receive greater heat, and indeed it does. With this heating, it first begins to emit smoke, and to crackle from time to time; and sometimes drops of water run out of it; and as it continues in this struggle and as the fire gains greater power over it, the rising smoke suddenly bursts into a flame, which at once dies away; and is quickly rekindled and likewise extinguished; and so a third and a fourth time, until at last the fire, penetrating deep into the wood and mastering it wholly, bursts out all together and everywhere lifts high its flames, which speedily and powerfully, roaring all around, make the wood seem one fire.

So human tears and sighings – the drops of water and the smoke, like those of Christ on fire with love in Robert Southwell's poem 'The Burning Babe' – yield to an experience of union, of total possession by God:

hasta que [el alma], sujeta ya del todo al dulzor, se traspasa del todo, y levantada enteramente sobre sí misma y no cabiendo en sí misma, espira amor y terneza y derretimiento por todas sus partes, y no entiende ni dice otra cosa si no es: *¡Luz, amor, vida, descanso sumo, belleza infinita, bien inmenso y dulcísimo, dame que me deshaga yo, y que me convierta en Ti toda, Señor!*   (670)

until the soul, subject completely to the sweetness, completely transported, and wholly lifted above herself and no longer contained within herself, breathes forth love and tenderness and melting away in her every part, and neither speaks nor understands anything save: *light, love, life, supreme rest, infinite beauty, immense and sweetest good, let me be utterly undone and converted wholly into you, o Lord!*

This is the most mystical passage in the *Nombres*, and Marcelo's silence the only adequate response. The rest of 'Esposo' follows a familiar track, as Marcelo briefly expounds the allegorical and mystical meaning of the Song, and Sabino recites Fray Luis's translation of Psalm xliv, a hymn to the mystical marriage. Night is far advanced, and the friends return home.

The writing has been as ardent as the theme. Once more, Fray Luis has used the language of Christian mysticism and its greatest source, the Song of Songs. His images – iron or wood in the fire, the ever-flowing river – point to a transformation for which he yearns but has not yet achieved, since for him it lies beyond death. It is the same yearning that we shall see in his most mystical poem, 'Alma región luciente' (xviii), where he longs for Christ to descend into his senses so that he may be converted wholly into Love.[31] The verbal parallels are striking – 'y que me convierta en Ti toda, Señor', and 'y toda en ti, oh Amor, la convirtiese' – the more so because the different objects of address, the Lord and Love, are in reality one and the same.

The third book

The discourses of the first two books of the *Nombres* had spanned a complete day, from dawn to nightfall; so the third book, though it did not appear until two years after the first edition, takes place the following day, the feast of St Paul. Sabino has risen very early and, meeting Juliano, wonders why the name Jesus was not on the paper. From this delightful and natural introduction, with its human and humorous touches, we learn that Marcelo will remedy the omission after Juliano has expounded a name of his choice.[32]

Juliano presents the fruits of his pensiveness in 'Hijo de Dios', the longest and most theologically developed of all the names. He outlines some of the texts which apply it to Christ, notably Psalm lxxi.17, supported by Heb. i.4–5, Psalm ii.7, Isa. i.2 and Hos. xi.1. The first section, establishing why this name is proper to Christ, is divided into the meaning of sonship and how it is demonstrated in Christ; the second, setting out what God teaches us through it, describes the five ways in which we can understand the birth of Christ, and forms the substantive part of the exposition.

It is to images and metaphors that Juliano, like Marcelo, first turns. Sons are like the portraits painters make of an original. They are formed from the substance and inherit the nature and likeness of the one who engenders them. In the realm of nature, some beings are temporal; and others eternal. The former reproduce through their offspring; the latter in such a way that their origin finds visible reflection: the sun does not perish, but sends forth its rays so that we can perceive it. Sonship requires four elements: a father's substance, likeness to him in every way, a birth in which this is made visible, and the ability to substitute for the father when the father dies. Perhaps because we sense the genetic or astronomical flaws in the argument, the analogies cannot have the same force for us; but they are a good example of the way in which the chosen images actually control its direction. For Juliano wants to conclude that only in Christ are all these essentials present. In his divinity he is of the Father's substance; in his humanity, of ours, made in the divine likeness. He alone reveals the eternal Father, as the ray reveals the sun; he obeys him even to the Cross, where as man laden with humanity's sins he does what God cannot do, which is to die.

Juliano now outlines the five births of Christ: his divine begetting of the Father, his human birth of Mary, his rebirth in resurrection, his birth in the sacred Host and his birth in us. They have all appeared in previous dialogues; now they are brought together, as the birth of the Son is shifted away from any narrow concentration on the Christmas story to enfold the whole history of salvation, past, present and to come, in its personal and its cosmic dimensions.

Juliano begins with an objection. Jews and Muslims regard God as so entirely perfect that he has no need to engender a Son. But, he says, sterility is a form of weakness and poverty, whereas God, fertile and rich above all else, cannot but give of himself in an overflow of his being. It is a curiously anthropomorphic answer, of Platonic ancestry, but one still widely held in the sixteenth century. Out of his infinite fertility comes the infinite perfection of the Son, to whom God is as both father and mother.[33] This Son, unlike human sons, who partly resemble and partly differ from their fathers, is the complete likeness of his Father. His engendering has no beginning or end, since temporality is a limitation; it is completely pure, without admixture of passion. One of the texts quoted (Micah v.2) introduces the ancient symbol of the fountain ceaselessly flowing, hymned by St John of the Cross in his beautiful 'Que bien sé yo la fonte' ('How well I know the fountain'). Juliano describes this birth 'como un manar de una fuente, y como una luz que sale con suavidad del cuerpo que luce, y como un olor que, sin alterarse, espiran de sí las rosas' (703), 'like a flowing of a fountain, and like a light softly emanating from a shining body, and like a scent which roses, without changing, give forth from themselves'. It proceeds from the all-seeing, all-understanding mind of God and is a painting of that mind from within it – he brings us back to the image of sonship he drew at the start of the name. Only thereafter do the creatures appear, as a later picture, which in comparison with the first are 'como sombras obscuras . . . y como cosas muertas en comparación de la vida' (704), 'as dark shadows . . . and as things dead in comparison with life'. The Father paints the living image of himself in the Logos, a Son by excellence, through whom all else came and comes to be. Juliano expounds some of the more notable Pauline texts (e.g. Col. i.15–16) to give Scriptural grounding to his teaching.

Having plunged deep into Trinitarian theology, he has to make some account of the Godhead of the Holy Spirit. The Spirit is not divine by image and likeness to the Father, but 'como inclinación a El y como abrazo suyo' (707), 'as inclination to Him and as his embrace'. He uses a human analogy, like Augustine's argument from human personality in his *De Trinitate*: I can understand myself, love myself when I have understood, and be drawn towards this image of myself which my understanding has formed by this love. So the Father engenders the image of himself, and, loving himself and embracing all he understands in himself, produces this inclination towards, this embrace of all that he loves. With me, such images and inclinations are lifeless, merely ideas; but in the life of God they have a complete reality, three circles of light, distinctly, ineffably resplendent within one light. In a series of similes based on the light of the sun but gathering up several of the images already used, Juliano shows how, for example, we can see God in all that he has made but would be blinded if we gazed upon him, just as the sun lights everything up but its own light dazzles us. So it is that God can be said to be 'claro y obscuro, oculto y manifiesto' (708), 'bright and dark, hidden and manifest'. Like the sun, the Father is a fountain of light; like the sun's rays, the Son is a perfect, living portrait which streams eternally from the Father.

The second birth, as flesh from Mary, moves from orthodox Western Trinitarianism to orthodox christology. Juliano outlines how the Logos took flesh without forfeiting his divinity, becoming one person with two distinct natures, a perfect unfallen human nature and the nature of God. He uses a set of traditional paradoxes:

En un instante solo salió en el tálamo de la Virgen a la luz de esta vida un Hombre Dios, un niño ancianísimo, una suma santidad en miembros tiernos de infante, un saber perfecto en un cuerpo que aun hablar no sabía; y resultó en un punto, con milagro nunca visto, un niño y gigante, un flaco muy fuerte; un saber, un poder, un valor no vencible, cercado de desnudez y de lágrimas.

. . . Y vimos una mezcla admirable; carne con condiciones de Dios, y Dios con condiciones de carne; y divinidad y humanidad juntas; y hombre y Dios, nacido de Padre y de Madre, y sin padre y sin madre; sin madre en el cielo, y sin padre en la tierra; y, finalmente, vimos junta en uno la universidad de lo no criado y criado.   (713)

In one single instant there came forth on the marriage-bed of the Virgin into the light of this life a Man God, a very ancient child, the sum of holiness in the tender limbs of an infant, a perfect knowledge in a body which as yet could not speak; and in one moment there resulted, in a miracle never before seen, a child and a giant, weak and very strong; a knowledge, a power and an invincible valour surrounded by nakedness and tears.

. . . And we beheld a wondrous mixing; flesh with the condition of God and God with the condition of flesh; and divinity and humanity joined; and man and God, born of a Father and Mother, and without a father and mother; without a mother in heaven, and without a father on earth; and finally, we beheld joined in one the universality of the uncreated and the created.

The paradoxes are not, of course, merely decorative; they attempt to communicate in a startling way the christological paradox of the two natures in the one Christ, a doctrine which cannot be captured by human reason and is expressible therefore only in a language which appears to contradict it.

The Logos, Juliano now states, appeared to men long before the Incarnation, and, following a long Patristic tradition, looks back into the Old Testament to show how he conversed with Adam in Eden and later with Abraham, Jacob, Moses and Joshua. Allegorical exegesis yields Juliano a rich harvest of Biblical images for the union of God and man in Christ. The Ark of the Covenant was made of wood and finest gold; one ark, out of two different materials. When Moses was given the Law there was fire and glory on the summit of Sinai and smoke and thick darkness at the foot:

así Cristo naciendo hombre, que es *Monte*, en lo alto de su alma ardía todo en llamas de amor, y gozaba de la gloria de Dios alegre y descansadamente; mas en la parte suya más baja temblaba y humeaba, dando lugar en sí a las penalidades del hombre. (716)

so Christ, who is *Mountain*, being born as man, burned wholly in flames of love and enjoyed the glory of God gladly and peaceably in the higher part of his soul; but in his lower part he trembled and smoked, making room in himself for the travails of man.

Jacob's ladder, the crossing of the Jordan, the Lamb that was slain and the four horsemen of the Apocalypse provide further examples, and this second birth ends with a passage from St Basil and a series of parallel sentences from Juliano which show how the taking of our flesh by the Logos heals it and redeems it from its enslavement to sin.

As in the Virgin's womb the Logos was clothed with flesh, so in the womb of the grave, at Christ's third birth, God restored him to life, glorified and free of the hold of death, which was destroyed by his power: 'Y renació el muerto, más vivo que nunca, hecho vida, hecho luz, hecho gloria; y salió del sepulcro como quien sale del vientre, vivo y para vivir para siempre, poniendo espanto a la naturaleza con ejemplo no visto' (720), 'And the dead man was born again, more alive than ever, having become life, having become light, having become glory; and he came forth from the grave as one who comes forth from the womb, alive and to live for ever, confounding nature with an example never before seen'. In his human birth he had been subject to human needs and limitations, but in the Resurrection all is supernatural, for no natural power can turn ice to heat and bring fullness where emptiness reigned. A text Marcelo had earlier used to describe the Incarnation (Psalm cix.3) Juliano now applies to the

Resurrection. He fixes on the word 'resplandores' (AV Psalm cx, 'beauties') – the splendours of the divine and glorified body and soul of the risen Christ. By this birth many others are brought to birth, for he descended into hell to restore the spirits of the just who languished there, and he unites to his glorified body the mortal flesh of those who belong to him:

Así que no nació un rayo solo la mañana que amaneció del sepulcro este sol; mas nacieron en él una muchedumbre de rayos y un amontonamiento de resplandores santísimos, y la vida, y la luz, y la reparación de todas las cosas, a las cuales todas abrazó consigo, muriendo, para sacarlas, resucitando todas vivas en sí. Por donde aquel día fue de común alegría, porque fue día de nacimiento común.   (723)

Thus on the morning when this sun dawned from the grave there was born not one single ray; but from him were born a multitude of rays and an accumulation of holiest splendours, and life and light and the restoration of all things, all of which he, dying, embraced to himself to ransom them, all rising alive in him. Hence that was a day of general rejoicing, because it was a day of general birth.

Yet the wonder is greater still. Christ, so gloriously born in the light of his Resurrection, is born daily in the disguise of the sacred Host, the womb of his fourth birth, called into being by the power of the words of consecration uttered by the priest. The Scriptural proof seems rather indirect: behind the word translated 'firmness' in Psalm lxxi.16 Juliano detects a Hebrew word which includes *bar*, 'son'. It is worth pausing to note the series of verbal connections which have brought us to this point, because they reveal clearly a train of thought natural to Fray Luis but certainly not to us. The womb of the Virgin has become a metaphor for two further lodgings of Christ – the tomb and the Host, both of which, like Mary's womb, are places from which this hidden Son is born. 'Firmness', which we are told is a Scriptural metaphor for wheat, contains in the original text a syllable which means 'son'; a son born in the bread made out of wheat. Until we can sense this, we cannot follow the logic of an argument which ends: 'será el *Hijo* lo que parecerá un limpio y pequeño trigo, porque saldrá a luz en figura de él y le veremos así hecho y amoldado, como si fuese un panecito pequeño' (724), 'the *Son* will seem a simple, small grain, because he will come to light in its figure and we shall see him so made and fashioned, as if he were a little piece of bread'. Through these connections, this birth is the more closely linked with the previous ones: the generation of the Word, and here the word which consecrates; the

Resurrection to glorified flesh, and here the real presence of the flesh of Christ; the poor and humble issuing of the babe from the Virgin's womb, and here the smallness and ordinariness of bread which conceals the treasures of heaven. By eating Christ's flesh, ours is purified:

Apaga el fuego vicioso y pone a cuchillo a nuestra vejez y arranca de raíces el mal y nos comunica su ser y su vida, y, comiéndole nosotros, nos come El a nosotros y nos viste de sus cualidades.   (726)

He puts out the fire of vice, he cuts out our old life, he tears up evil by its roots and gives to us his life and being; and as we eat him, so he eats us and clothes us in his qualities.

The language is strong and vivid; the final, bold paradox suggests that our physical eating of the Host brings about Christ's spiritual consuming of all that is unlike him in us. This food recapitulates all his other great acts; for not content with having been born and put to death, and having risen and ascended for our sakes his presence here enables us to take him into our lives. Born in us under the figure of wheat, made fruitful by the warmth of the Spirit, so he is reborn within us in his fifth and final birth.

Sabino wants to know what the difference is between our being born in Christ and his being born in us. Juliano agrees that they are connected, but sees a distinction, as between a swift but brief rapture and Christ's quiet, continual presence working deep within the soul to remake us according to his likeness. He is born within us at the moment of our repentance, when he enters our soul, is there established and makes it beautiful. At first he is born in us as a child, adjusted to our infant capacities, and he grows as we grow in grace towards our proper perfection. This growth, from birth and childhood through increasing to complete perfection, linked with the three traditional ways of the mystical journey, is seen as a process of Christ's life spreading from the higher to the lower parts of the soul and into the whole body and soul; a process of sanctification. For the soul, as in standard scholastic theology, has a higher part which looks heavenward and a lower earthward, and they war like Jacob and Esau among themselves. Christ comes first to the former, to enlighten and strengthen it, so that it can help the lower, which often experiences 'contradicción y agonía y servidumbre y trabajo' (732), 'contradiction and agony and servitude and travail'. Moses is the figure of this: he converses with God on Sinai and his face shines; but he descends to find the people rebellious, and their sufferings in the wilderness must teach them the necessary obedience. It is a different interpretation of the event from that given in the second birth, where Moses's descent was a type of the Logos assuming the lowliness of humanity.

In the next stage, of grace, Christ overcomes the rebellions of the lower soul and is enthroned there. God's will is done on earth (this lower part) as in heaven (the higher). Jacob and Esau are reconciled, reason and the senses co-operate; Christ commands the soul's fortress and extends his pacific reign, till the final perfecting of body and soul. Juliano finds several Biblical pictures of this blessed state, and notes that the five births correspond with the five Hebrew words for 'son' used in Scripture, each of which he explains. It is at this point that the episode of the little bird so dramatically intervenes, to conclude 'Hijo de Dios'.[34]

Next in sequence, though not in order of publication, comes 'Cordero', which, since it is given Christ by John the Baptist, needs no proofs. This name, for which Marcelo is once again the commentator, has three main sections; the meekness of the Lamb's condition, his pure and innocent life, and his sacrificial self-offering.

Christ's meekness is first seen in his gentle dealings with others, above all with sinners, like the woman taken in adultery; although Scripture does portray him as castigating people. This, Marcelo maintains, was done without passion or anger, but Sabino thinks that at least one saying – the cursing of the goats in Matt. xxv.41 – surely inspires terror. Marcelo agrees that Christ's voice there is terrible to the wicked, but that in himself he remained meek. Sabino is also worried about the name 'Lion', ascribed to Christ in the Apocalypse. This, says Marcelo, is not a contradiction of 'Lamb' but complements it. Christ is a Lion when he defends us against our enemies; no one dare snatch his own from his grasp. He has overthrown the usurped tyranny of the demons and descended to their dark realms to break open their prisons. So Christ is a Lion to us precisely because he is first the loving and meek Lamb, meek towards us, implacable towards his enemies. There follows a eulogy of his sufferings for us, borne with exemplary patience. Like the sacrificial lamb of old, he was torn to pieces:

Porque no hubo cosa en nuestra Bien adonde no llegase el cuchillo y el diente: al costado, a los pies, a los manos, a la sagrada cabeza, a los oídos, y a los ojos, y a la boca con gusto amarguísima; y pasó a las entrañas el mal, y afligió por mil maneras su ánima santa, y le tragó con la honra la vida . . .

Siempre le espinamos nosotros, y siempre El trabaja por traernos a fruto.
                                                            (810–11)

For there was no part of our Good which knife and tooth did not reach: his
side, his feet, his hands, his sacred head, his ears, his eyes, and his mouth, with
bitterest taste; and the evil passed into his heart, and afflicted his holy soul in a
thousand ways, and swallowed up his life with his honour . . .
We ever crown him with thorns, and he ever works to bring us to fruition.

Such sanctity or purity as the creatures possess is a fragment of
Christ, the abyss and fount of all purity and innocence, the second
characteristic of this Lamb. Sinless from the beginning, Christ becomes the means of liberating us from our sin, as our wrongful desires
are healed by his perfect will. He is the universal principle of sanctity
and virtue, source of whatever the creatures have of either, and the
sufficient sacrifice for the sins of this world and of all other worlds.
Whether this means other spiritual realms (e.g. the angelic world, or
St Paul's 'principalities and powers'), future generations or worlds as
yet not created is not clear; if the latter, it is a surprising thought for the
sixteenth century, but wholly consonant with the universality of
Christ as Fray Luis, following Paul, perceives it. He certainly does not
envisage salvation as for humanity alone, for, following Aristotelian
and Thomist tradition, he believes that all created objects, inanimate
and animate, have souls proper to their being (819).

Christ's perfection is found in his body and soul and in their
conjunction. His body was altogether excellent and beautiful, since it
came of the pure, undefiled substance of the Virgin. Juliano sees all the
rites of the Mosaic law as a crucible in which was distilled the purest of
physical bodies. He apparently believes that the Incarnation must
reveal physical human perfection as well as spiritual. Mary's virginal
blood gave Christ physical life, her milk nourished him; yet, in a
remarkable conceit, it is she who, by contemplating her infant son,
receives divine life: 'Y como se encontraban por los ojos las dos almas
bellísimas, y se trocaban los espíritus, que hacen paso por ellos, con los
del Hijo, deificada la Madre más, daba al Hijo más deificada su leche'
(817), 'And as these two most beautiful souls met one another through
the eyes, and their spirits, which find passage through them, were
exchanged, the Mother, more deified with the Son's, gave the Son
more deified her milk'. Christ's soul, as the perfect image of God,
'contiene lo bueno todo, lo perfecto, lo hermoso, lo excelente y lo
heroico, lo admirable y divino' (821), 'contains all the good, the
perfect, the lovely, the excellent, the heroic, the wondrous and the

divine'. It is a fountain which 'tiene manantiales tan no agotables y ricos, que en infinitos hombres más y en infinitos mundos que hubiese, podría derramar en todas excelencia de virtud y justicia, como un abismo verdadero de bien'(820), 'has springs so inexhaustible and rich that it could pour down upon whatever infinite numbers of men and infinite worlds there might be the excellence of virtue and justice, as a true abyss of good'. The images pile up: the union of his humanity to the Word is so intimate that it is like iron heated in a forge till it is indistinguishable from the glowing coals around it; his soul is 'un dechado de aquella suma bondad, y un sol encendido y lleno de aquel Sol de justicia, y una luz de luz, y un resplandor de resplandor, y un piélago de bellezas cebado de un abismo bellísimo' (822), 'a model of that highest goodness, a burning sun filled with that Sun of justice, a light from light, a splendour from splendour, and a sea of beauties fed by a most beauteous abyss'.

Then, as if to drive home the shock of the Passion, Marcelo brings us down from these heights to the Lamb who suffers death on the Cross he ascends to bring us life. His atonement theology follows Paul's closely. It was not enough for another to die in our place; rather, we ourselves have to die, grafted into one so completely just that as he dies bearing our sins so our sins are put to death. He has the suffering; we, the forgiveness: 'como acaece a los árboles que son sin fruto en el suelo do nacen, y transplantados de él fructifican, así nosotros, traspasados en Cristo, morimos sin pena y fuénos fructuosa la muerte', 'as happens to trees barren in their own soil but fruitful when transplanted, so we, transported into Christ died without pain and death was fruitful to us.' For a soul pure and free of sin, the agony and torment of the enormity of human transgression through the ages was unbearable, worse than any physical suffering:

Y subido y enclavado en ella [la cruz], no le rasgaban tanto, ni lastimaban sus tiernas carnes los clavos, cuanto le traspasaban con pena el corazón la muchedumbre de malvados y de maldades, que ayuntados consigo y sobre sus hombros tenía; y le era menos tormento el desatarse de su cuerpo, que el ayuntarse en el mismo templo de la santidad tanta y tan grande torpeza. A la cual por una parte su santa ánima la abrazaba y recogía en sí, para deshacerla por el infinito amor que nos tiene; y por otra parte esquivaba y rehuía su vecindad y su vista movido de su infinita limpieza; y así peleaba y agonizaba y ardía como sacrificio aceptísimo, y en el fuego de su pena consumía eso mismo que con su vecindad le penaba . . . De suerte que, ardiendo El, ardieron en El nuestras culpas . . . y muriendo el *Cordero*, todos que estaban en El . . . pagaron lo que el rigor de la ley requería. Que como fue justo que la comida de Adán, porque en sí nos tenía, fuese comida nuestra, y que su pecado fuese nuestro pecado y que, emponzoñándose él, nos emponzoñásemos todos, así fue justísimo que ardiendo en la ara de la cruz y sacrificándose este dulce *Cordero*, en quien estaban encerrados y como hechos uno todos los suyos . . . quedasen abrasados todos y limpios.   (824–5)

Having ascended and been nailed to it [the Cross], the nails did not tear him nor wound his tender flesh as much as his heart was pierced with pain by the multitude of evil men and deeds which united to himself he bore upon his shoulders; and the dissolution of his body was less torment to him than the joining to the temple of holiness itself so much and so great a baseness. On the one hand his holy soul embraced and took this to itself, to undo it by the infinite love he bears us; and on the other it shunned and fled its proximity and sight, moved by its own infinite integrity; and thus he fought and agonized and burned as a most acceptable sacrifice, and in the fire of his suffering he consumed the very fire which by its proximity afflicted him . . . So that as he burned, so our sins burned in him . . . and in the death of this *Lamb* all who were in him . . . paid what the rigour of the law demanded. For as it was just that Adam's food, because he had us in him, should be our food and his sin our sin, so that when he was poisoned we should all be poisoned, so it was supremely just that all his own, enclosed and united in this sweet *Lamb*, should have been consumed and cleansed as he burned upon the altar of the Cross and sacrificed himself.

The images of fire and poison, first noted in 'Padre del siglo futuro', here reach their climax. Beginning as metaphors for Satan's work and Adam's sin, they have spread to become the whole of human transgression, present in every human life. But now their focus is once more individual, for all the power they represent, Satan's and all the power derived from him, is concentrated on this single man who hangs on the Cross. He bears their full force for those who through the waters of baptism into him will find the antidote to poison and through the purifying fire be made like him. Once again, as in 'Rey de Dios', we are given a picture of the Crucifixion which is powerful and compelling, even shocking, yet which is constructed with great beauty. But this time it goes further, for through Marcelo Fray Luis is making his most eloquent statement of the meaning of Christ's sacrifice. Christ may well have come if Adam had not sinned; but Adam did sin, and Christ's coming therefore had to be in such a way that it could enter the darkness and the suffering which that sin began, and take it to himself that the light might shine for ever. Whatever view we may take of Fray Luis's Scotist preference, we cannot now presume that it led him to see Calvary as other than central to the drama of salvation.

The penultimate name, 'Amado', like 'Esposo', comes from the

Song of Songs, and it is a hymn to this Lamb, who was and is and always will be most beloved of all. The connection with 'Cordero' is clear from the last of Marcelo's texts – the Beloved is the Lamb slain from the foundation of the world (Rev. xiii.8). This Lamb is the true sacrifice of which all other sacrifices were but figures, 'porque todos ellos eran imagen del único y grande sacrificio de este nuestro Cordero' (749), 'because all were an image of the one great sacrifice of this our Lamb'. He is Beloved or Desired because all sacrifices, from the beginning of time, were a desire for God, a looking for Christ. Aristotle tells us to have few friends, because friendship is so precious a commodity; but he is thinking of earthly friendship, whereas the number of Christ's friends and lovers is vast, and his resources are limitless.

The centrality of Christ does not only touch the human world. Inanimate objects are also drawn to him as their Beloved, since they were created through him and tend towards him, ideas we have found embedded in the dialogues:

Las [cosas] que no tiene ni razón ni sentido, apetecen también a Cristo y se le inclinan amorosamente, tocadas de este su fuego, en la manera que su natural lo consiente . . . Porque todas las cosas, guiadas de un movimiento secreto, amando su mismo bien, le aman también a El y suspiran con su deseo y gimen por su venida. (753)

Things which have neither reason nor sense also desire Christ and are lovingly drawn to him, touched by this his fire, in a manner consistent with their natures . . . For all things, guided by a secret movement, loving their own good also love him and sigh with desire for him and groan for his coming.

The Pauline inspiration of this passage – Rom. viii.19–22 – is quoted in full, and allegorical exegesis of Song iii.9–10 confirms Christ's place at the heart of creation: Solomon's litter of cedar represents the universe in all its rich variety, and Solomon seated in its midst is Christ, governing the temple of the universe. The very word for 'love' used in this text, Marcelo says, conveys an intensity of burning, a consuming in the fire of love. Indeed, it is the Holy Spirit who kindles in our hearts our love for Christ (Rom. v.5), a fire in comparison with which all other human kinds of love are as shadows. This love, which leads to our deification, is truly a divine alchemy, as it transforms 'en oro fino nuestro lodo vil y bajísimo' (757), 'our vile and basest mud into the finest gold'. This truly is to 'eat' Christ (John vi.21): the reference to the Mass in 'Hijo de Dios' is recalled to show how Christ penetrates the hearts of those who love him.

The greatness of this love is seen, however, in the number and the difficulty of its requirements – keeping Christ's commandments, denying oneself, taking up one's cross, despising all that delights the senses alone. Song viii.7 and I Cor. xiii show how far this is from an ordinary affection, and Marcelo expounds Paul's great hymn to charity quality by quality, and with a passage from St Macarius of Egypt's *Homilies*. The exposition culminates in a catena of quotations from lovers of Christ – Paul, Ignatius, Gregory, Augustine, and those who chose poverty, solitude and martyrdom for his sake:

Por El les ha sido la pobreza riqueza, y paraíso el desierto, y los tormentos deleite, y las persecuciones descanso . . .
    Por Ti, Señor, las tiernas niñas abrazaron la muerte. Por Ti la flaqueza femenil holló sobre el fuego. Tus dulcísimos amores fueron los que poblaron los yermos. Amándote a Ti, ¡oh dulcísimo Bien!, se enciende, se apura, se esclarece, se levanta, se arroba, se anega el alma, el sentido, la carne.

(766)

For him poverty has been wealth to them, the desert paradise, torments delight and persecutions rest . . .
    For you, Lord, tender girls embraced death. For you feminine weakness trod on fire. Your sweetest loves were those who peopled the wastelands. Loving you, o sweetest Good, soul, sense and flesh are kindled, purified, illumined, raised, enraptured, drowned!

This final exclamation brings us close to the spiritual ecstasy into which the music of Salinas leads Fray Luis the poet ('A Francisco de Salinas'; iii):

> Aquí la alma navega
> por un mar de dulzura y finalmente
> en él ansí se anega,
> que ningún accidente
> estraño y peregrino oye y siente.

> Here the soul sets sail
> upon a sea of sweetness till at last,
> there drowned to such avail,
> nothing of foreign cast
> it feels or hears, all chance and strangeness past.

This love of Christ within us means that when God looks on us he sees Christ there, so that all Christ's beloved become as Christ to him.
    Marcelo anticipates the final name as he concludes 'Amado', by referring to Jesus who is our health. For that is what his personal name means. We have already studied his explanation of the name, but not what it signifies.[35] The health he brings contains within itself an

'impregnation' of good things, a metaphor which takes us back to the curious exegesis in 'Monte' of Christ as a womb pregnant with infinite treasures. For every disease, Christ is healing – cleansing of guilt, freedom from tyranny, ransoming from hell. The Biblical exegesis and the imagery Marcelo uses are very rich as he develops his thought and one example must suffice, because of its closeness to the role of music as a means to contemplation in the Salinas ode: 'Es la melodía acordada y dulce sobre toda manera, a cuyo santo sonido todo lo turbado se aquieta y compone' (783), 'He is the well-tuned melody, sweet above all else, at whose holy sound all that is disordered becomes quietened and composed'.

Jesus is health because he cures the cause of our disease and not its symptoms. Hence outward observance of ritual and ceremony cannot themselves bring about healing. The discussion that follows between the three friends shows Fray Luis at his most Erasmian, as each in turn insists on the essential practice of an interior spirituality.[36] The fact that this occupies a considerable portion of the dialogue indicates how important its author felt it still to be, and each of the speakers has words of criticism for the Church as he sees it. Marcelo makes a strong attack on over-reliance on outward show: the Christian's journey cannot stop until inner concord of the soul is reached. Until it is, he cannot consider himself healthy, that is, Jesus:

Que no ha de parar, aunque haya aprovechado en el ayuno, y sepa bien guardar el silencio, y nunca falte a los cantos del coro; y aunque ciña el cilicio y pise sobre el hielo, desnudos los pies, y mendigue lo que come y lo que viste paupérrimo, si entre esto bullen las pasiones en él, si vive el viejo hombre y enciende sus fuegos, si se atufa en el alma la ira, si se hincha la vanagloria, si se ufana el propio contento de sí, si arde la mala codicia; finalmente, si hay respetos de odios, de envidias, de pundonores, de emulación y ambición. Que si esto hay en él, por mucho que le parezca que ha hecho y que ha aprovechado en los ejercicios que referí, téngase por dicho que aún no ha llegado a la *salud*, que es *Jesús*.   (787)

He must not stop, though he has fasted beneficially and can well keep silence and is never absent from choir; and though he gird the hair shirt and walk barefoot on ice and beg what he eats and wear but the poorest clothes, if in the midst of all this his passions are raging, if the old man lives and kindles his fires, if anger rises in his soul, if vainglory swells, self-satisfaction boasts, if evil greed burns; if in sum, he is a respecter of hatred, envy, points of honour, rivalry and ambition. For if this is found in him, however much he thinks he has performed and benefited from the exercises I mentioned, let it be said that he has not yet reached that *health* which is *Jesus*.

There is a mean to be found between the inward and the outward. External practices are not rejected, any more than they were by

Erasmus, but the motivation must be right and the great trap of spiritual pride be avoided. Only when I am totally transformed in Christ can I find healing, Marcelo says, as he bursts into praise of such wholeness and in yearning for his own life to be free of all the sickness which prevents Christ from being his all in all. A passage from Job gives voice to his lament, and he begs pardon of Juliano and Sabino for the fact that 'el dolor que vive de contino en mí, de conocer mi miseria, me salió a la boca ahora y se derramó por la lengua' (791), 'the grief which dwells continually in me from knowing my misery, came now to my mouth and was uttered by my tongue'.

Marcelo now looks to Jesus as the Bread of life who by kneading the poverty and suffering of humanity with the grace and wisdom of divinity, produces food which truly satisfies and heals us. In a passage of great stylistic compression, he shows to us the effect of our eating of this bread of his two natures:

De arte que, comidas en El sus espinas, purgasen nuestra altivez; y sus azotes, tragados en El por nosotros, nos limpiasen de lo que es muelle y regalo; y su cruz, en El comida de mí, me apurase del amor de mí mismo; y su muerte, por la misma manera, diese fin a mis vicios. Y al revés, comiendo en El su justicia, se criase justicia en mi alma; y traspasando a mi estómago su santidad y su gracia, se hiciese en mí gracia y santidad verdadera; y naciese en mí substancia del cielo, que me hiciese hijo de Dios, comiendo en El a Dios hecho hombre, que, estando en nosotros, nos hiciese a la manera que es El, muertos al pecado y vivos a la justicia, y nos fuese verdadero *Jesús*.   (792)

So that having eaten in him his thorns, our pride might be purged; and that his scourging, swallowed by us in him, might cleanse us from comfort and indulgence; and that his Cross, eaten by me in him, might purify me of self-love; and his death, in the same way, put an end to my vices. And contrariwise, that by eating his justice in him, justice might be nourished in my soul; and by his holiness and his grace passing into my stomach, true grace and holiness might be created in me; and that heavenly substance might be born in me, to make me a son of God, by eating in him God made man, who, by being in us, might make us as he is, dead to sin and alive to justice, and be to us a true *Jesus*.

Many of the logical connections in the passage are suppressed. To understand it, we have to remember that the Christian is in Christ and he in the Christian, in the kind of union described in several of the names. The Host conveys to the believer, as we have seen in 'Hijo de Dios', the whole reality of Christ, so that we are remade according to his likeness. We can therefore be said to *eat* the crown of thorns because it is worn by the *bread* of life, and to *swallow* his scourging, because we receive his wounded body in Communion. It is clearly intended to startle us into comprehension, by uniting the language

of bodily digestion through the emblems of the Passion to the life
of sanctification.

Everything about this Jesus is health – his wounds, his spilt blood,
his example, his inspiration. The trees of the heavenly Jerusalem, with
leaves for the healing of the nations and bearing fruit each month
(Rev. xxii.2), stand for Jesus, who heals every sickness of body and
soul. Another dramatic passage sets our sins against the Passion:

Que a nuestra soberbia es Jesús, con su caña por cetro; y con su púrpura, por
escarnio vestido para nuestra ambición, es *Jesús*. Su cabeza, coronada con
fiera y desapiadada corona, es *Jesús*, en nuestra mala inclinación al deleite; y
sus azotes y todo su cuerpo dolorido, en lo que nosotros es carnal y torpe, es
Jesús. Eslo, para nuestra codicia, su desnudez; para nuestro coraje, su
sufrimiento admirable; para nuestro amor propio, el desprecio que siempre
hizo de sí.   (793–4)

For to our pride he is Jesus, with his reed for sceptre; dressed in mocking with
his purple, he is *Jesus* to our ambition. His head, crowned with a cruel and
pitiless crown, is *Jesus* in our evil inclination to pleasure; and his scourging
and his whole pain-racked body is *Jesus* in whatever is carnal and lewd in us.
His nakedness is such to our greed; his wondrous forbearance, to our passion;
his constant self-abasement, to our self-love.

Marcelo finds this depicted in the mysterious 'cluster of camphire'
(Song i.14), which he believes God made obscure so that by having to
ponder the meaning of its Hebrew root we should discover that it
signified pardon and satisfaction for sins.[37]

Marcelo ends with a question Sabino finds unrelated: are all things
created from nothing? It is another of those sudden shifts in the
dialogue, and we can be sure that he has a conclusion already in mind;
but it is also a means of recapitulating many of its main themes. Sabino
knows that all creatures receive their being from God, have no power
of their own, are created out of nothing, decay, die and are consumed
in nothingness. Marcelo explains: God, their author, needed to ordain
a means whereby all things should be restored to health. Such was the
Logos, begotten from all eternity and made man in time. The one
through whom all things were created becomes in his humanity the
one through whom their universal restitution takes place. The whole
creation – angels, humans, creatures animate and inanimate – will
come to new life through him, better than that they now possess. The
power of the Word sufficed to create them all, but to heal and restore
them the sickness of the human condition had to be assumed.[38] A fresh
typology is established, in which the two trees of Eden (knowledge,

life) become the types of two wonderful plants, of wisdom (the Logos) and of healing (Jesus), to whom we are united in the flesh. So in every situation we encounter, in joy and prosperity or in adversity and suffering, we have 'Jesus', health and restoration, in Jesus. 'Habíamos nacido en el Poniente de Adán; traspusístenos, Señor, en tu Oriente, Sol de justicia' (800), 'We had been born in the West of Adam; you transported us, Lord, to your East, the Sun of justice' (1, 800). This universal healing is foretold in Psalm cii, briefly expounded by Marcelo, before Sabino recites it in Fray Luis's Spanish verse translation. There is silence; and the *Nombres* are done.

Language and theology in the *Nombres*

In the course of our journey through the *Nombres*, we have noted many characteristics of the prose style of Fray Luis.[39] We know that he took the greatest care over the construction of his prose, and may recall both his own statement that he paid particular attention to rhythm and Pacheco's comment that he was the first to write in Spanish with measure and elegance.[40] The melodiousness of his prose is carefully achieved and owes much to his sensitivity to Spanish as a stressed language and to balance, contrast and climax in the construction of his phrases, clauses and sentences, some of which are very long. He regularly uses the three kinds of cadence standardized in the medieval *cursus*, the *cursus planus* (stressed /--/-), the *tardus* (/--/--) and the *velox* (/----/-). The first is by far the commonest and almost all the developed passages we have cited will reveal many examples. Yet we must remember that the harmony of the writing is intended to serve that larger harmony which is centred on Christ, who brings all created things into their proper and therefore harmonious relationship with each other and with God: 'En la forma del decir, la razón pide que las palabras y las cosas que se dicen por ellas sean conformes' (686), 'In the form of expression, reason demands that the words and the things expressed by them should be in conformity.'

There can be no doubt that Fray Luis was the first writer of Spanish prose to use the inheritance of classical and Renaissance rhetorical theory so comprehensively and to apply its precepts with such fine results. But we must not forget that as an Augustinian he was familiar with a more specifically Christian tradition of rhetoric. While the influence of Cicero is clearly seen in many of the passages we have looked at, in terms of the frequency of pairs of synonyms, parallelisms and antitheses, he follows the precepts St Augustine laid down in *De doctrina christiana* (IV, 20–1), with examples from Scripture and the Fathers, on the three styles appropriate for teaching, for delighting and for moving the reader – the 'estilo llano', 'simple style', for exposition and proof, the 'templado', 'moderate', for his more developed and ornate passages, and the 'sublime', with its exclamations and rhetorical questions, for moving his readers to repentance, prayer and praise.

Inevitably, we can but hint at the stylistic beauty and conceptual richness of so long and complex a work as the *Nombres*. Each of the names deserves more attention than we have been able to give to them all. But it is important to look at the *Nombres* as a whole, if only to become aware of an unfolding theology which the detail may conceal. The first five names are largely concerned with the purpose of God in creation, seen in Scotist terms as the revelation of himself in the person of the Word made flesh, the greatest and most glorious gift of all, from whom all the creatures came to be and to which all tend. But by the end of 'Monte' the more sombre story of the entry of sin into human experience begins, first in Lucifer's mind, then in Adam and Eve, till it spreads to infect the whole human race. From that moment, the purpose of God can only be achieved through suffering and sacrifice, and it is the death of the Incarnate Son on Calvary that the dialogues now reveal. This death is the appointed means of reconciling God's invincible purpose with his absolute justice. At the Resurrection Christ is reborn, triumphant over death. The sins of the Christian, now grafted on to Christ, die with him and their penalty is paid; at his rising the Christian is born to new life, and in his glorification enters at last the destiny which God had ordained. This new life is characterized by growth, from spiritual infancy to maturity. It grows too among human kingdoms, slowly but inexorably, until the end of time.

Such is the theological framework of the *Nombres*, an overarching span from Creation to Eschaton. Its remarkable christocentricity, so strongly influenced by St Paul's theology, which was itself so prominent in Erasmus and in sixteenth-century Lutheran and Reformed theology, is a rare treasure of post-Tridentine Spain. Mystical writers may have found Paul and Erasmus valuable allies in their stress on a life of personal, interior devotion, and there are passages in the *Nombres* which belong very much to that tradition. But few if any writers of this period in Spain saw with such clarity or described with such power the social, political, ecclesiological and universal dimensions of life in Christ. From the vastness of the heavens and worlds that are not yet in being, through the angelic to the human realms of nations, monarchs and the Christian commonwealth, down to the animal, vegetative and inanimate creation, all exists through Christ and is drawn towards him. The Scotist understanding of the Incarnation undoubtedly reinforced the christocentricity of Fray Luis, since it made Christ's coming the end of a gradually unfolding process of bringing the universe to glory, rather than an emergency measure to counter the baleful effects of sin. But stronger than the voice of Duns Scotus is that of Paul, and especially Paul when he writes of the mystery of the universe's destiny finally disclosed through Christ.

There is a great deal more to the theology of the *Nombres*, but to grasp its framework is essential if we are not to become confused by detail. The names themselves are intended to witness to it. The use Fray Luis makes of Scripture, which yields them in the first place, is therefore ordered to the same end. His task as an expositor is to uncover the names he has chosen, often hidden in obscure words and expressions, often requiring the assistance of other texts to clarify their meaning, and sometimes of the Hebrew original, in which so much mystery lay concealed. Even where they obviously apply to Christ, their depth cannot be plumbed without reference to Biblical texts which provide them with new and richer meanings. Fray Luis moves through the Bible at ease, finding in what seem to us the most unlikely places images of the truth he wishes to express. Some passages of the *Nombres* are nothing other than the kind of exegesis we meet in his Latin commentaries. We might remember that although in the *Cantar* and above all *Job* he was also expounding the Bible in Spanish, neither work was published in his lifetime, whereas the *Nombres* went into three editions. The only other work which approaches it in terms of bringing the Bible to the people is *La perfecta casada*, much more restricted in its intention and its scope.

We have seen how the Bible provided Fray Luis with some extraordinary metaphors, how exegesis enabled him to connect series of images which appear to have no relationship yet are united by their derivation from Scripture and its common witness to the will of God, and how he could combine them in strange patterns. 'Pimpollo' establishes at the outset from Scripture the metaphor of seed and fruit, to which he often returns. 'Monte' especially stands out, with its metaphors of mountains as wombs pregnant with treasures, of corn and trees as representing Christ's wisdom and that of ancient philosophy, and its use of Daniel's vision of the stone and the statue to express the smallness and hardness of Christ as he smites all idolatry. The womb metaphor assumes importance again in 'Hijo de Dios', where Christ has five births; Daniel's vision is also alluded to in 'Braço de Dios' and receives further exposition in 'Rey de Dios'.

Biblical imagery provides Fray Luis with a range of expressive language from beyond the normal bounds of sixteenth-century Spanish prose writing and with a divinely inspired authority. In a similar way the influence of the Song of Songs gives the poetry of St John of the Cross its mysterious and exotic lyricism. But the *Nombres* was not intended to be a work to be read only by theologians and Biblical scholars. It was for the literate, to enable them to know and love the Scriptures they were not allowed to read in their own tongue. Its many similes and metaphors illustrate and explain its difficult truths, and make them beautiful and attractive to believe. Many of them are of the simplest and most elemental kind – light, fire, the sun; water, fountains, oceans; seed, flowers and fruit; the night sky, the breeze; mirrors and paintings; poison and sickness. They are part of universal human experience, though all of them are to be found in the language of Scripture too; in both respects, they are like the patterns of imagery in Fray Luis's poetry. While they do not require the exegetical treatment of the Biblical images, their significance has nonetheless to be made clear.

Fray Luis uses them for many purposes. There are images of inexhaustibility and identity, which portray the relationship between the persons of the Trinity or the eternal quality of their gifts to humanity – the sun and its rays, which communicate its light without diminishing it; the fountain which is fed from a ceaseless spring; the bottomless abyss. There are images of relationship and likeness – the painter and the portrait; the seed and the fruit; the mother whose arms steady the child's feet; the fragrance of the rose; the night sky reflected in the water. There are images of growth and transformation – the physical language of bodily digestion for receiving Christ; iron or wood in the fire. There are images too of sin and evil – poison, fire, death itself. The same image may be used to convey different ideas at various points in the exposition: fire may be Satanic envy or the burning love of God. But there is often a common thread: water as the antidote to Satanic poison in baptism is related to tears shed for sin, since both flow from the unfathomable ocean of divine grace. Christ the fruit of all creation is the source of the fruitfulness of the Christian life, because all true Christian living grows from its union with him. Fray Luis uses this image to help his readers gain some awareness of the great theological division of the age and by doing so enables this to be expressed in a more approachable and eirenic way, opening out a possibility of reconciliation which only now, four centuries later, is becoming a reality. Almost all his images are ancient, and come from the traditional language of mysticism. Almost all, like the imagery of his poems, could be called commonplace, yet neither the concepts towards which they are intended to draw us nor the artistry which shapes them has anything of the commonplace about it.

For such reasons, the *Nombres* is a bridge between the specialized and technical work of Fray Luis as a Biblical scholar and theologian, which we have looked at closely, and his poems, so much more accessible and widely read, which as yet we have but glanced at. Now, having crossed the bridge, we may approach them with more open eyes.

6

The language of heaven

At first sight, Fray Luis's attitude towards his own poetry seems puzzling.[1] In the dedication he wrote for his collection of original poems and sacred and secular translations he assumes the thin disguise of 'Luis Mayor' and, as the name implies ('mayor' can mean 'adult', 'grown-up'), introduced his poems as an indulgent father viewing his youthful aberrations:

Entre las ocupaciones de mis estudios en mi mocedad, y casi en mi niñez, se me cayeron como de entre las manos estas obrecillas, a las cuales me apliqué más por inclinación de mi estrella que por juicio o voluntad.

(*Obras* II, 737)

Among the occupations of my studies in my youth, almost in my childhood, these little works slipped as it were out of my hands, and I applied myself to them more by the inclination of my star than through judgement or will.[2]

He pretends to have been persuaded to gather them together by an old friend who, through the allusions made to his suffering, must also be Fray Luis. The dedication has a light, playful tone and need not be taken at face value; it is more in the nature of a conventional disclaimer, in which the older, wiser author apologizes for the follies of his younger self, rather as in 'Padre del siglo futuro' Marcelo regrets his inability to forsake his 'less useful' works.[3] Yet it is not devoid of serious comment. Fray Luis observes that poetry can be a worthy art when applied to fit subjects, and that the real proof of this is the frequent use of poetic forms in the Bible. He also took his poetry sufficiently seriously to prepare a collection which excluded works wrongly attributed to him and to correct errors which had crept into copies of the poems as they circulated among his friends.[4]

Given what we know about Fray Luis's approach to Biblical language such comments are not to be ignored, especially when, as in 'Monte', they appear in an unexpected context. Marcelo has just recited part of a translation of Psalm lxxi by a 'común amigo nuestro'

(1, 492), 'a common friend of ours'. Juliano is impressed and wants to know who this friend might be – Fray Luis is evidently not beyond a little discreet boasting. Marcelo avoids telling him and instead remarks that such subjects alone are worthy of poetry. Those who use it for frivolous ends corrupt it and offend morality:

La poesía corrompen, porque sin duda la inspiró Dios en los ánimos de los hombres, para con el movimiento y espíritu de ella levantarlos al cielo, de donde ella procede; porque poesía no es sino una comunicación del aliento celestial y divino; y así, en los profetas casi todos, así los que fueron movidos verdaderamente por Dios, como los que incitados por otras causas sobrehumanas hablaron, el mismo espíritu que los despertaba y levantaba a ver lo que los otros hombres no veían, les ordenaba y componía y como metrificaba en la boca las palabras, con número y consonancia debida, para que hablasen por más subida manera que las otras gentes hablaban, y para que el estilo del decir se asemejase al sentir, y las palabras y las cosas fuesen conformes.

(492)

They corrupt poetry, because God doubtless inspired it in men's souls to raise them by its movement and spirit to heaven, whence it proceeds. For poetry is nothing other than a communication of the celestial, divine breath; and thus among almost all the prophets, those who were truly moved by God, and also those who spoke aroused by other supernatural causes, the same spirit which awoke them and lifted them up to see what other men did not see ordered, composed and as it were versified the words in their mouth, with due measure and consonance, so that they might speak in a loftier manner than the other peoples, and so that the style of their discourse might resemble what they felt, so that words and things might be in conformity.

This is more than a commonplace Renaissance expression of Plato's doctrine of poetic inspiration. To begin with, it stresses the moral and spiritual value of both the content and style of poetry, since it proceeds from God and when rightly used points towards heaven. Worthy poetry must therefore be a form of contemplation, and imitate the pattern Fray Luis sees written into the whole creation, which issues from the Father through the Word and returns through the Word made flesh to the Father. It also clarifies Fray Luis's understanding of the unique nature of Biblical poetry, for the Spirit not only inspires the prophetic content, but ensures that the words themselves are adequate to their theme. Divine inspiration is therefore equally present in the literary features of the text. Conformity between words and the objects they represent, so important an element of Fray Luis's theory of names, will therefore be exhibited to the highest degree in Biblical poetry.

Now comes a second puzzle. In spite of all this, Fray Luis's original poems seem to show surprisingly little influence of his understanding of poetry as a divine gift or the Bible as a treasury of divinely inspired words and images, and to owe more to secular and classical traditions. But the puzzle begins to disappear when we look more closely at the relationship between his Biblical and classical translations and his own poetry, and see that any neat distinction of secular from sacred influences breaks down.

As a translator of the classics and the Psalms he was already well known in Salamanca before his trial.[5] A well-attested story tells how he was invited to adjudicate an informal competition between three Salamanca classicists, El Brocense, Juan de Almeida and Alonso de Espinosa, for the best translation of the fourteenth ode in the first book of Horace's *Odes*. He claimed it was impossible to judge between three such good versions and instead submitted his own, which both for faithfulness to the original and elegance of diction bettered them all.[6] Four of his translations of Horatian odes were published anonymously while he was in prison, in El Brocense's commentary on the poetry of Garcilaso, by way of illustrating Garcilaso's dependence on Horace.[7] El Brocense thought highly of them, and they are indeed accomplished works, displaying sensitivity towards the originals, a sure handling of the Spanish, and a mastery of the *lira* form, used so often for his own compositions.

Fray Luis's translations of the first Psalm and of the famous *Beatus ille* from the *Epodes*, of interest in their own right, both relate to his own ode '¡Qué descansada vida!' (1), which we have already seen as carrying a greater profundity of meaning than is often recognized.[8] The translation of Horace is faithful, though lacking some of the bite of the original, in which the eulogy of country life and nature's bounty is spoken by a moneylender who, in spite of all that he has said, returns to his former occupation at the end. Horace's poem was partly the model for Fray Luis's ode, which nevertheless abandons its ironical tone to become a lyrical evocation of the simple country life as a metaphor for the pathway to virtue. Nor did Horace's moneylender, with his almost greedy delight in the harvest of farm and field, provide the image of the 'hidden path'. Indeed, instead of praising the natural abundance of the land, Fray Luis stresses a life of simplicity – 'one poor table', sufficient for every need – and prefers to give a lyrical description of the beauty of the countryside. Only in one place do his translation and ode correspond to any notable degree, where the happy man is shown enjoying his rest:

Debajo un roble antiguo ya se asienta,
ya en el prado florido.
El agua en las acequias corre, y cantan
los pájaros sin dueño;
Las fuentes, al murmullo que levantan,
despiertan dulce sueño.

(II, 949; lines 23–8)

Now beneath an ancient oak he sits,
now in the flowering meadow.
Water flows in the channels,
and the birds who have no master sing;
the fountains, with the murmuring they stir,
awaken sweet sleep.

Fray Luis's ode is more concerned with life away from the hidden path, with its restless search for satisfaction through lust for possessions, riches and power; but Horace's picture of flowering fields, flowing stream, birdsong, sound sleep and peace in the shade of a tree all pass into it, though changed: the birdsong is untutored; the poet sings reclining in the shade, crowned with ivy and laurel; unbroken sleep is not caused by the sound of water but the whole scene, and the image of the fountain and the stream becomes more prominent.

The reason for the difference in tone is surely that Fray Luis has another poem in mind, the first psalm, 'Beatus vir', which begins and ends with the image of the path, just as he had expounded it in 'Camino', as a metaphor for a way of life. In his translation, the first two lines of the psalm in the Vulgate are expanded into a *lira*:

Es bienaventurado
varón el que en concilio malicioso
no anduvo descuidado,
ni el paso perezoso
detuvo del camino peligroso.

(II, 971)

He is a blessed man
who in wicked counsel
walked not idly
nor turned his lazy step
from the dangerous way.

Like the original, the translation ends by contrasting the way of the just, which God knows, with the way of the ungodly, which will perish, a theme which becomes substantial in Fray Luis's ode.

The next verse, the flight from those who mock the virtuous and good and speak and nurture poisonous words and thoughts, is Fray Luis's paraphrase of the Psalmist's 'seat of the scornful'. The blessed man 'huye', 'flees' from their seat, just as in the ode the life of peace 'huye' from worldly clamour. The psalm, therefore, rather than Horace, has suggested the portrayal in the first four verses of '¡Qué descansada vida!' of the flattery and deceit found among the great and powerful. The third verse (AV: 'And he shall be like a tree planted by the rivers of water, that bringeth forth his fruit in his season; his leaf also shall not wither . . .') is translated succinctly, though its tone is classical, not Hebraic, with its four epithets and its everlasting crown of foliage:

> Será cual verde planta,
> que, a las corrientes aguas asentada,
> al cielo se levanta
> con fruta sazonada,
> de hermosas hojas siempre coronada.
>
> (II, 971)

> He shall be as a green plant,
> which, established by the running waters,
> rises to the heavens
> with seasonable fruit,
> with beautiful leaves ever crowned.

Each image in the psalm is artfully reworked by Fray Luis, and he adds the idea of upward growth to the sky or heaven (the Spanish 'cielo' means both): the tree is green, the characteristic Hebrew phrase 'rivers of water' is rendered by two different words referring to water ('corrientes', 'aguas'), and the leaves which never wither become, more positively, leaves ever crowning the plant.[9] The picture of the garden watered by a stream is at the heart of the ode:

> Del monte en la ladera,
> por mi mano plantado, tengo un huerto,
> que con la primavera,
> de bella flor cubierto,
> ya muestra en esperanza el fruto cierto.
>
> (II, 743)

> Upon the mountain side
> I have an orchard by my own hand made
> where newly each springtide
> fair flowers are arrayed,
> the certainty of fruit in hope displayed.

This planting (for once Fray Luis, the Vulgate and English use the same root word) is bound to recall the planting of Eden in Gen. ii, especially as the garden of the ode symbolizes a place of simplicity and innocence, like that of Eden, to which the poet can retreat away from the fallen world.

We may thus begin to sense how both the Horatian and Biblical poems have contributed to Fray Luis's ode. But if he sometimes borrows a classical idiom to translate parts of a Hebrew poem, his classical translations may equally attract Biblical material. One small example is the lovely ending of Horace's ode 1.22:

> dulce ridentem Lalagem amabo
> dulce loquentem.

This is translated:

> Lálage amada,
> la del reir gracioso,
> la del parlar muy más que miel sabroso. (ii, 924)

> Beloved Lalage,
> She of the gracious laughter,
> she of the voice more delightful by far than honey.

The comparison is suggested by the Bible, e.g. Psalm xviii.11 (AV xix.10), where, as Fray Luis himself translated, God's laws are called 'más dulces . . . que miel' (ii, 979), sweeter than honey.

But a more significant example of this confluence of classical and Biblical models is found by comparing Fray Luis's translation of Horace's ode iv.13 with his own 'De la Magdalena' (vi). Horace writes in a cruel and mocking way of a woman once beautiful and loved by the poet, whose wish that she should become old and ugly has now been fulfilled. Another woman has inherited her once vaunted attractions; her former rival is dead, before her beauty had time to decay. She can only compete with the old crow, and be the butt of youthful jokes, who see her once burning torch turned to ashes. Fray Luis addresses a woman who has likewise grown old. He retains some of the Horatian imagery and themes: the snow of white hairs, the blackened teeth, the suitors who have abandoned her, the passage of time, swift as a bird's flight. But the whole Horatian tone is replaced with a Christian morality, prominent already by the third verse:

> ¿Qué tienes del pasado
> tiempo sino dolor? ¿cuál es el fruto

> que tu labor te ha dado,
> si no es tristeza y luto,
> y el alma hecha sierva a vicio bruto?
>
> What have you of time past
> but grief? What is the fruit
> your toil has given you,
> but sorrow and mourning
> and your soul enslaved to brute vice?

The ideas belong to that constellation of thought we have already identified in Fray Luis. Life ordered to a wrongful end (in this case the satisfaction of the flesh) will bring only misery, not the fruit it promises; the soul will be entirely governed by the desires of the senses and become their servant, having forgotten its origin and goal. If only you had looked instead for heavenly beauty, he exclaims (verse 7). Yet there is hope:

> Mas hora no hay tardía,
> tanto nos es el cielo piadoso,
> mientras que dura el día;
> el pecho hervoroso
> en breve del dolor saca reposo;
>   que la gentil señora
> de Mágdalo, bien que perdidamente
> dañada, en breve hora
> con el amor ferviente
> las llamas apagó del fuego ardiente,
>   las llamas del malvado
> amor con otro amor más encendido . . .
>
>   (II, 754)

> There is no hour too late,
> so much is heaven merciful toward us,
> while the day lasts;
> the troubled breast
> fast finds respite from its grief;
>   for the gracious lady of Magdala,
> though desperately hurt, in a brief hour
> with fervent love
> put out the flames of burning fire,
>   the flames of wicked love
> with another love more ardent.

Mary Magdalene is here introduced as the Biblical model of a woman who lived for sensual love, but who discovered heavenly beauty in Christ. Fray Luis, following closely the Gospel story (e.g. Luke

7.36ff.), goes on to describe how she entered unbidden the house of
Simon the Pharisee, washed Christ's feet with her tears, wiped them
with her hair and anointed them with oil, to the disapproval of the
onlookers. But whereas in the Gospel Mary is silent as Christ gently
reproves his host and even when he turns to her to assure her that her
sins have been forgiven, Fray Luis gives her a long speech of repentance. He uses antithesis and paradox to create a series of conceits
which relate the hands, hair, mouth and eyes performing this act of
devotion to the medicine of forgiveness which will heal her:

> La que sudó en tu ofensa
> trabaje en tu servicio, y de mis males
> proceda mi defensa;
> mis ojos dos mortales
> fraguas, dos fuentes sean manantiales.
>
> Bañen tus pies mis ojos,
> límpienlos mis cabellos; de tormento
> mi boca, y red de enojos,
> les dé besos sin cuento,
> y lo que me condena te presento:
>
> preséntote un sujeto
> tan mortalmente herido, cual conviene,
> do un médico perfeto
> de cuanto saber tiene
> dé muestra, que por siglos mil resuene.

> May she who sweated in your offence,
> labour in your service, and from my evils
> let my defence proceed;
> let my eyes, two mortal forges,
> become two flowing fountains.
>
> Let my eyes bathe your feet,
> let my hair cleanse them; let my mouth,
> a snare of torment and troubles,
> give them countless kisses;
> and what condemns me I offer to you:
>
> I offer you a subject
> wounded so mortally, as is right,
> so that a perfect doctor
> may show a sign of all the knowledge he possesses,
> which may resound through a thousand ages.

The fire of sensual love – the same metaphor used in the *Nombres* for the
sin which Lucifer has spread throughout humanity – made her eyes

forges because in and through them her desires took form and shape. Her tears are the flowing fountains which extinguish this fire, but they come from the 'more burning fire' with which the Satanic flame has been put out. By using the same image of fire for both loves, and by differentiating them according to its intensity, Fray Luis is able to express the relationship between the two forms of loving in a way which is refreshingly different from the denunciation of physical love but also consistent with Christian morality and with his own sense of life as a searching after a peace which can only be found in Christ. Both loves are fiery; divine love has the greater power, power first to inspire her repentance and the tears she sheds which put out the flames of physical passion, and then to turn her life towards the true beauty for which she has been searching, unbeknown, and in the wrong places. Her visible tears also express the paradoxical nature of her repentant behaviour:

> Lavaba larga en lloro
> al que su torpe mal lavando estaba . . .
>
> Long in weeping she washed
> the one who was washing her base evil . . .

They can do no more than wash physically the one who invisibly, but completely, washes away her sin, yet that does not make her action vain. They are the equivalent of the drops of water forced out of the wood set on fire before the flames have wholly mastered it,[10] or the outward sign of water through which the sacramental regeneration of baptism is effected. But both metaphors, fire and water, with their ambiguities, give way to another, central to the name 'Jesus', that of the doctor who brings medicine for the healing of humanity. The apparently weak expressions 'cual conviene' and 'que por mil siglos resuene' also have their point. The first suggests that sinners rightly turn to Christ to find forgiveness; the second is a gloss on the Gospel story, where Jesus says that the woman's actions will be remembered wherever the Gospel is preached. Here it is the sign of Christ's healing power which is to resound through time.

So it is that Fray Luis transforms the Horatian original into a Christian poem which offers a vivid meditation on a Gospel story. In doing this, he does not however desert classical tradition. The ode uses hyperbaton frequently and contains many rhetorical questions and exclamations; its vocabulary is very Latinate, as are many of its expressions: it begins with the commonplace image of the woman's hair which once was gold and now has turned to snow, and Elisa, the ostensible subject of the poem, is asked: '¿por quién uno,/el cielo fatigaste/con gemido importuno?', 'for which one did you weary heaven with importunate lament?'. Here Fray Luis has adapted classical tradition for Christian use; in other poems, like his heroic odes ('A don Pedro Portocarrero', II, XIII; 'Canción al nacimiento de la hija del Marqués de Alcañices', IV; 'Profecía del Tajo', VII), a more secular tone is heard. Other poets could use the same metaphors and conceits as those in 'De la Magdalena' to portray sexual love: a prime example would be Góngora's ballad 'En un pastoral albergue', which recounts the love story of Angelica and Medoro from Ariosto's *Orlando furioso*, and in which eyes, tears, wounds and medicine all play their part in a celebration of erotic love.[11]

Many of the original poems of Fray Luis show the same kind of fusion of Biblical and classical source material. We need not imagine there was anything self-conscious or deliberate about it, for given what we know about him, it would have been quite natural. But we do need to take account of it when we read his poetry. It is the equivalent there of his use of classical poets to provide secondary illustrations in his Biblical commentaries, or his sense of classical literature at its best as a kind of Gentile Old Testament, pointing the way to Christ. Instead of assuming that his poetry bears little relationship to his Latin or Spanish prose works, we may see in both its themes and language some of the constant preoccupations of the author. The most telling example of all comes from his reworking of the traditions of pastoral literature.

Much has been written about the pastoral mode in sixteenth-century European literature – its popularity, its thematic and stylistic conventions, the prose romances and the poetry it inspired.[12] It seems to belong to the humanistic side of the Renaissance, using the pagan, classical past (Theocritus, Virgil) to explore the nature of human love, fidelity and jealousy. But some pastoral literature moved far beyond pretty pictures of shepherds and shepherdesses wandering lovelorn through idealized landscapes of meadows, groves and streams. It began to reflect the concerns of thinkers and writers of the age through its own particular artifice, and became a vehicle for the new thinking of the period, less concerned with religious orthodoxy or the super-natural, more open to the human and to new currents of thought and taste. It might exist in tension with religion: after all, did not the first and greatest of the Spanish pastoral poets, Garcilaso de la Vega, have to be rewritten, alongside his more prolix friend Boscán, to render him acceptable to the more pious readers of post-Tridentine Spain? The vogue for 'divinizing' poetry, about which much has also been written, appears to support the view that the pastoral evocation of human love and loss was intolerable from a Christian point of view.[13] Profane love poetry was a poison because it idolatrized a carnal approach to love: we have heard Fray Luis himself say much the same. Therefore it had to be spiritualized. The more beautiful it was, the more dangerous, and the more pressing the need to revise it. Why should the Devil have all the best tunes?

The argument was an old one, stretching back to the Fathers and their differing attitudes towards the poets of antiquity and the pagan culture in which Christianity began to grow. Many had condemned profane literature; others could not bear to reject those examples at least which showed beauty, grace and nobility. The revival of classical learning in the Renaissance gave fresh impetus to the old debate. Erasmus, for example, in his *Enchiridion*, recommended a number of classical authors as good preparation for the Christian life.[14] But the canon of Ubeda who addressed the reader in a preface to Sebastián de Córdoba's divinized version of Boscán and Garcilaso thought otherwise, and did not mince his words. The poems as they stood, he declared, were a pestilential danger to the soul, for the deceitful serpent lay hiding in the attractive style.[15] Nonetheless, some pastoral literature used the conventions of the form to explore moral and even spiritual themes, such as innocence and corruption, virtue and vice, countryside and cities, nature and art, and the transience of human experience.

Fray Luis uses pastoral imagery, following a long and venerable tradition, as a metaphorical mode representing the life of heaven. The Bible and classical antiquity (Virgil especially) provide him with his raw materials, and the result is an expression in poetry and prose of what is properly termed Christian pastoral. Evidence of this process in his works will show how subtle the fusion between them became, and how in the end it confronts us with the art of Fray Luis the poet, rather than the sources from which the scholar drew his inspiration.

Just as poets of both human and divine love frequently used the same images, so pastoral language could be used about the heavens in the secular sense. In the seventeenth century, Góngora developed to a sophisticated degree the art of transposing metaphors, something he learnt from classical tradition. The oceans, for example, were *ploughed* as though they were fields but of water, by ships, as though they were furrowing the surface. The heavens could also become fields: the Elysian Fields had moved from the underworld or the Isles of the Blessed (the abode of dead heroes) to become a classical version of the Christian heaven. If the heavens were fields, it required no great leap of the imagination for the stars to become flowers or crops. Hence, Góngora begins the first of his *Soledades* by describing spring as the time when 'el mentido robador de Europa/ . . . en campos de zafiro pace estrellas', 'Europa's perjured robber [Taurus] strays . . . Through sapphire fields to feast on stellar corn.'[16] The sign of the bull in the heavens, moving among the stars, is represented by the earthly bull grazing the pastures.

But a Christian parallel already existed long before this. In his *Confessions* (x.6). St Augustine wondered what his God might be and found that all creatures gave the same answer, 'God is he who made us', an answer read from their beauty, on which man could gaze. The fourth verse of St John of the Cross's *Cántico espiritual*, entitled 'Pregunta a las criaturas', 'Question to the creatures', is modelled on this. The Bride, searching for the Bridegroom, cries out:

> ¡Oh bosques y espesuras
> plantadas por la mano del Amado,
> oh prado de verduras
> de flores esmaltado!,
> decid si por vosotros ha pasado.[17]

> O woods and crowded thickets,
> By the hand of the Beloved raised,
> O meadow spread with verdure,
> With sheen of blossom glazed,
> Speak, tell me if he has passed your way.[18]

The picture seems clearly enough to evoke the beauty of the countryside, but that is not how St John understood it. He takes the woods to be the four elements and the thickets to be the great variety of creation, while of the 'prado de verduras' he writes:

Esta es la consideración del cielo, al cual llama prado de verduras, porque las cosas que hay en él criadas siempre están con verdura inmarcesible, que ni fenecen ni se marchitan con el tiempo, y en ellas como [en] frescas verduras se recrean y deleitan los justos.[19]

This is the consideration of heaven, which she [the Bride] calls a meadow of green because the things created in it ever exist with an unfading greenness and do not die or wither with time, and in them, as in fresh green places, the just find pleasure and delight.

This 'meadow' includes the differing beauties of the stars and planets; its green plants are also interpreted as the souls of the faithful departed, through a sentence from the funeral service, itself an allusion to our twenty-third Psalm, 'Constituat vos Dominus inter amoena virentia', ('God keep you in green and pleasant places'). On this reading the flowers become the angels and the souls of all the blessed, who adorn the heavenly places 'como un gracioso y subido esmalte en [un] vaso de oro excelente', 'like a lovely and noble enamel on a excellent golden vase.' St Bernard portrayed heaven similarly:

> They stand, those halls of Zion,
> Conjubilant with song,
> And bright with many an angel,
> And all the martyr-throng;
> The prince is ever in them,
> The daylight is serene,
> The pastures of the blessed
> Are decked in glorious sheen.[20]

Not only does San Juan use pastoral imagery to describe heaven, but the transition from green fields to blue skies is effected through using 'green' as a symbol of all that lives, fading on earth, unfading in heaven, and 'flowers' as an earthly symbol both for stars and blessed spirits. If flowering meadows on earth are beautiful, they are but a shadow of the beauty of heaven, where fields adorned with everlasting flowers remain eternally fresh and green.

This rich and suggestive exposition of apparently straightforward imagery, more or less contemporary with the writing of the *Nombres*, shows how readily a pastoral scene could be interpreted as a vision of heaven. Fray Luis consistently uses pastoral imagery in the same way, for the foretaste of knowledge and bliss enjoyed in heaven by the blessed and experienced on earth, however rarely or fleetingly, by the soul in contemplation.

At the end of his 'Noche serena' ode (VIII), for example, the journey upwards into the night sky reaches its climax with five exclamations invoking a fertile, pastoral landscape. Contemplation of the beauty of the starlit heavens has led the poet, as it led Marcelo in 'Príncipe de la paz', to meditate on the miseries of earthbound humanity, lost in sleep, of which physical sleep is but the symbol of the sleep of existence itself and of all the vain and foolish things for which men strive. He then looks upwards to the beauty and harmony of the heavens, an image of the true home of the imprisoned soul. There is to be found the reality of peace, happiness and love which men seek in empty, illusory substitutes like wealth and honour. This ignorance, accounted knowledge in our earthly life, is contrasted with the knowledge of a better world gained from contemplation of heaven, which the last three verses of the ode hymn as the place of 'inmensa hermosura', 'immense beauty', of 'clarísima luz pura/que jamás anochece', 'pure and brightest light which never darkens', where eternal springtime flowers. It is this last image which introduces the exclamations of the final verse:

> ¡Oh campos verdaderos!
> ¡Oh prados con verdad frescos y amenos!
> ¡riquísimos mineros!
> ¡oh deleitosos senos!
> ¡repuestos valles de mil bienes llenos![21]

> O pastures truly fair!
> O fresh and pleasant meadows, where truth dwells!
> O mines most rich and rare!
> Sweet shelter of the hills!
> Secluded vales abundant goodness fills!

The emphasis on truth, through the 'verdad'/'verdaderos' *polyptoton* in the first two lines, implies a Platonic contrast with 'false' fields, making the pastoral scenes of earth but shadows of the reality now glimpsed. The reference to mines, which some commentators take to mean springs of water, may also be connected with the mines of wisdom in Job xxviii and the treasures concealed in mountains in 'Monte'.[22]

This vision of heaven is thus a pastoral landscape of meadows, hills and valleys, but qualified as the dwelling-place of truth and good gifts. The night sky and stars have been transmuted into this daylight idyll through a series of links which are not always easy to detect. Night enables us to see the heavens, so that terrestrial darkness becomes the means whereby we contemplate celestial light. But that same darkness is also a symbol of the blind folly of human life and the vanity of its aspirations. It has two contradictory meanings – sight of earth and blindness to heaven, as light does (human blindness, heavenly radiance). Fray Luis creates a tension between them which governs the sense of the ode. The vision of the night sky does not merely show us the stars; it awakens us to understand that what we assume to be the light of our daily lives is itself a pervasive darkness, by opening our inward eyes to our true home, the spiritual heavens. Once our eyes are released from the blindness of earthly light they see the light of heavenly truth even though they remain physically in the darkness. That light is everlasting, our source and our goal; yet in the ode we can reach it only through one kind of darkness (the night sky) which reveals a deeper darkness (the soul's bondage). We ascend from the darkness we call light to the light which shines in the darkness, a paradox not unconnected with the tradition of apophatic theology associated with the pseudo-Dionysius and so strongly present in St John of the Cross. It opens out into the pastoral imagery of the final verse, a landscape which is no longer the shadow but the reality.

To understand this better, we must look at the significance Fray Luis gives to the name 'Pastor'. He defines the office of the shepherd as leading a quiet life removed from the vice and clamour of cities, one of innocent pleasure in the joys of the country – the open skies, the fresh air, the beauty of plants and flowers, the birdsong and the streams. It is a natural way of life, a very ancient one: Jacob and the Patriarchs were shepherds and so was David.[23] It is also celebrated by poets, especially Theocritus and Virgil, while in Scripture the Holy Spirit depicts Christ's love for us in the pastoral love-song of the Song of Songs. The cities may yield finer speech, but fine feeling belongs to the solitude of the countryside.

Fray Luis is not just repeating a commonplace of Renaissance pastoral literature about the freedom and innocence of country life in contrast to the ruinous corruption of city and court. Theocritus and Virgil take second place to the Bible, and there is again that strong hint, here in the word 'innocence', that something of the unfallen world of Eden can still be experienced in the country but which has been forever banished from city life. Love, Fray Luis continues, may be found in its pure and uncontaminated form in the country, whereas in the city it is artificial and becomes corrupted. Country love, open to the skies and close to the earth and the elements, is 'una como escuela de amor puro y verdadero' (i, 468), 'like a school of pure and true love', where everything exists in a harmonious relationship. The shepherd can therefore know the true meaning of love.

Moreover, his office is to govern 'en apacentar y alimentar a los que gobiernan', 'by feeding and nourishing those who govern', without imposing laws, but by ministering to each need as it arises and by exercising a personal care over the whole flock rather than delegating others to do some of the work. He finds them food and water, washes and shears them, heals, disciplines and calms them, gives them rec-reation and protection, and gathers all the scattered sheep into a single flock. Fray Luis's inspiration here is the book of Ezekiel (e.g. xxxiv) and the parable of the Good Shepherd (John x), and he carefully selects the details which will form the basis of his exposition. For he now asks if all these qualities are found in Christ.

There follows a lyrical and idealized portrayal of Christ the country-dweller:

Vive en los campos Cristo, y goza del cielo libre, y ama la soledad y el sosiego; y en el silencio de todo aquello que pone en alboroto la vida, tiene puesto El su deleite. Porque, así como lo que se comprende en el campo es el más puro de lo visible, y es lo sencillo y como el original de todo lo que de ello se compone y se mezcla, así aquella región de vida adonde viva aqueste nuestro glorioso bien, es la pura verdad y la sencillez de la luz de Dios, y el original expreso de todo lo que tiene ser, y las raíces firmes de donde nacen y adonde se estriban todas las criaturas. Y si lo habemos de decir así, aquéllos son los elementos puros y los campos de flor eterna vestidos, y los mineros de las aguas vivas, y los montes verdaderamente preñados de mil bienes altísimos, y los sombríos y repuestos valles, y los bosques de la frescura, adonde, exentos de toda injuria, gloriosamente florecen la haya y la oliva y el lináloe, con todos los demás árboles de incienso, en que reposan ejércitos de aves en gloria y en música dulcísima, que jamás ensordece. Con la cual región, si comparamos este nuestro miserable destierro, es comparar el desasosiego con la paz, y el desconcierto y la turbación, y el bullicio y disgusto de la más inquieta ciudad, con la misma pureza y quietud y dulzura. Que aquí se afana y allí se descansa; aquí se imagina y allí se ve; aquí las sombras de las cosas nos atemorizan y asombran; allí la verdad asosiega y deleita; esto es tinieblas, bullicio, alboroto; aquello es luz purísima en sosiego eterno. (469)

Christ lives in the fields and enjoys the open skies, and loves solitude and repose; and he puts his delight in the silencing of all that makes life restless. For as all that the countryside contains is the purest form of the visible, the simplest and as the original of all that is compounded and mixed with it, so that region of life where our glorious good now dwells is the pure truth and simplicity of the light of God, the express original of all that have being, and the firm roots from which they spring and on which they are stayed. And if we must so put it, those are the pure elements, the fields adorned with eternal flowers, and the fountains of living water, and the mountains verily pregnant with a thousand loftiest gifts, and the shaded and secluded valleys, and the freshness of the woods, where, free of all damage, there flourish gloriously the beech, the olive and the aloe, with every other incense-bearing tree, in which armies of birds rest in glory and sweetest music which never falls silent. To compare this our woeful exile with that region is to compare disharmony with peace, and the disorder, trouble, tumult and vexation of the most restless city with purity, calm and sweetness themselves. Here is boasting and there is resting; here is imagining and there is seeing; here the shadows of things frighten us and make us afraid; there truth brings repose and delight; this is darkness, tumult, disturbance; that is purest light in eternal rest.

Beginning with the Christ of the Gospels as he roams the Galilean countryside, Fray Luis quickly moves to the vision of heaven itself in a passage which is a commentary on the verse we have been examining from the 'Noche serena' and on the whole of the 'Alma región luciente' ode (XVIII); indeed, on all his longing to exchange the frailty and shadow of human life for the glory of heaven. The simplicity of the natural creation is closer to God's original than the works and arts of man, symbolized by the city; closer too to the *simplicitas* of the divine being than the fragmented, manifold existence of man in his cities. The imagery has many parallels with both odes; by now we should be used to the equation of mountains with pregnancy. Heaven is contrasted with earthly exile as in many of his poems, but here with the explicit introduction of the country–city antithesis.

Obviously, Fray Luis has endowed the country with a moral and spiritual significance. Life is simpler and purer there than in the city, as so many writers repeated; but for Fray Luis, unlike most of them, this becomes a pointer to the realm of peace and beauty above. He explains how rightly the Bride pleads with the heavenly Shepherd to show her the place of his pasture: 'Tell me, O thou whom my soul loveth, where thou feedest, where thou makest thy flock to rest at noon' (Song i.7). In the passage above, exotic incense-bearing trees stand amidst the western pastoral landscape, and here a Biblical text completes this section of the exposition. Fray Luis sees no conflict, only continuity, and expounds noon as the place:

... adonde está la luz no contaminada en su colmo, y adonde, en sumo silencio de todo lo bullicioso, sólo se oye la voz dulce de Cristo, que, cercado de su glorioso rebaño, suena en sus oídos de El sin ruido y con incomparable deleite, en que, traspasadas las almas santas y como enajenadas de sí, sólo viven en su *Pastor*.   (470)

where uncontaminated light reaches its zenith and where in profoundest silence of everything disturbing, the sweet voice of Christ alone is heard which, surrounded by his glorious flock, sounds noiselessly and with an incomparable delight in his ears, and in which blessed souls, transported and as if ravished from themselves, live only in their *Shepherd*.

'Pastor' continues with a eulogy of Christ's love for us, beyond all other kinds of loving. It includes a finely-wrought passage which weaves together fire and fountain imagery by portraying Christ as the Bridegroom wet with the dews of night (Song v.2), as also a living, ever-flowing fountain of love, whose flames we can behold as Moses saw the burning bush and St John the Divine the figure of the Son of Man shining like the sun. The images complement one another instead of cancelling each other out, as fire and water actually would. Then the shepherd's work is explained: Christ feeds us to immortality, cares for the needs of each member of the flock, rules by the spirit, not the letter, and brings his flock into a more intimate unity than any other. Christ is the good and perfect shepherd who calls his own flock, gives up his life for the sheep and himself becomes their food; a shepherd by birth and a shepherd for ever.

Fray Luis therefore has two principal sources for his pastoral images and themes, the western tradition of classical and Renaissance literature and the oriental tradition of the Bible. Bucolic poetry was for him the most appropriate form for the poetry of divine love because the Bible itself so uses it; as we know, he regarded the Song on the literal level as a pastoral eclogue.[24] And because the Bible, unlike poetry, was the authoritative record of divine revelation, it is reasonable to suppose that he saw the secular pastoral idiom of the west through its eyes. That is why he can so easily connect pastoral landscapes through mystical exegesis with the innocence of Eden and the vision of heaven.

His version of Christian pastoral is best represented by 'Alma región luciente', often called 'De la vida del cielo' ('Of the life of heaven'). Its final verse has been criticized for placing awkwardly together three expressions with very distinctive ancestries. Yet it is this very fact which provides insight into the structure and meaning of the ode. The verse answers a plea not actually made in the poem, but arising from the exclamation of the preceding verse: '. . . Siquiera/pequeña parte alguna descendiese/en mi sentido . . ./y toda en ti, ¡oh Amor!, la convirtiese!', 'If only the merest fragment [of that music] might descend into my senses and convert [my soul] wholly into Love!' Then:

> Conocería dónde
> sesteas, dulce Esposo; y desatada
> desta prisión, a donde
> padece, a tu manada
> viviera junta, sin vagar errada.[25]

> Then would it know, sweet Spouse,
> where you repose and breaking free, away
> from this its prison-house
> of woe, at one would stay
> united with your flock, nor wandering stray.

The plea, of course, is that of Song i.7, where the Beloved is urged to reveal the place of his noontide rest. Exegetes generally understood this to refer to the Bride's search for her absent Beloved, one which continues elsewhere in the Song, as in her night-time wanderings through the city, the germ of St John of the Cross's 'Noche oscura' poem, 'Upon a dark night'. Fray Luis's meaning here can be paraphrased as 'If only I could hear the voice of the Good Shepherd and be enraptured by it, then I would be wholly united with Christ'. The Spanish flavour of the verb 'sestear' (from which 'siesta' comes, and which harks back to line 23 of the ode, 'él, sesteando', 'He, resting'), should not mislead us. This is the Christ the Bridegroom, pictured here, as in the Song, as the shepherd at rest feeding his flock. The text is the very one Fray Luis chose in 'Pastor' as his Biblical warrant for Christ the lover of the countryside.

The second expression, literally 'unloosed from this prison where she suffers', is the Platonic commonplace of the soul as imprisoned in the flesh, a frequent theme in the poetry of Fray Luis. We have already encountered it in the 'Noche serena' (VIII), where the light and beauty of the heavenly temple, seen through the darkness of the night sky, is contrasted with the blind sleep of mortals below. But the tyranny of the senses clips the wings of the soul and it cannot fly home.[26] The beginning of the Ode to Salinas (III) is more explicitly Platonic, with the musician's art stirring the soul's 'memoria perdida', 'lost memory' of its 'origen primera esclarecida', 'first noble origin'. The Platonic theory of anamnesis here carries its later Christian overtones, because the soul's 'first origin' suggests its lost innocence and communion with God after the Fall, rather than its pre-embodied life, while the sphere-music becomes a symbol for the everlasting music of heaven. The third expression, 'it would live joined to your flock, without wandering astray', depends on Biblical pastoral themes (John xi.16, and the parable of the lost sheep in Matt. xviii/Luke xv, sometimes linked with the twenty-third Psalm in Christian devotion).[27]

These three sources, the Song, Platonic tradition and the pastoral mode, inform the whole poem and are reunited in this last verse. Fray Luis sees connections between them which we may not, as the exposition of 'Pastor' shows, and he uses them interchangeably as metaphors for the subject of the poem, Christ's presence in heaven as the true home of the earthbound soul. So a Platonic perception of earthly life as shadow and heavenly life as reality is joined with the pastoral poetic tradition of east and west, with its moral and spiritual significance, to evoke the life of immortality and to desire to grasp hold of it by knowing the heavenly Christ in the immortal region, of which every Christian possesses an image and a likeness through the presence of that same Christ in the soul.

The 'alma región luciente', 'beloved radiant region', of the opening apostrophe, in which 'alma' has an adjectival function, as elsewhere in Fray Luis, is of course heaven.[28] But the poem needs to be read with this movement between a heaven beyond the skies and heaven's imprint in the soul in mind, because heaven is the origin and goal of each person and the transcendent, heavenly Christ is one with the immanent Christ indwelling each Christian soul. The imagery of the first verse establishes the contrast between earth as a place of change and decay and the changelessness of heaven:

> Alma región luciente,
> prado de bienandanza, que ni al hielo
> ni con el rayo ardiente
> fallece: fértil suelo,
> producidor eterno de consuelo:

> Fair realm of radiant light,
> O meadow of the blest, that neither hail
> Nor lightning-flash may blight,
> But solace without fail
> Springing from richest soil doth e'er prevail.[29]

This radiant region is also a meadow of blessedness, a fertile land which is ever yielding consolation – physical images defined by abstract ones which give a moral and spiritual significance to the place. In contrast stand earthly pastures, prone to the destructive force of frost and lightning blast. Purely human aspirations after temporal goals are threatened by destructive forces as earth's crops are by extremes of weather; the natural pastures of the soul in heaven are self-sufficient and never fail.

The main verb is delayed until midway through the second verse, its subject till the end. This heightens its mystery: a figure begins to emerge before we know his identity or what he is doing:

> De púrpura y de nieve
> florida, la cabeza coronado,
> a dulces pastos mueve
> sin honda ni cayado,
> el Buen Pastor en ti su hato amado.

> With purple flowers and white
> His head is crowned as, onward journeying,
> To pastures of delight,
> With neither crook nor sling,
> The Good Shepherd his loved flock in thee doth bring.

The verse describes how the Good Shepherd moves his beloved flock through the radiant region to sweet pastures. But at first we see, literally, only 'with purple and with flowering snow, his head crowned'. The Greek accusative of the last phrase, a stylistic device associated with the later, *culto* poets, has a double effect. It makes plain that the figure being revealed is male, because it places the masculine 'coronado' up against the feminine 'cabeza' in a way which seems to transgress the elementary rules of agreement of gender. And it shows a crowning which is figurative or otherwise a nonsense, with purple and flowering snow (or flowering purple and snow; the syntax allows both). This is a poetic paraphrase of the kind found in Góngora, who often used 'coronar', a Latinism, and enjoyed creating paradoxical confusions of colours:

> Púrpuras rosas sobre Galatea
> la Alba entre lilios cándidos deshoja:
> duda el Amor cual más su color sea,
> o púrpura nevada o nieve roja.

> Encrimsoned roses mixed with lilies white
> On Galatea's beauty Dawn bestows,
> Till Love can hardly tell her hue aright,
> Whether a rosy snow or snowy rose.[30]

Galatea has the white innocence of the lily and the red beauty of the rose, but although the picture is highly stylized, it is realistic in the sense that the human complexion is a subtle combination of both colours. But the 'púrpura' and 'nieve florida' of Fray Luis's ode combine classical diction with Christian symbolism. Purple is associated with the kingship of Christ, and especially the mocking robe placed on him before his crucifixion. Snow is the colour of the Son of Man's raiment (Dan. vii.9) or hair (Rev.1.14). Moreover, there is a Biblical precedent for the mixing of the colours red and white, and we hardly need guess where: 'Dilectus meus candidus et rubicundus' (Song v.10), 'My beloved is white and ruddy.' We do not suppose Góngora to have been thinking consciously of this; but Fray Luis surely is, because, as we are about to learn, he is describing the one called Beloved in the Song and 'Amado' in the *Nombres* (the name here applied adjectivally to his flock), who is the Good Shepherd of St John, and 'Pastor'.

This Good Shepherd is moving his flock towards sweet pastures. 'Dulce' is one of the commonest of all adjectives in pastoral poetry, as in the opening of Garcilaso's first eclogue, 'El dulce lamentar de dos pastores', 'The sweet lamenting of two shepherds'. He moves them 'without sling or crook', because he is the perfect shepherd who, as

'Pastor' explains, governs his flock by feeding them and attending to individual needs, rather than by imposing laws, here symbolized by the necessary instruments of the shepherd's office on earth. There are no wild beasts to be fought off with slings, and the flock is held together by him in perfect love, so no crook is required. As he moves his flock towards the heavenly pastures, so he is moving within the earthbound soul, to lift it thither. This relationship is clarified in 'Pastor':

> O porque los tiene en sí, por esta misma causa, lanzándose en medio de su ganado, mueve siempre a sí sus ovejas; y no lanzándose solamente, sino levantándose y encumbrándose en ellas. . . Porque apacentándolas las levanta del suelo, y las aleja cuanto más va de la tierra, y las tira siempre hacia sí mismo, y las enrisca en su alteza, encumbrándolas siempre más y entrañándolas en los altísimos bienes suyos. Y porque El uno mismo está en los pechos de cada una de sus ovejas, y porque su pacerlas es ayuntarlas consigo y entrañarlas en sí . . . por eso le conviene también lo postrero que pertenece al *Pastor*, que es hacer unidad y rebaño. . . No está la vestidura tan allegada al cuerpo del que la viste, ni ciñe tan estrechamente por la cintura la cinta, ni se ayuntan tan conformemente la cabeza y los miembros, ni los padres son tan deudos del hijo, ni el esposo con su esposa tan uno, cuanto Cristo, nuestro divino *Pastor*, consigo y entre sí hace una su grey. (479–80)

For this very reason, because he possesses them in himself, he ever moves his sheep towards himself; not only by entering but by raising and uplifting himself in them . . . For by feeding them he lifts them from the ground and takes them away the further he goes from the earth, and draws them ever towards himself, and gives them refuge on his heights, ever uplifting them ever more and leading them to penetrate his highest gifts. And because He only himself is in the breast of each of his sheep and because his feeding them is to join them to him and lead them intimately into himself . . . he is rightly ascribed the final quality of the *Shepherd*, of creating unity and a flock . . . No clothing clings so closely to the body which wears it, no belt girds so tightly the waist, nor are head and limbs so fitly joined, no parents are such kindred to their child nor husband so at one with his wife as Christ our divine *Shepherd* makes his flock one with himself and one other.

As he moves in heaven, so he stirs within the soul – a simple yet profound statement of the classic tension in Christian theology and spirituality between the transcendent and the immanent, the risen and ascended Christ in heaven and the Christ who indwells human hearts. This is not far from the mystical journey described by St John of the Cross at the beginning of the *Cántico espiritual*, the way of introspection and self-knowledge, and St John uses the same text from the Song: '¡Oh, pues, alma hermosísima entre todas las criaturas, que tanto deseas saber el lugar donde está tu Amado para buscarle y unirte con él, ya se te dice que tú misma eres el aposento donde él mora', 'Oh soul, loveliest among all the creatures, so desirous of knowing the place where your Beloved is to seek him and be united with him! He is telling you that you yourself are the lodging where he dwells.'[31]

The third verse shows the flock following their shepherd and the pasture he gives them:

> El va, y en pos dichosas
> le siguen sus ovejas, do las pace
> con inmortales rosas,
> con flor que siempre nace
> y cuanto más se goza más renace.

> He goes, and after him
> Follow the happy sheep: their pasturage
> Are flowers that wax not dim,
> But their desire assuage
> And cropped still suffer neither change nor age.

The shepherd feeds his flock 'with immortal roses, with a flower ever born, and the more it is enjoyed, the more it is reborn.' Roses are usually a metaphor for fleeting beauty, and sheep do not eat them. By this double paradox, Fray Luis takes the rose, symbol of transience, old age and death, and turns it into a symbol of eternal and divine beauty which feeds the soul and which – like the sun, fountain and abyss metaphors of the *Nombres* – never ceases to give of itself. The eternity of such roses is reinforced by the three expressions of the last three lines of the verse. They are immortal; their flower is ever new; and they flower more freely the more they are enjoyed. In other words, he turns the rose metaphor inside out, and he does so because he is looking to the rebirth of what is mortal into immortality, the earthly rose of human life into the heavenly rose of the soul at one with Christ. The sheep hunger for and now feed upon divine beauty, which is eternal and ever being born.

This transmutation of a commonplace image into something much more subtle is one of the hallmarks of Fray Luis's poetic creativity. It exists in many forms. In the Ode to Salinas (III) the music played by the blind musician lifts the poet's soul into a higher world, where it hears:

> . . . otro modo
> de no perecedera
> música, que es de todas la primera.[32]

> . . . another kind
> of imperishable
> music, which is of all the first.

The sphere music of the classical heavens becomes the divine music of the Christian God; the music of the world below, played in time, with a beginning and an ending, is a distant echo of the music of heaven, out of which it flows in a fragmented and limited measure, retaining only the power to arouse the soul to memory of its source. His conclusion, 'que todo lo visible es triste lloro', 'for all that is seen is a sad weeping', acquires a particular pathos since the ode is addressed to a blind man whose music proves the point. And we have already noted how in the 'Noche serena' (VIII) darkness and light are likewise inverted. Images which express what is partial, transient and mortal on earth characteristically but also paradoxically represent what is eternal in the realm of truth. It is not therefore that life below is to be rejected as unbearably coarse; rather, that one must learn to respond sensitively to those treasures in it, like the rose, the night sky and beautiful music, which are the signposts to the life of heaven.

It is at such points that Fray Luis has perhaps been insufficiently appreciated. Elegant in style and diction, he is sometimes thought of as conventional in theme. But his use of these images of transience tells us otherwise, when, as here, we are faced with sheep who feed on ever-blooming roses. The images convey the theme instead of illustrating it, as a comparison with two quite different examples from English poetry may show. Robert Herrick's charming version of the *Carpe diem* topos, 'Gather ye rosebuds while ye may', is well known and follows a long tradition of advising lovely young women to take advantage of their beauty before its rose blows over and becomes ugly and shrivelled in old age. There are other famous examples – Ronsard's 'Mignonne, allons voir si la rose' and Góngora's humorous 'Que se nos va la Pascua, mozas' ('Easter's on the way out, girls'). By way of contrast, T.S. Eliot, so heavily indebted to the lyrical and mystical imagery of the European past, treats the image of the rose in his *Four Quartets* much more subtly and symbolically. At the beginning of 'Burnt Norton' (lines 15–17), as he wrestles with the relationship of past, present and future, he comments:

> But to what purpose
> Disturbing the dust on a bowl of rose-leaves
> I do not know.

He imagines the rose after its flower has died and fallen, and only the dying leaves and stem are left to gather dust. Why probe its message? The past is gone, beyond recall; memory cannot make what is lost live again. But this is the start of a journey consummated only at the end of

'Little Gidding', when 'the fire and the rose are one'. The purifying
and transforming power of fire, used in other parts of the poem as a
symbol for divine love, has consumed the fragile, ephemeral beauty of
the rose, but in order to fulfil its beauty, not to destroy it. Divine and
human love are at one from the moment time and eternity intersect in
the Incarnation. The true meaning and loveliness of the rose is
understood only when its shadow has been burnt away and it is no
longer a child of matter and of sense but is caught up into immortal
beauty. Only the Incarnation can make this possible, for only there
are divinity and humanity united, so that love both human and divine
passes through death and rises to glory. The 'inmortales rosas' of Fray
Luis have something of that order of complexity, though in a much
more concentrated span – beautiful but transient on earth, symbols of
the eternal beauty of heaven.

Yet there is more to them than that. In the fourth verse we reach the
place where the shepherd has guided his flock for refreshment:

> Ya dentro a la montaña
> del alto bien las guía; ya en la vena
> del gozo fiel las baña,
> y les da mesa llena,
> pastor y pasto él solo y suerte buena.

> In the blest mountain's fold
> He guides, and zealous for their welfare goes,
> Bathes them in waters cold
> And plenteous fare bestows,
> The Pastor–Pasture whence all blessing flows.

Like the 'radiant region' of the first verse, this is clearly allegorical:
they enter the mountain 'of lofty goodness', where the mountain's
characteristic epithet 'alto' is applied instead to the quality it
represents. The flock is bathed 'in the vein of faithful joy', a hint
perhaps of the cleansing power of baptism or Christ's blood, or of the
living water he brings. They pass 'dentro', 'within', deeper within the
'beloved region', which now contains this mountain sanctuary – the
name 'Monte' applied again to Christ, in a slightly different form.
They are given 'mesa llena', a 'furnished table', another echo of the
twenty-third psalm, so often used as an image of Holy Communion,
the altar table on which the food of Christ's body is set forth. The
ancient christological paradox of the shepherd who is also the pasture
is expounded through Fray Luis's mystical Pauline theology at the

end of 'Pastor', where he connects Christ's feeding with at least four of
the five births of the Son of God:

Es así *Pastor*, que es pasto también, y . . . su apacentar es darse a sí a sus ovejas.
Porque el regir Cristo a los suyos y el llevarlos al pasto, no es otra cosa sino
hacer que se lance en ellos y que se embeba y que se incorpore su vida, y hacer
que con encendimientos fieles de caridad le traspasen sus ovejas a sus
entrañas, en las cuales traspasado, muda El sus ovejas en sí. Porque,
cebándose ellas de El, se desnudan a sí de sí mismas y se visten de sus
cualidades de Cristo . . .
   Porque antes que naciese en la carne, apacentó a las criaturas luego que
salieron a luz; porque El gobierna y sustenta las cosas, y El mismo da cebo a
los ángeles . . . Y . . . nacido ya hombre, con su espíritu y con su carne
apacienta a los hombres, y luego que subió al cielo llovió sobre el suelo su
cebo; y luego y agora y después, y en todos los tiempos y horas, secreta y
maravillosamente y por mil maneras los ceba; en el suelo los apacienta, y en el
cielo será también su *Pastor*, cuando allá los llevare; y en cuanto se revolvieren
los siglos y en cuanto vivieren sus ovejas, que vivirán enteramente con El, El
vivirá en ellas, comunicándoles su misma vida, hecho su *Pastor* y su pasto.

(481–2)

Such a *Pastor* is he, that he is also pasture, for his feeding lies in giving himself
to his sheep. For Christ's governing of his own and his leading them to pasture
is none else than his entering into them so that his life is absorbed and
incorporated, and his transporting them into his very heart with faithful
kindlings of love, whither so transported he changes his sheep into himself.
For, feeding upon him, they are stripped of themselves and put on Christ's
qualities . . .
   For before he was born in the flesh, he fed the creatures as soon as they came
to light; for he governs and sustains all things, and himself gives food to the
angels . . . And . . . once born man, he feeds men with his spirit and his flesh;
and once ascended into heaven, he rained his food upon earth; and then and
now and afterwards, at all times and in every hour, secretly and wondrously
he feeds them in a thousand ways; on earth he feeds them and in heaven,
when he carries them there, he will likewise be their *Shepherd*; and as long as
the ages roll and his sheep live who will live eternally with him, he will live in
them, communicating to them his very life, their *Pastor* become their pasture.

The shepherd who in the second verse was guiding the flock to 'sweet
pastures' can only be leading them to himself if he is their food. When
he feeds them with immortal roses, he is feeding them with himself,
and the roses assume a fresh significance, not simply as symbols of
eternity but of the eternal food which is Christ himself. Fray Luis does
not state this overtly, but by the progression from 'immortal roses' to
the 'furnished table' of the one who is both shepherd and pasture he
implies it, and if we read the poem sensitively the train of thought

across the shifting images becomes apparent. The 'suerte buena' ('good fortune') the sheep enjoy is union with Christ in heaven, and like the 'bienandanza' of the first verse and the 'dichosas', 'bien' and 'gozo' of the third and fourth, it adds a positive content to the ode even when its language is abstract.

The syntax at the start of the fifth verse is disrupted; literally, 'And of its sphere when the summit reaches, ascended to the highest point, the sun', that is, when the sun reaches its noontide position:

> Y de su esfera, cuando
> la cumbre toca altísimo subido
> el sol, él sesteando,
> de su hato ceñido
> con dulce son deleita el santo oído.

> When in the highest sphere
> The sun to heaven's zenith doth attain,
> His flock around him here
> Resting, will he sustain
> His sacred ear's delight with music's strain.

This poetic paraphrase for noon marks the fulfilment of the quest, for at last we come to the Beloved's noontide resting-place with his flock. The place is hard to find because of its intimate seclusion, and it is easy to overlook here, in the heart of the ode, unless we are alert to the significance of the phrase 'él, sesteando' as the answer to the plea of Song i.7. It is a scene of idyllic pastoral peace. The shepherd rests 'girt by his flock': 'ceñido', used in an earlier passage from 'Pastor', suggests here as there the closeness of the union between them.

Now the imagery changes. Shepherds have pipes and make music, and the Good Shepherd is no exception, except that his music is of the imperishable kind: 'with sweet sound he delights the holy ear'. He plays on his 'rabel' ('pipe'):[33]

> Toca el rabel sonoro,
> y el inmortal dulzor al alma pasa
> con que envilece el oro,
> y ardiendo se traspasa,
> y lanza en aquel bien libre de tasa.

> Immortal ecstasy
> The soul drinks as he strikes the sounding lyre,
> Gold is mere mockery
> In this consuming fire
> Of endless blessings that outrun desire.

The verse contains several phrases which develop out of earlier ones. The sweet sound of the previous one becomes the 'sonorous pipe' which brings 'immortal sweetness': '*dulces* pastos', '*dulce* son', now '*dulzor*'; 'producidor *eterno*', 'rosas *inmortales*', now '*inmortal* dulzor'. The 'alto *bien*' of the mountain has become 'aquel *bien* libre de tasa', meaning 'unrestricted' rather than the literal 'tax-free', which has other connotations for us. This music puts all earthly treasure – symbolized by gold – into perspective. There is further syntactical difficulty in the line 'con que envilece el oro', because it is not clear from the Spanish what the subject of the verb is: whether it is gold which grows tarnished, or the immortal sweetness which tarnishes the gold; or, as seems likely, whether 'envilece' does not rather mean 'despises', so that the sweetness makes the soul despise gold.[34] This negative effect, however it takes place, is paralleled by a positive one, for the soul 'burning is transported and leaps into that goodness free of price.' Mystical experience may find it hard to express itself through images, but it also seems to cause disruption and ambiguity in the normal syntactical flow, a marked feature of the poetry of St John of the Cross.[35]

The journey has been both upwards and inwards until the shepherd's music is heard at the point of stillness in the middle of the poem; yet that very stillness is ambiguous, for in it the soul presses on upwards in the fire of ecstasy till it reaches its goal. The soul has ascended to the radiant region were the sheep rest secure and the shepherd plays sweet, intoxicating music, Christ's music, the fire of divine love which catches the soul up. The pastoral heaven has become an inferno of bliss.

But the movement cannot be sustained. The descent to where the soul remains trapped is swift and painful; significantly, the word 'alma', now with its substantive meaning, appears for the first time since the first word of the poem:

> ¡Oh son! ¡oh voz! Siquiera
> pequeña parte alguna descendiese
> en mi sentido, y fuera
> de sí el alma pusiese,
> y toda en ti, ¡oh Amor!, la convirtiese!

> O voice! O music! might
> But some faint strain descend into my sense
> In transports of delight,
> That my soul, journeying hence
> Might lose itself in thee, O love immense!

'If only!' the poet cries. If only the merest fragment of what the soul experiences there might enter 'my sense', all of me that is constrained and frustrated by life in the flesh. For the first time, the poem becomes personal – '*mi* sentido'. We sense the poet's pain: his imagination has travelled far but his soul remains grounded. He has come close to his destination, glimpsed it, but has yet to experience its reality. This expression of an unfulfilled longing is even more poignant than in Fray Luis's other poems, through the personal tone, which attaches to his senses but not to his soul, the five imperfect subjunctives, and the near impossibility of the wish. Not just 'if', but 'if only'; not just 'a part' or even 'a small part', but 'the smallest part'. These qualifications measure the poet's distance from his desired end, and emphasize it dramatically and emotionally. We remember, perhaps, Marcelo's outburst of grief at his sins in 'Jesús'.

The 'Noche serena' ode has the same theme of flight into freedom and knowledge, but ends more confidently with what the poet will see when he reaches the celestial regions inhabited by blessed spirits. He will see and know those things which Job could never understand when God spoke to him out of the whirlwind and asked 'Who is this that darkeneth counsel without knowledge?' (xxxviii.2). There Fray Luis uses some of the Biblical imagery – the stars, the seasons – which God uses to reveal Job's ignorance of the divine design, and the full effect of the ode will not be felt without seeing the closing chapters of the Biblical poem behind it. In the Ode to Salinas, the heavenly music to which the blind musician's playing opens his ears leads to the prayer:

> ¡Oh! suene de contino,
> Salinas, vuestro son en mis oídos![36]
>
> Oh, ever may your sound,
> Salinas, be sounded in my hearing!

But in 'Alma región luciente' it is so much more conditional. If only . . . then the soul would be 'fuera de sí', 'beyond herself', and be wholly converted into you, o Love. The tiniest fragment would cause the longed-for transformation; but it remains a longing, not an experience. That the poet remains alienated from what he so ardently desires calls into question the ecstatic picture of the sixth verse. Was it fuelled by what he had read, perhaps, of the saints and mystics? Or was it some briefest foretaste of what he longs to possess in its fullness? We cannot know.

So we return to where we started, to the fusion of images and concepts in the last verse of the ode, a fitting conclusion because it unites the separate strands: the midday rest of one who is the Good Shepherd and the sweet Husband; the ties which bind the soul to earth; and the pastoral mode as an image of heaven. The desire to find the Beloved's resting-place is one and the same with the desire for some fragment of Christ's presence to descend into the senses, purify them of their wrongful desires, and restore the soul to its rightful position of supremacy. If I were wholly transformed in Love, then I would be free of all that prevents my rising to where my sweet Husband, Christ the Good Shepherd and the Bridegroom, entrances his flock in his mountain pastures with his music. After the brief soaring in the fire of love, the ode returns us to the poet's prison, still haunted by the conditionality of 'If only!', on which the last verse depends. Its final word, 'errada', 'lost', carries all the weight of error and foolish searching among lesser goods of which Fray Luis so often wrote. But that is where the poet belongs. He is not united with Christ's flock, but wanders astray. Only 'Amor', the God who is Love, can lead the soul to the secret place of noontide rest, where she may soar in burning ecstasy to the sound of his eternal music.

Fray Luis is a more difficult poet than is sometimes admitted. He weaves together many traditional elements into a complex pattern of images and ideas which deceive us by its apparent simplicity. What seems to be decorative, like the language of the pastoral mode, comes supported by a foundation of the theological reflection beneath the surface, as we have seen not only in this ode but in several others, by reference to parallel passages in the *Nombres*. The clarity of his poetic diction is deceptive too. He uses many stylistic features of the *culto* poets of the following century. The history of Spanish Golden Age poetry as one of an increasing difficulty and deliberate obscurity, from Garcilaso through Herrera to Góngora and Quevedo, can only be accepted if the poetry of Fray Luis, let alone St John of the Cross, is excluded from the reckoning. With him, we find links both with the humanistic side of Renaissance literature, especially in the influence of classical poetry, and with a much older Christian tradition, both in terms of its Biblical and devotional content. If there is a bridge between these two worlds in Spanish Golden Age literature, then Fray Luis is that bridge. If we want to make some overall sense of a culture which could produce the ardent outpourings of St John of the Cross and the linguistic and conceptual obscurities of Góngora or Quevedo, then Fray Luis gives us an abundance of clues.

It is in his handling of commonplace images and ideas that his originality is best appreciated, as we have tried to show through a close reading of 'Alma región luciente', supported by other poems and the *Nombres*. In the ode we encounter the central character crowned with crimson and white flowers before we know his identity; we meet him feeding his sheep with everlasting roses before we learn that he is himself their pasture. But it is no more than we might expect from one who pressed his classical and Biblical scholarship so completely into the service of his Christian faith. If that is not as evident in his poetry as in his prose works, that is because he is an artist of subtlety and grace, who knows that sometimes to suggest and hint at the mystery of beauty and of love through a language of image and symbol is a surer road to winning his reader's allegiance than the plain assertion of the truth.

Notes

1. Seeing through words

1 The best study of Luis de León in English remains A.F.G. Bell, *Luis de León* (Oxford, 1925). For his biographical information Bell was indebted to a long series of articles by P. Gregorio de Santiago Vela in *AHHA*, 6–20 (1916–23), which remain fundamental. Bell discusses the doubts some critics have expressed about the date and place of the birth of Fray Luis, pp. 88–92. For the cult of Mary at Belmonte, see W.A. Christian, *Local Religion in Sixteenth-Century Spain* (Princeton, 1981), pp. 77, 97.

2 He gives details of his early years in *CDIHE* x, 180–2.

3 See D. Gutiérrez, 'Del origen y carácter de la escuela teológica hispano-agustiniana de los siglos XVI y XVII', *CD*, 153 (1941), 227–55; M. Andrés' 'Reforma y estudio de teología entre los agustinos reformados españoles (1431–1550)', *Anthologica Annua*, 4 (1956), 439–62, and also his *La teología española en el siglo XVI*, 2 vols. (Madrid, 1976–7), I, 140–58. On Fray Luis's early promise, see J. Román, 'Chronica de la Orden de los Ermitaños del Glorioso Padre Sancto Agustín', BNM MS R 30177, dated Salamanca, 1569, ff. 136^r, 148^v; also D. Gutiérrez, 'Textos y notas acerca de Fray Luis de León y Francisco Cornejo', *AnalAug*, 30 (1967), 332–40.

4 He was proclaimed a Doctor of the Church by Pius V in 1567.

5 See Fernández de Castro, 'Fr. Cipriano de la Huerga, maestro de Fray Luis de León', *REEB*, 2 (1928), 269–78.

6 Bell, *Luis de León*, p. 103.

7 Quoted in E. Asensio, 'Fray Luis de León y la Biblia', *Edad de Oro* 4 (1985), 5–31, p. 21.

8 Francisco Pacheco, *Libro de descripción de verdaderos retratos de ilustres y memorables varones*, eds. P.M. Piñero Ramírez and R. Reyes Cano (Seville, 1985), pp. 69–70.

9 The three sermons were first published in *Declaración de los mandamientos de la ley, artículos de la fe, sacramentos, y ceremonias de la Iglesia* (Madrid, 1792), as an appendix to thirty-two sermons by the sixteenth-century Spanish Dominican Juan de la Cruz, translated from Latin into Spanish (translator and editor unknown). There is an eighteenth-century MS copy of the Soto and Augustine sermons in RAH (9–9–8 2091). The copyist does not seem to have known the earlier, Zaragoza MS, since the corrections he suggests sometimes agree and sometimes do not agree with the Zaragoza corrections. The Zaragoza MS, described in *Manuscritos e incunables de la Biblioteca del Real Seminario de San Carlos de Zaragoza* (Zaragoza, 1943), p. 46, is the seventeenth-century MS 74, entitled 'Luysii Legionensis. . . Orationes tres ex codice manuscripto'. Each copyist must have been working from a different, older MS.

10 This is most easily available in A. Coster, 'Discours prononcé par Luis de León au chapître de Dueñas', *RH*, 50 (1920), 1–60.

11 References to this sermon are from the 1792 edition, above, appendix pp. 49–87. See also J.M. Becerra, 'Panegírico de San Agustín por Fray Luis de León', *Augustinus*, 26 (1981), 35–65.

12 Quotations from San Juan de la Cruz follow *San Juan de la Cruz. Obras completas*, ed. L. Ruano, OCD, 11th edn (Madrid, 1982); p. 27.

13 R. Lapesa, *Poetas y prosistas de ayer y de hoy* (Madrid, 1977), pp. 110–45, is especially valuable on Fray Luis as a *culto* writer.

14 St Augustine's views on the 'usefulness' of the obscurity of Biblical language became very influential (*De doctrina christiana* II, vi).

15 So I am told by the Augustinians of Salamanca.

16 W. Repges, *Philologische Untersuchungen zu den Gesprächen über die Namen Christi von Fray Luis de León* (Münster, 1959), pp. 408–12.

17 See M. Bataillon, *Erasmo y España* (Mexico, 1966), pp. 345–404; A. de Valdés, *Diálogo de las cosas ocurridas en Roma* and *Diálogo de Mercurio y Carón* (Madrid: *CC*, 1965); J. de Valdés, *Diálogo de doctrina cristiana* (Mexico City: Universidad Nacional de México, 1964).

18 All references to the published Spanish prose works of Luis de León are, unless otherwise indicated, from *Fray Luis de León. Obras completas castellanas*, ed. F. García, 2 vols., 4th edn (Madrid, 1967).

19 From Isaac Watts (1674–1748); the last hymn in book 1 of his *Horae Lyricae* (1709), 'Eternal Power, whose high abode' (based on AV Psalm lxv. 1).

20 Quotations from the original poems of Fray Luis come from *Fray Luis de León. Poesías*, ed. A.C. Vega (Barcelona, 1980); here, pp. 20–1. Some versions read 'la India' for 'la mina' in the second verse.

21 Both 'todo lo demás' and 'todo lo visible' have MS support; see Vega, *ibid.*, p. 17.

22 T. O'Reilly, 'The Ode to Francisco Salinas', in *What's Past is Prologue. A Collection of Essays in Honour of L.J. Woodward*, eds. S. Bacarisse et al. (Edinburgh, 1984), pp. 107–13.

23 *The Solitudes of Don Luis de Góngora*, verse trans. E.M. Wilson (Cambridge, 1965), p. 29.

24 *CDIHE* x, 477, 491–3; xi, 293–4. On Montano, see A.F.G. Bell, *Benito Arias Montano* (Oxford, 1922); B. Rekers, *Arias Montano* (Madrid, 1973).

25 *CDIHE* x, 26–7. In the *Cantar*, see, for example, i, 141–2, 187–90, 195–7, 210.

26 *Ibid.*, p. 565.

27 The defence he made of his interpretation from his prison cell is in *Obras* i, 211–18.

28 E.R. Curtius, *European Literature and the Latin Middle Ages* (London, 1953), pp. 46–7.

2. The strife of tongues

1 The trial record is printed in *CDIHE* x–xi; references in the text give volume and page numbers only.

2 *CDIHE* x, 6–7. On Vatable and Pagnini see below, note 7 and p. 39.

3 Bell, *Luis de León*, gives a full account of his involvement in university affairs, pp. 168–93.

4 See C.P. Thompson, 'A little-studied manuscript of Luis de León: the *Quaestiones Variae*'. *BHS*, 61 (1984), 5–6. The *quaestio* was a recognized form for the logical discussion of philosophical or theological issues.

5 The Tunisian refugee Jacob ben Chayin: 'the greatest step forward yet taken towards establishing the best text of the Hebrew Bible' (*CHB* iii, 52).

6 C.P. Thompson, '*Quaestiones*', 2.

7 *CHB* III, 45. On Pagnini, see also T. Centi, 'L'attività letteraria di Santi Pagnini (1470–1536) nel campo delle scienze bibliche', *Archivum Fratrum Praedicatorum*, 15 (1945), 5–51.

8 On Estienne, see E. Armstrong, *Robert Estienne, Royal Printer* (Cambridge, 1954).

9 H. Jedin, *A History of the Council of Trent*, trans. E. Graf, 2 vols. (London, 1957–61); II, 92.

10 E.F. Sutcliffe, in 'The Council of Trent on the "Authentica" of the Vulgate', *Journal of Theological Studies*, 49 (1948), 35–42; p. 36.

11 In 'El decreto tridentino sobre la Vulgata y su interpretación por los teólogos del siglo XVI', *Estudios Bíblicos*, 5 (1946), 137–69; p. 145.

12 *CDIHE* x, 287; M. de la Pinta Llorente, *Proceso criminal contra el hebraísta salmantino Martín Martínez de Cantalapiedra* (Madrid, 1946), p. 4.

13 E. Asensio, 'Fray Luis', 20–1.

14 *De fide* is in *Opera* V, 223–323.

15 *Opera* V, 259.

16 *Opera* V, 280.

17 See C.P. Thompson, 'The Lost Works of Luis de León: (2) *Expositio in Genesim*', *BHS*, 57 (1980); 206.

18 Quoted in F. Cantera, 'Arias Montano y Fr. Luis de León', *BBMP*, 22 (1946), 299–338; p. 328; also in *Obras* I, 963. Fray Luis wrote also of his desire to escape from University business and to 'vivir lo que resta en sosiego y en secreto aprendiendo lo que cada día voy olvidando más' (I, 964), 'live what remains in tranquillity and privacy, learning what each day I am increasingly forgetting.'

19 *Commentaria in Esaiam Prophetam* (Salamanca, 1570); see also V. Pinto Crespo, *Inquisición y control ideológico en la España del siglo XVI* (Madrid, 1983), p. 195.

20 BM MS Egerton 1871, ff.9^r–16^v (untitled).

21 BM MS Egerton 1871, ff.2^r–4^r.

22 Quoted in F. Pérez Castro, *La Biblia Políglota de Amberes* (Madrid, 1973), p. 32.

23 Castro was for example mentioned as a possible collaborator with Diego de Vera in the preparation of a new Inquisitorial catalogue and involved in revising Montano's Polyglot; Pinto Crespo, *Inquisición*, pp. 192; 71–2.

24 M. de la Pinta Llorente, *Estudios y polémicas sobre Fray Luis de León* (Madrid, 1956), p. 59.

25 H. Kamen, *The Spanish Inquisition* (New York, 1965), p. 174. Pinto Crespo, *Inquisición*, is the most accessible full-scale work on the Inquisition and its effect on Spanish intellectual life.

26 For brief details about Pérez, see G. de Andrés, *Proceso inquisitorial del padre Sigüenza* (Madrid, 1975), p. 206, note 125.

27 B.J. Gallardo, *Ensayo de una biblioteca española de libros raros y curiosos*, 4 vols. (Madrid, 1863–89), IV, 1328–9; Bell, *Luis de León*, p. 162.

28 Pinta Llorente, *Proceso contra . . . Martínez*, p. 212.

29 See below, pp. 147–50.

30 Published in M. de la Pinta Llorente, 'Agustinos renacentistas en la Inquisición española', *AA*, 60 (1976), 3–42.

31 Christmas Eve, 1568. See J. Lynch, *Spain under the Habsburgs*, 2 vols., 2nd edn (Oxford, 1981), I, 224–33.

32 Pedro de Fuentidueñas, quoted in Ben Rekers, *Arias Montano* p. 82.

33 Prohibition began as early as 1233, during the Cathar troubles, and was renewed at the end of the fifteenth century. On Spanish attitudes in the sixteenth century, se J.I. Tellechea Idígoras, 'Biblias publicadas fuera de España secuestradas por la Inquisición de Sevilla', *BH*, 64 (1962), 236–47, and 'La censura inquisicional de Biblias de 1554', *Anthologica Annua*, 10 (1962), 89–142.

34 *Obras* I, 408. Others felt the same need for a vernacular Bible. The best-known Spanish apologia of the period is Fadrique Furió Ceriol, *Bononia, sive de libris sacris in vernaculam linguam convertendis* (Basle, 1556).

35 In his polemical *Alla Serenissima Madama la Granduchessa Madre*; see *Opere de Galileo Galilei*, 13 vols. (Milan, 1808–11), XIII, 49–50. Zúñiga's commentary does not seem to have been singled out for expurgation until the Papal Index of 1616, according to *Catalogue des ouvrages mis à l'Index* (Paris, 1825).

36 1591 edition, pp. 318–19.

37 M. de la Pinta Llorente, *Causa criminal contra el biblista Alonso Gudiel, catedrático de la Universidad de Osuna* (Madrid, 1942); see also Santiago Vela, 'El P.M. Fr. Alonso de Gudiel', *AHHA*, 7 (1917), 178–92.

38 C. Muiños Sáenz, *Fr. Luis de León y Fr. Diego de Zúñiga* (El Escorial, 1914).

39 I. Aramburu Cendoya, 'Fr. Diego de Zúñiga, O.S.A. Biografía y nuevos escritos', *AA*, 55 (1961), 51–103, 329–84.

40 *Ibid.*, 93.

41 François Titelman(s) (1502–37), a Franciscan and later a Capuchin, held a Chair at Louvain, wrote many philosophical works and Biblical commentaries, and supported the Vulgate against Erasmus.

42 D. Gutiérrez, 'Fray Luis de Alarcón († p. 1554) y la provincia agustiniana de España en el siglo XVI', *AnalAug*, 24 (1961), 30–90; 74. See also *CDIHE* x, 369.

43 Steuch, or Augustinus Eugubinus (*c.* 1497–1548), an Italian theologian and Biblical scholar, coined the expression *philosophia perennis*, according to P.O. Kristeller, *Renaissance Thought and its Sources* (New York, 1979), p. 131.

44 Lindanus (Willem van der Lindt, bishop of Ghent) was a Biblical scholar and an anti-Lutheran controversialist; this work was published Cologne, 1558.

45 Quotation from M. Durán, *Luis de León* (New York, 1971), p. 143. The psalm commentary is in *Opera* I, 118–68.

46 Kamen, *Spanish Inquisition*, p. 92.

47 *Obras* II, 177.

48 AHN MS Inq. 4427, no.1; contractions resolved, punctuation modernized.

49 Bell, *Luis de León*, pp. 174–5, assumes, probably rightly, that the Dominican Castillo felt that Fray Luis had suffered enough and in any case had many influential friends.

50 AHN MS Inq. 4444, no.10; see Santiago Vela, 'Delación del libro "De los Nombres de Cristo" de Fr. Luis de León', *AHHA*, 12 (1919), 114–15.

51 Vega, *Fray Luis de León. Poesías*, p. 49; from XV, 'Esperanzas burladas'.

52 E.L. Rivers, *Fray Luis de León: The Original Poems* (London: Grant & Cutler, 1983), p. 16.

53 Vega, *Fray Luis de León. Poesías*, p. 49.

54 *Ibid.*, p. 70.

55 *Ibid.*, p. 35.

56 *Ibid.*, p. 29.

57 *Ibid.*, p. 31.

58 His opinion is in *Obras* I, 987–91 (1587–8).

59 The second trial is studied fully by S. Múñoz Iglesias, *Fray Luis de León, teólogo* (Madrid, 1950), pp. 135–85, following the documents given by F. Blanco García, *CD*, 41 (1896), 16–37, 102–12, 182–91, 273–83. Bell gives a brief account, *Luis de León*, pp. 175–80.

60 Múñoz Iglesias, *Fray Luis de León*, p. 157.

61 *Ibid.*, p. 164. On Castillo's role in the affair, see *CDIHE* XI, 228–9. In 1576 he had found Fray Luis's views quite orthodox but thought he was unwise to raise such contentious issues; in 1580 he had supported him (see note 49, above) and had approved the Latin commentary on Psalm 26.

62 Múñoz Iglesias, *Fray Luis de León*, pp. 167–9.
63 *Ibid.*, pp. 181–5.
64 It is in such controversies that an implicit Catholic theology of 'double predestination' might be seen. Calvin developed the idea of election to reprobation, rather than inventing it.
65 This concerned the way in which God's grace operated; see *ODCC*, 383.
66 'Doluimus de captura magistri Ludovici Legionensis et ad eum adiuvandum hortati sumus' – see D. Gutiérrez, 'Textos y notas acerca de Fray Luis de León y Francisco Cornejo', *AnalAug*, 30 (1967), 332–40; 334.
67 The atmosphere is well summed up by a future Pope, a member of an unsuccessful Roman delegation to Spain in 1565, to get Carranza handed over to Rome: 'Nobody dares to speak in favour of Carranza for fear of the Inquisition. No Spaniard would dare to absolve the archbishop, even if he were believed innocent, because this would mean opposing the Inquisition. The authority of the latter would not allow it to admit that it had imprisoned Carranza unjustly. The most ardent defenders of justice here consider that it is better for an innocent man to be condemned than for the Inquisition to be disgraced' – Kamen, *Spanish Inquisition*, p. 162.
68 On Villavicencio, see M. Andrés, *La teología española en el siglo XVI*, 2 vols. (Madrid, 1976–7); II, 407–9; and for the Inquisition's interest in him, Pinta Llorente, 'Agustinos renacentistas . . .', *AA*, 60 (1976), 16–17.
69 Pinta Llorente, *ibid.*, 19.
70 *Ibid.*, 16.
71 G. de Andrés, *Proceso . . . Sigüenza.*
72 *Ibid.*, pp. 99, 117, 133, 150.
73 *Ibid.*, pp. 64, 110, 113, 123, 129, 131.
74 *Ibid.*, p. 127.

3. The language of revelation

1 Santiago Vela, 'Oposiciones de Fr. Luis de León a la cátedra de Biblia', *AHHA*, 6 (1916), 192–209, 255–68, 325–37; also Bell, *Luis de León*, pp. 171–2.
2 Some idea of this vast subject may be gained from R.M. Grant, *The Letter and the Spirit* (London, 1957); R.M. Grant and D. Tracy, *A Short History of the Interpretation of the Bible*, 2nd edn (London, 1984). For the medieval period, see B. Smalley, *The Study of the Bible in the Middle Ages*, 3rd edn (Oxford, 1983); G.R. Evans, *The Language and Logic of the Bible: The Earlier Middle Ages* (Cambridge, 1984); H. de Lubac, *Exégèse mediévale. Les quatre sens de l'Ecriture*, 4 vols. (Paris, 1959–64); and *CHB* II, vi, 'The exposition and exegesis of Scripture'.
3 O. García de la Fuente, 'Un tratado inédito y desconocido de Fr. Luis de León', *CD*, 170 (1957), 258–334. My translations follow this text. The treatise ends with the note 'Explicit Tractatus . . . in vigilia Nativitatis Beatae Virginis Mariae, anno 1581' (334), i.e. 7 September. Though not specifically attributed to Fray Luis, it is found in an unnumbered MS in the private library of the Augustinian community at El Escorial, who kindly permitted me to examine it, alongside other Biblical expositions of his. Judging by the decorated headings, the large, clear hand and the abundance of marginal notes and references, it is a fair copy made from lecture notes.
4 In 'Hijo de Dios' (*Nombres*, third book), Fray Luis expounds each of these births and adds two more, in the Host and in the Christian soul; see below, pp. 212–18.
5 *CDIHE*, x, 9, 65.
6 *The Sunday Times*, Review Section, 20 June 1982.

7 *In Abdiam Prophetam* (Salamanca, 1589); in *Opera* III, 5-174.

8 Bell, *Luis de León*, p. 259, note 3, says that Fray Luis's 1580 commentaries had been plagiarized by Fray Jerónimo Almonacid in his *Commentaria in Canticum Canticorum Salomonis* (Alcalá, 1588). He follows Santiago Vela, 'El "Libro de los Cantares", comentado por Fr. Luis de León', *AHHA*, 12 (1919), 257-68.

9 On Kimhi, see *CHB* II, 269-71; also F.E. Talmage, *David Kimhi: The Man and the Commentaries* (Cambridge, Mass., 1978).

10 Josephus is referred to as Joseph ben Gorion, or Gorionis. The fate of the ten lost tribes has continued to interest certain groups: the British Israelites identify them with the white Anglo-Saxon races, the Mormons with the ancestors of the American Indians.

11 J. Prest, *The Garden of Eden* (New Haven, 1981), p. 38; see also H. Levin, *The Myth of the Golden Age in the Renaissance* (New York, 1969), pp. 175-6. On the American Indians, see A. Pagden, *The Fall of Natural Man* (Cambridge, 1982).

12 C.P. Thompson, '*In Genesim*', 206; Levin, *The Myth of the Golden Age*, pp. 183-4.

13 *Don Quixote* I, xi.

14 Levin, *The Myth of the Golden Age*, pp. 93, 190-1.

15 That historians as well as theologians looked for evidence of the foretelling of a new world is seen in the fact that Agustín de Çarate quotes a verse from Seneca's *Medea* as a secular prophecy of this in the dedication (dated 1555) to his *Historia del descubrimiento y conquista de las provincias del Perú* (Seville, 1577).

16 *Commentaria in Epistolam II Beati Pauli Apostoli ad Thessalonicenses*, in *Opera* III, 423-81.

17 A view put forward by K. Kottman, in *Law and Apocalypse: The Moral Thought of Luis de León* (The Hague, 1972), p. 79.

18 *In Canticum Canticorum Triplex Explanatio*, in *Opera* II.

19 For example, E.A. Peers, 'Mysticism in the poetry of Fray Luis de León', *BSS*, 19-20 (1942-3), 25-40; Crisógono de Jesús, 'El misticismo de fray Luis de León', *Revista de espiritualidad*, I (1942), 30-52; D. Gutiérrez, 'Fray Luis de León, autor místico', *RyC*, 93-4 (1976), 409-33.

20 References from *Bernard of Clairvaux on the Song of Songs*, trans. K. Walsh, 4 vols. (Kalamazoo, 1979-83).

21 Prest, *The Garden of Eden*, pp. 21-4; Curtius, *European Literature*, pp. 195-200.

22 From one of his 'Divine Love' poems, in *The New Oxford Book of Christian Verse*, ed. D. Davie (Oxford, 1981), pp. 148-9.

23 See below, pp. 160-1.

24 St Teresa of Avila, though she knew no Latin, gives the same interpretation of the kiss in her *Meditaciones sobre los Cantares*; see *Obras completas de Santa Teresa de Jesús*, eds. E. de la Madre de Dios and O. Steggink, 2nd edn (Madrid, 1967), p. 337.

25 Isaac Watts, at the start of the poem in note 22 above.

26 *Obras completas*, p. 31.

27 *Paradoxes of Paradise, Identity and Difference in the Song of Songs* (Sheffield, 1983), p. 272.

28 *Ibid.*, p. 275.

29 Places and dates of composition, recorded in the hand of Fray Luis on the Salamanca MS (see note below) are as follows: chapters 34-5, Valladolid, 10 and 14 December 1580; 36-40, Madrid, 27 October, 29 November, 14 December 1590 and 6 January, 1 February 1591; 41-2, Salamanca, 19 February, 8 March 1591. See Santiago Vela, 'El *Libro de Job*, del P.M. Fr. Luis de León', *AHHA*, 12 (1919), 132-47, 193-205. *Job* has attracted few studies, the most notable being M. Nerlich, *El hombre justo y bueno: Inocencia bei Fray Luis de León* (Frankfurt a/M, 1966) and J. Baruzi, *Luis de León, interprète du livre de Job* (Paris, 1966).

30 Salamanca University Library, MS M/219 JOB, 518ff.

31 On the exact identity of Basilio Ponce de León (b. 1570), see Bell, *Luis de León*, p. 94; P.M. Vélez, *Observaciones al libro de Aubrey F.G. Bell sobre Fray Luis de León* (El Escorial, 1931), p. 64; on his lack of success in getting the unedited works of Fray Luis published, see Santiago Vela, 'El *Libro de Job*'. It is to Ponce de León that we owe a number of references to works by Fray Luis subsequently lost; see J. Zarco Cuevas, 'Bibliografía de Fr. Luis de León', *REEB* 2 (1928), 287–413; especially 295, 298.

32 AHN MS Inquisición legajo 4444, no. 9; published by Santiago Vela in 'El *Libro de Job*', 138–40.

33 See A Sister of Notre Dame de Namur (Sister Anne Hardman), *Life of the Venerable Anne of Jesus* (London, 1932).

34 His correspondence on the Reform with Juan Vázquez del Mármol, January–July 1590, is in *Obras* I, 942–50. He took a keen interest in the internal politics of the Discalced and strongly supported the nuns in their desire to retain the privileges they enjoyed under the Teresan constitutions (e.g. to choose their own confessors and have a large measure of independence of the male Discalced hierarchy). He probably wrote the *Discurso sobre la diferencia que ay entre Frayles y Monjas Carmelitas Descalços, acerca del gouierno*, a short but masterly exposition of the reasons for permitting the nuns to retain their original constitutions. This appeared early in 1591 and could therefore be among his very last works. See Santiago Vela, 'Fr. Luis de León y los catedráticos de propiedad en la Universidad de Salamanca', *AHHA*, 8 (1917)–19 (1923), a long series of articles including material on his involvement in the Reform. His concerns no doubt grew out of his editing of St Teresa's works and the impression they made upon him: *Los libros de la Madre Teresa de Iesus* appeared in 1588 at Salamanca, and his finely written and moving appreciation of her work is in *Obras* I, 921–41. His 'Apología de los *Libros* de Santa Teresa de Jesús', *Obras* I, 915–20, is much more favourable than the judgement given by Báñez; see G. del Niño Jesús, 'Censores de los manuscritos teresianos: las correcciones de la Autografía teresiana, de Báñez a Fray Luis de León', *MC*, 65 (1957), 42–60.

35 Félix García; *Obras*, II, 8.

36 Baruzi, *Luis de León*, p. 6.

37 See e.g. J. Barr, *Fundamentalism*, 2nd edn (London, 1981); G.B. Caird, *The Language and Imagery of the Bible* (London, 1980).

38 Again we note how naturally the link between Virgil and the Bible was made. See H. de Lubac, *Exégèse médiévale*, II, 233–62, 'Virgile philosophe et poète'.

39 See H. Ettinghausen, *Francisco de Quevedo and the Neo-Stoic Movement* (Oxford, 1972).

40 *Obras* II, 1021–39, 'El Cantar de los Cantares en octava rima'. There is also a *lira* translation the authenticity of which has been disputed; the original is in Wadham College, Oxford, MS 52, ff. 191ʳ–205. See J. Múñoz Sendino, 'Los Cantares del Rey Salomón, en versos líricos, por Fr. Luis de León', *BRAE*, 28 (1948), 411–61; 29 (1949), 31–98. The matter remains unresolved.

41 The *terceto* has hendecasyllabic lines rhyming aba, bcb, cdc and so on, and normally ends, as here, with a quatrain, to complete the versification scheme.

42 This is discussed with reference to Fray Luis in I. Caramuel (Lobkowitz; bishop of Vigevano), *Primus Calamus*, 2 vols. (Rome, 1663–8), II, 529–30, who says it is a frequent device among the Greeks and gives examples from Horace and Fray Luis, quoting Quevedo's defence of the practice: if Fray Luis did it, that is sufficient authority. See also A. Quilis, 'Los encabalgamientos léxicos en "–mente" de Fray Luis de León y sus comentaristas', *HR*, 31 (1963), 22–39.

43 Following the classification of L.A. Sonnino, *A Handbook to Sixteenth-Century Rhetoric* (London, 1968).

44 At the end of the magnificent Ode to Juan de Grial (XI; Vega, *Fray Luis de León. Poesías*, p. 39) Fray Luis uses the whirlwind as a metaphor for treachery and his own consequent suffering:

> que yo, de un torbellino
> traidor acometido, y derrocado
> del medio del camino
> al hondo, el plectro amado
> y del vuelo las alas he quebrado.

Bell translates (*Luis de León*, p. 294):

> For me a treacherous blast,
> Suddenly assailing in a whirlwind dire,
> From out the way has cast
> To the depths, and my loved lyre
> Has broken, and the wings of my desire.

But the whilwind is also a sign of the presence of the omnipotent God, as supremely in Job xxxviii, discussed by Fray Luis in *Obras* II, 615–17. Storm imagery, like other metaphors, thus has several possible meanings.

4. The language of mystery

1 A. Mackay, *Spain in the Middle Ages* (London, 1977), p. 196.

2 J.N.D. Kelly, *Jerome: His Life, Writings and Controversies* (London, 1975), p. 134.

3 Smalley, *Study of the Bible*, especially pp. 112–95.

4 de Lubac, *Exégèse mediévale*, II, ii, 344–67.

5 See J.H. Bentley, *Humanists and Holy Writ* (Princeton, 1983), p. 74.

6 Bentley, *ibid.*, p. 75. There is some discrepancy in the information given about these *conversos* between von Hefele, *The Life of Cardinal Ximénez,* trans. J. Dalton (London, 1860), p. 138, and E. Esperabé Arteaga, *Historia pragmática e interna de la Universidad de Salamanca*, 2 vols. (Salamanca, 1914–17), II, 296–300.

7 *CHB* III, 48–56.

8 This, with much useful background information, is well surveyed by G. Lloyd-Jones, *The Discovery of Hebrew in Tudor England* (Manchester, 1983), especially pp. 26–35.

9 *CHB* III, 43.

10 See K.R. Stow, 'The burning of the Talmud in 1553, in the light of sixteenth-century Catholic attitudes towards the Talmud', *BHR*, 34 (1972), 433–59.

11 *CHB* III, 48.

12 For this ambivalence, see O.H. Green, *Spain and the Western Tradition*, 4 vols. (Madison, 1963–6), e.g. I, 5–26.

13 *CDIHE* XLI, 137–9; A.F.G. Bell, *Benito Arias Montano*, pp. 14–18; G. Andrés Martínez, 'Gestiones de Felipe II en torno a la compra de la Biblioteca del Cardenal Sirleto para El Escorial', *Revista de Archivos, Bibliotecas y Museos*, 67 (1959), 635–60.

14 BM MS Egerton 1871, ff. 5ʳ–8ᵛ. Another glimpse into contemporary attitudes is seen in Escorial MS H.I.II, ff. 20–1, 29; J. Zarco Cuevas, *Catálogo de los manuscritos castellanos de la Real Biblioteca de El Escorial*, 3 vols. (Madrid & El Escorial, 1924–9), I, 344. This contains correspondence in 1584–5 between Miguel de Alaejos, Prior of El Escorial, Dr Valverde, Arias Montano and the Archbishop of Toledo about

certain Hebrew notebooks (*cuadernos*) containing prohibited works and where these should be kept. It is clear from Alaejos and Valverde that they contained Kabbalistic material – 'cosas místicas, de la escriptura diuina, fundadas en arithmética y números' (f. 20ʳ), 'mystical things from divine Scripture based on arithmetic and numbers' – and that they had aroused some interest.

15 Perhaps the catalogue of 1583–4; see Pinto Crespo, *Inquisición*, pp. 197–233.

16 See P.E. Russell, 'Secular literature and the censors: a sixteenth-century document re-examined', *BHS*, 59 (1982), 219–25.

17 J.M. Millás Vallicrosa, 'Probable influencia de la poesía sagrada hebraico-española en la de Fr. Luis de León', *Sefarad*, 15 (1955), 261–86.

18 A parallel case might be the suggested Islamic influences on St John of the Cross; see L. López Baralt, *San Juan de la Cruz y el Islam* (El Colegio de México: Universidad de Puerto Rico, 1985).

19 A. Habib Arkin, *La influencia de la exégesis hebrea en los comentarios bíblicos de Fray Luis de León* (Madrid, 1966), p. 4.

20 W.J. Entwistle, 'The scholarship of Luis de León', *RR*, 26 (1935), 3–11; D. Gutiérrez, 'Fray Luis de León y la exégesis rabínica', *Augustinianum*, 1 (1961), 533–50. An interesting case for the influence of Kabbalism on some poetic expressions of Fray Luis is made out by L.J. Woodward, 'Hebrew tradition and Luis de León', *BHS*, 61 (1984), 426–31.

21 Kottman, *Law and Apocalypse*; see also his articles 'Fray Luis de León, O.S.A.: Notebook on the promises of the Old Law', *Augustiniana*, 22 (1972), 583–610', and 'Fray Luis de León and the universality of Hebrew: an aspect of 16th and 17th century language theory', *Journal of the History of Philosophy*, 13 (1975), 297–310.

22 See the review of the book by R.W. Truman, *EHR*, 89 (1974), 433.

23 C.G. Noreña, *Studies in Spanish Renaissance Thought* (The Hague, 1975), especially chapter 3, 'Fray Luis de León and the concern with language', pp. 150–209.

24 BNM MS 721, entitled 'Papeles tocantes a la Inquisición', f. 73. The MS also contains a 'Discurso sobre la dissension que ay entre los christianos viejos y christianos nuevos' (ff. 15ʳ–37ᵛ), an account of the conversion of Pablo de Santa María (f. 71), material on the 1559 Valladolid and 1588 Toledo *autos* and on the Carranza trial (ff. 105ʳ–114ᵛ; 117ʳ–120ᵛ).

25 On *limpieza de sangre* see Kamen, *Spanish Inquisition*, pp. 123–39.

26 *Ibid.*, p. 186.

27 G.G. Scholem, *Major Trends in Jewish Mysticism* (Jerusalem, 1961); *On the Kabbalah and its Symbolism* (London, 1965); *Kabbalah* (Jerusalem, 1974).

28 Scholem, *Major Trends*, p. 18.

29 *The Shaking of the Foundations* (Harmondsworth, 1962), pp. 166–9.

30 *CHB* III, 51.

31 In Letter 57 to Pammachius, Jerome set out his principles as a translator, stressing the need to render the sense of the words rather than to give a word-for-word version. He did however suggest that in the Bible the order of words itself contained mystery. See *CHB* II, 96–100, and *Saint Jérôme, Lettres*, trans. J. Labourt, 8 vols. (Paris, 1953), III, 59.

32 The definitive study is F. Secret, *Les Kabbalistes chrétiens de la Renaissance* (Paris, 1964); see also J.L. Blau, *The Christian Interpretation of the Cabala in the Renaissance* (New York, 1944).

33 Ficino quoted the *Bahir* against the Jews, while the French humanist Lefèvre d'Etaples (*c.* 1455–1536) wrote a treatise *De magia naturali* (1492–4) which modifies Secret's view that the first description of Kabbalism in France was Champier's *Ars parva Galeni* of 1516. Lefèvre evidently regarded Kabbalism 'as a way of manipulating the numerical value of Hebrew letters, especially those in sacred names, in order to work wonders of learning and magic'; see B.P.

Copenhauer, 'Lefèvre d'Etaples, Symphorien Champier, and the secret names of God', *Journal of the Warburg and Courtauld Institutes*, 40 (1977), 189–211.

34 Kottman, *Law and Apocalypse*, p. 32.

35 Andrés, *La teología española*, II, 75–6.

36 On Medina, see C. Gutiérrez, *Españoles en Trento* (Valladolid, 1951), pp. 848–69.

37 An unfinished translation, partly in Spanish, partly in Latin of Kimhi on Isaiah, Jeremiah and Malachi; MS a.IV.20; Zarco Cuevas, *Catálogo*, I, 19.

38 C.P. Thompson, *'Quaestiones'*, 4–5.

39 See e.g. Smalley, *Study of the Bible*, p. 104; *CHB* II, 266.

40 C.P. Thompson, *'In Genesim'*, 207, 210–11.

41 In *John Donne: Selected Prose*, eds. H. Gardner and T. Healey (Oxford, 1967), p. 244.

42 Studied by S. Múñoz Iglesias, 'Una opinión de Fr. Luis de León sobre la cronología de la Pascua', *Estudios Bíblicos*, 3 (1944), 79–96.

43 Failure to appreciate this explains the form 'Jehovah', in which the vowels of the pious paraphrase *Adonai*, 'the Lord', were mistakenly read with the consonants of the tetragrammaton YHWH. It is a good, if difficult point to raise with Jehovah's Witnesses.

44 See above, pp. 75–6.

45 The translation is by G. Cunningham, in A.A. Parker, *Polyphemus and Galatea* (Edinburgh, 1977), pp. 130–1.

46 Erasmus and Luther disputed the meaning of the hardening of Pharaoh's heart in relation to free will; see *Luther and Erasmus: Free Will and Salvation* (Philadelphia, 1969), pp. 64–5, 223–31.

47 As I was preparing this chapter, two pamphlets came into my possession from an American fundamentalist source, purporting to show how the name Jesus is present in the Old Testament and how he can be proved to be the Messiah from a hundred primary Old Testament references. Some of the texts they mention are expounded by Fray Luis. The old polemic is enjoying a long twilight.

5. The names of the Word

1 See especially Repges, *Philologische Untersuchungen*.

2 *PG* 6, e.g. 651, 767–71.

3 *PG* 14, e.g. 60–1, 64–5.

4 *PL* 4, especially 727–8, 740–3, 751–3.

5 *PL* 34 (*De Genesi ad litteram* IV.28); *PL* 35 (*In Joannis Evangelium*), e.g. 1727–31, 1735.

6 *PL* 82, 264–8.

7 Repges, *Philologische Untersuchungen*, pp. 316–77.

8 Iᵃ. 13.

9 *Opera* IV, 7–485.

10 For the influence of Duns Scotus on Fray Luis, see A. López, 'La idea cristocéntrica en Fr. Luis de León', *RyC*, 23–4 (1961), 564–82; Segundo Folgado, *Cristocentrismo teológico en Fr. Luis de León* (El Escorial, 1968); E. Rivera de Ventosa, 'El primado de Cristo en Duns Escoto, y Fr. Luis de León', *RyC*, 93–4 (1976), 485–502.

11 See above, pp. 9–11.

12 *La pensée de Fray Luis de León* (Paris, 1943); shortened as *El pensamiento filosófico de Fray Luis de León* (Madrid, 1960).

13 Hebrew, for Fray Luis, is thus the first language not merely because it came first in time but because its words are the nearest of any to representing the divine

meaning of things. See Kottman, 'Fray Luis . . . and the Universality of Hebrew'.

14 See above, p. 166.

15 Much has been written about this piece of paper. Some critics have identified it with an opuscule by Blessed Alonso de Orozco, *De nueve nombres de Cristo*, first published by Muiños Sáenz, 'De los *Nombres de Cristo*, de Fr. Luis de León y del beato Alonso Orozco', *CD*, 16 (1888); also in *Obras* 1, 827–64. They have believed this was either a summary of the *Nombres* or its source, the 'paper' on which Fray Luis based his work. See also Santiago Vela, 'De Nueve Nombres de Cristo', *AHHA*, 17 (1922), 137–49 (attacking the views of Muiños Sáenz), and E.J. Schuster, 'Alonso de Orozco and Fray Luis de León: *De los nombres de Cristo*', *HR*, 24 (1956), 261–70. My own view is that the 'paper' is a literary convention and that far too much significance has been attached to it; I am equally sure that Orozco's work is a summary of the *Nombres*, not a source. The practice of copying out or summarizing books found to be valuable was widespread. In the Escorial, for example, is a MS entitled 'Entre muchos nombres que Christo tiene el más propio y principal es llamarse Jesús' (MS d. III.25; Zarco Cuevas, *Catálogo*, 1, 119). This contains a verse translation of Psalm cii ('Benedic, anima mea') different from that of Fray Luis, but the whole work is clearly based on 'Jesús' from the *Nombres*. MS z.IV.12, ff. 248–335 (Zarco Cuevas, *Catálogo*, 11, 164–5) is even more curious, as it has a verse translation of eight of the *Nombres*, perhaps by the Jeronymite Juan de la Puebla.

16 See below, p. 219.

17 See above, pp. 22–6.

18 Solomon's temple fascinated many writers of the period and continues to form the basis of Masonic ritual through an allegorical interpretation of its architecture which has a long history. Some scholars have maintained that the Escorial itself was built to its proportions and that its principal architect, Herrera, was influenced by its mysteries; see R. Taylor, 'Architecture and Magic: considerations of the *Idea* of the Escorial', in *Essays in the History of Architecture Presented to Rudolf Wittkower* (London, 1967), pp. 81–109. G. Kubler counters this in his magisterial *Building the Escorial* (Princeton, 1982), pp. 43, 128–30. Apart from the imagintive reconstruction of the Temple by the Jesuits Villalpando and Prado (Kubler, *ibid.*, fig. 22), published 1598–1604, the Escorial library also contains an unpublished treatise of 1581 by the Premonstratensian Diego de Vergara, 'De la grandeza y la magnificencia de aquel templo tan famoso que el rey Salomón edificó' (MS J.II.13; 88ff).

19 See below, pp. 232–3.

20 See below, pp. 210–11.

21 It is thus a plan existing in his mind before he can carry it out; compare e.g. Calderón, *No hay más fortuna que Dios*, ed. A.A. Parker (Manchester, 1949), pp. xxvi–xxix.

22

> Born to raise the sons of earth,
> Born to give them second birth.
> (Wesley; 'Hark! the herald angels sing')

> A second Adam to the fight
> And to the rescue came.
> (Newman; 'Praise to the Holiest in the height')

23 See J.L. de Orella y Unzue, *Respuestas católicas a las Centurias de Magdeburgo (1559–1588)* (Madrid, 1976), especially pp. 347–87.

24 Santiago Vela, 'La Universidad de Salamanca y Fr. Luis de León (Datos para la

historia)', *AHHA*, 6 (1916), 11–26, 92–102; 'Oposiciones de Fr. Luis'; 'Fr. Luis de León y los catedráticos de propiedad'; 'La Universidad de Salamanca y Fr. Luis de León', *AHHA*, 13 (1920), 5–21, 133–43, 261–72; 14 (1920), 17–29; also Bell, *Luis de León*, especially pp. 182–93.

25 See above, pp. 160–1.

26 We are reminded of Lear's flash of insight during the storm:

> Poor naked wretches, wheresoe'er you are,
> That bide the pelting of this pitiless storm,
> How shall your houseless heads, and unfed sides,
> Your loop'd and window'd raggedness, defend you
> From seasons such as these? O! I have ta'en
> Too little care of this. Take physic, Pomp;
> Expose thyself to feel what wretches feel . . .
>
> (III.iv. 28–34)

Or of the astonishment of Montaigne's cannibals when they visited France and found that the few gorged themselves while the many starved.

27 See above, pp. 98–101.

28 See Thompson, *El poeta y el místico* (El Escorial, 1985), pp. 235–6.

29 See above, pp. 15–26; below, pp. 234–41.

30 See *Calderón de la Barca: Autos Sacramentales*, 2 vols., ed. A. Valbuena Prat (Madrid, 1957–8), I, 71–195.

31 See below, pp. 259–60.

32 The rather *conceptista* conversation they have about the correspondence between birds and fish is studied by M.J. Woods, *The Poet and the Natural World in the Age of Góngora* (Oxford, 1978), pp. 126–7, and is paralleled in the lectures on Genesis; see Thompson, *'In Genesim'*, 204–5.

33 The motherhood of Jesus or of God has become a much-debated issue in theology, and it is interesting to observe that Fray Luis makes reference to it here: 'Y porque es infinitamente fecundo, el mismo [Dios], como si dijésemos, se es el padre y el madre' (701), 'and because he [God] is infinitely fertile, he is, we might say, both father and mother to himself'. The idea is popularly associated with Mother Julian of Norwich, but Fray Luis could have found it in St Anselm's 'Prayer to St. Paul' (see *The Prayers and Meditations of Saint Anselm with the Proslogion*, trans. Sister Benedicta Ward, SLG (Penguin, 1973), pp. 153–6).

34 See above, pp. 75–6.

35 See above, pp. 161–5.

36 For the Erasmian influence on Fray Luis, see M. Bataillon, *Erasmo y España*, pp. 760–70.

37 Another example of the equation of obscurity with deep and hidden meaning.

38 Cf. the old Patristic dictum 'What is not assumed is not healed' –if Christ did not assume full humanity, then there can be no healing for the human condition.

39 The one full study of this remains available only in Spanish – H.D. Goode, *La prosa retórica de Fray Luis de León en "Los Nombres de Cristo"* (Madrid, 1969).

40 See above, pp. 7, 133.

6. The language of heaven

1 The most important recent critical editions are those of E. Sarmiento, *Fray Luis de León. The Original Poems* (Manchester, 1953); A.C. Vega, *Fray Luis de León. Poesías. Edición crítica* (Madrid, 1955); and the shorter version, Vega, *Fray Luis León*.

Poesías (Barcelona, 1980); O. Macrí, *La poesía de Fray Luis de León* (Salamanca, 1970); M. de Santiago, *Fray Luis de León. Obra poética completa* (Sant Cugat del Valles: Libros Río Nuevo, 1981); and *Obras* II, 697–1039.

Recent studies of the poetry include: L.J. Woodward, '*La vida retirada* of Fray Luis de León', *BHS*, 31 (1954), 17–26, and 'Fray Luis de León's *Oda a Francisco Salinas*', *BHS*, 39 (1962), 69–77; K. Maurer, *Himmlischer Aufenthalt* (Heidelberg, 1958); A. Quilis, 'Los encabalgamientos léxicos'; G.A. Davies, 'Notes on some classical sources for Garcilaso and Luis de León', *HR*, 32 (1964), 202–16, and 'Luis de León and a passage from Seneca's *Hippolytus*', *BHS*, 41 (1964), 10–27; D.J. Figueroa, 'La "Oda a la Ascensión" de Fray Luis', *RyC*, 10 (1965), 211–28; D. Alonso, *Poesía española*, 5th edn (Madrid, 1966), pp. 109–98; R. Ricard, 'Le Bon Pasteur et la Vierge dans les poésies de Louis de León. Notes et commentaires', *Less Lettres Romanes*, 22 (1968), 311–31; R. Lapesa, *Poetas y prosistas*, pp. 110–45; R. Senabre, *Tres estudios sobre Fray Luis de León* (Salamanca, 1978); C.P. Thompson, '"En la Ascensión": Artistic tradition and poetic imagination in Luis de León', in *Mediaeval and Renaissance Studies on Spain and Portugal in Honour of P.E. Russell* (Oxford, 1981), pp. 109–20; E.L. Rivers, *Fray Luis de León. The Original Poems* (London, 1983); T. O'Reilly, 'The Ode to Francisco Salinas'.

2 On the dedication, see Rivers, *Fray Luis de León*, pp. 13–15.

3 See above, p. 193.

4 On the MSS prepared by Fray Luis, see the editions of Sarmiento, pp. xxviii–xxxi, 70; Macrí, pp. 155–8; Vega (Madrid, 1955), pp. 361–412.

5 For his work as a classical translator, see C. Casanova, *Luis de León como traductor de los clásicos* (Barcelona, 1936); M. Fuertes Lanero, 'Versión de la I Olímpica de Píndaro', *RyC*, 11 (1966), 181–99; 12 (1967), 93–105; 13 (1967), 107–17; 14 (1969), 273–86; V. Bocchetta, *Horacio en Villegas y en Fray Luis de León* (Madrid, 1970); *Fray Luis de León. Obra poética completa*, ed. Santiago pp. 99–109.

6 In *Escritores del siglo XVI, ii: Obras del maestro fray Luis de León*, ed. G. Mayans y Síscar, *BAE* 37 (Madrid, 1872), p. xiii; the versions and Fray Luis's judgement appear in Caramuel, *Primus Calamus*, II, 528–31.

7 These were Odes ii.10, iv.13, i.22 and the second of the Epodes; see A. Gallego Mórell, *Garcilaso de la Vega y sus comentaristas* (Madrid, 1972), pp. 266, 269, 271–2, 286–7; also *Obras* II, 929–30, 947–8, 923–4, 949–51. El Brocense introduces the first with the words: 'Y porque un docto de estos reinos la tradujo bien, y hay pocas cosas de estas en nuestra lengua, la pondré aquí toda', 'And because a learned man of these realms has translated it well and there are few such examples in our tongue, I shall give it here in full' (Gallego Morell, *Garcilaso de la Vega*, p. 266).

8 See above, pp. 19–26.

9 Again we note the use of the *culto* 'coronar'.

10 See above, p. 210.

11 Entitled 'A Angélica y Medoro'. As Angélica tends the wounded Moor, Love enters her hitherto stony heart through the eyes, and the flint (of her heart) gives off sparks of water (tears); Love gives her his blindfold, but with it she bandages Medoro's wounds.

12 See most recently for the Spanish tradition F. López Estrada, *Los libros de pastores en la literatura española. La órbita previa* (Madrid, 1974); pp. 152–205 deal with Christian pastoral.

13 On divinization, see B. Wardropper, *Historia de la poesía lírica a lo divino en la cristiandad occidental* (Madrid, 1958); J. Crosbie, 'Amoral "a lo divino" poetry in the Golden Age', *MLR*, 66 (1971), 599–607.

14 See e.g. *The Essential Erasmus*, trans. J.P. Dolan (New York, 1964), p. 36.

15 Sebastián de Córdoba, *Las obras de Boscán y Garcilasso trasladadas en materias Christianas y religiosas* (Granada, 1575), f. 7ʳ.
16 *The Solitudes of Don Luis de Góngora*, p. 7.

276   NOTES TO PAGES 242–60

17 *San Juan de la Cruz. Obras completas*, p. 25.
18 Translated by Lynda Nicholson, in G. Brenan, *St. John of the Cross. His Life and Poetry* (Cambridge, 1973), p. 149.
19 *San Juan de la Cruz. Obras completas*, p. 591 (*Cántico* B, 4.4).
20 In a long poem entitled 'De contemptu mundi'; this verse is from John Mason Neale's well-known translation of parts of it, which begins 'Jerusalem the golden'.
21 Vega *Fray Luis de León. Poesías*, p. 31.
22 See above, pp. 186–9.
23 Juan del Encina (1468–1530) makes this point too; see López Estrada, *Los libros de pastores*, p. 153.
24 See above, pp. 28–9.
25 Most editions follow this reading, but Vega (*Fray Luis de León. Poesías*, p. 56) gives the last line as 'junta, no ya andara perdida, errada', 'united, would no longer walk lost and astray.'
26 See above, pp. 27–9.
27 As in H.W. Baker's popular paraphrase:

> Perverse and foolish oft I strayed,
> But yet in love he sought me,
> And on his shoulder gently laid,
> And home, rejoicing, brought me.

28 The other example is from '¡Qué descansada vida!' (1), line 24: 'A vuestro almo reposo', 'To your soul-repose'. The adjectival nature of 'almo' is clear because it has acquired a masculine form.
29 The rest of the translation of this poem is from Bell, *Luis de León*, pp. 294–5. A less archaic one is in *The Unknown Light. The Poems of Fray Luis de León*, trans. Willis Barnstone (Albany, 1979), pp. 87–9.
30 Cunningham's translation, *Polyphemus and Galatea*, pp. 114–15; see M.J. Woods, *The Poet and the Natural World*, p. 112.
31 *Cántico* B, 1.7; ed. cit., pp. 575–6.
32 Vega, *Fray Luis de León. Poesías*, p. 16; other editions read 'que es la fuente y la primera', 'which is the fountain and the first'. For 'todo lo visible es triste lloro', below, Vega, p. 17, has 'que todo lo demás es triste lloro', poetically less satisfying, in spite of his defence.
33 Defined as a three-stringed musical instrument, or a pipe. Barnstone, *The Unknown Light*, p. 87, translated 'rebec'.
34 Discussed by Vega, *Fray Luis de León. Poesías*, p. 56; Macrí, *La poesía de Fray Luis de León*, p. 356; Rivers, *Fray Luis de León*, p. 67.
35 See Thompson, *El poeta y el místico*, pp. 201, 205–6.
36 Vega, *Fray Luis de León. Poesías*, p. 17.

Bibliography

1. Manuscript sources

a Spain

i El Escorial
MS a.iv.20 'Comentarios de David Kimhi sobre Isaias, Jeremias y Malaquias, traducidos del hebreo en castellano'
MS ç.iii.6 'De las grandezas de Christo Rey. Libro segundo. Fr. Lucas de Alaejos, 1610'
MS d.iii.25 'Entre muchos nombres que Christo tiene el más proprio y principal es llamarse Jesús'
MS h.i.11 'Representación del prior de San Lorenzo, fr. Miguel de Alaejos, a S.M. sobre unos cuadernos hebreos. 12 de agosto de 1584' (ff.20–1)
MS j.ii.13 [Treatise on the magnificence and greatness of Solomon's Temple, Fr. Diego de Vergara, 1581]
MS z.iv.12 [Verse translation of parts of the *Nombres de Cristo*, ff. 248–335, ?Juan de la Puebla]
Unnumbered MS, Biblioteca de la Comunidad 'Obras d[] Maestro [ ] De Scriptura Sacra'

ii Archivo Histórico Nacional, Madrid
These MSS are untitled.
AHN MS Inq 3712
AHN MS Inq 3713
AHN MS Inq 4427
AHN MS Inq 4444

iii Biblioteca Nacional de Madrid
BNM MS 721 'Papeles tocantes a la Inquisición'
BNM MS 1243 'Historia de la Ciudad de Toledo', by P. Gerónimo de la Higuera, SJ, 9 vols.
BNM MS R 30177 'Chrónica de la Orden de los Ermitaños del Glorioso Padre Sancto Agustín', Fray Hieronymo Román, Salamanca, 1569

277

iv Madrid, Real Academia de la Historia
RAH MS 9-9-8 2073 (formerly 11-2-7 451)
'Quaestiones variae cum dogmaticae tum expositivae, necnon quodlibeticae
    per Magistrum Luisium Legionensem Eremitam Augustinianum'
RAH MS 9-9-8 2076 (formerly 11-1-3 fª 1ª 112)
'Codice de S Felipe'
RAH MS 9-9-8 2081 (formerly 11-1-3 fª 1ª 116)
'Papeles pertenecientes a la causa del Mro Fr. Luis de León'
RAH MS 9-9-8 2091 (formerly 11-1-3 fª 1ª 102)
'Obras latinas' and 'Oratio funebris in exequiis Magistri Dominici Soli per
    Magist. L. Leonense'

v Pamplona, Biblioteca de la Catedral
MS Cod. 83 'Expositio in Genesim'
MS Cod. 111 'De simonia'

vi Salamanca, Biblioteca de la Universidad
MS M/219 'Libro de Job a la muy religiosa madre Ana de Jesús'
MSS A.U.S. 940–4; 948–9; one unnumbered. 'Libros de visitas de cátedras'
    (1560–3, 1564–7, 1567–9, 1569–71, 1571–2; 1576–7, 1578–80; 1589–91)

vii Zaragoza, Real Seminario de San Carlos
MS 74 'Fr Luysii Legionenis Augustiniani, Orationes Tres. Ex codice
    manuscripto'

b Portugal

i Coimbra, Biblioteca de la Universidad
MS 1834 (Untitled)
MS 1984 (Untitled; 'De libero arbitrio', ff. 517–32)

ii Evora, Biblioteca Pública
MS cxxiii 2–27 'Scholia Super tertiam partem S. Tho. de Sacr[ament]is in
    Comuni. a Mancio Salmanticae – 1568' ('De sacramentis', ff. 193–211)

iii Oporto, Biblioteca Municipal
MS 1202 ('De simonia', ff. 146–74)

c England

i British Library
MS Egerton 1506 'Papeles del Consejo de la General Inquisición – Consultas
    al Rey Filippo II. 1574–1596'
MS Egerton 1871 'Mariana 3. Tractatus varii et collectanea, vol. 1'

ii Wadham College, Oxford
MS 52 'Los Cantares del Rey Salomón, en versos líricos, por Fr. Luis de León'
   (ff. 191^r–205)

II Books printed before 1800

Caramuel, Ioannis. *Primus Calamus*, 2 vols. Rome, 1663, 1668
Çarate, Agustín de. *Historia del descubrimiento y conquista de las provincias del Perú.*
   Seville, 1577
Castro, León de. *Commentaria in Esaiam Prophetam.* Salamanca: Mathias
   Gastius, 1570
   *Apologeticus pro lectiones apostolica, et evangelica, pro Vulgata Diui Hieronymi, Pro
   translatione LXX virorum, Proque omni Ecclesiastica lectione contra earum
   obtrectatores.* Salamanca: Haeredes Mathiae Gastij, 1585
   Commentaria in Oseam Prophetam. Salamanca, 1586
Córdoba, Sebastián de. *Las obras de Boscán y Garcilasso trasladadas en materias
   Christianas y religiosas.* Granada, 1575; Zaragoza, 1577
Crusenius, F. Nicolaus. *Monasticon Augustinianum.* Munich: Ioan. Hertsroy,
   1623
Furió Ceriol, Fadrique. *Bononia, sive de libris sacris in vernaculam linguam
   convertendis.* Basle: Oporinus, 1556
Herrera, Tomás. *Alphabetum Augustinianum.* Madrid: Gregorio Rodríguez,
   1644
   Breve compendio de los prelados eclesiásticos y ministros. Madrid: Francisco
   Maroto, 1643
   Historia del Convento de S. Augustín de Salamanca. Madrid: Gregorio
   Rodríguez, 1652
Juan de la Cruz, Fray. *Declaración de los mandamientos de la ley, artículos de la fe
   . . . Añádense al fin tres sermones latinos del maestro Fray Luis de León.* Madrid:
   Benito Caro, 1792
Múñoz, Luis. *Vida, y obras espirituales del venerable padre maestro Fr. Luis de
   Granada*, 3 vols. Madrid: Herederos de la Viuda de Juan García
   Infanzón, 1753
Soto, Domingo. *De natura et gratia.* Venice, 1547; Paris: Ioannes Foucher,
   1549; facsimile, Ridgewood, NJ: Gregg, 1965
Titelman(s), François. *Paraphrastica Elucidatio in librum D.Iob.* Paris: apud
   Audeonum Paruum, 1547
Zúñiga, Fray Diego de. *De Vera Religione.* Salamanca: Mathias Gastius, 1577
   In Zachariam Prophetum Commentaria. Salamanca: Mathias Gastius, 1577
   In Iob Commentaria. Toledo, 1584; Rome: Franciscus Zannettus, 1591
   Philosophiae prima pars. Toledo: Petrus Rodríguez, 1597

III Significant editions of the works of Fray Luis de León

In Psalmum vigesimum sextum Explanatio. Salamanca: Lucas a Junta, 1580
In Cantica Canticorum Salomonis Explanatio. Salamanca: Lucas a Junta, 1580;
   2nd edn, 1582

De los nombres de Christo and *La perfecta casada*. Salamanca: Juan Fernández, 1583
  2nd edn. Barcelona: Iuan Pablo Manescal, 1586
  3rd edn. Salamanca: G. Foquel, 1587
  4th edn. Salamanca: Iuan Fernández, 1595
  5th edn. Salamanca: Antonia Ramírez, 1603
Los libros de la Madre Teresa de Iesús, edited by Fray Luis. Salamanca: Guillermo Foquel, 1588
In Canticum Canticorum triplex Explanatio. Salamanca: Guillermo Foquel, 1589
In Abdiam Prophetam Expositio. Salamanca: Guillermo Foquel, 1589
In Epistolam Pauli ad Galatas. Salamanca: Guillermo Foquel, 1589
In Epistolam II Pauli ad Thessalonicenses. Salamanca: Guillermo Foquel, 1589
  [The above four works were published together under the general title *F. Luysii Legionensis Augustiniani Theologiae Doctoris, & Divinorum Librorum primi apud Salmanticenses interpretis explanationum in eosdem.*]
De utriusque agni typici atque veri immolationis legitimo tempore. Salamanca: Guillermo Foquel, 1590
Obras propias, y traducciones latinas, griegas y italianas, ed. Francisco de Quevedo. Madrid: Imprenta del Reyno, 1631
Obras propias i Traducciones, con la paráfrasis de Algunos Psalmos de David y capítulos de Iob. Milan: Guisolfi, 1631
Exposición del Libro de Job. Madrid: Pedro Marín, 1779
Traducción literal y Declaración del Libro de los Cantares. Salamanca: Francisco de Toxar, 1798
Obras del M.Fr. Luis de León, ed. Fray Antolín Merino, 6 vols. Madrid: Viuda de Ibarra, 1804–16
Epistalario español, ed. Eugenio de Ochoa. *BAE* 62; Madrid: M. Rivadeneyra, 1870
Obras del maestro fray Luis de León, ed. Gregorio Mayans y Síscar. *BAE* 37; Madrid: M. Rivadeneyra, 1872
Mag. Luysii Legionensis . . . Opera, ed. P. Marcelino Gutiérrez, OSA, 7 vols. Salamanca: Episcopali Calatravae Collegio, 1891–5
De los nombres de Cristo, edited by Federico de Onís, 3 vols. Madrid: *CC*. 1914–21
Fray Luis de León. The Original Poems, ed. Edward Sarmiento. Manchester University Press, 1953
Poesías. Edición crítica, ed. Angel C. Vega. Madrid: SAETA, 1955
Obras completas castellanas, ed. Félix García, OSA, 4th edn, 2 vols. Madrid: BAC, 1957
De Legibus, ed. Luciano Pereña. Madrid: CSIC, 1963
La poesía de Fray Luis de León, ed. Oreste Macrí. Salamanca: Anaya, 1970
Fray Luis de León. Poesías, ed. Angel C. Vega. Barcelona: Planeta, 1980
Fray Luis de León. Obra poética completa, ed. Miguel de Santiago. Sant Cugat del Valles: Libros Río Nuevo, 1981

IV Translations into English

Bell, Aubrey F.G. *Luis de León*, pp. 284–304. Oxford: Clarendon, 1925
The Unknown Light. The Poems of Fray Luis de León, trans. Willis Barnstone.
  Albany: State University of New York Press, 1979
Luis de León. The Names of Christ, trans. Manuel Durán and William Kluback.
  Classics of Western Spirituality, London: SPCK, 1984
  Reviewed by Colin P. Thompson in *New Blackfriars*, 66 (1985), 201–2

V Works published since 1800

Acosta y Lozano, Zacarías. 'Crítica de las obras poéticas de Fr. Luis de León'.
  AHHA, 15 (1921), 291–302
Alaejos, Abilio, C.M.F. 'En torno de la *Perfecta Casada*', *REEB*, 2 (1928).
  151–69
Aldana, J.A. de, S.I. 'Manuscritos teológicos postridentinos de la biblioteca
  provincial de Cádiz'. *Archivo teológico granadino*, 2 (1939), 25–33
Alonso, Dámaso. *Poesía española*, 5th edn. Madrid: Gredos, 1966
Alvárez Turienzo, Saturnino. *Fray Luis de León: valor de actualidad de su estilo
  intelectual y humano*. Salamanca: Universidad Pontificia, 1973
Andrés, Gregorio de. *Proceso inquisitorial del padre Sigüenza*. Madrid: FUE,
  1975
Andrés, Melquíades. 'Manuscritos teológicos de la Biblioteca Capitular de
  Palencia'. *Anthologica Annua*, 1 (1953), 477–550
'Reforma y estudio de teología entre los agustinos reformados españoles
  (1431–1550)'. *Anthologica Annua*, 4 (1956), 439–62
La teología española en el siglo XVI, 2 vols. Madrid: BAC, 1976–7
Andrés Martínez, G. 'Gestiones de Felipe II en torno a la compra de la
  Biblioteca del Cardenal Sirleto para El Escorial'. *Revista de Archivos,
  Bibliotecas y Museos*, 67 (1959), 635–60
Anselm, Saint. *The Prayers and Meditations of Saint Anselm*, trans. Sister
  Benedicta Ward, SLG. Harmondsworth: Penguin Classics, 1973
Aramburu Cendoya, Ignacio. 'Fr. Diego de Zúñiga, O.S.A. 1536–c. 1599.
  Biografía y nuevos escritos'. *AA*, 55 (1961), 51–103, 329–84
'El Capítulo Toledano de 1504 fin de la Claustra en la Provincia de
  España'. *AA*, 57 (1963), 67–92
'La Provincia de Castilla o de España en los años 1505–1525'. *AA*, 57
  (1963), 289–326
Armstrong, Elizabeth. *Robert Estienne, Royal Printer*. Cambridge University
  Press, 1954
Asensio, Eugenio. 'Fray Luis de León y la Biblia'. *Edad de Oro*, 4 (1985), 5–31
Augustine, Saint. *Obras de San Agustín XV. Tratados escriturarios*, ed. Balbino
  Martín, OSA. Madrid: BAC, 1969
Barr, James. *Fundamentalism*, 2nd edn. London: SCM, 1981
Baruzi, Jean. *Luis de León, interprète du livre de Job*. Paris: Presses Universitaires
  de France, 1966

Bataillon, Marcel. *Erasmo y España*. Mexico: Fondo de Cultura Económica, 1966

Becerra, J.M. 'Panegírico de San Agustín por Fray Luis de León'. *Augustinus*, 26 (1981), 35–65

Bell, Aubrey F.G. *Benito Arias Montano*. Oxford University Press, 1922
Francisco Sánchez El Brocense. Oxford University Press, 1925
Luis de León. Oxford: Clarendon, 1925

Beltrán de Heredia, Fr. Vicente, OP. 'Los manuscritos de los teólogos de la Escuela Salmantina'. *CT*, 42 (1930), 327–49
'Hacia un inventario analítico de manuscritos teológicos de la Escuela Salmantina, siglos xv–xvii, conservados en España y en el extranjero'. *RET*, 3 (1943), 59–88

Bentley, Jerry H. *Humanists and Holy Writ*. Princeton University Press, 1983
Bernard of Clairvaux on the Song of Songs, trans. Kilian Walsh, OCSO, 4 vols. Kalamazoo: Cistercian Publications Inc., 1979–83

Biblia Sacra iuxta Vulgatam Clementinam, ed. Alberto Colunga, OP and Lorenzo Turrado, 4th edn. Madrid: BAC, 1965

'Bibliographie historique de l'Ordre de Saint Augustin 1954–1975'. *Augustiniana*, 26 (1976), 1–340

Blanco García, Francisco. *Fr. Luis de León*. Madrid: Sáenz de Lubera, 1904

Blau, J.L. *The Christian Interpretation of the Cabala in the Renaissance*. New York: Columbia University Press, 1944

Bocchetta, Vittore. *Horacio en Villegas y en Fray Luis de León*. Madrid: Gredos, 1970

Brenan, Gerald. *St John of the Cross. His Life and Poetry*. Cambridge University Press, 1973

Brown, Jonathan. *Ideas and Images in Seventeenth-Century Spanish Painting*. Princeton University Press, 1978

Caird, George B. *The Language and Imagery of the Bible*. London: Duckworth, 1980

Calderón de la Barca, Pedro. *No hay más fortuna que Dios*, ed. A.A. Parker. Manchester University Press, 1949
Autos Sacramentales, ed. Angel Valbuena Prat, 2 vols. *CC* 69–70, Madrid: Espasa-Calpe, 1957–8

Cambridge History of the Bible, The. eds. S.L. Greenslade, G.W.H. Lampe, P.R. Ackroyd and C.F. Evans, 3 vols. Cambridge University Press, 1963–70

Campbell, Roy. *St John of the Cross: Poems*. Harmondsworth: Penguin, 1960

Cantera, Francisco. 'Arias Montano y Fr. Luis de León'. *BBMP*, 22 (1946), 299–338

Casanova, Concepción. *Luis de León como traductor de los clásicos*. Barcelona, 1936

Castrillo y Aguado, Tomás. 'La "Inmensa Cítara"'. *REEB*, 2 (1928), 173–8

Catálogo de los libros manuscritos que se conservan en la Biblioteca de la Universidad de Salamanca. Salamanca, 1855

Catálogo de manuscritos. Coimbra, 1955

Catalogue des ouvrages mis à l'Index. Paris: Imprimerie Ecclésiastique de Beaucé-Rusand, 1825

Centi, Timoteo, OP. 'L'attività letteraria di Santi Pagnini (1470–1536) nel campo delle scienze bibliche', *Archivum Fratrum Praedicatorum*, 15 (1945), 5–51

Christian, William A. *Local Religion in Sixteenth-Century Spain*. Princeton University Press, 1981

Colección de documentos inéditos para la historia de España, vols x–xi, eds. Miguel Salvá and Pedro Sáinz de Baranda. Madrid, 1847; vol. xli, eds. Marqueses de Pidal and Miguel Salvá. Madrid, 1862

Copenhauer, Brian P. 'Lefèvre d'Etaples, Symphorien Champier, and the secret names of God'. *Journal of the Warburg and Courtauld Institutes*, 40 (1977), 189–211

Copleston, Frederick, SJ. *A History of Philosophy*, 9 vols. London: Search Press, 1947–74

Coster, A. 'Discours prononcé par Luis de León au chapître de Dueñas'. *RH*, 50 (1920), 1–60

Crisógono de Jesús, OCD. 'El misticismo de fray Luis de León'. *Revista de espiritualidad*, 1 (1942), 30–52

Crosbie, John. 'Amoral "a lo divino" poetry in the Golden Age'. *MLR*, 66 (1971), 599–607

Cunha Rivara, Joaquin Heliodoro da. *Catálogo dos manuscriptos da biblioteca pública eborense*, 4 vols. Lisbon, 1850–71

Curtius, Ernst R. *European Literature and the Latin Middle Ages*. London: Routledge & Kegan Paul, 1953

Davies, Gareth A. 'Notes on some classical sources for Garcilaso and Luis de León'. *HR*, 32 (1964), 202–16

'Luis de León and a passage from Seneca's *Hippolytus*'. *BHS*, 41 (1964), 10–27

Domínguez Berrueta, Juan. 'Paralelo entre Fr. Luis de León y San Juan de la Cruz'. *REEB*, 2 (1928), 253–65

Domínguez Carretero, P.E. 'La escuela teológica agustiniana de Salamanca'. *CD*, 169 (1956), 638–85

Donne, John. *John Donne: Selected Prose*, eds. Helen Gardner and T. Healey. Oxford: Clarendon, 1967

Durán, Manuel. *Luis de León*. New York: Twayne, 1971

Ehrle, Franz. *Los manuscritos vaticanos de los teólogos salmantinos del siglo XVI*. Madrid: Biblioteca de Estudios Eclesiásticos, 1930

Entwistle, W.J. 'The scholarship of Luis de León'. *RR*, 26 (1935), 3–11

Erasmus. *The Praise of Folly*, trans. Betty Radice. Harmondsworth: Penguin, 1971

The Essential Erasmus, trans. J.P. Dolan. New York: Mentor, 1964

Esperabé Arteaga, Enrique. *Historia pragmática e interna de la Universidad de Salamanca*, 2 vols. Salamanca: F. Núñez Izquierdo, 1914–17

Estebáñez, Maximiliano, P. 'El P. Muiños y su obra póstuma Fr. Luis de León y Fr. Diego de Zúñiga'. *España y América*, 47 (1913), 129–39

Ettinghausen, Henry. *Francisco de Quevedo and the Neo-Stoic Movement*. Oxford University Press, 1972

Evans, G.R. *The Language and Logic of the Bible: The Earlier Middle Ages*.

Cambridge University Press, 1984

Fernández de Castro, Eduardo Felipe. 'Fr. Cipriano de la Huerga, maestro de Fray Luis de León'. *REEB*, 2 (1928), 269–78

Figueroa, D.J. 'La "Oda a la Ascensión" de Fray Luis'. *RyC*, 10 (1965), 211–28

Fitzmaurice-Kelly, James. *Fray Luis de León*. Oxford University Press, 1921

Folgado, Avelino, OSA. 'Los tratados *de legibus* y *de justitia et jure* en los autores españoles del siglo XVI y primera mitad del XVII'. *CD*, 172 (1959), 275–302

Folgado, Segundo, OSA. *Cristocentrismo teológico en Fr. Luis de León*. El Escorial: Biblioteca 'La Ciudad de Dios', 1968

Foulché-Delbosc, R. 'Manuscrits hispaniques de bibliothèques dispersées'. *Revue des Bibliothèques* 22 (1912), 430–72; 23 (1913), 81–108

Fresno, Leonides, OSA. 'Sentido afirmativo de *Los Nombres de Cristo*'. *RAE*, 10 (1969), 493–514

Fuertes Lanero, Miguel, P. 'Versión de la I Olímpica de Píndaro'. *RyC*, 11 (1966), 181–99; 12–13 (1967), 93–105, 107–17; 14 (1969), 273–86

Galileo Galilei. *Opere de Galileo Galilei*, 13 vols. Milan: 1808–11

Gallardo, Bartolomé José. *Ensayo de una biblioteca española de libros raros y curiosos*, 4 vols. Madrid: M. Rivadeneyra, 1863–89

Gallego Morell, A. *Garcilaso de la Vega y sus comentaristas*. Madrid, 1972

García, Paul, OSB. 'El concepto de la persona en *La Perfecta Casada*'. *RAE*, 9 (1968), 17–32

'Orden contra caos en Fray Luis de León'. *RAE*, 9 (1968), 201–20

'La expresión de la naturaleza en la *Perfecta Casada*'. *RAE*, 10 (1969), 87–107

García Alvárez, Jaime, OSA. 'Los fundamentos filosóficos de la obra literaria de Fray Luis de León'. *Burguense*, 13 (1972), 129–98

García de Castro, Rafael G. '*Los Nombres de Cristo*'. *REEB*, 2 (1928), 95–107

García de la Fuente, Arturo, P. 'Arias Montano'. *CD*, 153 (1941), 5–56

García de la Fuente, Olegario, P. 'Un tratado inédito y desconocido de Fr. Luis de León'. *CD*, 170 (1957), 258–334

García Lorca, Francisco. *De Fray Luis a San Juan: la senda escondida*. Madrid: Castalia, 1972

García Oro, José. *La reforma de los religiosos españoles en tiempo de los Reyes Católicos*. Valladolid: Instituto "Isabel la Católica" de Historia Eclesiástica, 1969

Góngora, Luis de. *Poems of Góngora*, ed. R.O. Jones. Cambridge University Press, 1966

The Solitudes of Don Luis de Góngora, verse trans. Edward Meryon Wilson. Cambridge University Press, 1965

Polyphemus and Galatea, ed. Alexander A. Parker, with a verse trans. by Gilbert F. Cunningham. Edinburgh University Press, 1977

Goñi Gaztambide, José, P. 'Catálogo de los manuscritos teológicos de la Catedral de Pamplona'. *RET*, 18 (1958), 61–85

Goode, Helen Dill. *La prosa retórica de Fray Luis de León en 'Los Nombres de Cristo'*. Madrid: Gredos, 1969

Grant, Robert M. *The Letter and the Spirit*. London: SPCK, 1957
  and Tracy, D. *A Short History of the Interpretation of the Bible*, 2nd edn.
  London: SCM, 1984
Green, Otis H. *Spain and the Western Tradition*, 4 vols. Madison: University of
  Wisconsin Press, 1963–6
Gustavo del Niño Jesús, OCD. 'Censores de los manuscritos teresianos: las
  correcciones de la Autobiografía teresiana, de Báñez a Fray Luis de
  León'. *El Monte Carmelo*, 65 (1957), 42–60
Gutiérrez, C. *Españoles en Trento*. Valladolid: CSIC, 1951
Gutiérrez, David, OSA. 'Del origen y carácter de la escuela teológica
  hispano-agustiniana de los siglos XVI y XVII'. *CD*, 153 (1941), 227–55
  'Un comentario inédito de fray Luis de León'. *Augustinianum*, 1 (1961),
  273–309
  'Fray Luis de León y la exégesis rabínica'. *Augustinianum*, 1 (1961), 533–50
  'Fray Luis de Alarcón († p. 1554) y la provincia agustiniana de España en
  el siglo XVI'. *AnalAug*, 24 (1961), 30–90
  'Autenticidad de las lecturas *De spe* y *de caritate* de Fray Luis de León'.
  AnalAug, 25 (1962), 340–50
  'Sobre la autenticidad de algunos escritos atribuídos a Fray Luis de León'.
  AnalAug, 27 (1964), 341–79
  'Españoles del siglo XVI en el epistolario de Seripando'. *CD*, 177 (1964),
  234–66
  'Textos y notas acerca de Fray Luis de León y Francisco Cornejo'.
  AnalAug, 30 (1967), 332–40
  'Fray Luis de León, autor místico'. *RyC*, 93–4 (1976), 409–33
Gutiérrez, Marcelino, P. *Fr. Luis de León y la filosofía española del siglo XVI*.
  Madrid, 1885
Guy, Alain. *La pensée de Fray Luis de León*. Paris: Joseph Vrin, 1943
  El pensamiento filosófico de Fray Luis de León. Madrid: Ediciones Rialp, 1960
Habib Arkin, Alexander. *La influencia de la exégesis hebrea en los comentarios
  bíblicos de Fray Luis de León*. Madrid: CSIC, 1966
Hefele, von, Revd. Dr. *The Life of Cardinal Ximénez*, trans. the Rev. Canon
  Dalton. London: Catholic Publishing and Bookselling Company, 1860
Höpfl, Hildebrando, OSB. 'Fr. Luis de León y la Vulgata'. *REEB*, 2 (1928),
  221–30
Ibáñez, Diosdado, CMF. 'La versión del libro de Job de Fr. Luis de León'.
  REEB, 2 (1928), 211–17
Jedin, Hubert. *A History of the Council of Trent*, trans. Ernest Graf, 2 vols.
  London: Nelson, 1957–61
Jerome, Saint. *Saint Jérôme, Lettres*, trans. J. Labourt, 8 vols. Paris: Belles
  Lettres, 1953
Juan de la Cruz, San. *San Juan de la Cruz. Obras completas*. ed. Lucinio Ruano,
  OCD. 11th edn. BAC, Madrid: 1982
Kagan, Richard L. *Students and Society in Early Modern Spain*. Baltimore: Johns
  Hopkins University Press, 1974
Kamen, Henry. *The Spanish Inquisition*. New York: New American Library,
  1965

Kelly, J.N.D. *Jerome: His Life, Writings and Controversies*. London: Duckworth, 1975

Kottman, Karl A. 'Fray Luis de León, O.S.A.: Notebook on the promises of the Old Law'. *Augustiniana*, 22 (1972), 583–610

Law and Apocalypse: The Moral Thought of Luis de León. The Hague: Nijhoff, 1972

'Fray Luis de León and the universality of Hebrew: an aspect of 16th and 17th century language theory'. *Journal of the History of Philosophy*, 13 (1975), 297–310

Kristeller, Paul Oskar. *Renaissance Thought and its Sources*. New York: Columbia University Press, 1979

Krynen, Jean. 'De la teología humanista a la mística de las luces'. *RyC*, 93–4 (1976), 465–83

Kubler, George. *Building the Escorial*. Princeton University Press, 1982

Landy, Francis. *Paradoxes of Paradise, Identity and Difference in the Song of Songs*. Sheffield: The Almond Press, 1983

Lapesa, Rafael. *Poetas y prosistas de ayer y de hoy*. Madrid: Gredos, 1977

Lawrence, C.H. *Medieval Monasticism*. London: Longman, 1984

Lea, Henry Charles. *A History of the Inquisition of Spain*, 4 vols. London: Macmillan, 1906–7

Levin, Harry. *The Myth of the Golden Age in the Renaissance*. New York: OUP, 1969

Llamas, Enrique, OCD. *Documentación inquisitorial*. Madrid: FUE, 1975

Llamas-Martínez, Enrique. 'Instrucciones sobre procedimientos inquisitoriales, según un MS. del 'British Museum'. *Salmanticensis*, 18 (1971), 121–53

Lloyd-Jones, G. *The Discovery of Hebrew in Tudor England*. Manchester University Press, 1983

López, A. 'La idea cristocéntrica en Fr. Luis de León'. *RyC*, 23–4 (1961), 564–82

López Baralt, L. *San Juan de la Cruz y el Islam*. El Colegio de México: Universidad de Puerto Rico, 1985

López Estrada, Francisco. *Los libros de pastores en la literatura española. La órbita previa*. Madrid: Gredos, 1974

Lubac, Henri de. *Exégèse mediévale. Les quatre sens de l'Ecriture*, 4 vols. Paris: Aubier, 1959–64

Luther, Martin. *Luther and Erasmus: Free Will and Salvation*. Philadelphia: Westminster, 1969

Lynch, John. *Spain under the Habsburgs*, 2nd edn, 2 vols. Oxford: Blackwell, 1981

Mackay, Angus. *Spain in the Middle Ages*. London: Macmillan, 1977

Macrí, Oreste. *La poesía de Fray Luis de León*. Salamanca: Anaya, 1970

Maurer, Karl. *Himmlischer Aufenthalt*. Heidelberg: Carl Winter, 1958

Menéndez Pidal, Ramón. 'Cartapacios literarios salmantinos del siglo XVI'. *BRAE*, 1 (1914), 43–55, 151–70, 298–320

Miguel, Raimundo de. *Biografía del maestro Francisco Sánchez, El Brocense*. Madrid: 1859

Millás Vallicrosa, José María. 'Probable influencia de la poesía sagrada hebraico-española en la de Fr. Luis de León'. *Sefarad*, 15 (1955), 261–86

Muiños Sáenz, Conrado. *El 'Decíamos ayer' de Fray Luis de León*. Madrid: 1908

Fr. Luis de León y Fr. Diego de Zúñiga. El Escorial: Administración de 'La Ciudad de Dios', 1914

Múñoz Iglesias, Salvador. 'Una opinión de Fr. Luis de León sobre la cronología de la Pascua'. *Estudios Bíblicos*, 3 (1944), 79–96

'El decreto tridentino sobre la Vulgata y su interpretación por los teólogos del siglo XVI'. *Estudios Bíblicos*, 5 (1946), 137–69

Fray Luis de León, teólogo. Madrid: CSIC, 1950

'Manuscritos teológicos de Fray Luis de León'. *RET*, 15 (1955), 97–9.

Múñoz Sendino, José. 'Los Cantares del Rey Salomón, en versos líricos, por Fr. Luis de León'. *BRAE*, 28 (1948), 411–61; 29 (1949), 31–98

Nerlich, Michael. *El hombre justo y bueno: Inocencia bei Fray Luis de León*. Frankfurt a/M: Klostermann, 1966

New Oxford Book of Christian Verse, The. ed. Donald Davie. Oxford University Press, 1981

Niño Jesús, G. del. 'Censores de los manuscritos teresianos: las correcciones de la Autografía teresiana, de Báñez a Fray Luis de León', *MC*, 65 (1957), 42–60

Noreña, Carlos G. *Studies in Spanish Renaissance Thought*. The Hague: Nijhoff, 1975

O'Reilly, Terence. 'The Ode to Francisco Salinas' in *What's Past is Present. A Collection of Essays in Honour of L.J. Woodward*, eds. S. Bacarisse et al. Edinburgh University Press, 1984

Orella y Unzue, José L.de. *Respuestas católicas a las Centurias de Magdeburgo (1559–1588)*. Madrid: FUE, 1976

Oxford Dictionary of the Christian Church, The, 2nd edn, eds. F.L. Cross and E.A. Livingstone. Oxford University Press, 1974

Pacheco, Francisco. *Libro de descripción de verdaderos retratos de ilustres y memorables varones*. eds. P.M. Piñero Ramírez and R. Reyes Cano. Seville, 1985

Pagden, Anthony. *The Fall of Natural Man*. Cambridge University Press, 1982

Parker, Alexander A. *The Allegorical Drama of Calderón*. Oxford: Dolphin, 1968

Patrologia Graeca. ed. J.P. Migne, 162 vols. Tournai, 1857–66

Patrologia Latina. ed. J.P. Migne, 221 vols. Tournai, 1844–64

Peers, E. Allison. 'Mysticism in the poetry of Fray Luis de León'. *BSS* 19–20 (1942–3), 25–40

Pereña, Luciano. 'El descubrimiento de América en las obras de Fray Luis de León'. *Revista española de derecho internacional*, 8 (1955), 587–604

Pérez Castro, Federico. *La Biblia Políglota de Amberes*. Madrid: FUE, 1973

Pinta Llorente, Miguel de la, OSA. 'Investigaciones inquisitoriales contra el biblista español Gaspar de Grajal. Notas inéditas para el estudio de la cultura española en el siglo XVI'. *Cruz y Raya*, 33 (1936), 329–79

Causa criminal contra el biblista Alonso Gudiel, catedrático de la Universidad de

Osuna. Madrid: CSIC, 1942

Proceso criminal contra el hebraísta salmantino Martín Martínez de Cantalapiedra.
Madrid: CSIC, 1946

Estudios y polémicas sobre Fray Luis de León. Madrid: CSIC, 1956

Crítica y humanismo. Madrid: Archivo Agustiniano, 1966

'Agustinos renacentistas en la Inquisición española'. *AA*, 60 (1976), 3–42

Pinto Crespo, Virgilio. *Inquisición y control ideológico en la Espana del siglo XVI.*
Madrid: Taurus, 1983

Prest, John. *The Garden of Eden.* New Haven: Yale University Press, 1981

Quilis, Antonio. 'Los encabalgamientos léxicos en "–mente" de Fray Luis de
León y sus comentaristas'. *HR*, 31 (1963), 22–39

Rekers, Ben. *Arias Montano.* Madrid: Taurus, 1973

Repges, W. *Philologische Untersuchungen zu den Gesprächen über die Namen Christi
von Fray Luis de León.* Münster, 1959

Revilla, Mariano, OSA. 'Fr. Luis de León y los estudios bíblicos en el siglo
XVI'. *REEB*, 2 (1928), 27–81

Ricard, Robert. 'Le Bon Pasteur et la Vierge dans les poésies de Louis de
León. Notes et commentaires'. *Les Lettres Romanes*, 22 (1968), 311–31

Ríos, Ramón, OSB. 'Fr. Luis de León, el poeta bíblico'. *REEB*, 2 (1928),
181–208

Rivera de Ventosa, Enrique. 'El primado de Cristo en Duns Escoto, y Fr.
Luis de León'. *RyC*, 93–4 (1976), 485–502

Rivers, E.L. 'A new manuscript of a poem hitherto attributed to Fray Luis de
León'. *HR*, 20 (1952), 153–8

Fray Luis de León: The Original Poems. London: Grant & Cutler, 1983

Rubio, Fernando, OSA. 'Breves noticias de algunos conventos agustinianos
del siglo XVI en España'. *Analecta Augustiniana*, 34 (1971), 171–84

Russell, P.E. *Temas de 'La Celestina'.* Barcelona: Ariel, 1978

'Secular literature and the censors: a sixteenth-century document re-
examined'. *BHS*, 59 (1982), 219–25

ed. *Spain: A Companion to Spanish Studies.* London: Methuen, 1973

Salazar Rincón, Javier. *Fray Luis de León y Cervantes.* Madrid: Insula, 1980

Sandalio, Diego, SJ. 'Cronología de los comentarios del Mtro. Fray Luis de
León'. *REEB*, 2 (1928), 87–91

San Pedro García, J. 'Principios exegéticos del Mtro. Fray Luis de León'.
Salmanticensis, 4 (1957), 51–74

Santiago Vela, Gregorio de. 'La Universidad de Salamanca y Fr. Luis de
León (Datos para la historia)'. *AHHA*, 6 (1916), 11–26, 92–102

'Convento de San Agustín de Salamanca: Protocolo del P. Antonio de
Solís'. *AHHA*, 5 (1916), 165–75

'Magisterio en artes de Fr. Luis de León'. *AHHA*, 5 (1916), 325–36

'Oposiciones de Fr. Luis de León a la cátedra de Biblia'. *AHHA*, 6 (1916),
192–209, 255–68, 300–17

'Proceso original seguido ante el Maestrescuela de la Universidad de
Salamanca por Fr. Luis de León sobre el derecho de asistir a grados'.
AHHA, 7 (1917), 86–94

'El P.M. Fr. Alonso de Gudiel'. *AHHA*, 7 (1917), 178–92

'Capítulo de la Provincia de Castilla celebrado en Toledo el 3 de Diciembre de 1588'. *AHHA*, 7 (1917), 212–15

'El P. Mtro. Fr. Juan de Guevara'. *AHHA*, 7 (1917), 267–80, 333–45

'Fr. Luis de León y los catedráticos de propiedad en la Universidad de Salamanca'. *AHHA*, 8 (1917), 10–27, 182–98, 257–67, 347–60, 412–24

'Delación del libro "De los Nombres de Cristo" de Fr. Luis de León'. *AHHA*, 12 (1919), 114–15

'El *Libro de Job*, del P.M. Fr. Luis de León'. *AHHA*, 12 (1919), 132–47, 193–205

'El "Libro de los Cantares", comentado por Fr. Luis de León'. *AHHA*, 12 (1919), 257–68

'La Universidad de Salamanca y Fr. Luis de León'. *AHHA*, 13 (1920), 5–21, 133–43, 261–72; 14 (1920), 17–29

'Libros de matrícula de la Universidad'. *AHHA*, 14 (1920), 364–5; 15 (1921), 107–9

'Autógrafos de Fr. Luis de León'. *AHHA*, 15 (1921), 38–52

'Capítulo de la provincia de Castilla en 1586'. *AHHA*, 16 (1921), 15–32

'Sobre una sustitución en Salamanca'. *AHHA*, 16 (1921), 140–56, 293–308

'De Nueve Nombres de Cristo'. *AHHA*, 17 (1922), 137–49

'Discurso sobre la diferencia que ay entre Frayles y Monjas Carmelitas Descalços, acerca del gouierno'. *AHHA*, 19 (1923), 39–56

'Fr. Luis de León en libertad'. *AHHA*, 19 (1923), 295–309; 20 (1923), 23–37, 137–53, 300–17

Santos Olivera, Balbino. 'Fr. Luis de León y el Eclesiastés'. *REEB*, 2 (1928), 111–15

Scholem, Gershom G. *Major Trends in Jewish Mysticism*. Jerusalem: Schocken, 1961

On the Kabbalah and its Symbolism, trans. Ralph Manheim. London: Routledge, 1965

Kabbalah. Jerusalem: Keter, 1974

Schuster, E.J. 'Alonso de Orozco and Fray Luis de León: *De los nombres de Cristo*'. *HR*, 24 (1956), 261–70

Secret, François. *Les Kabbalistes chrétiens de la Renaissance*. Paris: Dunod, 1964

Senabre, Ricardo. *Tres estudios sobre Fray Luis de León*. Salamanca: Universidad de Salamanca, 1978

Shakespeare, William. *King Lear*, ed. Kenneth Muir. London: Methuen, *The Arden Shakespeare*, 1972

Sister of Notre Dame de Namur, A. (Sister Anne Hardman). *Life of the Venerable Anne of Jesus*. London: Sands, 1932

Smalley, Beryl. *The Study of the Bible in the Middle Ages*, 3rd edn. Oxford: Blackwell, 1983

Solana, Marcial. *Historia de la filosofía española*, 3 vols. Madrid: Aldus, 1941

Sonnino, Lee A. *A Handbook to Sixteenth-Century Rhetoric*. London: Routledge & Kegan Paul, 1968

Stegmüller, Friedrich. 'Spanische und portugiesische Theologie in englischen Bibliotheken'. *Spanische Forschungen der Görresgesellschaft*, 5 (1936), 372–89

Stow, K.R. 'The burning of the Talmud in 1553, in the light of sixteenth-century attitudes towards the Talmud'. *BHR*, 34 (1972), 433–59

Sunday Times, The Review Section, 20 June 1982 (George Steiner)

Sutcliffe, E.F. 'The Council of Trent on the "Authentica" of the Vulgate'. *Journal of Theological Studies*, 49 (1948), 35–42

Talmage, Frank E. *David Kimhi: The Man and the Commentaries.* Cambridge, Mass.: Harvard Judaic Monographs 1, 1978

Taylor, René. 'Architecture and Magic: considerations on the *Idea* of the Escorial', in *Essays in the History of Architecture presented to Rudolf Wittkower.* London: Phaidon, 1967

Tellechea Idígoras, J.I. 'Biblias publicadas fuera de España secuestradas por la Inquisición de Sevilla'. *Bulletin Hispanique*, 64 (1962), 236–47

'La censura inquisicional de Biblias de 1554'. *Anthologica Annua*, 10 (1962), 89–142

Tiempos recios: Inquisición y heterodoxias. Salamanca: Ediciones Sígueme, 1977

Teresa de Avila, Santa. *Obras completas de Santa Teresa de Jesús*, eds. Efrén de la Madre de Dios, OCD and Otger Steggink, OCarm, 2nd edn. Madrid: BAC, 1967

Thompson, Colin P. 'The Lost Works of Luis de León: (1) *De simonia. BHS*, 57 (1980), 95–102

'The Lost Works of Luis de León: (2) *Expositio in Genesim*'. *BHS*, 57 (1980), 199–212

'La huella del proceso de fray Luis de León en sus propias obras', in *Actas del Sexto Congreso Internacional de Hispanistas.* Department of Spanish and Portuguese, University of Toronto, 1980

'"En la Ascensión": Artistic tradition and poetic imagination in Luis de León', in *Mediaeval and Renaissance Studies on Spain and Portugal in Honour of P.E. Russell.* Oxford: The Society for the Study of Mediaeval Languages and Literature, 1981

'A little-studied manuscript of Luis de León: The *Quaestiones Variae*'. *BHS*, 61 (1984), 1–12

The Poet and the Mystic. Oxford University Press, 1977

El poeta y el místico, revised and expanded edn, trans. Susana Hurtado and Guillermo Lorenzo. El Escorial: Swan, 1985

Tillich, Paul. *The Shaking of the Foundations.* Harmondsworth: Penguin, 1962

Torre, Martín de la and Pedro Longas. *Catálogo de códices latinos de la Biblioteca Nacional.* Madrid: Patronato de la Biblioteca Nacional, 1935

Tovar, Antonio and Pinta Llorente, Miguel de la. *Procesos inquisitoriales contra Francisco Sánchez de las Brozas.* Madrid: CSIC, 1941

Valdés, Alfonso. *Diálogo de las cosas ocurridas en Roma*, ed. José F. Montesinos. Madrid: *CC*, 1928

Diálogo de Mercurio y Carón, ed. José F. Montesinos. Madrid: *CC*, 1929

Valdés, Juan de. *Diálogo de doctrina cristiana*, ed. Domingo Ricart. Mexico City: Universidad Nacional Autónoma de México, 1964

Vallejo, Gustavo, OCD. *Fray Luis de León: su ambiente, su doctrina espiritual, huellas de Santa Teresa.* Rome: Colegio Internacional de Santa Teresa, 1959

Vega, Angel Custodio, OSA. *Los manuscritos de Fray Luis de León que se conservan en la biblioteca de la Academia de la Historia.* Madrid: Maestre, 1953

'Capítulo de una obra inédita de Fray Luis de León'. *CD*, 166 (1954), 127–57

'Un autógrafo del "Cantar de los Cantares" de fray Luis de León olvidado'. *CD*, 172 (1959), 166–77

Cumbres místicas. Madrid: Aguilar, 1963

'Fray Luis de León y Fray Juan de Guevara'. *CD*, 180 (1967), 313–49

Vélez, Pedro M., P. *Observaciones al libro de Aubrey F.G. Bell sobre Fray Luis de León.* El Escorial: Imprenta del Monasterio, 1931

Ventosa-Sotiello-Villalmonte, P.P.R. de. 'Actualidad y doctrina de Juan Duns Escoto'. *Salmanticensis*, 17 (1970), 639–66

Vossler, Karl. *Fray Luis de León.* Madrid: Espasa-Calpe, 1960

Wardropper, Bruce W. *Historia de la poesía lírica a lo divino en la cristiandad occidental.* Madrid: Revista de occidente, 1958

Wilson, Edward M. *Spanish and English Literature of the 16th and 17th Centuries.* Cambridge University Press, 1980

Woods, Michael J. *The Poet and the Natural World in the Age of Góngora.* Oxford University Press, 1978

Woodward, L.J. '*La vida retirada* of Fray Luis de León'. *BHS*, 31 (1954), 17–26

'Fray Luis de León's *Oda a Francisco Salinas*'. *BHS*, 39 (1962), 69–77

'Hebrew tradition and Luis de León'. *BHS*, 61 (1984), 426–31

Zarco Cuevas, Julián. *Catálogo de los manuscritos castellanos de la Real Biblioteca de El Escorial*, 3 vols. vols 1–2. Madrid: Imprenta Helénica, 1924–5; vol. 3. El Escorial: Imprenta del Monasterio, 1929

'Bibliografía de Fr. Luis de León'. *REEB*, 2 (1928), 287–413

Index of Biblical references

All references are to the Vulgate
    numbering, unless otherwise indicated.

Genesis, 158
  i, 150
  i.1, 102, 162
  i.26, 9
  ii, 237
  ii.8, 45, 159
  ii.19–20, 33, 177
  iii.17–19, 134
  xii, 114
  xxi, 90
  xlix.10, 157

Exodus
  xii.37, 114
  xii.46, 90
  xxxii, 23

Leviticus, 91, 160, 195

Numbers
  vi, 182
  xxi.6–9, 23

II Samuel
  xii, 88

Job, 68, 70, 121–39, 141, 225, 260
  i.6, 126
  iii.7, 132
  iii.23, 127
  iv.13, 136
  v.22, 124
  v.23ff., 129
  viii.14, 124
  viii.20, 74
  ix.6, 66
  ix.18, 135

xi.8–9, 183
xiii, 127
xiii.6, 124
xvi.9, 127
xvi.22, 124
xvii, 132
xix.8–11, 206
xix.25–6, 129, 131
xx.5, 127
xx.17, 66
xx.18, 55
xxiv, 131
xxiv.5, 125
xxiv.6, 126
xxiv.11, 126
xxiv.13, 135
xxiv.21, 133
xxvi, 128
xxvi.14, 137
xxvii–xxviii, 131
xxviii, 99, 245
xxviii.4, 127
xxviii.4–5, 7–8, 99
xxviii.14, 127
xxix.22, 127
xxix.23, 132
xxx–xxxi, 131
xxx.20, 130
xxxi.35, 127
xxxi.39, 134
xxxii.3, 125
xxxv.10, 130
xxxvii.4, 130
xxxviii.2, 260
xxxix.27, 127
Psalms
  i, 235–6
  ii, 96, 203
  ii.1–2, 189

ii.7, 87, 212
viii.2, 60
xii, 62, 69
xviii.3, 205
xviii.11, 237
xxii.5, 25
xxiii (AV), 127, 244, 250, 256
xxvi, 70–4
xli, 62, 69
lxviii, 188
lxxi, 187–8
lxxi.16, 187, 216
lxxi.17, 212
lxxii, 179
lxxix, 182
lxxix.20, 167
lxxxix.4, 102
cix, 181
cix.3, 215
cx (AV), 216
cii, 227
ciii, 197
cxiii.4, 88
cxix.103 (AV), 120

Proverbs, 91, 106, 129
viii, 175
xxx.15, 89

Ecclesiastes, 106

Song of Songs (Song of Solomon), 10,
    26–36, 38, 61, 69–70, 94, 103–21, 124,
    131, 145, 163, 211, 222, 230, 246,
    249–50, 253
i.1, 113
i.1–ii.7, 106
i.2, 113
i.3, 106, 114
i.5, 114
i.7, 114, 248–9, 258
i.14, 226
i.14–15, 114
ii.4, (AV), 106
ii.8, 114
ii.8–v.2a, 106
ii.9, 33
ii.10, 114
ii.10–13, 107
ii.15, 108
ii.17, 114
iii.1–3, 108

iii.3–4, 114
iii.6–11, 114
iii.9–10, 222
iv, 30
iv.1, 33–4
iv.1–2, 109
iv.4, 109
iv.5, 109
iv.6, 115
iv.11, 114, 120
iv.12, 98, 110
iv.12–v.1, 25, 115
iv.16, 25, 110
v.2, 115, 201, 248
v.2b, 111
v.5, 7–8, 115
v.7, 108, 112
v.10, 112, 252
v.10–16, 115, 182
v.11, 115
v.12, 31
v.14, 31
vi.1, 112
vi.4–9, 116
vi.9, 30
vi.11, 117
vii.1, 112, 117
vii.1–9, 117
vii.3, 4, 117
vii.5, 32
vii.6, 30
vii.11, 117
viii.1, 32
viii.6–7, 118
viii.7, 223
viii.8, 112, 118
viii.10, 118
viii.10–12, 112
viii.11–12, 118
viii.13, 118
viii.14, 119

Wisdom (Sapientia), 91

Ecclesiasticus, 91
xxvii.11, 8

Isaiah, 126, 160, 179, 185
i.2, 212
iv.2, 167, 179
v.1–7, 118
ix.6, 43, 155, 173, 189, 197–8

Isaiah (*cont.*)
xviii, 100–1
xviii.1–6, 100–1
xxxv.8–10, 184
xlv, 95
xlv.8, 167, 181
xlvii, 34
lii.10, 160
liii, 181
liii.1, 160
liii.8, 59
lx, 204
lxiii.1, 95
lxv, 204

Jeremiah, 179
ii.2–3, 115
xxxi.31–4, 202
xxxiii.15, 167, 179

Lamentations
iv.1, 64

Ezekiel, 69, 126, 247
i, 162
iii.3, 120
xxxiv, 247
xxxvii, 23

Daniel, 96, 126, 153, 198, 230
ii, 203
ii.34–5, 187–8
vii, 202
vii.9, 252

Hosea
ix.1–2, 115
xi.1, 212

Amos
v.25, 115

Obadiah, 94–101
4, 96
17–18, 97
20, 99

Micah
v.2, 213

Haggai
ii.7–8, 158

Zechariah, 68, 179
iii.8, 179
vi, 202
vi.12, 167, 179
xiv.14, 198

Matthew, 42
vii.14, 24
ix.15, 198
xviii, 250
xxii, 97
xxv.41, 218

Mark
xi, 92
xiii.10, 169

Luke
ii.34, 189
vii.11–17, 92
vii.36ff., 238–9
xv, 250

John, 159, 200, 252
iii.29, 198
vi.21, 222
viii.6, 166
ix, 158
x, 113, 247
xi.16, 250
xii.24, 188
xv, 113

Romans
v, 194
v.5, 222
viii.19–22, 222
ix–xi, 100, 169
xi.25–6, 169

I Corinthians
iii.2, 120
v.8, 23
xiii, 223

Galatians, 94
iv.22–6, 86
iv.24, 59

Ephesians
iv.13, 196

Philippians
  ii, 187

Colossians
  i, 175
  i.15–16, 213
  i.15–19, 180

II Thessalonians, 94, 102–3

Hebrews, 42
  i.4–5, 212

ii.10, 162
xi.1, 25

I Peter
  v.8, 92

Revelation
  i.14, 252
  v.5, 92
  xii, 96
  xiii, 202
  xiii.8, 222
  xxii.2, 226

General index

Aaron, 114
Abel, 89, 197
Abraham (Abram), 90, 114, 154, 215
Abulafia, Abraham, 151
Adam, 33, 102, 134, 158, 164, 175, 177,
    182, 189–92, 194–7, 201, 206, 215,
    221, 227–8
Advent, 115
Aegidius Romanus (Giles of Rome), 5
Aeneas, 95
Alcalá de Henares, university of, 5–6, 67,
    82, 141, 143–4, 153, 156
allegory, 76, 93, 256
    in Bible, 27–8, 34, 48, 86–93, 96, 104–5,
    115, 118, 120, 159, 211, 215, 222
Almeida, Juan de, 234
Almonacid, Fray Jerónimo, 268n
Alonso de Orozco, Blessed, 273n
Alvárez de Mármol, Juan, 122
Amminadib, 117
Ana de Jesús, Madre, 122
Anabaptists, 90
analogy, 161, 192, 194, 196, 212
anamnesis, Platonic theory of, 17, 250
Andrew of St Victor, 141
Annunciation, the, 164
Anselm, St, 274n
Antichrist, the, 103, 116, 156, 169
Antiochus Epiphanes, 153
anti-semitism, 37, 56, 58, 141, 185
Apocalypse, the, 215, 218
Apocrypha, the, 157
Apostles, the, 101, 197
Aquinas, St Thomas, 5–6, 41, 69, 81–2, 91,
    171, 173–4
    Summa theologica, 171
    see also Thomism
Aramaic, 42, 69, 84, 143, 166, 168, 179
    see also Chaldean

Arboleda, Fray Francisco de, 54
Arévalo, 152
    Ana de, 67
Ariosto, Ludovico, 241
    Orlando furioso, 241
Aristotle, 69, 87, 219, 222
Ark of the Covenant, the, 114, 215
Armada, the Spanish, 1
Assyria, 48
astrology, 64–5
astronomy, 65, 68, 212
Atlantic Ocean, the, 99
Atlantis, 100
Atlas, 200
Atonement, the, 220
Augustine, St, 8, 11–12, 26, 69, 81–2, 86,
    88, 90–2, 158, 171, 191, 204, 209, 213,
    223, 228, 243, 264n
    Confessions, 11, 243
    De doctrina christiana, 228, 264n
    De Genesi ad litteram, 158
    De Trinitate, 213
    Dialogues, 12
Augustinians (Hermits of St Augustine), 5,
    12, 41, 47, 61, 66–8, 80–1, 84, 145,
    156, 227
    Spanish, 5, 8, 67
    see also Dueñas
Augustinus Eugubinus (Steuch), 69, 266n
Authorized Version, see under Bible
Ávila, 152

Babylon, 95, 97, 153
Bahir, the, 150, 271n
    see also Kabbalah
Baker, H.W., 276n
Báñez, Domingo, 81–3
baptism, 76, 196, 240, 256
    see also sacraments

Bashan, 187–8
Basil, St, 167, 215
Bathsheba, 88
beatific vision, the, 112
beatus ille
    see under classical commonplaces
Bede, the Venerable, 35
Belmonte, 4, 149–50, 263n
Bembo, Pietro, 12, 69
    Prose, 12
Bernard of Clairvaux, St, 27, 69, 107–10,
    113, 119, 162, 171, 244, 276n
    On the Song of Songs, 107–9
Bible, the (Scripture) 1–2, 6, 8, 10, 12, 14,
    25–75, 79–80, 84–146, 150–63, 165–7,
    169–84, 186–9, 194–8, 200–7, 210–13,
    215–16, 218, 222–4, 226–42, 244–50,
    252–3, 256, 258, 260–2, 264n, 269n,
    271n
    Authorized Version (King James Bible),
        31, 38, 71, 106, 114, 120–1, 123, 157,
        197, 216, 236–7
    Estienne/Vatable, 39, 41–2, 45, 47–8, 52,
        59, 61
    Greek, 23, 38–9, 42–6, 48, 54, 67–9, 85,
        87, 143, 165; *see also* Septuagint
    Hebrew, 27, 30–5, 39, 42–9, 54, 56, 58,
        67–9, 80, 84–5, 87, 101, 141–3, 154,
        157–8, 160, 171, 179, 181–2, 186, 188,
        205, 216, 226, 229, 264n
    interpretation of, 8, 36, 59, 69–70,
        86–139, 175, 177–84, 186–9, 197–8,
        202–3, 212–13, 215–16, 218, 222, 229;
        Jewish, 36, 48–9, 56–9, 66, 84–5, 94,
        146, 150–3, 157–61, 179; *see also*
        Biblical exegesis
    Latin, 33, 38–40, 43–6, 54, 67–8, 143,
        165; *see also* Vetus Latina; Vulgate;
        other Latin versions
    names of Christ in, 12, 43, 161–2, 164–5,
        169, 171–231
    Polyglot, *see separate entry*
    Rabbinical, 39
    Soncino, 142
    Septuagint, *see separate entry*
    translation of, 8, 32–4, 36, 40, 55–6,
        62–4, 123–4, 126, 130, 154, 187, 206
    vernacular, 1, 8, 26–35, 40, 60–4,
        121–39, 266n
    Vetus Latina, 42
    Vulgate, *see separate entry*; other Latin
        versions, 39–40, 42, 44, 46, 54, 80

    see also allegory, in Bible; Biblical canon
        etc.; Epistles; Gospels; León, Fray Luis
        de, works; New Testament; Old
        Testament; prophecy; Scripture
Biblia Regia, the, 49–50, 144, 265n
    see also Polyglot Bibles
Biblical canon, 27
    exegesis (Biblical), 8, 35, 57, 59, 86–7,
        90–1, 93, 96–7, 101, 103, 105, 111,
        116–17, 120, 125, 130–1, 138, 141,
        146, 154, 157–61, 163, 165, 169, 171,
        179, 181–3, 188, 203, 215, 222, 224,
        229–30, 249
    inspiration, 14, 42, 46, 177, 234
    language, 10, 14, 23, 26–7, 30–2, 35, 37,
        86–139, 160–1, 170–1, 175, 177,
        179–81, 184, 195, 202, 210, 215–16,
        218, 224, 228–30, 252, 260, 264n
    see also imagery, Biblical; metaphor,
        Biblical; symbolism, Biblical
Bomberg, Daniel, 39
Borrow, George, 1–2
Boscán, Juan, 242
Bosphorus, the Straits of, 101
Brocense, el (Francisco Sánchez de las
    Brozas), 234, 275n
Byzantium, 96
    see also Constantinople

Cajetan, Cardinal, 65
    Summa, 65
Calderón de la Barca, Pedro, 135, 205
    autos sacramentales: La vida es sueño, 205; *El
        gran teatro del mundo*, 205
Calvary, 199, 221, 228
    see also Cross, Crucifixion
Calvin, John, 83, 267n
Calvinists, 39, 196
Cáncer, Dr, 53–4
cannibals, 98, 100, 274n
Cano, Melchor, 6, 42, 56, 70
Cántico espiritual
    see under John of the Cross, St
Çarate, Agustín de, 268n
Carmelites, 10, 108, 269n
    Carmelite Reform, 122, 269n
    Discalced Carmelites, 123, 269n
Carpe diem, see under classical commonplaces
Carranza, Bartolomé de (Archbishop of
    Toledo), trial of, 47, 64, 267n,
    271n
Catechismo christiano, 47

Cassian, John, 86
Castillo, Hernando de, 74, 81
Castro, Alfonso de, 62, 91–2
Castro, León de, 36, 47–51, 56, 58–60, 64,
    69, 76–7, 87, 91, 125, 143, 182,
    265n
    Commentaria in Esaiam, 48–9, 69
Catharism, 63
Catholics, *see under* Church, the Roman
    Catholic
Celestina, La, 63, 170
Centuries of Magdeburg, The, 193
Cervantes, Miguel de, 7
    Don Quixote, 98
    La Galatea, 7
Chaldaea, 202
Chaldean (Chaldee), 7, 42
    see also Aramaic
Chardin, Teilhard de, 176
Christ, 1, 11–14, 18, 27–8, 38, 48, 57–61,
    63, 71, 76, 80–1, 86–90, 92–3, 95–7,
    102–3, 107, 109–10, 112–19, 129, 138,
    155, 160–89, 192–209, 211–12, 215–25,
    227–30, 238–41, 246–54, 256–9, 261,
    274n
    see also exile, Christ's; kingship, Christ's;
    Messiah; sacrifice, Christ's; Second
    Coming; Son; soul, Christ's
Christmas, 199, 212
christology, 83, 172–3, 175, 179, 183, 214,
    256
Chrysostom, St John, 207
Church, the, 8, 27–8, 33–4, 42, 44–7, 59,
    61, 63, 85, 90, 95–7, 106, 109–20, 122,
    141, 143–4, 181, 197, 203, 207–8, 224
    Roman Catholic, 1, 37, 39–40, 44, 47,
    55–9, 65–6, 81, 83, 91, 110–11, 142,
    165, 185, 193, 197
    Western, 38, 80
Cicero, 227
Cisneros de Ximénez, Cardinal, 6, 141, 143
Cistercians, 6
classical allusions, 16, 200
    antiquity, 89, 93, 104, 242
    commonplaces; *beatus ille*, 77, 234; *carpe
    diem*, 255; *locus amoenus*, 13, 25, 99
    philosophy, 27, 87, 188, 201, 206,
    229–30
    tradition, 13–14, 29, 35, 89, 105, 113,
    116, 227, 234, 236–7, 240–2, 261–2
    wisdom, 66
Clement VIII, Pope, 80

Clementine Vulgate, 80
Cologne, 142
Columna, Pietro, *see under* Galatinus
conceit, literary, 31, 219, 239, 241
Confessions, see under Augustine, St
conquistadores, the, 1
Constantine the Great, 96, 115
Constantinople, 147
    fall of, 38
    see also Byzantium
contemplation, 10, 14, 17, 25–6, 106, 145,
    151–2, 244–5
conversion, 100, 146
    of Jews and Muslims, 141
    of the Jews, 103, 169, 185
    of the New World, 161
conversos (converted Jews), 56–7, 69, 140–3,
    146–50, 155, 157, 168, 170
Copernicus, Nicolas, 65, 67
Córdoba, Sebastián de, 242
creation, 8–11, 14, 24, 33, 43, 102, 104,
    112, 121, 128, 136–7, 145, 158–9,
    162–3, 173, 175–7, 180, 182–3, 189,
    205, 214, 219, 222, 226, 228, 230, 243,
    248
Creator, the, 11, 13, 23, 25, 112, 151–2, 243
Crivelli, Cardinal, 67
Cross, the, 90, 115, 137, 161, 168, 176,
    194–5, 197, 200, 212, 220–1, 225
    see also Calvary, Crucifixion
Crucifixion, the, 221, 252
    see also Calvary, Cross
Cuenca, Cathedral, 149
    province of, 4, 148–9
Curiel, Juan Alfonso de, 122
Cuzco, 61
Cyprian of Carthage, St, 171, 196
Cyrus, 95, 97

dark night (of the soul), 109, 130
Darwin, Charles, 93
David, king, 48, 71, 73, 88, 90, 246
De auxiliis controversy, 83
deification, 176, 194, 208–9, 222
Deucalion, 116
Devil, the, 89, 112, 117, 186–7, 206, 242
    see also Lucifer, Satan
Dionysius, the pseudo-, 152, 246
divinization of poetry, 242
Doctors, of the Church, 46, 59, 69, 84, 93,
    102, 144, 197
    Catholic, 56, 65

Hebrew, 95, 158, 167
Jewish, 165
doctrine, Christian, 11, 81, 90, 110, 119,
    123, 157, 166–7, 172, 176, 186, 192,
    197, 215
  of transubstantiation, 208
  Pauline, 196
  scholastic, 41
Dominicans, 36–7, 39, 41, 51, 53, 80–3, 142
  at Salamanca, 5–6, 36
  Colegio de San Esteban, Salamanca, 6
Donne, John, 158–9, 199
Dueñas, Augustinian Provincial Chapters
    at, 8, 67
Durandus de Saint-Pourçain, 6, 81, 173
  Commentary on the Sentences of Peter Lombard,
    173

Eckhart, Meister, 152
ecstasy, 17, 106–7, 111, 151–2, 258, 261
Eden, Garden of, 13, 98, 107, 118, 121,
    154, 159, 177, 189, 195, 215, 226, 237,
    246, 249
  see also paradise
Edom (Idumaea), 94–7
Egypt, 114, 198–9
  Egyptian wisdom, 154
Elijah, 102–3, 169
Eliot, T.S., 255–6
  Four Quartets, 255–6
Elisha, 169
Elysian Fields, the, 98, 243
End, the, 100–4, 113, 115, 152, 169
  see also eschatology
Enoch (Enosh), 102–3
Epistles, the, 91, 122, 167
  see also Bible, New Testament, Scripture
Erasmus, Desiderius, 12, 38–9, 114, 143,
    225, 228, 242, 266n, 272n, 274n
  editions of the Fathers, 38
  Enchiridion, 38, 242
Esau, 89, 95, 97, 217–18
eschatology, 100, 103, 138
  Eschaton, the, 228
  see also End
Escorial, el, 76, 84, 143, 157, 270n
Espinosa, Alonso de, 234
Estienne, Robert, 39, 41, 45, 47, 50, 61
Ethiopia, 100
Eve, 189, 228
Everyman, 127
exile, 247–8

Christ's, 198–9
  of Jews, 158; to Babylon, 97; from Spain,
    152–3; to Spain, 101
  see also expulsion of Jews from Spain
Exodus, the, 89–90, 114, 161
expulsion of Jews from Spain, 101, 140,
    152–3
  see also exile of Jews
Ezra the Scribe, 42

Fall, the, 33, 128, 134, 158, 175, 177, 189,
    191–3, 201, 206, 250
  see also sin, original
Father, God the, 88–9, 111, 155, 162–3,
    165–6, 168, 212–14, 233
Fathers, the, 38, 43, 59, 69, 80, 89, 93, 95,
    102, 117, 144, 165, 207, 228, 242
  see also Patristic writers
Fernández, Pedro, 36
Fernández de León, Gómez, 149
Ficino, Marsilio, 155, 159, 271n
Flanders, 39, 49–50, 143
Flecha, la, 12, 25
Flood, the, 98
Florentine Academy, the, 154, 159
Fludd, Robert, 156
Francis I of France, 39
Franciscans, 74
  at Salamanca, 5,
  at the Council of Trent, 46
  Franciscan theologians, 173
free will, 80–1, 164, 180, 272n
Freiburg, 142
Freud, Sigmund, 93
Fuentidueñas, Pedro de, 265n
Furió Ceriol, Fadrique, 266n
  Bononia, 266n

Gabriel (Biel), 81
Galatinus (Pietro Columna), 102, 144,
    155–7, 164–9, 175
  De arcanis catholicae veritatis, 155, 165–9
Galilee, 152–3, 248
Galileo Galilei, 66
Gallo, Gregorio, 70
Garcilaso de la Vega, 29, 80, 234, 241–2,
    252, 261
Geneva, 39
Gentiles, the, 97, 118, 168–9, 201, 241
Gerona, 152
Gethsemane, Garden of, 199
Gibralter, 101

Giles of Rome (Aegidius Romanus), 5
Glossa ordinaria, 69
Gnosticism, 150
God, 9–11, 14, 23, 26–7, 33–5, 56, 58, 63,
    70–3, 89–91, 96, 100–14, 116–17,
    120–1, 123–4, 126–30, 136–8, 150–6,
    160–83, 185, 187, 189–95, 197–8,
    200–3, 205–7, 209–10, 212–15, 217–18,
    222–3, 226–8, 230, 233, 247, 250, 255,
    257, 260–1, 267n, 274n
  as Creator, 9–11, 13–14, 23, 25–6, 33,
    112, 150–2, 174–5, 179–80, 189
  as first mover, 10
  as giver of language (Hebrew), 33, 56
  as inspiring poetry, 233
  as Judge, 125, 169
  attributes of, 151–2
  author of Scripture, word of God, 14,
    26–7, 33–5, 87, 89, 105, 120, 124, 126,
    becoming man, 27, 173–6, 183, 193–4,
    214; *see also* Incarnation, the
  contemplation of, 10, 25–6
  foreknowledge of, 80–3, 174
  Name of, 151–2, 155, 164–6, 178
  nature of, 88, 128, 182
Golden Age, 38
  myth of, 98, 107, 116
  of Spain, 1–4, 29, 137–8, 140, 261
Goliath, 90
Góngora, Luis de, 11, 24, 107, 168, 241–3,
    252, 255, 261
  'En un pastoral albergue', 241
  Polifemo, 107, 168, 252
  'Que se nos va la Pascua, mozas', 255
  Soledades, 24, 243
González, Diego (Inquisitor), 56–7
González, Diego (poet), 131
Good Shepherd, the, 251–2, 258, 261
Gospel, the, 27, 97–101, 103, 114, 116–18,
    137, 161, 169, 187, 203, 238–40
Gospels, the, 91, 122, 167, 176, 248
  Synoptic, 159
  see also Bible; New Testament; Scripture
grace, 14, 81, 83, 108, 111, 161, 175, 180,
    182, 190, 196, 201–3, 206, 217–18,
    225, 230, 267n
Grajal, Gaspar de, 6, 36–7, 51, 56–7, 69,
    85, 91, 148
Granada, 4–5, 60, 64
  Archbishop of, 47, 52
Granada, Luis de, 69
  Libro de oración y meditación, 69

Greek, 7, 23, 27, 32, 45, 69, 144, 151, 168,
    accusative, 252
  Apologists, 171
  Empire, 202
  wisdom, 154
  see also Bible, Greek
Gregory the Great, 115, 223
Gregory of Nyssa, 162
Guadalajara, 152
Gudiel, Alfonso de, 66
Guevara, Antonio de, 156
Guevara, Juan de, 70
Guzmán, Domingo de, 80

Haedo, Diego de, 51
Hagar, 90, 92
Handel, Georg Friedrich, 123
heaven, 21–2, 78–9, 102, 107, 130, 137–8,
    183–4, 189, 191, 201, 204, 209, 214,
    217–18, 226, 233, 236, 238, 241–6,
    248–51, 253, 255–9, 261
heavens, the, 136, 180, 206, 229, 255
Hebrew, 6–7, 23, 26–7, 30, 32–4, 42–3, 45,
    56, 66, 69–70, 84, 87, 92, 95,
    101–2, 117, 120–1, 123–6, 129–32,
    140–3, 145–6, 151–4, 157–8, 161–6,
    168, 170, 175, 177, 179, 181, 186, 188,
    216, 218, 226, 229, 237, 271n–273n
  as first language, 177, 272n
  doctors, 95, 167
  scholars, 34, 50, 141, 153, 175
  study by Christians, 140–4
  see also Bible, Hebrew; Jews; Judaism
hell, 187–8, 191, 216, 224
heresy, 45–6, 53–4, 62, 64, 67, 80–2, 103,
    117, 148, 173, 197
  heretics, 50, 88, 90–1, 108
Hermetic wisdom, 154
Hernández, Fray Vicente, 60–1
Herrera, Fernando de, 261
Herrick, Robert, 255
Hilary of Poitiers, St, 69
Hinduism, 206
Holocaust, the, 153
Holy Communion, 225, 256
  see also Host; Last Supper; Mass;
    sacraments
Holy Office, the, 62, 74, 144, 149
  see also Inquisition
Holy Spirit, the, 27–9, 44, 46, 54–5, 60–1,
    65, 79, 107, 111, 162, 165–8, 197, 208,
    213, 217, 222, 233, 246

Homer, 69, 143
Hopkins, Gerard Manley, 76
Horace, 17, 19, 29, 69, 74, 77, 143, 234–7, 240, 269n
  Epodes, 234
  Odes, 234, 237, 275n
hortus conclusus (Song iv.12–v.1), 25, 98, 110–11, 115
Host, the Sacred, 212, 216–17, 225
  see also Holy Communion, Last Supper, Mass, sacraments
Huerga, Cipriano de la, 6, 70, 142, 156
humanism, Renaissance, 41, 66, 69, 141, 156, 241, 261

idolatry, 97, 118, 161, 203, 230
Ignatius Loyola, St, 223
Illuminists (*alumbrados*), 64
imagery, Biblical, 27, 31–2, 93, 96, 100, 103–6, 109, 113–15, 119–21, 126, 131, 138–9, 160, 167, 175–6, 184, 187–8, 210, 215, 229–30, 234–5
  in poetry and prose of Luis de León, 15–17, 22–6, 76–9, 133, 170, 177, 183–5, 191, 194–7, 208, 212–14, 220–1, 224, 230–1, 234–7, 240, 244, 248, 270n
Incarnation, the, 26–9, 83, 113, 115, 146, 155, 161, 172–6, 178, 181, 189, 194, 203, 208, 215, 219, 229, 256
  see also God, becoming man
Index of Prohibited Books, 47–8, 63, 142–5
Indians, American, 98–101, 116
innocence, 70–2, 77, 124–5, 128, 154, 219, 237, 246, 250, 252
Inquisition, the Spanish, 1, 4, 6, 36–7, 47, 51–3, 57, 60–1, 70, 74–5, 78, 80, 84, 122, 140, 142, 144, 149–50, 265n, 267n
  Council of the Inquisition (*Suprema*), 36, 52–3, 57, 74, 122
  Inquisitor General, 53, 71
  Inquisitors, Cuenca, 148–9; Seville, 84; Toledo, 85; Valladolid, 36, 45, 52–6, 58, 60–1, 64–5, 74, 82, 150
  see also Holy Office
Isaac, 89, 195
Ishmael, 89–90
Isidore of Seville, St, 171
  Etymologiae, 171
Isles of the Blessed, the, 243
Israel, 89, 95, 97, 113–15, 119, 157, 169

Jacob, 89, 95, 97, 215, 217–18, 246
Jacob ben Chayin, 264n
Jared, 102
Jerome, St, 34, 38–9, 42–4, 48, 55, 79, 91, 97, 118, 140–1, 143, 154, 162–3, 170, 271n
  Quaestiones hebraice in Genesim, 154
Jeronymites, 37, 51, 81, 84, 273n
Jerusalem, 42, 95, 97, 99, 153, 178, 226
  see also Zion
Jesuits, 49, 80, 82–3, 143–4
Jesus, 42, 58, 75–6, 86, 88, 93, 155, 157–9, 161, 163–5, 167–8, 171, 180–1, 194, 205, 212, 223–7, 240, 272n, 274n
Jews, the, 36, 42–3, 45, 48–9, 54, 58–9, 65, 74–5, 95, 97, 100–1, 112, 116–18, 140–4, 146–8, 152–3, 155, 158–61, 168–71, 185, 213
  conversion of the, 103, 141–2, 169, 185
  Jewish culture, 145–6; dogma, 66; exegesis, 56, 59, 85, 94, 157, 160, 179; mysticism, 150–3; poetry, 145; practices, traditions, 48, 56, 142, 148–9, 157, 165; sacrifices, 116; scholars, doctors, 97, 150, 158–9, 165; wisdom, 154
  see also Hebrew; Judaism; Law, the Jewish
John the Baptist, 218
John the Divine, St, 248
John of the Cross, St, 10–11, 29, 108–9, 117, 122, 130, 152, 203, 213, 230, 243–4, 246, 250, 253–4, 259, 261
  Cántico espiritual, 10–11, 29, 117, 122, 243–4, 253–4
  'En una noche oscura', 250
Jordan, river, 215
Joseph, 97
Josephus, 97, 268n
Joshua, 215
Juan de Santa Cruz, Fray, 81
Judaism, 63, 141, 143, 147–9, 155, 170
judaizers, 48, 56–8, 60, 66–7, 84, 143, 148
Judas Iscariot, 199
Judgement, Day of, 101
Julian of Norwich, Dame, 274n
justice, 10, 37, 83, 100, 127–9, 173, 179, 181, 185, 190, 192, 195, 225, 227–8
justification by faith, 110–11, 185, 193
Justin Martyr, 43, 171
  Dialogus cum Tryphone Judaeo, 171

Kabbalah, the, 50, 145–6, 150–1, 153, 156–7, 165
Kabbalism, 151–4, 159, 165, 168, 271n
Kabbalistic techniques, 155
Kabbalists, 152, 155–9, 161–2, 165, 170; Christian, 102, 146, 153–6, 159, 163–6, 169, 175
Path of the Names, the, 151; of the Sefiroth, 151–2
see also Bahir; Zohar
kenosis, 187
Kimhi, David, 97, 157–8
King James Bible, the, 121, 123
see also Bible, Authorized Version
kingship, 74–5, 128, 158, 198
Christ's, 200–4, 252

Lamb of God, the, 90, 160, 215, 218–22
Last Supper, the, 159, 199
see also Holy Communion; Host; Mass; sacraments
Latin, 2, 7, 26, 32–3, 122–3, 141, 143–6, 151, 171–2, 179
see also Bible, Latin; Vulgate
Law, the Jewish, 62, 90, 92, 113–14, 129, 147–8, 184, 201–2, 205–6, 215, 219
see also Torah
law, international, 6
Lefèvre d'Etaples, 155, 271n
Leo I, Pope, 69
Leo X, Pope, 154
León, Francisco de, 4
Juan de, 149
Lope de, 4, 149
León, Fray Luis de: ancestry, 2, 4–5, 56–7, 146–50, 168, 170
early years, 4–5
trial and imprisonment, 1–2, 4, 6, 11, 28, 33–4, 36–86, 104, 109, 123, 138
works: Latin prose: De fide, 41–7; De incarnatione, 172–6, 180; In Abdiam, 94–101, 138; In Canticum Canticorum, 69–70, 104–21, 129, 138; In Genesim, 45, 158–9; In II Ad Thessalonicenses, 102–3, 138; Latin sermons, 8–12, 26, 263n; In Psalmum XXVI, 70–4, 77, 109, 124–5; Quaestiones, 39, 157–8; Tractatus, 87–94, 105, 117, 159, 267n
original poems: 'Qué descansada vida' (I), 19–26, 132, 138, 184, 234–7; A Francisco Salinas (III), 17, 191, 223–4, 250, 254–5, 260; A Felipe Ruiz (V),

15–17; De la Magdalena (VI), 237–41; Noche serena (VIII), 78, 132, 136, 204, 244–6, 248, 250, 255, 260; A Felipe Ruiz (X), 78, 135, 145; Al licenciado Juan de Grial (XI), 104, 270n; A Felipe Ruiz (XII), 77; 'Huíd, contentos' (XV), 76–7; 'Alma región luciente' (XVIII), 78, 145, 211, 248–62; A nuestra Señora (XXII), 77–8, 181; 'Aquí la envidia y mentira' (XXIII), 76
Spanish prose works: Cantar, 26–35, 37, 51, 60–3, 65, 90, 123, 146, 161, 229; Discurso, 123, 269n; edition of St Teresa, 269n; Job, 68, 70, 74, 99, 121–39, 146, 229; Nombres, 7, 12–15, 17–18, 25, 63–4, 70, 74–6, 83, 87–8, 96, 121, 125, 133, 137, 155–6, 160–7, 169–232, 239, 244–50, 252, 254, 260–2; La perfecta casada, 7, 229
translations of classical poems, 8, 70, 74, 127, 234–7; of Job in verse, 2, 130–2; of Psalms, 14, 187, 198, 211, 227, 232, 234–6
León, Moses de, 152
Lepanto, battle of, 67
Lewis, C.S., 176
Perelandra, 176
limpieza de sangre, 52, 74–5, 148
Linacre, Thomas, 69
Lindanus (Willem van der Lindt), 69, 266n
lira (verse form), 234–5
Llull, Ramón, 141
locus amoenus see under classical commonplaces
Logos, the, 83, 213–15, 218, 226–7
see also Word
Lot, 88
Louvain, 38, 143–4
university, 39
Lucifer, 114, 189, 228, 239
see also Devil; Satan
Luria, Isaac, 153
Luther, Martin, 85, 185, 193, 272n
Lutheranism, 80, 85
Lutherans, 39, 64, 82, 192, 196, 228
Lyra, Nicholas of, 65, 97, 141, 143, 158
Postilla, 141

Macarius of Egypt, St, 223
Homilies, 223

Madrid, 5, 147
Mahomet, 49
Mancio de Corpus Christi, 51, 53, 55
Marcus Licinius Crassus, 16
Mariana, Juan de, 49–50, 143–5
Martínez de Cantalapiedra, Martín, 36–7,
    51, 56, 58, 69, 85, 91, 142
Marx, Karl, 93
Mary, the Blessed Virgin, 4, 7, 62, 167–8,
    181, 194, 212, 214–17, 219, 263n
Mary Magdalene, 237–41
Masius, Andreas, 142, 155
Mass, the, 208, 222
    see also Holy Communion; Host; Last
    Supper; sacraments
Medina, Bartolomé de, 36, 51, 53, 60, 64,
    69, 76–7
Medina, Miguel de, 156
    Christianae Paraenesis, 156
Mediterranean Sea, the, 96
Meir, Samuel ben, 157
Mesopotamia, 45
Messiah, the, 42, 57–9, 86, 112–13, 116,
    129, 152–3, 155, 157–8, 160–1, 165,
    167–9, 175, 179, 272n
    Handel's Messiah, 123
    Messianic texts, 43, 60, 87, 95–6, 157–8,
    160, 167, 169, 181, 187; see also
    testimonia
metaphor, 8–12, 22–6, 31, 35, 76–9, 88–9,
    132–5, 174, 181–3, 185, 191, 197, 206,
    212, 216, 221, 224, 234–5, 239–42,
    250, 254, 270n
    Biblical, 28, 100–1, 106, 118, 121, 161,
    167, 171, 175–6, 179, 216, 229–30
Michael, St, 114
Middle Ages, the late, 155, 171
Milton, John, 121
Mishnah, the, 142
Molière, Jean, 134
    Tartuffe, 134
Molina, Luis de, 83
Montaigne, Michel de, 98, 274n
Montano, Arias, 26, 48–50, 61, 64–5, 70,
    79, 84, 97, 101, 142–3, 146, 157, 265n,
    270n
    Cantares, 70
Montemayor, Prudencio de, 80 82
Montoya, Gabriel de, 68
Moors, the, 185, 202
    Moorish craftsmen, 23
    moriscos, rising of the, 57

Mormon, Book of, 154, 268n
Moses, 89, 113–14, 154, 156, 201–2, 215,
    217–19, 248
music, 17, 20, 22, 25, 70, 79, 137, 151, 191,
    224, 247, 249–50, 254–5, 258–61
    of the spheres, 250, 255
Muslims, 141, 213
mysticism, 105, 108–9, 145–6, 150–3, 184,
    211, 231
    Christian, 211
    Jewish, 150–3
    Western, 184
mystics, 29, 108, 141, 260
    mystical experience, 27, 106, 259;
    imagery, 255; journey, 217, 253;
    literature, 65, 208
    see also theology, mystical
Myth of God Incarnate, The, 93
myth, 93
    of Atlantis, 100
    of the Golden Age, 98, 107, 116

Naples, 156
Nathan, 88
nature, 13–14, 88, 120, 209, 212, 215, 234,
    242
    and art, 13–14, 209, 242
Neale, J.M., 276n
Nebuchadnezzar, 186–7
neo-Platonism, 141, 145
    see also Platonism, Christian
neo-Stoicism, 128
    see also philosophy, Stoic
New Testament, the, 38–9, 42, 44–5, 59,
    86, 88, 90, 92, 117, 120, 129, 143, 155,
    174, 202
    Greek, 7, 42; see also Bible, Greek
    see also Bible; Epistles; Gospels;
    Scripture
New World, the discovery of the, 1, 61,
    98–101, 101, 103, 116, 118, 131, 146,
    161, 169, 202
    Gospel preached in the, 101, 103, 118,
    161, 169
    prophecies of the, 98–101, 202
Newman, John Henry, 190, 273n
Nicodemus, 189
Noah, 89
    Noah's ark, 89
nominalism, 5
Núñez, Jerónimo, 61

obscurity (in language), 11, 29, 32, 35, 38,
44, 90, 95, 102, 104, 123–4, 126, 129,
131, 138, 140, 154, 166, 226, 261, 264n
observantism, 5
Occam, William of, 5
Old Testament, the, 38, 42–4, 48–9, 57–8,
60, 86, 89–93, 96, 98, 117, 120, 127–9,
138, 141, 143–4, 155, 157, 160–1,
169–70, 202–3, 206, 215, 241, 272n
see also Bible, Hebrew; Scripture;
Septuagint
oposiciones, 6
Origen, 42–3, 102, 154, 159, 171
Hexapla, 42
Ortiz de Funes, Dr, 51
Osiander, Andreas, 39
Osorio, Isabel, 26, 61, 68
Osuna, University of, 66
Ovid, 28, 34, 60–1

Pacheco, Cardinal, 40, 62
Pacheco, Francisco de, 7
Pagnini, Santes, 36, 39, 48, 144
Palestine, 100, 115, 152
Palm Sunday, 199
pantheism, 11
parables, 88, 247
paradise, 45, 114, 120–1, 158–9, 194
see also Eden, Garden of
paradox, literary, 16, 88, 120, 183, 185,
214, 217, 239–40, 246, 252, 254–5
theological, 112, 121, 183, 214, 246, 256
Paris, 143–4
University of, 5, 39
Passion, the, 115, 175–6, 187, 189, 199–200,
220, 226
Passover, the, 92, 159–60
pastoral literature, 28–31, 99, 241–62
Path of the Names; of the Sefiroth, see under
Kabbalism
Patriarchs, the, 246
Patristic writers, 101, 170–1, 174, 181,
208–9, 215, 274n
see also Fathers, the
Paul, St, 14, 76, 92, 102, 117, 163, 169–70,
181, 188, 192, 201, 212, 219, 223,
228–9
see also theology, Pauline
Paul of Burgos (Pablo de Santa María), 95,
100, 141, 165, 271n; Additiones, 141
Paul of Heredia, 155
Crown of the King, The, 155

Epistle of Secrets, The, 155
peace, 14–15, 17–26, 108, 112, 125, 129,
161, 192, 203–7, 235–6, 240, 245,
247–8
see also shalom
Pelagianism, 81
Peña, Juan de la, 70
Pentateuch, the, 91, 160
Pérez, Sebastián, Dr, 52, 104
Peralta, Hernando de, 47
Persia, 16, 202
Peru, 61, 99
Perusa, Tadeo de, 84
Peter, St, 117, 178
Petrarch, 32
Pfefferkorn, Johann, 142
Philip II, King, 49–50, 85, 143, 156
Philo of Alexandria, 27, 159
philosophy, 79, 88
ancient, 188, 206, 229–30
Aristotelian, 87
Greek, 27
Indian, 206
nominalist, 5
pagan, 206
Stoic, 128
see also classical philosophy
pícaro, the, 67
Pico della Mirandola, 102, 141, 154, 159,
165
Pilate, Pontius, 200
Pindar, 69
Pius XII, Pope, 80
Divino Afflante, 80
Plantin, Christophe, 45
Plato, 12, 100, 206, 233
Platonic thought, 78, 182, 191, 213, 245,
250; theory of anamnesis, 17, 250
Platonism, Christian, 105
see also neo-Platonism
Poe, Edgar Allan, 1
Polyglot Bibles: Complutensian, 6, 49, 141,
144, 153–4
Hexapla, 42
Biblia Regia, 49–50, 144, 265n
Ponce de León, Basilio, Fray, 122, 269n
Portocarrero, Pedro, 94
Potosí, 99
prayer, 7, 108–9, 119
predestination, 80–3, 174, 196, 267n
prisci theologi, the 89, 154
Priscillianists, 90

prophecy, 28, 43, 46, 57–8, 71, 87, 91,
    94–7, 99–100, 102, 115, 123, 129, 131,
    138, 151–2, 160, 168, 181, 201–2, 233,
    268n
Protestantism, 63, 85, 91
Protestants, 2, 37, 39, 83, 110–11, 118, 142,
    185, 193, 197
    see also theology, Protestant
Protocols of the Elders of Zion, the, 147
Provence, 150
proverbs, 88
Puebla, Juan de la, 273n
Pyrrha, 116
Pythagoreans, 17, 43, 155, 204

quaestio, the 102–3
Quevedo, Francisco de, 7, 131, 261, 269n
Quintanar, 148–9
Quintanar, Gonzalo de, 148
Quiroga, Archbishop, 71, 82
Quito, 61
Qur'an, the, 58

Rabbis, the, 47–9, 97, 166
    Rabbinical works, 39, 57–8, 101–2,
        141–6, 151, 155, 157, 165, 167–8
Ramos, Nicolás, Fray, 53, 74
Rashi, 141, 157
reason, 9–10, 37, 100, 110, 125, 163, 205–7,
    215, 218, 222, 227
Red Sea, the, 114
Redeemer, the, 129, 131
redemption, 83, 89, 152, 173–4, 176, 184–5
Reformation, the, 39
    pre-Reformation period, 142
    Reformers, the, 142
Renaissance, the, 12–14, 30, 35, 38, 89, 93,
    99, 108, 116, 141–2, 146, 153–4, 227,
    233, 241–2, 246, 249, 261
Resurrection, the, 76, 88, 115, 129, 137,
    194–6, 203, 212, 215–17, 228
Reuchlin, Johannes, 142, 155, 157
    De arte cabalistica, 142, 155
    De rudimentis hebraicis, 142
revelation, 38, 64, 98, 124, 138, 152, 154,
    161, 170–1, 228, 249
rhetoric, 8, 30, 35, 88, 96–7, 99, 104, 127,
    133, 186, 227
    Biblical, 35, 93, 127, 133
rhetorical devices: acervatio, adnominatio, 133
    alliteration, 132
    anaphora, 133

antithesis, 22, 25, 73, 79, 110, 116, 121,
    134, 183, 196, 200, 209, 228, 239, 248
apostrophe, 30, 251
conformatio (personification), 127, 200
congeries, 186
epiphonema, 30
exclamation, 240, 244–5
Greek accusative, 252
hyperbaton, 127, 240
hyperbole, 30, 88
interpretatio, 133
litotes, 127
metonomy, 24, 30, 127, 188
occupatio, 97, 133
oxymoron, 210
parallelism, 132, 200, 227
polyptoton, 184–5, 245
rhetorical questions, 200, 228, 240
rogatio, sermonicatio, 133
synechdoche, 30, 115, 127
transitio, 133
Rimini, Gregory of, 5, 68
Rodríguez, Bartolomé, 67
    Diego, see under Zúñiga, Diego de
    Pero, 149
Rojas, Domingo de, 6
romances of chivalry, 63
Rome, 40, 50, 67, 83, 95–6, 117, 143–4,
    193, 202, 267n
    Romans, the, 74, 95–7, 99, 117
    Roman Empire, the, 202
Ronsard, Pierre, 255
    'Mignonne, allons voir si la rose', 255
Rousseau, Jean-Jacques, 98

sacraments, the, 53, 117, 195–6, 208, 240
    see also baptism; Holy Communion; Host;
        Last Supper; Mass
sacrifice, Christ's, 220–2, 228
Safed, 153
Saints, the, 59, 81, 84, 101–2, 115, 128,
    188, 197, 260
Salamanca, 4–5, 12, 25–6, 36, 57, 64, 68,
Sancti Spiritus convent, 26, 68
    University, 4–5, 36–7, 41, 47–54, 58, 65,
        67, 70, 79–80, 82–4, 86, 143, 193, 234;
        cátedras menores, 6; Chair of Durandus, 6,
        41; of Greek, 36, 47; of Hebrew, 36; of
        St Thomas, 6, 41; library, 122; Prime
        Chair of Bible, 6, 36, 41, 86, 103, 122; of
        Law, 4; of Theology, 6, 51; Rector, 62
Salinas, Francisco de, 17, 69

salvation, 27, 70, 73, 81, 95, 100, 108, 120, 128, 146, 164, 168, 173, 185, 191, 197, 200, 213, 221
sambenito, the, 149–50
Samuel, 157
Sánchez, Elvira, 148
Sánchez de Ciruelo, Pedro, 156
    Paradoxae quaestiones decem, 156
Sánchez de las Brozas, Francisco (el Brocense), 234, 275n
Sánchez de Villanueva Avivelo, Fernán, 148
Sancho, Francisco, 49
Sarai (Sarah), 154
Satan, 90, 126, 134, 161, 189, 191–2, 200, 203, 221, 230, 240
    see also Devil; Lucifer
Saul, 71, 88, 157
scholasticism, 6, 41, 82, 87
    see also theology, scholastic
Scotus, Duns, 81, 173–4, 221, 228–9
Scripture, 1, 12, 14, 27–8, 32, 40–1, 45, 58–9, 62–3, 66–7, 74, 85–7, 93, 100–3, 108, 111, 117, 119–24, 126, 130, 138–9, 154, 156–7, 159, 161–2, 165, 169–72, 175–80, 182–3, 195, 202, 207, 210, 213, 216, 218, 228–30, 246
    see also Bible; Epistles; Gospels; New Testament; Old Testament
Second Coming (of Christ), 102, 112
Second World War, the, 93
Seneca, 268n
Septuagint, the, 42–3, 45, 47–9, 58–9, 69, 138, 157
    see also Bible, Greek
Seripando, Girolamo de, 5, 156
Serna, Juana de la, 148
shalom, 125–6, 205
    see also peace
Shiloh, 157–8
Sicily, 155
Sigüenza, José de, 84–5
Siloam, pool of, 158
simile, 8, 30, 96, 196, 208, 210, 214, 230
Simon the Pharisee, 239
sin, 17, 63, 73, 80, 83, 108, 110, 114, 128, 161, 173–6, 182–3, 186, 189–92, 194–5, 201, 206, 212, 215, 219–21, 225, 228–30, 239–40
    original, 83, 189, 194, 196–7
    see also Fall, the
Sinai, 89, 113–14, 154, 156, 215, 217

Sixtus V, Pope, 79
Sixtus of Siena, 69, 156
    Bibliotheca sancta, 156
Solomon, king, 27–30, 48, 65, 104–6, 114, 222
    Solomon's temple, 184, 273n
Son, the, 83, 155, 162, 165–8, 171, 178, 180, 193, 212–14, 216, 228, 257
    Son of Man, the, 248, 252
Sophocles, 69
Soria, 5
Soto, Domingo, 6, 8
Sotomayor, Pedro, 70
soul, the, 11, 16–17, 25, 27, 34, 72–3, 78, 106–9, 111–12, 126, 130, 136–8, 145, 162, 177, 188–9, 191–2, 201, 203, 205–8, 210, 217–18, 221–5, 238, 242, 244, 246, 248–51, 253–5, 258–61
    Christ's, 182–3, 215–16, 219–21
Southwell, Robert, 211
    'The Burning Babe', 211
Steuch (Augustinus Eugubinus), 69, 266n
suffering, 2, 42, 70, 72–4, 107–8, 123–4, 128–30, 152, 161, 183, 189, 194–5, 198–202, 218, 220–1, 225, 227–8, 232, 270n
Suprema, the, *see under* Inquisition
Sybil, the Erythraean, 168
    Sybils, the, 102
symbolism, Biblical, 120–1
    Christian, 252
symbols, 12, 99, 105, 107, 111, 120, 244–5, 256–7, 259, 262
syntax, 11, 123, 258–9
Syriac, 7

Talmud, the, 43, 102, 142, 144, 151, 156, 158, 165
Tantalus, 16, 25
Targums, the, 42, 69, 144, 179
Teresa of Avila, St, 123, 129, 268n–9n
testimonia, 42, 45
    see also Messianic texts
tetragrammaton, the, 165–6, 168, 178
Theocritus, 29, 241, 246
theodicy, 128
theology, 1–2, 5–6, 8, 10, 12, 26, 79, 82, 84, 93, 99, 103, 108–11, 113, 117, 120, 122, 130, 152–3, 169, 172–6, 178–9, 181, 183–4, 189–90, 193, 195, 197, 203, 208, 213, 217, 220, 228–31, 246, 256, 261, 267n, 274n

apophatic, 246
early Greek, 175
Hebrew, 152–3
Jewish mystical, 152
mystical, 109, 260
Pauline, 100, 168, 185, 194, 196–7, 220, 228, 256
Protestant, 195, 208
Reformed, 228
scholastic, 41, 84, 109, 171, 175–6, 181, 192, 217
see also paradox, theological
Thomism, 82, 219
see also Aquinas, St Thomas
Tillich, Paul, 153
Titelman(s), François, 65, 68–9, 266n
Paraphrastica elucidatio in librum D. Iob, 68
Toboso, el, 148
Toledo, 68, 84
Archbishop of, 1, 47, 71, 270n see also Carranza, Bartolomé; Quiroga
Torah, the, 148
see also Law, Jewish
Tormes, river, 12–13
Tostado, el (Alonso de Madrigal), 143, 158
Tradition (of the Church), 40, 45–6, 66, 103, 117, 129, 138, 171, 173, 188, 201, 261
Transfiguration, Mount of, 162
transubstantiation, 208
Trent, Council of, 6, 62, 79–80, 91, 110, 156
decree on Scripture, 40–2, 44–6, 54, 60, 79–80, 85
Trinity, the, 155–6, 162, 165–6, 178, 193, 213–14, 230
Turks, the, 96, 118, 202–3
Turkish Empire, 202
Turkish fleet, 67
typology, 90, 160, 226

Ur, 114
usury, 127

Valdés, Alfonso de, 12
Juan de, 12
Valera, Inés de, 4
Juan de, 4
Valla, Lorenzo, 38
Adnotationes, 38
Valladolid, 5–6, 36, 53, 57, 74, 79, 84, 103, 150
see also Inquisition, Valladolid

Valverde, Dr, 79, 270n
Vatable, François de, 36, 39, 42, 47–8, 52, 58–9, 61, 97, 143
Vázquez del Mármol, Juan, 269n
Vega, Andrés de, 46, 70
Venus, 107
Vera, Diego de, 265n
Vergara, Juan de, 69
Vetus Latina, the, 42
Vienne, Council of, 141
Villalobos, Luis de, 70
Villanueva, Graviel de, 148–9
Juana de, 149
Leonor de, 5, 149
Pedro de, 148
Villavicencio, Lorenzo de, 84
Virgil, 29, 69, 127, 143, 167, 241–2, 246, 269n
Georgics, 127
Viterbo, Egidio de, 5, 156, 165
Vitoria, Francisco de, 5–6, 70
Vives, Juan Luis, 143
voyages of discovery, 99–101
Vulgate, the, 8–9, 33–4, 36–8, 40–2, 44–54, 56, 58, 60–1, 65–7, 69, 74, 79–80, 84–5, 99–100, 102, 123–4, 126, 138, 141–2, 157, 235, 237

Watts, Isaac, 15, 111, 115, 264n, 268n
Wesley, Charles, 190, 273n
Word, the, 113, 155, 161–4, 167, 171–2, 175, 178, 182, 208, 216, 220, 226, 228, 233
see also Logos

Ximénez de Cisneros, Cardinal, see under Cisneros de Ximénez

Zamora, Alfonso de, 156–7
Zamora, bishop of, 68
Zaragoza, 151
Zerubbabel, 167, 179
Zion, 97, 111, 244
see also Jerusalem
Zohar, the (Sefer ha-Zohar, The Book of Splendour), 151–2, 156
see also Kabbalah
Zúñiga, Fray Diego de, 37, 64–8, 70, 76, 84
family background, 67
In Iob Commentaria, 66, 68
Manera de aprender todas las ciencias, 68
Philosophiae prima pars, 68